Paving the Way:
Women's Struggle for Political Equality in California

Steve Swatt
Susie Swatt
Rebecca LaVally
Jeff Raimundo

Foreword by Greg Lucas

Berkeley Public Policy Press
Institute of Governmental Studies
University of California, Berkeley
2019

Library of Congress Cataloging-in-Publication Data

Names: Swatt, Steve, author. | Swatt, Susie, author. | LaVally, Rebecca, author. | Raimundo, Jeff, author.
Title: Paving the way : women's struggle for political equality in California / Steve Swatt, Susie Swatt, Rebecca LaVally ; with Jeff Raimundo.
Description: Berkeley : Berkeley Public Policy Press, 2019. | Includes index.
Identifiers: LCCN 2018028188 | ISBN 9780877724599
Subjects: LCSH: Women--Political activity--California--History. | Women--Suffrage--California--History. | Suffragists--California--Biography. | Feminists--California--Biography. | Women politicians--California--Biography. | Women social reformers--California--Biography.
Classification: LCC HQ1236.5.U6 S93 2019 | DDC 320.082/09794--dc23
LC record available at https://lccn.loc.gov/201802818

Dedicated to the California women who paved the way . . .

and to the women and men who supported them.

Also by Steve Swatt, Susie Swatt, Jeff Raimundo and
Rebecca LaVally:

Game Changers: Twelve Elections That Transformed California

Contents

They Paved the Way

Chapter 11: The Movement Heads into the Twenty-First Century

Doris Allen

Toni Atkins

Kathryn Barger

Karen Bass

Patricia Bates

Barbara Boxer

Grace Dorris

Delaine Eastin

Katherine Philips Edson

Dianne Feinstein

Carly Fiorina

Janice Hahn

Kamala Harris

Dolores Huerta

Sheila Kuehl

Barbara Lee

Margaret Levee

Doris Matsui

Kristin Olsen

Nancy Pelosi

Ellen Sargent

Libby Schaaf

Hilda Solis

Jackie Speier

Mimi Walters

Maxine Waters

Meg Whitman

Betty Yee

…and thousands more

Foreword

California is home to the most diverse collection of people ever brought together in the 6,000-year history of human civilization. Today, there are an estimated 300 languages and dialects spoken in this state. Forty percent of our families speak a language other than English at home. Nearly 30 percent were born in another country—about the same percentage as when California became a state.

In 1848, the Golden State wasn't even the Golden State. The Mexican land that would become California—after the Treaty of Guadalupe Hidalgo ended the Mexican-American War—was home to at least 150,000 Native Californians, 6,500 *Californios* of Mexican or Spanish descent and, by some accounts, fewer than a thousand white settlers.

By statehood in 1850, the nonnative population had exploded to more than 93,000—not counting records burned or lost in San Francisco and a couple of other Bay Area counties. Many of those newcomers, just like today's California immigrants, arrived from throughout the world.

We're learning more about the contributions of those early immigrants—and of indigenous Californians—as our history becomes more inclusive and comprehensive, a process fueled in part by a growing appreciation of the economic and social assets that California's diversity represents. This gives us an ever-deepening understanding of how our many million individual threads combine to create California's distinctive and enduring weave.

But like the old cliché says, history has been written by—and for—the winners for a long, long time. By definition that means the telling of California's story isn't as comprehensive or as inclusive as it should be. History often focuses on the achievement, the milestone, the point-in-time rather than the failed first attempts or the individuals whose contributions laid the foundation for future successes.

Paving the Way: Women's Struggle for Political Equality in California helps remedy those deficiencies by acquainting us with a number of women who helped shape California over the past centuries.

Fortunately, contemporary studies are training new lenses on gender and politics in America, and some of these inform *Paving the Way*. However, these works tend to have a national perspective or are grounded in particular periods of California history. In contrast, this book chronicles the work of female trailblazers in policy and politics across state history. It is not—and for practical reasons cannot be—a comprehensive encyclopedia of ground-breaking women, but much of the joy in moving through *Paving the Way* is meeting historically underappreciated individuals—of both sexes—and discovering their contributions to what California has become.

It is notable, for instance, that women received the right to vote in California's statewide elections in 1911—nine years before the Nineteenth Amendment guaranteed all American women this right. The California victory culminated six decades of effort by numerous women of grit and intellect who not only fought for enfranchisement but struggled to be taken seriously—let alone heard—in a male-dominated society. Among key suffragists was Clara Foltz, who became California's first woman lawyer at a time when legislation was necessary to make that happen. For proof that, indeed, the more things change, the more they stay the same, there's the book's vivid account of the final frenzied hours of the 1878 legislative session in which Foltz barely secures passage of a measure allowing women to be licensed to practice law in California. The lobbying scene, as described, could just as easily occur today in Sacramento.

A hundred years after the first four women were elected to the state assembly in 1918, *Paving the Way* establishes the solid record of women's policy achievements inside and outside government. It names dozens of women who stand as models of persistence and sometimes resistance, as doers who strived to promote public causes that ultimately endured. The Golden State's girls and women are anything but monolithic. Women historically have disagreed over such fundamental issues as the inevitability of female suffrage, the appropriateness of *Roe v. Wade,* and notions of feminism itself. This book respects that diversity, individually and ideologically. Even so, it finds that the women who made the biggest differences in shaping California's political landscape have had some qualities in common. Almost invariably, they were resilient, determined, and fierce.

Uncovering the stories of noteworthy Californians seemingly lost to history, or at least hidden away for generations, teaches us about ourselves.

Sure, plenty of famous white men, for better or worse, have shaped the California we know today. But we are all descendants, either literally or figuratively, of California's trailblazing women, including women of color.

While their images are missing from the hallways of the state capitol, among the portraits of an unbroken lineage of male governors, countless female groundbreakers have left their marks in deeds rather than in banner headlines.

What deepens our understanding of the tenacity of these progressive and persistent Californians is the research the authors have conducted of the worlds in which the women in this book operate. Whether describing Gold Rush mining camps, the halls of the nineteenth-century legislature, or a 1960s campus protest, there's an immediacy that amplifies appreciation for how much these women accomplished and exactly how hard it was to do that.

Part of the fun of being California's State Librarian is unearthing fascinating stories buried in the massive collections of the State Library, the State Archives, and other cultural heritage institutions—like the local library.

Paving the Way: Women's Struggle for Political Equality in California proves that names can be found and stories told if one is sufficiently persistent in digging. The authors perused newspapers from the 19th century, for instance, to track down colorful nuggets that reported, sometimes in shocked tones, the audacity of pioneer-era women who challenged cultural barriers to push for policy and social changes. The authors spent many, many hours poring over oral histories and personally interviewing key players who have borne witness to more recent history-making. Every page reflects that herculean effort.

Paving the Way takes us from early statehood all the way to present-day California. It not only helps us better understand the context of movements like #Me-Too but invites us to ponder why so few women have risen to the top of California's political hierarchy in nearly 170 years of statehood. The book acknowledges that women of color faced a double burden of gender and racial discrimination in early California, when nonwhites could be singled out for systematic abuse, repression, and, in the case of California Indians, government-sanctioned elimination. Public-school segregation dating from the 1800s was not abolished until the 1940s in some California cities.

This isn't the maiden voyage for Steve and Susie Swatt and Rebecca LaVally and Jeff Raimundo. Their 2015 book, *Game Changers: Twelve Elections That Transformed California*, demonstrates their solid grasp of California history and its sinuous political landscape as well as, ahem, clearly helping pave the way for the book that's now in your hands.

Finally, what this book also illustrates quite clearly is how many stories in our state's extraordinary history haven't been told as well or as often as they should be—or haven't been told at all. Large amounts of source material used in *Paving the Way* come from the California State Library and the California State Archives.

The precision, detail, and vividness of this book are testimony to the many timeless tales that these two institutions can share with Californians and the world. The State Library and the State Archives—and the state of California as whole— have a responsibility to make powerful stories that explain who Californians are more readily accessible to more Californians, online or otherwise.

Greg Lucas
California State Librarian

Introduction

Hallmarks of the Struggle

"And thou hast proved that woman can—
Who has the nerve, and strength, and will—
Work in the wider field of man,
And be a woman still."
—Madge Morris in praise of Clara Foltz, 1917

Sometimes it's easy to overlook the long and tortuous nature of the journey that California's political women, paralleling their sisters nationwide, have traveled across the generations since the mid-nineteenth century, without compass or timetable, to penetrate democracy's political hierarchy. Although California women have been breaking gender barriers since the dawn of statehood, we have lacked a coherent means of recognizing their names, struggles, and milestones in paving the way along this still-rocky road. This book is a journal of the journey, an attempt to pull together the big story, to help establish where the nation-state of California stands on an elusive path toward political gender equality.

We define political equality for women as parity with men in influencing the development of public policy—both inside and outside formal power structures. We recognize that gender can be fluid, rather than cast in stark binaries between female and male, masculine and feminine. We acknowledge, too, that girls and women do not fit any unified category of shared political, cultural, or social outlook, needs, or interests, socioeconomic status or educational attainment, nor any common sense of identity and experience. No matter how gender is defined or perceived, however, striving toward parity in gender representation remains an important if elusive challenge in democratic political life. In legislating, gender parity means reshaping the male cast that has molded policy ideas and outcomes since the genesis of democracy. In governing, it translates into wider inclusion in managing and imposing executive powers. In the judiciary, it enlarges perceptions in creating and handing down judgments.

Yet the prolonged struggle toward political gender parity in California sometimes seems barely out of its infancy, following the decades-long gestation for female suffrage a century ago.

No one has come closer than Dianne Feinstein, the grande dame of California politics, to winning the title of first elected female governor of the nation's most populous state. Only three women have ever been nominated by Republicans or

1

Democrats to make the try. Feinstein was the first woman mayor of San Francisco and the first woman president of the San Francisco County Board of Supervisors. She would become the first female US senator from California as well. However, any chance for Democrat Feinstein to govern the Golden State slipped away in 1990 with her loss to Republican Pete Wilson by just 3.5 percentage points. A *Los Angeles Times* poll found men disagreeing, three to two, that it was "time we had a woman governor." Women disagreed slightly.[1]

For the two women nominees who followed Feinstein, the losing margins were wide. Democrat Kathleen Brown failed to deny Wilson a second term in 1994 by a resounding 14.5 percentage points. Meg Whitman, who carried the banner for Republicans in 2010, lost to Democrat Jerry Brown by nearly 13 points.

We might be puzzled that a mega state of 40 million has seen no woman reach the political summit—none confidently stride across the threshold to take charge of the double-doored governor's suite at the state capitol. We might wonder, too, why only six women were governors among the nation's 50 states in 2018, the same number as eight years earlier or, for that matter, why only one major-party nominee for US president has ever been female.

Scholars of gender and politics who probe such questions have identified barriers to female elected leadership ranging from the deeply personal to the persistently cultural. More women than men tend to doubt their own qualifications and abilities to win elections, and female and male voters alike are influenced by cultural mores that perceive male leadership as the norm.

Women who wish to become leaders typically are expected to demonstrate more competence than men.[2] While people want women candidates to be warm, likeable, and feminine, those qualities clash with the take-charge attitude also expected of political leaders. Striking a workable balance means political women walk a tightrope that male leaders never encounter. Complicating this, people of both genders can perceive highly competent women as unlikeable and likeable women as incompetent.

Studies of hundreds of subjects show that perceptions of ambition and power-seeking in women candidates can generate a backlash of "moral outrage" among voters, although voters don't mind seeing those qualities in male candidates.[3]

---

[1] George Skelton, "Wilson, Feinstein about Even in Race for Governor," *Los Angeles Times*, June 22, 1990, OCA1.

[2] Susan J. Carroll, "Reflections on Gender and Hillary Clinton's Presidential Campaign: The Good, the Bad, and the Misogynic," *Politics & Gender* 5.1 (2009): 5–6.

[3] Tyler G. Okimoto and Victoria L. Brescoll, "The Price of Power: Power Seeking and Backlash against Female Politicians," *Personality and Social Psychology Bulletin* 36.7 (2010): 923.

Pushing Back against Restrictive Gender Mores and Laws

From the earliest days of California statehood in 1850, the frontier spawned white pioneer women willing to push back against the social mores that severely constricted expectations and permissible behaviors for most American women in the nineteenth century. Deeply embedded east of the frontier, these norms—dictating the standards of a "cult of true womanhood"—demanded that women be demure and confine their interests to the private sphere. Public matters, especially voting and engaging in civic affairs, but even addressing mixed audiences of men and women, were best left to male voices to spare women irreparable damage to their reputations and risk of derogatory labels such as prostitute.

Undeterred, Emily Pitts Stevens, co-owner of the West's first suffrage newspaper in the 1870s, argued that women should be revolutionaries. Pitts Stevens more than played the part herself, interrupting one antisuffrage event with derisive comments and loud applause at all the wrong times. A state assemblyman admonished Pitts Stevens to behave herself. Nevertheless, in the parlance of one of today's popular feminist slogans, she persisted.

Other newspapers were happy to cover such rabble-rousing behaviors, which is how we know of them today. A *Sacramento Daily Union* headline moralized: "A Shameful Scene at Platt's Hall—Women Suffragists Disgracing Their Sex."[4]

Another pioneering suffragist, Clara Foltz, helped overturn a prohibition on women lawyers in California. Foltz had a natural interest in law, but California restricted the legal profession to "any white male citizen" with good moral character. She tackled the barrier head-on by drafting legislation that substituted "any citizen or person" for "any white male citizen" and found a state senator to carry it. Foltz later recounted that she helped win the bill's passage through sheer force of will: "I coaxed, I entreated, I would have reasoned had they been reasonable men; I almost went down on my knees before them, asking for the pitiful privilege of an equal chance to earn an honest living in a noble profession!"[5]

Foltz and Laura de Force Gordon would become the first two female lawyers in California. Foltz drafted legislation to grant voting rights to women, and Gordon fruitfully lobbied lawmakers to put it on the 1896 ballot.

Erecting Racial and Ethnic Barriers to Participation

In the early years of statehood, women of color were repressed by laws that not only were sexist, using today's vernacular, but were racially and ethnically

---

[4] "A Shameful Scene at Platt's Hall—Women Suffragists Disgracing their Sex," *Sacramento Daily Union*, June 26, 1872, 1; "Anti-Woman Suffrage—Lecture by Mrs. Frost," *Sacramento Daily Union*, June 26, 1872, 3.

[5] Clara Foltz, "Struggles and Triumphs of a Woman Lawyer," *New American Woman*, August 1916, 11, https://archive.org/stream/newamericanwoman01losa#page/n139/mode/2up.

discriminatory, subjecting them to a dual set of constrictions. California was added to the Union as a free state in 1850, two years after Mexico surrendered what is now the southwestern United States under the Treaty of Guadalupe Hidalgo to end the Mexican-American War. Yet California's new legislature adopted a fugitive slave law that from 1852 through 1855 required runaway slaves to be returned to their masters. African Americans brought into California to mine goldfields or otherwise serve their owners thus could be held in slavery rather than freed when they entered the state's boundaries.

Even after the law lapsed, Bridget "Biddy" Mason—who had walked most of her two-thousand-mile journey to California behind her master's wagon in 1851— was forced to go to court to win her freedom in 1856. Her case was complicated by another state law forbidding nonwhites to testify in court against whites. Finally set free by a sympathetic judge, Mason would become a savvy and generous businesswoman. She accumulated substantial sums from her real estate dealings and donated the land for the first African-American church in Los Angeles.

Although California women were not granted the vote until 1911, the ragtag collection of state fathers who crafted California's first constitution in 1849 shared a common goal—they wanted to attract more marriageable white females to the frontier. By then, California's nonnative population of about 180,000 had five men for every woman. As an inducement, a law dating to the days of Mexican rule was incorporated into the new constitution—awarding women a right to retain their own separate property after marriage.[6]

Among the profound consequences of the Gold Rush of 1849, Californians were destined to become a remarkably diverse lot. Not only had California once been part of Mexico, but it now was a destination for east coasters, free blacks, European and Asian immigrants, and others who came to seek fortunes, whether literally in mines and rivers or metaphorically in fresh starts. Sacramento would become the terminus of a transcontinental railroad perilously blasted through the high Sierra by Chinese immigrants, opening the way for travel and commerce. But the state was more hierarchy than melting pot, and none suffered more than the indigenous population, nearly wiped out by hardship and slaughter. Given no chance to assimilate or even coexist in the rapidly evolving culture, California Indians had endured involuntary servitude under Spanish-Mexican rule, were felled by European diseases, and systematically hunted down and massacred by settlers, soldiers, and militias in state-sanctioned raids. Survivors were forced to relocate to barren mountain regions. Federal treaties were ignored. By the late 1880s, the number of California Indians had plummeted from a quarter of a million to just twenty thousand.[7]

---

[6] Steve Swatt, Susie Swatt, Jeff Raimundo, and Rebecca LaVally, *Game Changers: Twelve Elections that Transformed California* (Berkeley: Heyday, 2015), 25.

[7] Charles Wollenberg, "Ethnic Experiences in California History: An Impressionistic Survey," in *Neither Separate nor Equal: Race & Racism in California*, ed. Roger Olmsted and Charles Wollenberg (California Historical Society, 1971), reprinted from the *California Historical Quarterly*, September, 1971.

California's early years were marred by enforced patterns of bigotry against others as well, given that most of the state's white citizens held "a fixed belief in the innate superiority of whites over other races," write historians James J. Rawls and Walton Bean.[8] Discriminatory laws and practices described by Rawls and Bean are noted here because they infringed on the ability of women as well as men to obtain fair treatment, affected the quest for female suffrage, and kept some California schools segregated into the 1940s. The first constitution limited the vote to white male citizens. Asians, Mexicans, and other Latin Americans, were typically excluded from the goldfields that had lured them in the first place. If allowed to mine, they were penalized with extra taxes.

Although the Treaty of Guadalupe Hidalgo had promised holders of Mexican and Spanish land grants that they could keep their rancheros, their lands frequently were seized by incoming white settlers. Chinese immigrants were singled out for especially harsh treatment in San Francisco and elsewhere, often effectively relegated to Chinatowns. Echoing the theme, the federal Chinese Exclusion Act in 1882 banned additional laborers from China. California laws, targeting Asian immigrants forbidden to become citizens under federal law, prohibited noncitizens from owning land well into the twentieth century.

Within living memory, 90,000 Californians of Japanese ancestry, two-thirds of them American citizens, were removed by federal decree during World War II and incarcerated in remote compounds. Less known to most Californians, hundreds of thousands of Mexican Americans and Mexican immigrants were sent to Mexico in waves of US deportations and relocations, often carried out under inhumane conditions, from the 1930s into the 1950s. The Los Angeles County Board of Supervisors apologized in 2012 for the county's role in facilitating the roundups of the 1930s. Governor Arnold Schwarzenegger in 2005 signed a bill apologizing to some 400,000 US citizens and legal residents who were forcibly relocated south of the border during the Depression and World War II eras.[9]

Dating from early statehood, California had practiced its own brand of Jim Crow segregation. In 1860, the legislature granted the state superintendent of public instruction authority to withhold funds from schools that accepted nonwhites. State law held that "Negroes, Mongolians and Indians shall not be admitted into the public schools."[10] This prompted the state's first Chinese school in San Francisco, then California's most populous city. African-American schoolchildren also were segregated in San Francisco. A challenge to school segregation led by Chinese families in 1902 was unsuccessful.

---

[8] James J. Rawls and Walton Bean, *California, an Interpretive History* (9th ed.) (New York: McGraw-Hill Education, 2008), 140.

[9] "LA County Officials Apologize for Depression-Era Deportations," *Los Angeles Times*, February 21, 2012, http://latimesblogs.latimes.com/lanow/2012/02/la-county-officials-apologize-for-depression-era-deportations.html.

[10] "The Inferior Races in the Public Schools," *Sacramento Union*, May 3, 1864, 2.

Forging a Campaign for California Suffrage

Against this backdrop, the drive to win the vote for women in California—so grueling that it covers the first four chapters of this book—would be a largely white endeavor. Suffragists had splintered nationally over whether to support or resist the Fifteenth Amendment, ratified by the states in 1870 to prohibit denying the vote based on "race, color, or previous condition of servitude." Famed suffragists Susan B. Anthony and Elizabeth Cady Stanton lost their congressional fight to put voting rights for women into the Fourteenth and Fifteenth Amendments at the close of the Civil War, and bitterly opposed the Fifteenth Amendment for failing to include women. The amendment was actively endorsed by other prominent suffragists, however, who considered it consistent with the movement's early roots in the cause of abolition. Even after the split factions made amends in 1890, the movement's tactics could be exclusionary, devaluing immigrants and African-American women.[11]

Denied a national constitutional amendment for woman suffrage by Congress until 1919, the movement was forced to wage elections state by state, enduring dozens of defeats. Among them was the loss of the 1896 election in California.

The rejection was a bitter setback, given the state's substantial population of roughly 1.35 million by then, and it sent the drive for state-by-state suffrage into a tailspin for another 14 years. Like many of their sisters nationally, white suffragists at the helm of California's 1896 campaign believed white male voters, who held the power to enfranchise women, would balk at including foreign-born females and those of color. To assuage male voters, suffragists argued that educated women, if given the vote, would overwhelm the influence of illiterate foreigners. In postmortems, strategists realized one of several flaws in the campaign had been a failure to engage women and men across socioeconomic classes.

Still, California campaign leaders had called on Naomi Anderson, an African-American poet and author, to visit black churches and other venues, seeking support from black voters. Since African Americans weren't welcomed into white suffrage groups, Anderson formed black suffrage clubs. A passionate and powerful orator for the cause, she spoke on behalf of those "who have been compelled to kiss the dust and drink the dregs of womanhood."[12]

Many voters in San Francisco and other urban areas feared that enfranchising women would bring prohibition—a justifiable concern given alliances between suffrage advocates and the Women's Christian Temperance Union, which blamed alcohol for a variety of social ills. California's liquor industry battled hard against suffrage.

The campaign was hampered, too, by antisuffrage women, called "antis," who lent credence to opposition arguments that women didn't want the vote. An-

---

[11] National suffrage leader Alice Paul notoriously discouraged African-American women from participating in a massive suffrage parade in 1913 in Washington, D.C.
[12] "The Suffrage Convention," *Sacramento Record-Union*, May 31, 1896.

tis asserted that suffrage would change the very nature of women, who already had sufficient influence in the domestic sphere. Other suffrage foes contended women were too physically weak, mentally frail, and emotionally fraught to merit the vote—or that bringing women into the realm of public affairs would violate divine will.

Beating Back the Doldrums of Defeat

Only four states had awarded the vote to women by the turn of the twentieth century—Wyoming, Utah, Colorado, and Idaho. The fifth and sixth states to grant suffrage also were in the west: Washington state in 1910 and California, finally, in 1911. California's hard-fought victory was aided by a Progressive movement that had sent anticorruption, reform-minded legislators and Governor Hiram Johnson to Sacramento in the 1910 elections. The legislature had promptly put female suffrage and a spate of other civic reforms on a special statewide ballot.

The win was agonizingly narrow, and the final outcome—by a margin of just 3,587 votes—was in doubt for nearly two days. Even so, it proved a turning point for the national movement. Virtually overnight, the California success doubled the number of American women eligible to vote to more than a million.[13] Slim as it was, the victory ignited a resurgence that led to other state wins and—at long last, years after the deaths of both Anthony and Stanton—to congressional approval of the Nineteen Amendment. Its final ratification by a single vote in the Tennessee legislature achieved female suffrage across America in 1920.

In the years before they could vote, many middle-class and well-to-do white women, lacking an ability to craft public policy firsthand, joined women's social and civic clubs that collectively lobbied in Sacramento and Washington for causes that included health issues and environmental protections. Led by activists such as San Francisco clubwoman Catherine Hittell, they won safeguards for birds threatened by the fashion industry's penchant for adorning women's hats with them. Much later, in the 1950s, groups of women would lead the way in combatting the dangers of Los Angeles's choking smog.

A collection of women's clubs won permanent protections for thousands of acres of ancient redwoods along California's central and northern coasts and in the Sierra foothills of Calaveras County. To this day, nearly a million visitors annually experience the majestic beauty of Humboldt Redwoods State Park in the state's northern reaches. One popular attraction there: a grove of the towering trees named for the California Federation of Women's Clubs.

The federation's umbrella organization, the National Federation of Women's Clubs, reinforced its policy of excluding black membership in a vote at its national convention in Los Angeles in 1902. However, African Americans already had created their own thriving women's clubs in Oakland and elsewhere in the state.

---

[13] Robert P. J. Cooney, Jr., "Winning California for American Suffrage, 1911," *American Graphic Press*, http://americangraphicpress.com/articlesphotographs.html.

Figure 1. Lillian Harris Coffin, Mrs. Theodore Pinther, Jr., and Mrs. Theodore Pinther, Sr. (L-R) Lead Suffrage March in Oakland, 1908.
Credit: California Historical Society, CHS2010.22

Illustrating how they differed from the white clubs, the motto of the California Association of Colored Women was "Lifting as We Climb," echoing the slogan of its national association. Civically aware, the clubs supported African Americans in coping with societal barriers and were precursors to political activism in black communities.

Moving from Clubwoman to Governor's Appointee

Women's clubs continued to be vehicles for social change—and a way for individual women to magnify their voices—even after suffrage became inevitable.

In Los Angeles, for instance, former rancher Katherine Philips Edson, active in the Friday Morning Club, enlisted the California Federation of Women's Clubs in her crusade against milk contaminated by diseased cows. The women would win Governor Johnson's signature on legislation giving the state authority to oversee milk production.

Edson did not stop there. Appointed to the state Bureau of Labor Statistics, she documented the distressing working conditions of women and children in laundries, merchandising, and canneries. At the behest of Governor Johnson, she drafted legislation to create a state Industrial Welfare Commission, which still functions today to enforce laws that regulate wages and working conditions. Named by Johnson as one of its first members, Edson served on the commission through the administrations of three subsequent governors.

As these pages show, male-dominated decision-making in the political arena historically has determined what women will receive from their political system—whether it is the right to vote, congressional or state protections for redwoods, a minimum wage, or appointment to a state post. But the opportunity for California women to directly influence legislation would begin to change seven years after suffrage was won. It started with the election of 1918—which sent the first four women to the legislature.

The new assemblywomen—Grace Dorris, Esto Broughton, Elizabeth Hughes, and Anna Saylor—all had strong community ties, were adept at politicking, and railed against traditional gender roles and stereotypes. The quadruple victory seemed a promising start to the heady notion of one day winning political equality for women.

However, in the following 56 years, only 10 other women won assembly seats. Not until 1966 would the number of women candidates for state and congressional offices surpass the number of females who had run in 1914.[14] By the 50-year anniversary of state suffrage, only three California women had been elected to the US House of Representatives and none had served together. It wasn't until 1995 that a woman became assembly speaker. It took until 1976 for a woman to be elected to the state senate, and until 2018 for a woman to become the state senate leader.

Making a Difference Outside Elective Office

During the decades-long dry spell for women in elective state and federal office, savvy businesswoman Leone Baxter ascended to prominence by choosing to more directly affect political outcomes in California. She and partner Clem Whitaker applied their creative talents to influence who might get elected in the first place. The two are credited with inventing political consulting and campaign management strategies in the mid-1930s. Together, Baxter and Whitaker devised aggressive, expensive, and often cleverly manipulative strategies to elect or defeat

---

[14] California Statements of Vote 1914–1966 (Sacramento: State Printing Office).

state and local candidates and ballot measures—creating campaign templates still followed today.

Whether the women's movement made gains or losses, its bouts of fervent activity seemed punctuated by intervals of lethargy in advancing female rights. It was as if the populace periodically found some need to step back, mulling over prospects for further change. Even during these downtimes, however, female pathfinders still were making differences in public policies and social causes.

Among them was Felicitas Mendez, a Mexican immigrant angered at the segregation of her youngsters in a school for "barrio" children in the Orange County community of Westminster in the mid-1940s. She and her husband launched a legal fight that helped bring down the school segregation laws that had been on California's books since the Civil War. Californians of Mexican ancestry had become particular targets of segregation policies beginning in the early 1900s, when their numbers burgeoned as agribusiness increasingly sought cheap Mexican labor.

Felicitas and Gonzalo Mendez sued Westminster and four other districts in federal court, with strategic support from the League of United Latin American Citizens. They won a ruling in 1946 that mandatory separate schools for students with Spanish surnames violated the equal protection clause of the Fourteenth Amendment. An appellate court upheld the decision. Although the Mendez case was not appealed further, its impacts reverberated in Sacramento. Barely two months after the appellate ruling, Governor Earl Warren signed legislation to end all legally mandated school segregation in California.[15] Seven years later, as chief justice of the US Supreme Court, Warren would write the momentous decision in *Brown v. Board of Education* that ended enforced school segregation nationwide.

While Dolores Huerta is far better-known than Felicitas Mendez, her passion, commitment, and achievements too often have been overshadowed. During more than a half-century of activism on behalf of mostly Latino farmworkers, Huerta was spat upon, verbally assaulted, beaten, jailed numerous times, and thrown out of fields and vineyards.

After Cesar Chavez and Huerta formed the United Farm Workers union, Chavez went into the fields to persuade workers to sign union cards. Huerta negotiated with farmers, met with legislators, and led marches, strikes, and boycotts. Grape boycotts she organized in 1970 and 1975 ultimately won higher-paying jobs and better benefits for thousands of UFW members. Her Sacramento lobbying led to laws removing citizenship requirements for public assistance and making farmworkers eligible for disability and unemployment insurance.

Governor Jerry Brown, who signed UFW-sponsored legislation to create an Agricultural Labor Relations Board in 1975, praised Huerta for "embodying the spirit of Cesar Chavez." His words unwittingly underscored that Huerta's contributions to the cause typically were overwhelmed by public attention to Chavez.

---

[15] In the 1960s and '70s, large populations of Mexican Americans moved from rural areas to concentrated urban communities, prompting legal de facto segregation in which schools were separated along racial and ethnic lines.

"That's the history of the world," she told an interviewer. "I feel that has to change and women are going to have to change it."[16]

Renewing a Drive for Change in the Second Wave

A second-wave women's movement, following long after the first wave's campaign for suffrage, gradually began to make a difference in the number of women who ran for and won public office. Sometimes labeled the women's liberation movement, the second wave from the mid-1960s through the 1980s focused on achieving gains for women (especially white women of relative privilege, it would turn out) in male-dominated workplaces and other venues.

Women and people of color were inadvertently helped by a US Supreme Court ruling that forced California to overhaul its state senate and assembly districts for the 1966 elections—with the side effect of opening up more assembly seats. Shattering records, 32 women ran for state and congressional offices that year. It would become the first banner year for political women in California since the long-ago victories of the first four assemblywomen. The prolonged malaise had reached its depths in 1958, when only 11 California women sought state and federal offices.

(One reason many potential female candidates had snubbed electoral politics in 1958 might be traced to the lingering effects of a brutal US Senate race in 1950. The victor, US Representative Richard Nixon, virtually demolished the reputation of his female opponent, House colleague Helen Gahagan Douglas, by branding her a communist sympathizer. Nixon infamously contended Douglas was "pink down to her underwear." At the time, Douglas was only the third California woman ever elected to the House and the first to win without succeeding a deceased husband.)

Among the notable election victories of 1966, Ivy Baker Priest, a former US treasurer, captured a close contest for treasurer of California, becoming the first woman in state history to win statewide office. Although only two new women were elected to the assembly—just the thirteenth and fourteenth since statehood—both made history. March Fong became the legislature's first Chinese American. Yvonne Brathwaite became its first African-American woman.

Fong would solidify her credentials in the assembly as an advocate of women's causes by memorably smashing a toilet with a sledgehammer at a media event in front of the capitol in 1969, symbolizing her opposition to public pay toilets. Pay potties discriminated against women, she argued, given that urinals were free. Governor Ronald Reagan signed the ban on pay toilets in 1974, near the end of her eight years in the assembly.

March Fong Eu (she had married Henry Eu in 1973) would make history again with her election as California secretary of state—becoming the first Asian

---

[16] Lisa Genasci, "UFW Co-Founder Comes Out of Shadow," Associated Press in the *Los Angeles Times*, May 11, 1995, D8.

American in the nation to win a state executive office. During her five terms at the helm, Eu established a political reform division, adopted programs to boost voter registration, and made it easier for Californians to vote by mail. "Not too bad for a lady born behind a Chinese laundry," she once told the *Los Angeles Times*.[17]

Her onetime assembly colleague, Yvonne Brathwaite (later Yvonne Brathwaite Burke), also built a trailblazing career in public life, winning 10 elections and losing two. She became the first black woman from California to win a seat in the US House. After she lost a bid for state attorney general in 1978, Governor Brown appointed Burke to a vacant seat on the Los Angeles County board of supervisors, where she became the board's first female and first African-American member. Although Burke was defeated for a full term from the affluent, mostly white district, she won a seat on the board from a lower-income district in 1992 and served four terms.

Fracturing Still More Glass Ceilings

Not merely a glass ceiling but a veritable bell jar seemed to encase the state senate for 126 years, until Rose Ann Vuich's upset win from a district in the Central Valley made her California's first woman state senator in 1976. Vuich gently called attention to her gender by ringing a small porcelain bell that rested on her senate desk whenever any of her 39 male colleagues, out of long habit, addressed the "gentlemen of the senate."

With once-stubborn roadblocks beginning to crumble, it took only two years after Vuich's surprise victory for the senate to gain its second female member—Diane Watson of Los Angeles, elected the senate's first African-American woman in 1978. Three years earlier, she had become the first black woman elected to the Los Angeles school board as it dealt with the still-thorny issue of racial integration. One of her campaign advisers, Jerry Zanelli, recalled in an interview: "I think qualified women were starting to step up, and that was the big difference. They believed they could win. A lot of voters were probably thinking, 'The guys have screwed up so bad, let's try a woman.'"

The first Latina to join the legislature, Gloria Molina, considered herself the product of both the feminist and Chicano movements. She narrowly won her hotly contested Democratic primary election in a Los Angeles district that was heavily Latino, ensuring victory in the fall of 1982. After five years in the assembly—focusing on issues such as sexual harassment, school dropouts, and consumer protections—Molina spent the next quarter-century as Los Angeles's first Latina city councilwoman and first Latina county supervisor.

---

[17] Al Martinez, "Political World of March Fong Eu," *Los Angeles Times*, July 23, 1979, B3.

Appointing Record Numbers of Women

Katherine Philips Edson, the Hiram Johnson-appointed industrial welfare commissioner who served three ensuing administrations, belonged to what had been a miniscule club of women to hold key positions in state government until Jerry Brown succeeded Ronald Reagan in 1975. During his four terms in the governor's suite, Brown would prove himself one of California's most consistent assets to the feminist cause, although he typically allowed his record to speak louder than his words on the subject.

In his first two terms, from 1975 to 1983, Brown appointed more than 1,600 women to boards, commissions, state agencies, and departments, including two to his first cabinet. Most controversially, he picked Rose Bird early in his first term to become California's chief justice—the first woman ever appointed to the California Supreme Court. The judicially inexperienced Bird, who voted against imposing the death sentence in all 61 of the death-penalty cases that came before her as chief justice, was denied reconfirmation to the bench by voters in 1986. So were two of Brown's male appointees to the high court.

Brown in his third (2011–2015) and fourth (2015–2019) terms was appointing so many women to so many thousands of posts within the sprawling executive branch that—without fanfare or drumroll—by 2015 women had achieved appointment parity with men.[18] Illustrating that timing in politics may be nearly as important as substance, Californians barely noticed this high-water mark on the scale of political gender equality. In contrast, Dianne Feinstein was rebuked for pledging during her 1990 quest for governor to fill appointive posts with equal numbers of men and women as chief executive and to appoint people of color in numbers representative of their ratios in the population. Critics from pundits to everyday citizens accused her of seeking to govern by quota rather than quality. Californians opposed Feinstein's pledge by a margin of four to one. Even women were opposed, according to a *Los Angeles Times* poll, by two to one.[19]

A Silver Lining in Feinstein's Loss for Governor

Paradoxically, Feinstein's loss of the governor's race to Pete Wilson had a luminous upside. Barely two years later, she was sworn in as the first female US senator from California to fill the remaining two years of the Senate term that Wilson had abandoned to become governor. He was left struggling with gushing red ink in Sacramento. With Feinstein's election to a partial term and Barbara Boxer's open-seat win for a full term in 1992, California became the first state to send two women senators to Washington. Feinstein and Boxer had campaigned together at a time when women voters, especially, were still angered over the

---

[18] "The Status of Women in California Government in 2017," *California Women Lead.* http://www.cawomenlead.org/?page=StatewideReports.

[19] Skelton, "Wilson, Feinstein."

all-male Senate Judiciary Committee's dismissive treatment of Anita Hill. In her riveting, nationally televised testimony, Hill in 1991 told the committee that her former boss, Supreme Court nominee Clarence Thomas, had sexually harassed her. A backlash fueled by the committee's seeming insensitivity to abuses in the workplace sent so many women into elective offices in 1992 that it was dubbed the "Year of the Woman." In California, the ranks of female legislators rose from 22 to 27 and those in the state's House delegation more than doubled from three to seven. Female US senators increased from two to six, and Feinstein became the first woman on the Senate Judiciary Committee.

A quarter of a century after the Year of the Woman, however, gains by political women seemed to have largely plateaued—or even fallen. In 2017, men held majorities approaching 80 percent (or more) in governing bodies ranging from Congress to the California legislature to city councils across the state. The US Senate numbered 21 women among its 100 members.[20] In the US House, the female ratio was 19.3 percent. During the 2017 legislative session that wrapped up work in mid-September, just 21.7 percent of the 120 lawmakers were women, down from a high of nearly 31 percent in 2006. It was the lowest ratio since 1998 and put California behind more than 30 other states, by the calculations of the Center for American Women and Politics at Rutgers University.[21]

As it turned out, however, Hillary Clinton's unexpected loss to Donald Trump would have unforeseen consequences. As Trump took office in 2017, millions of American women were becoming politically galvanized in ways unseen since at least 1992, if ever. Amid record-setting women's marches and a #MeToo movement reminiscent of Anita Hill's long-ago battle against unwanted sexual advances, female advocacy and empowerment organizations began grooming unprecedented numbers of women to run in the midterm races of 2018.

Among dozens of nonpartisan California groups promoting female candidacies were California Women Lead, Run Women Run, Black Women Organized for Political Action, and Hispanas Organized for Political Equality.[22] The June primary elections for the US House drew 62 female major- and minor-party candidates in California—over 26 percent more than in 2012, when a previous record

---

[20] In early 2018, Tina Smith and Cindy Hyde-Smith became the twenty-second and twenty-third women in the Senate, each setting a Senate record when sworn in—Smith in January and Hyde-Smith in April. Smith was appointed by the governor of Minnesota and Hyde-Smith by the governor of Mississippi to fill vacated seats pending the outcome of the November elections. Each was running to keep her seat. Smith replaced Al Franken, who resigned over accusations of sexual misconduct, while Hyde-Smith replaced Thad Cochran, who left because of health issues.

[21] "State Fact Sheet—California," Center for American Woman and Politics, http://www.cawp.rutgers.edu/state_fact_sheets/ca.

[22] For an extensive list of advocacy groups for political women in California, see "Political and Resource Leadership Map," Center for American Women and Politics, Eagleton Institute for Politics, Rutgers University, http://www.cawp.rutgers.edu/education/leadership-resources.

had been set.[23] An overview of results and impacts from the 2018 elections is offered in the Epilogue.

High and Low Points in Closing the Political Gender Gap

In what would prove a mixed blessing for political women, California voters in 1990 had limited the number of terms that legislators and state officeholders could serve. Initially, more women and people of color successfully ran for open seats vacated by "termed-out" incumbents, who were often white males, increasing the legislature's diversity. Then—as we will see in more detail in Chapter 11—the law began terming women out, too. In 2012, voters tweaked the limits by allowing incumbents to serve a total of 12 years, either in one house or a combination of both legislative houses. The result: open seats, those most receptive to women and other newcomers, will be scarce until 2024.

California's experience in Congress—which has no term limits—suggests that restricting the number of times an incumbent can seek reelection ultimately may hurt political women more than it helps. As evidence, the composition of California's 55-member congressional delegation, including Senators Kamala Harris and Feinstein, was 34.5 percent female in 2017—significantly higher than the ratio in the term-limited legislature. Since members are free to run as often as they choose, some of the state's most enduringly popular female leaders serve in Washington. Most notably, Nancy Pelosi, a San Franciscan first elected to the House in 1986, was chosen by her peers to be the first female House speaker from 2007 to 2011. Even after Democrats lost control of the House in the 2010 elections, Pelosi as minority leader arguably remained the nation's top woman officeholder into 2018.

Scholarship finds that when women run, they can win.[24] Yet all but one of California's eight elected state officeholders, such as governor or treasurer, were men in 2017. The lone exception was state controller Betty Yee. (Kamala Harris, California's first woman state attorney general and the first African American in the office, left Sacramento for Washington after her election in 2016 to succeed Boxer.) Heading into the 2018 elections, no woman had ever been elected governor or lieutenant governor in California.

Among local governments, just five of California's 58 counties had female majorities on their elected boards of supervisors in 2017, according to figures compiled by California Women Lead. On an upside, though, one of these was vast

---

[23] Statement of Vote at Primary Election held on June 5, 2012, California State Printing Office, Sacramento, 2012; Statement of Vote at Primary Election held on June 5, 2018, California State Printing Office, Sacramento, 2012.

[24] Danny Hayes and Jennifer L. Lawless pursue this argument in their 2016 book, *Women on the Run: Gender, Media, and Political Campaigns in a Polarized Era* (New York: Cambridge University Press). In today's politics, they assert, "candidate sex plays a minimal role in the vast majority of U.S. elections" (7).

Los Angeles County. Across the state's nearly 500 cities, just 15 percent had majorities of city councilwomen; 50 percent had only one councilwoman or none. Of the 10 largest cities in California, only one had a woman mayor—Libby Schaaf of Oakland.[25]

Coinciding with the Year of the Woman in 1992 had been the rise of a third wave of the feminist movement, one that had sought to be at once more inclusive and more individualistic than its predecessors. Bent on overcoming the shortcomings of the second wave, especially, it put its emphasis on individual choices. This wave could readily embrace rights and freedoms for women of color, LGBTQ communities, and personal expressions of sexuality. Perhaps because it was less concerned with united action, however, collectively won political gains would slow or stagnate.

Given the promise of today's resurgent feminism, some scholars see an emerging fourth wave, reliant on social media to promote interactive responses on multiple fronts of interest to women (and men). It is manifested in women's marches, #MeToo causes, and arguably in social justice and reformist movements such as Black Lives Matter and the student-led "March for Our Lives" campaign against gun violence.

In her book, *The Paradox of Gender Equality*, Kristin Goss observes that the wave metaphor has likened the long quest for women's rights to ocean waters that alternatively crest and recede. However, Goss argues, the metaphor overlooks the many ways women have influenced policy on social issues during supposed lulls between the waves. Instead, Goss and some others suggest, a *river* metaphor would more accurately describe how women's activism has flowed, branching into streams that may gain their own force.[26] This book seeks to capture this sense of flow, even as we track the waves.

The State Senate's First Woman Leader

Even before the ballots were cast in the much-anticipated midterms, political women were continuing to break longstanding glass ceilings. Former San Diego Mayor Toni Atkins was sworn in as the first woman—and first openly lesbian or gay senator—to lead the 40-member state senate on March 21, 2018. Her election by senate colleagues smashed a barrier that had endured 168 years. "It's the first time. And it's about time," Atkins declared to well-wishers, family members, and legislators from both houses who packed into the senate chamber. In remarks that could describe the trailblazing women whose stories are told in this book, she added:

---

[25] "The Status of Women in California Government—2017," *California Women Lead*, http://c.ymcdn.com/sites/www.cawomenlead.org/resource/resmgr/files/7.26.2017_Status_of_Women_in.pdf.

[26] Kristin A. Goss, *The Paradox of Gender Equality: How American Women's Groups Gained and Lost Their Public Voice* (Ann Arbor: University of Michigan Press, 2013), 7.

But if I'm touching any part of the sky today, it's because I'm standing on the shoulders of couriers of courage. Individuals who refused to accept closed doors, hidden closets or glass ceilings. They weren't waiting—they were working. Marching in streets. Battling in courtrooms. Speaking out. Stepping up.[27]

Atkins also holds the unique distinction of having served as California governor for 12 hours when she was the assembly speaker in 2014, while the governor and lieutenant governor were out of the state.

When women take office, public policies can change to benefit girls, women, families, and often boys and men. In California, these have produced paid family leave, tougher treatment of sexual harassment and domestic violence, insurance coverage of contraceptives, and greater equity between the genders in costs for retail services. People, including politicians, are influenced by their own experiences and their familiarity with others. In 2017, there was enough support to pass a female-sponsored bill—signed by Brown—requiring public schools in low-income areas to stock bathrooms with free tampons and menstrual pads. The topic would have been unthinkable for floor debate without a critical mass of women lawmakers.

This Introduction has been drawn largely from the chapters that follow. *Paving the Way* tells the stories and backstories of remarkable women pathfinders who left their marks along the elusive trail to political gender equality in California. Unanswerable, however, is what it might take to one day close that gender gap.

As the country prepared to honor the centennial of national woman suffrage in 2020, the question was not only timely but quintessentially American—fundamental to the nation's continuing struggle to move ever closer to the evolving vision of equality enshrined in its founding documents. Many hoped a reinvigorated women's movement—this time more consciously promoting advances by women of color—could translate into new gains in voting booths, governing chambers, and beyond. California is more populous than many nations and more prosperous than most, with an economy bigger than all but a handful. It is geographically immense as well, fronting more than 800 miles of Pacific Ocean. Beyond all that, however, as the end destination of the nation's westward movement since the days of the Gold Rush, California has signified a sense of challenge, change, and destiny (although too often at the expense of persecuted native peoples and others of color).

An ending to the collective story of women paving the way inside and outside of California's formal political structures is still unwritten. To appreciate what

---

[27] "Toni Atkins' Remarks on Being Sworn in as 48th President pro Tempore of the California State Senate," March 21, 2018, http://sd39.senate.ca.gov/news/20180321-toni-atkins%E2%80%99-remarks-being-sworn-48th-president-pro-tempore-california-senate.

California women have achieved and not achieved since statehood in 1850 is, in some ways, to understand how American women of diverse racial and ethnic backgrounds have fared overall. These pages tell an overarching story of struggle that, by nearly any measure, has no end in sight.

Chapter 1

1854–1896
Equal Rights Pioneers Challenge Traditional Gender Roles

> "I coaxed, I entreated. I would have reasoned had
> they been reasonable men."
>
> —Clara Foltz

One newspaper denounced her as a free-lover and a socialist. Another called her "Pittsey." Emily Pitts Stevens was making news instead of covering it. She had wormed her way into San Francisco's fraternal order of ink-stained newspaper editors in 1869 when she was a 25-year-old schoolteacher who had moved to California from New York. She bought a half interest in the *California Weekly Mercury*—which called itself a "Journal of Romance and Literature," and turned it into the West's first suffrage newspaper, later changing its name to *The Pioneer* to better reflect its mission of fearlessly defending the rights of women. She charged three dollars for a yearly subscription and was praised by that icon of suffrage, Susan B. Anthony, as a forceful writer, "a nervously organized, pleasing little woman, with dark eyes, curly hair, refined manners and features."[1]

Pitts Stevens referred to women as revolutionists, and in her first issue as publisher, she left no doubt about the newspaper's editorial policy. "The wrongs of woman, the many abuses she has suffered," she wrote, "have at last [been] aroused from their lethargic sleep. . . . We shall claim for her the right of suffrage—believing by this she will gain the position for which God intended her—equality with man."[2]

Pitts Stevens backed up her talk with action, hiring women to set type for her newspaper in defiance of the "arbitrary and unjust laws of the Printers' Union"[3] and pushing for an eight-hour workday for women. She wrote about "young, industrious, and pure-minded girls" heading to work before seven o'clock in the morning, then "trudging homeward, not tripping so lightly as in the morning . . .

---

[1] Roger Levenson, *Women in Printing: Northern California* 1857–1890 (Santa Barbara: Capra Press, 1994), 90.

[2] *California Weekly Mercury*, January 24, 1869, 2, quoted in Levenson, 91.

[3] Advertisement for *The Pioneer* in Nevada County Directory for 1871–1872, quoted in Levenson, 95.

they are tired—very tired."[4] She wondered why young working men in San Francisco were establishing an eight-hour reform for themselves but saw fit to ignore the plight of young women.

Despite her "refined manners," the feisty editor refused to back down from a fight and created a nineteenth-century version of a media frenzy the evening of June 24, 1872, when she and four fellow suffragists strode into San Francisco's venerable Platt's Hall at Montgomery and Bush streets on a mission to confront the featured speaker, a noted antisuffragist. While a brass band played music outside the auditorium, the five women took seats up front and were primed for a fight. A newspaper advertisement that day heralded the appearance of Mrs. J. Blakesley Frost, the noted author of a Civil War history. Frost was described as a "champion of her own sex . . . [who] testily throws down the gage of battle." The ad ridiculed "the masculine traits so strongly characteristic of the 'Susan Anthony' school." And it took on Emily Pitts Stevens by name, saying she and her suffragist colleagues "have triumphantly fulminated their peculiar doctrines, defying the 'Lords of Creation.'"[5]

At the outset of her lecture, Frost suggested suffrage would be destructive to the family, church, and state. She accused suffragists of supporting free love and rejecting the Bible, and she argued that women already possessed all the power they would ever need. In a show of defiance, Pitts Stevens and compatriots laughed sarcastically, made loud derisive comments, and frequently interrupted the talk with applause when it was not intended.

The speech had attracted an audience of about 40, and from the back of the hall a man shouted, "I move those ladies behave themselves." Also in the audience was David Meeker, a state assemblyman representing San Francisco, who jumped to his feet. "Second that motion," he shouted. Pitts Stevens fired back, "We have a right to applaud, if we please," to which Meeker responded, "I intend to make you behave yourselves, Mrs. Stevens. You are behaving disgracefully." To a combination of cheers and hisses, Pitts Stevens defiantly replied, "You will find it difficult to make us do anything we don't like." Frost then joined the fray: "This is the class of women who would elbow their way to the polls. I suppose we have here a sample of what we might expect if women were in power."[6]

The argument continued for a few minutes, and then abated until the end of the lecture when an angry Pitts Stevens made a bee-line for Meeker as he began to exit the hall and astonished onlookers by challenging him to a duel. "You insulted me in a public hall and I demand the satisfaction usual among gentlemen." Meeker laughed at the woman, but she stood her ground. "Will you apologize?" she demanded. "Of course not," Meeker replied, at which point Pitts Stevens reached

---

[4] *California Weekly Mercury*, April 18, 1869, 2, quoted in Levenson, 92.

[5] "The Champion against Woman Suffrage, Mrs. J. Blakesley Frost," *Daily Alta California*, June 24, 1872, 2.

[6] "A Shameful Scene at Platt's Hall—Women Suffragists Disgracing Their Sex," *Sacramento Daily Union*, June 26, 1872, 1; "Anti-Woman Suffrage—Lecture by Mrs. Frost," *Sacramento Daily Union*, June 26, 1872, 3.

into her pocket, pulled out a derringer and aimed it directly at the assemblyman's chest. A bystander grabbed hold of it, and Pitts Stevens agreed to put the pistol back in her pocket.

It was a scandalous scene, and the newspapers loved it. The *Sacramento Daily Union* called it, "A Shameful Scene at Platt's Hall—Women Suffragists Disgracing Their Sex." The newspaper concluded: "The ladies allowed their zeal for the cause to make them forget the rules of politeness and good order, and Meeker forgot that he was talking in public to a woman." In its account of the confrontation, the *Mariposa Gazette* characterized the newspaper publisher's behavior as "naughty," but it clearly admired her fighting spirit. "[*The Gazette*] cannot indorse her radical views about suffrage. But when it comes to a fight between her and old Meeker, we are a Stevens man all the time."[7]

A couple of days after the incident, Pitts Stevens tried to correct the record with a statement to the newspapers. She denied drawing a gun on Meeker. "She says she is afraid to open the drawer where her husband keeps his derringer, and belongs to the peace society. What she did have in her hand she does not state. Her friends claim it was only a dummy pistol, but others think different."[8]

Emily Pitts Stevens occupies a hallowed position in the pantheon of early suffrage advocates and opinion leaders. She used her newspaper as a pulpit to unabashedly preach against gender inequality and forcefully urged the all-male legislature to give women the vote. She and her colleagues were considered novelties by the popular press. Once, after a series of capitol speeches by Pitts Stevens and others, which packed the galleries, the *San Francisco Chronicle* mockingly reported on the women's efforts "to cackle on the subject of their rights and wrongs." The newspaper said the crowd "received her remarks with good humored and frequent—too frequent—applause. Another old lady followed. Her voice was cracked, and she lifted it very high, and people laughed immoderately. Pitts looked daggers, and the applause increased." Finally, the *Chronicle* continued, the chairman "declared the séance adjourned. The audience enjoyed the performance; it was better, they all declared, than a circus." The newspaper declared that the prospects for female suffragists did not improve. "Let us crow," it concluded.[9]

"A Good Spokeswoman for Her Cause"— ## Sarah Pellet

California was late to the suffrage debate. More than two decades earlier, in 1848, the famed Seneca Falls Convention in New York—the nation's first women's rights convention—had passed a resolution in favor of woman suffrage. But

---

[7] "Pittsey Stevens in a Desperate Attitude," *Mariposa Gazette*, June 28, 1872, 2.

[8] "By State Telegraph—Mrs. Stevens," *Sacramento Daily Union*, June 28, 1872, 1.

[9] "Sacramento: The Female Suffragists," *San Francisco Chronicle*, March 15, 1872, 1.

in frontier California, women activists at first were concerned with other issues, and a young Ohio transplant, Sarah Pellet, was leading the way.

When Pellet took the stage at San Francisco's Musical Hall on September 29, 1854, she caused an immediate sensation. Charging one dollar admission, she was a fascinating rarity—the first female lecturer ever seen in the fast-growing center of the nation's newest state. Newspaper accounts described Pellet as a small, neat woman in her thirties. An advance story in the *Daily Alta California,* characterized her as "a woman of considerable intellectual power, a clear mind, and a pleasing address." Mere curiosity, readers were told, should ensure a large audience.[10]

Educated at Oberlin College, the first US college to offer coeducation, Pellet was a friend of Susan B. Anthony and the vanguard of California's nascent movement that sought to rally women and persuade the ruling male class on the need for such reforms as temperance, women's rights, and spiritualism—the controversial belief that spirits communicated with the living and even instructed humans about ethics and morals. She and others also hit the lecture circuit arguing for clothing reform, specifically, the need to replace tight-laced corsets with less-restrictive undergarments, called Bloomers. Pellet had arrived in California after a lengthy and arduous voyage from New York, through 70 miles of the mosquito-infested Panama jungle, then up the Pacific coast by steamship. She had raised eyebrows by wearing brown linen Bloomers on the ship.

Pellet's lecture that night, "Political Reform and the Means of Obtaining It," was witnessed by about 150 curious San Franciscans, half of whom were women. Despite the favorable build-up, much of the male press turned quickly. According to one account, many in the audience "seemed in agony; but they controlled themselves, and took another chew—the men did—while the ladies smiled and yawned. . . ."[11] The *Daily Alta California* decided not to "question the propriety of women becoming public lecturers, but it called her talk rambling and dull, suggesting that Pellet had "decidedly mistaken her profession." It noted that only the lecturer's head appeared above the podium. "Her voice is not pleasant, and her manner of delivery anything but pleasurable . . . nobody appeared to be able to understand what she was driving at."[12] Readers of the city's leading newspapers had no idea, either; accounts of her speech omitted anything substantive from Pellet's discussion. The next evening, Pellet gave a second lecture. The audience shrunk to 22. "This must be rather discouraging to the lady's prospects of reform," the *Daily Alta California* snickered, "if her work is to be limited to twenty-two persons each night."[13]

---

[10] Miss Pellet's Lecture, *Daily Alta California*, September 29, 1854, 2.

[11] Levenson, 43–44.

[12] "Miss Pellet's Lecture on Political Reform," *Daily Alta California*, October 7, 1854, 6.

[13] "Miss Pellet's Second Lecture, *Daily Alta California,* October 2, 1854. 2.

Undaunted, Pellet headed to California's sprawling mining camps, lecturing hard-drinking prospectors in lawless Gold Country about the evils of alcohol. Overnight, tiny clearings adjacent to foothill rivers had become powerful magnets for fortune hunters. Famed historian Hubert Howe Bancroft estimated California's nonnative population at the start of 1848 to be 14,000, of whom 7,500 were Spanish Californians and 6,500 were "foreigners."[14] Four months after James Marshall's January 24th gold discovery, the *San Francisco Californian*—initially published in Monterey and the first newspaper printed on the Pacific Coast between Oregon and the Equator—notified readers that if they were about to leave town for the gold region, they could have their newspapers forwarded to New Helvetia (Sacramento).[15] Five days later, the newspaper reported that a miner had recently pulled "$128 worth of the real stuff in one day's washing." The stampede was on. "The whole country, from San Francisco to Los Angeles, and from the sea shore to the base of the Sierra Nevada, resounds with the sordid cry of 'gold, GOLD, GOLD!'" while the field is left half planted, the house half-built, and everything neglected but the manufacture of shovels and pickaxes."[16]

By 1852, California's nonnative population had increased about 13-fold to 181,000—with five men for every woman. Bancroft noted that during the onset of the Gold Rush, one could scarcely find a single woman in the rough-and-tumble mining camps, "and where one was found she proved too often only the fallen image, the center of gyrating revelry and discord."[17]

Saloons and gambling halls were the centerpiece of a miner's off-hours existence. Alcohol was blamed for crime, poverty, abuse, and disease. *The Pioneer* reported on a series of letters that Louise Amelia Knapp Smith Clapp wrote to her sister in Massachusetts, which described the influence of alcohol on lives in the camps and how formerly wealthy miners—earning hundreds of dollars a day—had become drunken gamblers who saw their fortunes disappear. Even worse, "In the short space of twenty-four days, we have had murders, fearful accidents, bloody deaths, a mob, whippings, a hanging, an attempt at suicide, and a fatal duel." She told of a stabbing incident involving a Spaniard and a naturalized citizen from Ireland. The Spaniard had a "Mejicana hanging on his arm." The first act of the camp's Vigilance Committee was to try the woman—not the combatants. "Some went so far as to say, she ought to be hung, for she was the indirect cause of the fight. You see always," she wrote, "it is the old, cowardly excuse of Adam in Paradise: 'The woman tempted me and I did eat.'" The woman was exiled from the camp.[18]

---

[14] Hubert Howe Bancroft, *The Works of Hubert Howe Bancroft*, Vol. XXII (San Francisco: The History Company, 1886), 643.

[15] "The Gold Mine—Newspapers," *San Francisco Californian*, May 24, 1848, 1.

[16] "To Our Readers," *San Francisco Californian*, May 24, 1848, 4.

[17] Bancroft, Vol. XXIII, 232.

[18] Shirley, "California in 1852," *The Pioneer or, California Monthly Magazine*, Vol. IV (July-December 1855): 103, 104–06.

It was this environment that Sarah Pellet encountered on Christmas Eve, 1854, as she arrived, likely on horseback, in Doten's Bar on the banks of the North Fork of the American River. Doten's Bar, built 80 feet above the river, was nestled among a series of mining camps—among them Rattlesnake Bar, Whiskey Bar, Milk Punch Bar, Deadman's Bar, and Condemned Bar. By 1854, Sierra foothill miners were still extracting upwards of $70 million in gold annually, but the easily found deposits had been worked over, and the state's gold take would gradually recede in the ensuing years. In Doten's Bar, canvas tents had been replaced by a trading post and hotel, saloons, livery stables, two bakeries, a drug store, and a two-story building that housed the town hall, a concert hall, and ballroom. California was in the midst of one of its periodic droughts, but it was bitterly cold that night. More than 30 miles down the foothills in Sacramento, water froze "to the thickness of glass."[19]

In her lecture, Pellet praised the state of Maine, which had enacted a tough law prohibiting the manufacture and sale of alcohol. And she received some positive coverage. The *Sacramento Daily Union*'s Placer County correspondent praised her "pleasing but modest style," calling her a tolerably fair speaker" with fairly distinct articulation. She was, the reporter concluded, "a good spokeswoman for her cause."[20]

Pellet, the fearless vagabond, continued to lecture and make news in California for another 11 months. In April, she delivered another talk on temperance in the remote Placer County town of Washington, again earning praise from the *Daily Union* as "the distinguished female lecturer." The following morning, in a daring move for a young, unmarried female, "she left on horseback for another lecture at Cache Creek in Yolo County," more than 80 miles to the southwest.[21] In a whimsical bit of story placement, the article on Pellet's speech appeared next to a news item on a giant pound-and-a-half mushroom on exhibit in San Francisco.

In the ensuing months, there were speeches at Mokelumne Hill, Sonora, Weaverville, and other mining sites, and she shared the dais with California's third governor, John Bigler, at a Sacramento May Day celebration. In Spanish Flat, Pellet's mere presence drew an astounding crowd of 500 respectful men—nearly half of the town's entire population—to her speech in Poker Hall, a converted gambling den. When she finished her address, she asked listeners to come forward and sign a pledge and petition for the organization of a local Sons of Temperance lodge. She proposed to import 5,000 young, marriageable girls from the New England states, who would be "consigned to the various divisions of the Sons of Temperance, who are to provide for their wants, husbands, included."[22]

In the fall of 1855, Pellet took her reform message to southern Oregon, but her timing was unfortunate. The US Army and local militias were fighting Native

[19] "The City," *Sacramento Daily Union*, December 23, 1854, 2; December 29, 2.
[20] "Placer County Correspondence," *Sacramento Daily Union*, December 29, 1848, 3.
[21] "Temperance," *Sacramento Daily Union*, April 24, 1855, 3.
[22] *Red Bluff Beacon*, May 26, 1858, 1.

Americans in the Rogue River Wars. A dispatch in the *San Francisco Sun* announced the unceremonious end of her lecture tour: "Miss Sarah Pellet, lecturer on Temperance, left on the Golden Age yesterday. She despaired of converting the Oregon Indians, and narrowly escaped ornamenting one of their wigwams with her hair."[23]

The temperance movement in California was a harbinger of the women's rights battles to come, emboldening increasing numbers of women to push back against cultural strictures that confined them to the political shadows. In time, California's temperance crusaders would work with elite white women's clubs to curb prostitution, end child labor, and censure "impure books."[24]

The Beginning of California's Suffrage Movement— Laura de Force Gordon

Sarah Pellet eventually would return to the East Coast, teach school, and become a reporter. Her departure would not leave a vacuum. A year before Emily Pitts Stevens first used her newspaper to champion women's voting rights, Laura de Force Gordon was raising the issue in speeches up and down California. Susan B. Anthony credited Gordon with giving more than 100 speeches in a single year. She delivered what is believed to be the first speech on suffrage in California on February 19, 1868 at San Francisco's Platt's Hall.

Outspoken and fiercely dedicated to her numerous causes, Laura de Force was one of nine children born to a Pennsylvania couple in 1838. She and her grief-stricken family had turned to spiritualism after one of her brothers died when she was a teenager. A mostly self-taught young woman gifted in oral and written communication skills, she toured the Northeast giving lectures about contacting the departed. It was on one of her speaking trips that she met, and later married, Charles Gordon, a doctor. The couple traveled to Civil War hospitals, and after the war they rode a converted hospital wagon across the nation's mid-section and settled first in White Plains, Nevada, and later in the San Joaquin Valley town of Mokelumne (later Lodi). In 1867, while on the lecture circuit in Northern California, the *Grass Valley Union* said "the lady talks like a book though she looks like a woman."[25]

Spiritualists had a substantial following in those pioneer days, but they also were mocked and ridiculed for their beliefs, including one tenet of spiritualism that espoused gender equality. Days before her watershed San Francisco appearance, Gordon placed a small newspaper ad that invited guests to hear a new topic

---

[23] "Gone," *Marysville Daily Herald (*from *San Francisco Sun),*" December 8, 1855, 2.

[24] Mary Ann Irwin, *California Women in Politics*, Robert W. Cherny, Mary Ann Irwin, and Ann Marie Wilson, eds. (Lincoln: University of Nebraska Press, 2011), 346.

[25] Ralph Lea and Christi Kennedy, "Laura de Force Gordon was Lodi's Early Suffragette," *Lodi News-Sentinel*, October 1, 2011, http://www.lodinews.com/features/vintage_lodi/image_ef87b69b-54bc-5e44-b194-d417ead4cba6.html.

Figure 1.1. Laura de Force Gordon
Credit: Courtesy of California State Library

in California lecture circles. It proved to be just as divisive as communicating with the dead. "Subject: 'The Elective Franchise,' Who Shall Vote?" the ad said. Tickets cost 25 cents.[26] Accounts of the audience size are contradictory. Anthony, in her exhaustive history of the suffrage movement, characterized the attendance for this landmark event as "small." However, a San Francisco newspaper reporter suggested it was a "tolerably large audience." In a brief mention near the bottom of a lengthy column reviewing opera performances, a masquerade ball, and a large rock on display at Montgomery and California Streets, the *Daily Alta California* said the lecture that launched the state's suffrage movement "was well received." The newspaper said her arguments were "handled with ability."[27]

Gordon had found a new and exciting calling—a zealous passion to bring full equality to California women. The state's constitution, written before statehood during the Gold Rush, was progressive in many respects. It provided for freedom of assembly, speech, and press, and prohibited imprisonment for debt, slavery, and all legal distinctions between individuals on religious grounds. A particularly forward provision allowed wives to own their own property. But it limited voting rights to white male citizens over the age of 21 who had been residents of the states for six months and, according to Anthony, it made "outlaws and pariahs of all the noble women who endured the hardships of the journey by land or sea

---

[26] "Lecture," *Daily Alta California*, February 16, 1868, 4.
[27] "Amusements, etc.," *Daily Alta California*, February 20, 1868, 1.

. . . that instrument cannot be said to secure justice, equality and liberty to all its citizens."[28]

Racial Divisions and Heroic Struggles—Maria Amparo Ruiz de Burton, Biddy Mason, and Mary Ellen Pleasant

The national outlook was equally bleak. Thousands of women had participated in the antislavery movement, delivering petitions to Congress and writing articles for abolitionist newspapers. But suffragists were particularly disheartened after the recent ratification of two post-Civil War amendments to the US Constitution that turned their backs on women. The Fourteenth Amendment (1868) penalized states that denied the vote to adult males, while the Fifteenth Amendment (1870) officially banned race as a barrier to voting, but didn't mention sex. The nation's leading suffrage organization, the American Equal Rights Association, split bitterly during the ratification process for the Fifteenth Amendment. One angry faction—led by Susan B. Anthony and Elizabeth Cady Stanton—campaigned against ratification, because it omitted women. "I will cut off this right arm of mine before I will ask for the ballot for the Negro and not for the woman," Anthony said. An indignant Anna Howard Shaw, president of the National Woman Suffrage Association, argued that the Fifteenth Amendment made black men political superiors of white women. "Never before in the history of the world have men made former slaves the political masters of their former mistresses!"[29]

It is an inconvenient truth that during the nineteenth and early twentieth centuries, California's women's movement was mostly a white endeavor. When middle-class and wealthy white women formed social and suffrage clubs to advocate for reforms, minorities were excluded. Many women of color, however, faced more daunting challenges that dealt with freedom and basic rights, and they turned to the legal system to redress wrongs.

Famed author Maria Amparo Ruiz de Burton, who was born into an aristocratic Mexican family, spent decades in court trying to hold on to land holdings near San Diego that she and her husband had acquired in 1854. Her legal issues remained in doubt when she died in 1895.[30]

Bridget "Biddy" Mason used the legal system to win her freedom. She was born a slave in Georgia, and in 1851 walked most of the two-thousand-mile journey to California behind her master's wagon. California's constitution outlawed slavery, but in a move that belied the myth of western freedom, state lawmakers

---

[28] Susan B. Anthony, *History of Woman Suffrage, 1876–1885*, Vol. III (Rochester, N.Y.: Charles Mann Printing Co., 1886), 750.

[29] Evette Dionne, "Women's Suffrage Leaders Left Out Black Women," *Teen Vogue*, August 18, 2017, https://teenvogue.com/story/womens-suffrage-leaders-left-out-black-women.

[30] "Maria Ruiz de Burton," *History of American Women*, http://www.womenhistory-blog.com/2014/10/maria-ruiz-de-burton.html.

in 1852 approved a fugitive slave law that put the freedom of many transported African Americans in jeopardy. Even after the law elapsed in 1855, Mason's owner continued to claim her as property. She challenged him in court even though state law prohibited blacks from testifying against whites. She won her freedom in 1856, with Judge Benjamin Hayes declaring, "All men should be left to their own pursuit of freedom and happiness."[31]

Settling in Los Angeles, a small town with a few thousand residents, Mason worked as a midwife and nurse. Diligently, she saved her money and bought two parcels of land in what would become the city's downtown business district. She bought and sold real estate, becoming wealthy and using much of her fortune to help the less fortunate. After a devastating flood that left many people homeless, Mason paid for groceries for the victims—black or white. She provided financial aid for the poor in the city's slums, and she founded a church and paid its taxes and expenses.[32]

Shortly after "Biddy" Mason won her freedom, another former slave—Mary Ellen Pleasant—used the courts to advance minority rights. She had inherited a substantial sum of money from her first husband, much of which she used to help escaped slaves. Arriving in San Francisco in 1852, Pleasant found work as a cook and opened boardinghouses for influential and well-to-do men in the city. Investing wisely in Wells Fargo, mining companies, and laundries, Pleasant amassed a fortune and helped finance abolitionist John Brown's raid on Harper's Ferry in West Virginia.[33] She rescued slaves and badgered San Francisco merchants to hire African Americans.

In the mid-1860s, Pleasant put her stamp on the era's civil rights movement by lobbying the state legislature to rescind the law that prevented black people from testifying in court, and she challenged the discriminatory practices of a San Francisco transportation company. One day in 1866, as she stood on Folsom Street awaiting a street car, Pleasant was refused admittance. The conductor told her that the company policy prohibited "colored" people from riding in its cars. Pleasant sued the company, dropping the action only after it "agreed to convey colored people over their road in the cars the same as white persons," according to a news report.[34] Later, in the 1880s, a few Chinese immigrant women successfully used the court system to circumvent provisions of the Chinese Exclusion Act (1882) and school segregation.

---

[31] "Biddy Mason: They Had a Dream," *Lincoln Star*, June 5, 1975, 4.

[32] Jeri Chase Ferris, "The Story of Biddy Mason," *Los Angeles Times*, February 9, 2001, E9.

[33] Susan Spano, "Stitching Together Fragments of Clues in a California Mystery Woman's Life," *Los Angeles Times*, May 6, 2001, L7.

[34] *Marysville Daily Appeal*, July 6, 1866, 2; Claran Conliffe, "Mary Ellen Pleasant, Businesswoman and Civil Rights Activist," August 18, 2017, https://headstuff.org/history/terrible-people-from-history/mary-ellen-pleasant-black-businesswoman-civil-rights-activist.

Opening Doors for Women at the University of California

Privileged white activists, meanwhile, started advancing the cause of woman suffrage in California only months after the Fifteenth Amendment became part of the US Constitution. Laura de Force Gordon helped organize the first state woman suffrage convention in San Francisco. The local press gave it ample coverage, at times mixing the trivial with the substantive. "Much confusion seemed to prevail as to whether the Lady President should be called 'Mrs. Chairman' or Mrs. Chairwoman,'" noted the *Daily Alta California*. Gordon told the 120 delegates about her travels on the lecture circuit, but she admonished the women to be more forceful. "Mrs. Gordon said she had noticed that when questions had been put to the meeting not more than a dozen timid voices were heard to be saying 'aye' or 'no.' Let the ladies not be afraid to open their mouths. Let them not sit by like so many mummies."[35]

In setting forth its principles, the convention called attention to the fact that women were being denied natural rights that had been awarded to men, which tended not only to "humiliate, impoverish, degrade and debase women, but also to rob Governments of her elevating, purifying, attractive and humanizing presence and influences. . . ." Another convention resolution excoriated the fledgling University of California for barring females from the school. The university had been founded in 1868 and opened the following year in Oakland while the first buildings on its new, sprawling Berkeley campus were being built. The resolution said "barring females from the University is a direct insult to women, and merits our condemnation, etc., etc."[36]

A year after that first suffrage convention, the university changed its policy and opened its doors to women. The class of 1873—the first to graduate from the university—comprised 12 men, including James Budd, who would enter a career in politics and be elected California's governor in 1894. Budd was sympathetic to the women's movement. He signed legislation that placed woman suffrage on the 1896 ballot, which failed, and he appointed Phoebe Apperson Hearst, wife of mining tycoon George Hearst, the first female regent of the university. Hearst became one of the university's most beloved figures. She was a tireless advocate of women's education, having established the school's first scholarships for female students, and she dedicated a sizeable portion of her family fortune to the young university's physical development.

The women didn't confine their efforts merely to securing the franchise. They built coalitions and joined with others to advance the cause of women's equality in other ways. One of their advocacy partners was Clara Foltz—a remarkable women's rights pioneer, largely unknown today, who would be celebrated by famed poet Madge Morris:

---

[35] "The Woman Suffrage Convention," *Daily Alta California*, July 27, 1870, 1.
[36] "The Woman Suffrage Convention," *Daily Alta California*, July 29, 1870, 2.

And thou hast proved that woman can—Who has the nerve, and strength, and will—Work in the wider field of man, And be a woman still.[37]

Expanding Access for Women in the Workplace— Clara Shortridge Foltz

Clara Shortridge grew up in Indiana and Iowa in the 1850s and early '60s, the daughter of an itinerant preacher who had been trained as a lawyer. She boasted that she was "descended from the heroic stock of Daniel Boone and never shrank from contest nor knew a fear."[38] Her biographer Barbara Babcock writes that as a young girl, Clara heard a speech by renowned suffragist Lucy Stone and later would describe that event as a defining moment in her life. With an incredible backstory that shines a bright spotlight on her intellect, tenacity, and strategic vision, she overcame nineteenth-century gender biases to lead the way for generations of women to come.

In 1864, at the age of 15, Clara eloped with Jeremiah Foltz, a Civil War veteran who struggled to keep their Iowa farm afloat. Eventually, the young family moved first to Oregon, then settled in San Jose. In 1878, Jeremiah abandoned the family for another woman in Portland. Clara was 29 years old, a single mother with five children, aged two to 11. She faced a daunting future. She knew that traditional woman's work—sewing dresses and making hats—provided insufficient funds for her family, so she created a niche for herself as a public speaker on woman suffrage.

The novelty of a woman lecturer, and Clara's ability to deliver passionate talks with rhetorical flourishes, led to numerous engagements, although not without controversy. Before a scheduled lecture in a church in the small town of Gilroy, the minister had instructed women to stay away. Suffragists, he said, were "free loves, poor mothers, dissatisfied wives and spinsters seeking annuities." The warning backfired, for more people attended Foltz's lecture than had ever heard the minister speak. Already wise in the way of media relations, Foltz stopped at a local newspaper after her lecture to reiterate some of the fine points of her suffrage speech and enhance her chances of getting coverage.[39]

The "Lady Lawyer" Bill

It was the law, however, that fascinated Foltz the most. While continuing her lectures to earn money to feed her family, she sought to study the law but quickly

---

[37] Madge Morris, *The Lure of the Desert Land: And Other Poems* (San Francisco: Harr Wagner Publishing Company, 1917), 90.

[38] Clara Foltz, "Struggles and Triumphs of a Woman Lawyer," *New American Woman*, January 1918, 16, https://archive.org/stream/newamericanwoman02losa#page/n325/mode/2up.

[39] Barbara Babcock, *Woman Lawyer* (Stanford: Stanford University Press, 2011), 17.

Figure 1.2. Clara Foltz: California's First Female Lawyer
Credit: Courtesy of California State Library

discovered how difficult the task would be. At that time, it was important for aspiring attorneys to apprentice at a law office, because California didn't have a law school. Decades later, in a serialized autobiographical sketch for *The New American Woman*, which she founded and edited, Foltz said she applied with a prominent San Jose lawyer and received a humiliating letter in response. He refused to encourage her "in so foolish a pursuit, wherein you would invite nothing but ridicule if not contempt. A woman's place is at home, unless it is as a teacher."[40] Foltz later found another law office where she could study, but no amount of preparation or apprenticeship would have helped her become an attorney. California law limited the practice to "any white male citizen" of good moral character with at least six months residence in the state.

---

[40] Foltz, "Struggles," June 1916, 5, https://archive.org/stream/newamericanwoman-01losa#page/n85/mode/2up.

Recognizing that state law was a roadblock that prevented her and other women from working in their chosen field, Foltz wrote what the press called the "Lady Lawyer" bill. It merely substituted "any citizen or person" for "any white male citizen" as a prerequisite for admission to the state bar. Her friend and representative in the state senate, Bernard Murphy, agreed to carry the legislation, one of a record 1,500 bills introduced in the 1878 legislative session. Attracting little attention at first, the measure sailed through the senate, and a confident Foltz left Sacramento for a six-week lecture tour in Oregon. When the measure was brought to the assembly floor, opponents argued that they merely were trying to protect women from being exposed to unsavory courtroom events. W. M. DeWitt of Yolo County said he opposed the bill as "a friend of the fair sex. He thought the sphere of women was infinitely more important than that of men, and that sphere was home." Byron Waters of San Bernardino said it was "well enough for women to practice medicine, but it was no place for them in the law."[41] Some opponents feared that women lawyers would use their feminine charms to convince susceptible male jurors to vote for their clients. Absent Foltz's aggressive lobbying efforts during assembly debate, the measure was defeated 30 to 33. It seemed dead, but following the arcane rules of legislative procedure, the bill was permitted to be reconsidered at a later date.

This was the political reality that greeted Foltz upon her return from Oregon. Her bill was in shambles—alive but on life support as the legislature raced toward adjournment. A lengthy expose in the *Sacramento Record-Union* described the last-minute frenzy of lobbyists—"voluble of tongue, oily of speech"—as legislators prepared to vote on pending legislation before the session deadline:

> Hundreds of men were circulating through the halls and chambers, whispering in corners, closeted in alcoves, consulting in knots, buzzing in groups, bending over legislators at their desks, buttonholing, counseling, advising, plotting, working every plan, pulling every wire, and bringing to bear every influence known to the lowest grade of the lobby art.[42]

Foltz and Laura de Force Gordon, who also sought a career in the law, were among the lobbyists pacing the capitol halls and cajoling lawmakers in an effort to resurrect the "Lady Lawyer" bill. Actually, Gordon did double duty, because she also was a reporter covering the legislative session, a position that enabled her to keep up with the break-neck pace of business at the capitol. In customary chaos three days before adjournment, lawmakers agreed to reconsider the bill, and after a few procedural ballots, they reversed their original vote and sent it to Governor

---

[41] *"California Legislature:* Assembly,*"* *Sacramento Record-Union*, February 26, 1879, 1.

[42] "Another Last Chapter," *Sacramento Record-Union*, March 30, 1878, 8.

William Irwin with two votes to spare.[43] Foltz later would describe her ordeals as a lobbyist: "I coaxed, I entreated, I would have reasoned had they been reasonable men; I almost went down on my knees before them, asking for the pitiful privilege of an equal chance to earn an honest living in a noble profession!"[44]

Tantalizingly close to victory, Clara Foltz and her cadre of supporters needed only to get Governor Irwin's signature on the bill to secure for women the opportunity to become members of the legal profession. One nineteenth-century historian described Irwin as "large, strong and presentable in person. . . . Though not brilliant, nor much of a speaker, he was dignified in deportment."[45] According to Foltz's retelling of the story years later, she had joined a throng of people outside the governor's office awaiting his action on numerous bills. A mere 15 minutes before the midnight deadline for gubernatorial action, she recalled, a cigar-chomping race track lobbyist, described as "a great big ignoramus," emerged from the governor's office and shouted that the lawyer bill was dead. That's when Foltz sprang into action. "I made a break through the solid ranks of men for the door of the chamber," she said. Foltz elbowed her way into the office and "undaunted, though hesitatingly" confronted the governor. "I said, 'Governor, won't you please sign the Woman Lawyer's bill?'" Apparently, the bill was in a pile destined to be vetoed. At the governor's request, a clerk fished it out of the pile, at which point the governor picked up his pen, dipped it in the ink well and said to a trembling Foltz, "This bill to entitle women to practice law is wise and just, and I take great pleasure in signing it." At that instant, Foltz said, the clock struck twelve.[46]

Armed with legislative sanction, Foltz and Gordon pursued legal careers and became the first two female lawyers in California. At that time, a law school education wasn't a prerequisite to becoming an attorney. Foltz undoubtedly saw part of herself in her first clients, who tended to be young women placed in vulnerable financial circumstances because of desertion or extremely low-paying jobs. Both women, however, wanted formal legal educations so as to better serve their clients. On January 9, 1879, Foltz paid her 10 dollars tuition and began attending classes at the new Hastings College of Law in San Francisco, a department of the University of California and the only law school in the state. Two days later, however, she was barred from classes because of a school policy against admitting women. Foltz and Gordon sued the school and represented themselves.

During a packed Fourth District Court hearing in San Francisco, Foltz argued that the Hastings ban on woman students violated the university's open-door pol-

---

[43] *Assembly Journal: 22nd Session of the California Legislature* (Sacramento: State Printing Office, 1879*)*, 430–31, 732–34; Anthony, 758.

[44] Foltz, "Struggles," August 1916, 11, https://archive.org/stream/newamericanwoman01losa#page/n139/mode/2up.

[45] Theodore Hittell, *History of California* (San Francisco: N.J. Stone & Co. 1897), 567.

[46] Foltz, "Struggles," September 1916, 10, https://archive.org/stream/newamericanwoman01/losa#page/n165/mode/2up.

Figure 1.3. *Oakland Tribune,* October 12, 1880
Credit: Courtesy of Newspapers.com

icy. In opposition testimony, a judge argued that women "would be found so entirely unfitted from the rough-and-tumble of legal practice, that they would soon
find it was not the field to earn a livelihood or to win honor." Then, in a curious
twist of logic, he further argued that Foltz might be too accomplished a lawyer:
"[I]f this lady should go before the jury with as good a speech as she made in her
own behalf, she would have an advantage at which the Bar might complain."[47]
Much of the press, mesmerized by the novelty of women lawyers arguing in court,
at times seemed more concerned with the physical appearances of the plaintiffs
than the legal arguments. In the opening paragraph of its hearing recap, the *San
Francisco Chronicle* commented how Foltz's "profuse hair was done in braids,
which fell backward from the crown of her head like an Alpine glacier lit by a
setting sun." As for Gordon, "she wore a stylish black silk dress, with some suggestions of masculinity in the make . . . and curls enough to supply half the thin-
haired ladies of San Francisco with respectable switches."[48]

Foltz and Gordon won their case at trial, but Hastings appealed. At the California Supreme Court, the justices unanimously agreed with Foltz's argument
that since qualified women were allowed entrance to the University of California,
they also should be allowed to enter its affiliated law school. It was a pyrrhic victory, however. When Foltz finally won her court decision, she was broke and had
to forego law school in order to work full-time to support her family. Foltz and

---

[47] "Aspiring Lady Lawyers," *Daily Alta California*, February 25, 1879, 1.
[48] "Woman's Rights: Two Lady Lawyers Who Demand Admission to the Hastings
Law College—How They Dress," *San Francisco Chronicle*, February 25, 1879, 1.

Gordon often commiserated together about making ends meet, particularly if they had to spend several weeks at a time away from home lobbying in Sacramento or going on the lecture circuit. In late 1878, Gordon had expressed her financial fears to Foltz. In a handwritten response, Foltz talked about her own cash shortage. "O, how terribly awful it is . . . that not one dollar of your expenses are paid by the wealthy woman whose cause you so ably champion," Foltz wrote. "My poverty is so extreme, and with all the expenses of my great family of little ones. I find it utterly impossible to spend my money in that direction though I would gladly help to pay your expenses."[49]

Victories and Defeat at the 1879 State Constitutional Convention

As the Hastings events unfolded, California's constitutional convention was meeting simultaneously in Sacramento over 157 days. One-hundred-fifty-two delegates, all white and all male, attended the often-raucous proceedings. Members of the Workingmen's Party of California (WPC), led by the rabble-rousing and charismatic Denis Kearney, comprised about a third of the delegation. Their primary goal was to fashion a constitutional document that excluded the Chinese—who they blamed for high unemployment and other ills—and cracked down on corporate misbehavior. But Foltz, Gordon, and other activists saw an opening for their issues, since most of the WPC delegates also supported woman suffrage.

Two suffrage measures were up for consideration. One would grant full voting rights to all qualified women. At one point, the convention's Committee on Suffrage floated compromise language that would let the legislature decide if women should have the right to vote. The major opponent of that proposal was James Caples, a farmer who owned 3,200 acres of land about 20 miles east of Sacramento. Caples had come to California in 1849 and sold merchandise to prospectors. By the time of the convention, he was in his mid-fifties and had nine children. Imploring the convention delegates, Caples painted the picture of future legislatures attracting a "corrupting, degrading, demoralizing lobby, forever besieging our Legislature about this supposed right."[50]

Delegates turned down both suffrage proposals, but advocates for women's equality secured two notable victories. Inspired by Foltz's "Lady Lawyer" bill, the delegates adopted language that precluded a person's sex from disqualifying anyone from pursuing a lawful business, vocation, or profession. Delegates also wrote into the constitution the right of women to attend all departments of the University of California, and they reaffirmed language in the state's 1849 con-

---

[49] Letter from Clara Foltz to Laura de Force Gordon, November 20, 1878, Laura Gordon Papers, Stein Collection, Bancroft Library, University of California, Berkeley.

[50] *Debates and Proceedings of the California Constitutional Convention, Vol. II*, (Sacramento: State Printing Office, 1881), 1007; *Thompson and West's History of Sacramento County 1880* (Berkeley: Howell-North), 1960, 268.

stitution that women were entitled to their own property, separate from their husband's. Foltz's victory set the stage for battles to come. Writing of the California developments, Susan B. Anthony boasted, "California stands to-day [as] one of the first States in the Union, as regards the educational, industrial and property rights of women, and the probability of equal political rights being secured to them at an early day, is conceded by the most conservative."[51] Anthony wrote those words in 1886. It would take another quarter-century before California men would give women "equal political rights."

Laura de Force Gordon would specialize in criminal law and become the second woman admitted to practice law before the US Supreme Court. She ran unsuccessfully for the state senate, campaigning aggressively and receiving several hundred votes. She was the first woman in the nation to own and run a daily newspaper, the *Stockton Daily Leader,* and she remained a suffrage leader the rest of her life. (Pitts Stevens's suffrage newspaper had been a weekly.) In the 1880s, she was nominated but declined to run for attorney general. Emily Pitts Stevens, the newspaper editor who used the pages of her newspapers to argue fervently for suffrage, became a temperance lecturer and an organizer for the Women's Christian Temperance Union and remained active in the state suffrage society and the Equal Rights League.

Clara Foltz continued to have a remarkable law career. In 1893, at a forum at the Chicago World Columbian Exposition, she introduced the concept of the public defender system to ensure adequate representation for indigent defendants who could not afford an attorney. She wrote legislation creating the position, which years later became law in California and more than 30 other states. In a 1910 news article, the *Los Angeles Herald* referred to her oratorical and legal skills and said she "once convinced a jury of twelve males that a woman has a perfect right to go through her husband's pockets and confiscate the bank roll."[52] Foltz became the state's first female prosecutor and founded a daily newspaper in San Diego, all the while remaining an ardent advocate for suffrage. She played an important role in the 1911 campaign that gave women the vote in California, but she always considered the battle of Hastings to be the highlight of her career. Of the four nineteenth-century pioneers—Pitts Stevens, Pellet, Gordon, and Foltz—she was the only one who would live long enough to see woman suffrage become a reality.

Discussion Questions

1. For what reasons do you believe Emily Pitts Stevens and Sarah Pellet received coverage in the era's newspapers? Given the attention they attracted, as well as Pitts Stevens's status as a journalist, for what reasons do you think they are so little-known today?

---

[51] Anthony, 760.

[52] Mrs. Foltz Sworn in by District Attorney," *Los Angeles Herald*, April 26, 1910, 1.

2. What ideas did Pitts Stevens preach and live regarding feminism? For what reasons might she have been a controversial or even threatening figure to some men and women? How might her style be compared with today's feminists?
3. For what reasons is Sarah Pellet described as "a fearless vagabond"?
4. How persuasive do you believe Pellet's ideas may have been to her audiences in the mining camps? What opposing arguments might have surfaced?
5. For what reasons did national suffrage icons Susan B. Anthony and Elizabeth Cady Stanton oppose the Fifteenth Amendment? Do you believe their decision had any lasting effect on the way the suffrage movement and some of its leaders are remembered?
6. Outspoken suffragist Laura de Force Gordon helped organize an early women's rights convention in San Francisco. What were its impacts?
7. Clara Foltz is described as "a remarkable women's rights pioneer" who managed to face down the gender biases of the 1800s. In what ways did Foltz and Gordon team up to make a lasting difference for future generations of girls and women in California?
8. What rights did California's two early constitutions grant to women that frequently were denied in other states? Why do you suppose California was more progressive than other states on women's rights?

Recommended Reading

Babcock, Barbara A. *Woman Lawyer: The Trials of Clara Foltz*. Stanford: Stanford University Press, 2011.

Gullett, Gayle. *Becoming Citizens: The Emergence and Development of the California Women's Movement, 1880–1911*. Urbana: University of Illinois Press, 2000.

Stanton, Elizabeth Cady, Susan B. Anthony, and Matilda Joslyn Gage, eds. *The Concise History of Woman Suffrage: Selections from History of Woman Suffrage*. Urbana: University of Illinois Press, 2005.

Chapter 2

1896
Debacle of 1896 Leaves Suffrage Movement in Shambles

> "The power of the ballot is given to all but
> criminals, idiots, and women."
> —Susan B. Anthony

Henry Harrison Markham, California's eighteenth governor, spent much of March 1893 closeted in his capitol office as he raced to beat a constitutional deadline to sign or veto hundreds of bills sent to him by the legislature. In fact, one newspaper reported, "The Governor is besieged from the moment he enters the office until he leaves again."[1] With a horde of lobbyists clamoring for action—or inaction—Markham signed legislation allowing prison inmates out on parole and cut $2 million from the state budget as California coped with drought and a national depression. With an active veto pen, the governor invalidated legislation to move the state capital from Sacramento to San Jose, angered dairy counties by striking down a bill to limit the sale of oleomargarine in the state, and removed funds for a monument to the Donner Party at the site of their frozen demise in the Sierra Nevada. But it was a bill that Markham neither signed nor outright vetoed that earned him a place in the suffragists' hall of shame.

Markham had taken a circuitous route to California. Born and raised on a farm in upstate New York, Markham enlisted in the Union army during the Civil War and participated in General William Tecumseh Sherman's devastating 250-mile march from Atlanta to Savannah, Georgia. A few weeks later, Markham was severely wounded at the Battle of Whippy Swamp Creek in South Carolina. After the war, he and his wife responded to a newspaper ad and bought 23 acres in Pasadena in the belief that Southern California weather would improve his health. A Republican, Markham practiced law, was elected to the House of Representatives and, in 1890, ran for governor as "the dashing colonel from Pasadena," defeating his Democratic rival by a scant 8,000 votes. He was an enthusiastic campaigner who personally greeted thousands of voters with what became known as

---

[1] "Before the Governor: Signed and Unsigned," *Sacramento Daily Union*, March 22, 1893, 2.

39

the "Markham Glad-hand." One historian called it "his signature move—a firm, hearty handshake evoking sincerity."[2]

Markham never mentioned the suffrage issue during his inaugural address, instead concentrating on the economic climate, water, and Chinese exclusion.[3] But the suffragists thought the governor was an ally. He had four daughters and seemed to have a warm place in his heart for vulnerable women and children. According to lore, Markham once happened upon a woman and her son on the street who couldn't pay their rent and had just been evicted from their apartment. He walked up to the door and then returned to the boy and his mother, telling the child that he had seen a key in the lock. The mother and boy returned to the apartment to find a $100 bill sticking out of the keyhole as Markham slipped away quietly.[4]

In 1891, early in Markham's first year in office, five senators had introduced legislation to give women the vote, and the influential Women's Christian Temperance Union (WCTU) presented 15,000 petition signatures to the legislature in support of suffrage. The national WCTU had been created in the mid-1870s to attack the social ills caused by alcoholism, including prostitution, domestic abuse, public health threats, and labor exploitation. The California chapter, with 200 members, held its first convention in 1879 and grew rapidly in the '80s. At first, the members were reluctant to support woman suffrage, but Sarah Severance, who would become the WCTU's energetic state superintendent of suffrage, convinced the more conservative members that voting was the key to achieving their reform agenda.

Severance and two other prominent suffragists, Laura de Force Gordon and Emily Pitts Stevens, testified before lawmakers on the suffrage legislation and won an initial victory when the state senate narrowly approved it, 21 to 17. However, in a procedural setback, the bill had been delayed so long that there was insufficient time for the state assembly to act.

At the next legislative session in 1893, the women came back with a compromise and a new strategy. Although women had been granted eligibility to hold school offices 20 years earlier, they couldn't vote in school elections. Since prospects for full suffrage looked bleak, they decided to settle for less. Several large states—including New York, Michigan, and Minnesota—already had granted suffrage in school elections. The suffragists agreed to push for limited suffrage and then seek the full vote once they secured their partial victory. Advocates had every reason to believe Markham would look favorably on legislation that incrementally inched forward the franchise for women. The governor delighted suffragists when he announced he was "fully in accord with the purpose and intent of this

---

[2] Lawrence P. Gooley, "Henry Markham: New York's Governor of California (Part 2)," The New York History Blog, July 17, 2012, http://newyorkhistoryblog.org/2012/07/17/henry-markham-nys-governor-of-california-part-2/.

[3] "Inaugural Address," January 8, 1891, The Governors' Gallery, California State Library, http://governors.library.ca.gov/addresses/18-Markham.html.

[4] "Did You Know?," The Governors' Gallery, California State Library, http://governors.library.ca.gov/18-Markham.html.

measure,"[5] but he also raised a red flag about a potential constitutional issue. Since the state constitution limited voting privileges to males, the argument went, it would take a voter-approved state constitutional amendment, not merely a legislative statute, to secure the franchise. When discussing the pending legislation, Markham was coy, refusing to tip his hand.

Lobbying on the bill was fierce. With three paid lobbyists, the WCTU presented 23,000 signatures to the legislature in favor of the school suffrage measure. Severance wrote columns for the Sacramento newspapers. The Republican senate approved the measure easily. The vote was much closer in the assembly, which passed and sent it to the governor. That's when Markham took the unusual step of trying to determine the bill's constitutionality himself instead of letting the courts decide its validity. The Republican governor asked the state's Democratic Party chair, who opposed the bill, to consult with a law firm about the measure's constitutionality.

The debate reignited while the law firm presumably did its research. Opponents not only questioned the measure's constitutionality, but they also suggested that if given the vote, women merely would choose the best-looking candidates. Clara Foltz and others, meanwhile, stepped up their pressure on the governor. "Chinese, idiots, insane persons, etc., are mentioned by the constitution as classes barred from suffrage, but women are not mentioned," lawyer Foltz argued. "Since woman is not within the classes barred she must be in a class not barred, and certainly the Legislature may confer the privilege by statute."[6] She also peppered Markham with telegrams. One read, "Please sign the woman suffrage bill. Let the Supreme Court pass on its constitutionality."[7] In an editorial, the *Santa Cruz Daily Sentinel* agreed, arguing that the courts had the sole responsibility of deciding the measure's constitutionality. The governor, it said, "should not rest his veto on the ground of alleged unconstitutionality . . . merely because he imagines" that a measure might not be sustained by the courts.[8] The court never got the chance to hear the case.

In a move that was viewed with suspicion at best, and evil chicanery at worst, the law firm doing the research failed to report before the governor's legal deadline to sign or veto the measure. Markham decided to take no action at all—a step called a pocket veto—which prevented the bill from becoming law. Suffrage advocates felt betrayed and were furious with the governor. Severance wrote succinctly, "Tricked! Tricked!"[9]

---

[5] Gayle Gullett, *Becoming Citizens: The Emergence and Development of the California Women's Movement, 1880–1911* (Urbana and Chicago: University of Illinois Press, 2000), 81.

[6] "An Appeal for Women," *San Francisco Call*, March 17, 1893, 5.

[7] "The Female Suffrage Bill," *San Francisco Call*, March 24, 1893, 6.

[8] "The Governor's Vetoes," *Santa Cruz Daily Sentinel*, March 30, 1893,1.

[9] Gullett, 82.

A Voting-Rights Champion in Congress—Aaron Sargent

Decades before Governor Markham's treachery, California women had mobilized and pressured the male power structure on voting rights—without success—with one of the state's most visible power couples leading the way. Aaron
and Ellen Sargent, who wielded clout on both sides of the continent, put down
roots in Nevada County. As a young adult, Aaron, had been intoxicated by tales of
the gold discovery in Northern California. In 1849, the 22-year-old Philadelphia
printer borrowed $125 from his uncle and booked passage on a ship bound for San
Francisco. He had met Ellen Clark years earlier when they taught Sunday school
together in Massachusetts, and he promised to marry her once he improved his
financial situation in the gold fields.

Aaron Sargent settled in the foothill mining hamlet of Nevada, which for
short periods was also called Caldwell's Upper Store, Creek Dry Diggings, and,
finally, Nevada City. During the first brutal winter in his new home, roads were
nearly impassible and four-foot snowdrifts were common. The huge influx of
miners, working the nearby Yuba and Bear Rivers and needing food and supplies,
drove prices skyward. A pair of boots cost $40, shovels were $16, potatoes were
75 cents a pound, and the cost of getting a letter from Sacramento 60 miles away
was $2.50.[10] The social center of town catered to drinkers and gamblers. "Gam-
bling saloons arose in splendor and numbers, and were thronged. Liquors were
sold and fights were common. Claims were jumped; pistols and knives were worn
and drawn; murder was committed; lawyers came into use. . . ."[11]

In a sketch of Nevada City, Sargent described a scene along the town's main
street one day in October, 1850, in which drinkers and gamblers poured out of the
saloons, "then in full glory," to take in church services from a street preacher (the
town didn't have a church yet). A short distance away, an auctioneer tried to sell
a mule, up the street a Swiss girl entertained miners with a hand organ, all while
two dogs were engaged in a "savage" fight.[12]

Like so many contemporary fortune hunters, Sargent didn't strike it rich in
the mine fields. However, he found a more public-minded calling and turned to
newspaper work, becoming a partner with several others in the *Nevada Journal*,
the county's first newspaper. In the center of town, he built a small four-room
house, then returned to Massachusetts to fulfill his promise of marriage to Ellen.
The couple arrived in Nevada City in October 1852. Ellen later wrote that the
only drawback to her new frontier home were the "large sized rats which made
their nests and performed their activities on the dark side of the muslin above our

---

[10] Edwin Bean, *Bean's History and Directory of Nevada County, California* (Nevada:
Daily Gazette Book and Job Office, 1867), 78.
[11] Ibid.
[12] A. A. Sargent, quoted in Bean, 80.

heads."[13] Aaron started to make a name for himself in local politics, becoming a leader in the new Republican Party after the Whigs broke up. He was elected district attorney and was vice chairman of the Republican National Convention that nominated Abraham Lincoln in 1860. The same year Lincoln won the presidency, Sargent was elected to the House of Representatives, which soon would approve construction of the transcontinental railroad to connect eastern commerce with Sacramento. When President Lincoln signed the legislation on July 3, 1862, Sargent broke the story, wiring the *Sacramento Daily Union:* "The President has signed the Pacific Railroad Bill. Let Californians rejoice."[14] After three terms in the House, Sargent was elected to the Senate where he was a fervent proponent of the discriminatory Chinese Exclusion Act, which restricted Chinese workers from entering the US—a popular position in nineteenth-century California. During a senate floor speech, Sargent argued "the Chinaman can live on a dead rat and few handfuls of rice [and] work for ten cents a day. . . . There can be no remedy except for general exclusion."[15]

At considerable political risk, and at a time when women enjoyed few of the rights and privileges that benefited men, Sargent was an early champion of the women's movement. In 1878, his last year in the US Senate, Sargent introduced a US constitutional amendment that addressed—for the first time—full voting rights for women: "The right of citizens of the United States to vote shall not be denied or abridged by the United States or by any State on account of sex." It was defeated without much fanfare. The same language would be re-introduced by a succession of lawmakers in the following four decades without success.

A New Leader in the Suffrage Movement— Ellen Sargent

Sargent's proposed amendment had the clear imprint of his wife and adviser, Ellen Clark Sargent, who had begun to build her own legacy in the women's movement. In 1869, as the idea of women's voting rights was starting to attract attention in California, Sargent founded a suffrage organization in Nevada City and the following year, she circulated petitions that were delivered to state lawmakers. She quickly caught the eye of national voting-rights matriarch Susan B. Anthony, who often hosted Sargent when the Californian visited Washington, DC. In a letter to fellow suffragist Isabella Beecher Hooker, Anthony referred to Ellen Sargent as an "excellent sound sense woman—splendid."[16] While her husband

---

[13] Gary Noy, *Sierra Stories: Tales of Dreamers, Schemers, Bigots, and Rogues* (Berkeley: Heyday, 2014), 132.

[14] "Pacific Railroad Bill Approved," *Sacramento Daily Union*, July 4, 1862.

[15] Noy, 136.

[16] Letter from Susan B. Anthony to Isabella Beecher Hooker, dated January 18, 1874. Ann Gordon, ed. *Selected Papers of Elizabeth Cady Stanton and Susan B. Anthony, Vol. III* (New Brunswick, NJ: Rutgers University Press, 1997), 36.

was toiling in the senate, Ellen spent six years as treasurer of the National Women Suffrage Association.

Once Aaron's political career ended, the Sargents returned to California and Ellen assumed a leadership role in the in the state's budding suffrage movement. In a letter to a fellow suffragist in Palo Alto, Sargent said she was incensed that women couldn't enjoy "the great privileges and responsibilities of full American citizenship" and placed part of the blame on apathetic women. "Why cannot women see their low estate in the scale of humanity! And to think they could change it if they would."[17]

"We asked for a loaf . . . and received a chunk of dough."

The push for woman suffrage in California was becoming a cohesive movement by the 1890s, but it was complicated by the fact that the nation was plunged into a four-year depression that began in 1893 and was marked by gross economic inequities. The so-called Gilded Age of the 1870s and '80s had brought dramatic economic growth, spurred by innovations by such business titans as Andrew Carnegie (steel), J. P. Morgan (finance), Leland Stanford (transportation), Cornelius Vanderbilt (railroads and shipping), and John D. Rockefeller (oil). The boom brought the innovators great wealth, and the higher wages for workingmen and women attracted a huge influx of immigrants from Europe. But much of the prosperity had been driven by railroad expansion and speculation, and when the overextended Philadelphia and Reading Railroad went bankrupt, the dominoes began to fall. Stock prices dropped precipitously, and other railroads, farms, and businesses failed, prompting frightened depositors to wait in long lines to take their savings out of banks. At the height of the panic, national unemployment hovered around 20 percent. Workers and farmers protested in large numbers as the class divide widened.

Within a few months, the panic in the East hit California. Southern California banks were the first to fail. When bankers refused requests for new loans, growers couldn't pay to harvest their crops and many canneries shut down. Fifty-thousand Californians eventually lost their jobs. The state's vaunted weather and fertile fields attracted thousands of desperate unemployed workers from other states who had hitched rides in railroad freight cars, but many cities evicted the "vagrants" who wandered the state in search of relief. In mid-1894, the Southern Pacific, Central Pacific, and Santa Fe railroads were paralyzed by a "Pullman" rail strike that affected more than 11,000 railroad workers and cost SP an estimated $200,000 a day in losses over the length of the nearly one-month work stoppage. During this "widespread and unprecedented business depression," the Interstate Commerce

---

[17] Noy, 134.

Commission reported that nearly 200 railroads, operating 42,000 miles, "were in the hands of receivers."[18]

Laura de Force Gordon saw the depression as particularly harmful to women who, she said, were worried about the safety and wellbeing of their households. "Millions of men and women in this land of plenty are reduced to absolute want . . . there is a vast army of unsheltered, unemployed tramps roaming over the country; a larger army of men, women, and children unfed, unclothed, and suffering for want of a little, while thousands have more than they can enjoy."[19]

As the nation sank deeper into malaise, many working-class men worried that offering women more political power might cost them their already-precarious jobs. But suffragists were preparing for battle when the 1895 legislature convened, asserting that Californians should "seriously consider the right uses of the ballot" in solving the state's problems. In a circular released in the fall of 1894, the California State Woman's Suffrage and Educational Association argued that politics needed an infusion of purity. To that end, it said, "women have proven themselves a potent factor in work for public good in the advancement and accomplishment of necessary reforms."[20]

Although the state's suffrage movement routinely had endured legislative setbacks over the years, national leaders, who were closely watching California, felt "the time seemed to be highly propitious for securing woman suffrage" during the 1895 session.[21] Republicans had large majorities in the senate and the assembly, and the GOP had endorsed woman suffrage the year before. A Democrat, James Budd, had been elected governor, but he was a populist and considered friendly to the suffrage cause.

In early January, women at the weekly meeting of the Equal Rights League were read the language of draft legislation written by Clara Foltz. It was only two sentences in length: "Sec. 1. Women citizens of this State who have complied with the elections law thereof, who are of the age of 21 years and upward, shall be entitled to vote at all elections, and shall have the same rights and duties as male citizens. Sec. 2. This act shall take effect immediately." The women in the audience "loved its brevity, which they remarked would make it impossible for any politician to plead that he had not had time to read the bill."[22]

---

[18] R. Hal Williams, *The Democratic Party and California Politics 1880–1896* (Stanford: Stanford University Press, 1973), 178–80, 194–95; "Railroad Statistics," *San Francisco Call,* June 25, 1895, 6; Gullet, 89.

[19] Laura de Force Gordon, "Woman's Relation to the State," *Sacramento Bee,* February 2, 1895, 2.

[20] "To the People of California," California State Woman Suffrage and Educational Association, October 1, 1894, California State Library.

[21] Elizabeth Cady Stanton, Susan B. Anthony, Matilda Joslyn Gage, and Ida Husted Harper, *The History of Woman Suffrage, Vol. IV 1883–1900* (Indianapolis: The Hollenbeck Press, 1902), 485.

[22] "Equal Rights League: A Document That Contained a Great Deal in Small Space—Plans for Sacramento," *San Francisco Call,* January 9, 1895, 5.

Gordon lobbied hard. For her, it was simply a matter of human rights. She scoffed at suffrage opponents who suggested that women were too good and pure to be contaminated by the filthy world of politics. In a lengthy, angry, and sarcastic by-lined opinion piece for the *Sacramento Bee*, Gordon argued that woman long had been considered "an inferior being whose happiness, welfare, and life even were entirely subject to the will of her self-constituted superior—man . . . degraded to the level of a mere voiceless serf, classed with idiots, lunatics, criminals and Chinamen, politically."[23]

It wasn't smooth sailing, however, as Republicans sent mixed messages. The measure easily passed the assembly but ran into trouble in the senate. The senate's judiciary committee reprised the argument that only a voter-approved state constitutional amendment—not a legislative statute—could secure the vote for women. Mass meetings were held in Sacramento to rally support, and Foltz, Gordon, and the WCTU lobbied intensively for passage. Gordon warned that the same men who would deny women the vote could also decide to deny it to male laborers and nonproperty owners. To no avail, Gordon filed a brief with the legislature arguing that since the constitution was silent on women, lawmakers were empowered to authorize the vote. The bill never made it to the senate floor, but majority Republicans pushed through a compromise that placed a state constitutional amendment before voters on the 1896 ballot.

Contemplating months of labor, stress, and fundraising to promote the ballot measure in the midst of an economic depression, Foltz was described as downcast and gloomy. "[We] asked for a loaf in the shape of suffrage and received a chunk of dough instead," she told the *San Francisco Call*. She excoriated Republicans who voted "against the measure indorsed by the Republican convention and advocated by the best and brainiest men in the state." Now, the amendment would be decided by an all-male electorate. "The women who own property and pay taxes," Foltz declared, "ought to boycott the State until they are given justice and equity the same as men." If it weren't for the upcoming statewide vote, a despondent Foltz said, "I should now feel like leaving the State forever." Gordon saved her venom for Napa senator Henry Gesford, a Democrat, who was the women's foremost enemy during the legislative debate. "If I live long enough I'll see that he is properly punished. If not I shall haunt him when I am dead."[24]

The Suffrage Election of 1896

California activists recognized that getting a state constitutional amendment approved by voters would be a tough slog. They'd have to set up volunteer campaign organizations throughout the state, raise funds in a challenging economic environment, and educate "the masses of the people in the cities [who] were still

[23] Gordon.
[24] "Just a Glimmer of Light Ahead," *San Francisco Call, March 21*, 1985, 4.

in a state of deadly apathy," according to suffrage chronicler Selina Solomons.[25] They knew they needed help and called in the cavalry—the biggest attractions in the women's movement—Susan B. Anthony, president of the National American Woman Suffrage Association, and the organization's vice president, Anna Howard Shaw. The association would help raise funds, provide speakers and an electoral strategy.

The pair caused a sensation when they were featured at the state's annual Women's Congress, as 2,500 women "struggled and tore their clothing in their determination" to hear the women speak, one newspaper reported. "Nobody ever supposed that the women of San Francisco cared for ought except their gowns, their teas, and their babies. But they do. They like brains, even in their own sex."[26] Anthony and Shaw then hit the road for a lengthy speaking tour, using free railroad passes courtesy of Jane Stanford, the widow of railroad baron Leland Stanford.[27]

National suffragists agreed the campaign was a long-shot, but they felt a California victory would be an important milestone in a fast-growing state that was approaching a population of 1.5 million. Before Election Day 1896, only three small western states had allowed women to vote—Wyoming, Colorado, and Utah. Wyoming, in fact, enacted suffrage before statehood when it was a territory inhabited by 6,000 men and only 1,000 women. Some Wyoming legislators hoped publicity from the suffrage vote would attract young, single women to the rugged and isolated frontier territory.[28]

Anthony and Shaw arrived in California and found a fractured contingent of suffragists in Northern California, particularly in San Francisco, the state's population hub. Since mid-1894, Laura de Force Gordon and Nellie Holbrook Blinn had run competing factions of the state suffrage society—Gordon, the fiery radical, and Blinn, a charismatic former stage actress and teacher. Critics were accusing Gordon of being all talk and no action. She lobbied the legislature and gave speeches, but her detractors were impatient with her "musty classical rhetoric, idiosyncratic leadership, and legalistic approach, all of which discouraged grassroots mobilization."[29] Gordon dismissed them as "kindergarteners." When her old compatriot, Clara Foltz, cast her lot with Blinn, Gordon struck back. "She never did take any interest in the cause," she said of Foltz. "She would just come in like a bluejay, ruffle her plumes, and say she was devoting her life to women."

---

[25] Selina Solomons, *How We Won the Vote in California* (San Francisco: The New Woman Publishing Co., 1912), 3.

[26] Quoted in Ida Husted Harper, *The Life and Work of Susan B. Anthony, Vol. II* (Indianapolis: The Hollenbeck Press, 1898), 828.

[27] Ibid., 830.

[28] "December 10, 1869: Wyoming Grants Women the Vote," History.com, www.history.com/this-day-in-history/wyoming-grants-women-the-vote, 2009.

[29] Rebecca Mead, *How the Vote Was Won: Woman Suffrage in the Western United States 1868–1914* (New York: New York University, 2004), 77.

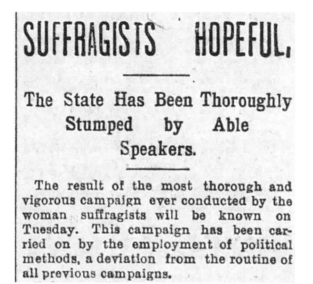

SUFFRAGISTS HOPEFUL.

The State Has Been Thoroughly Stumped by Able Speakers.

The result of the most thorough and vigorous campaign ever conducted by the woman suffragists will be known on Tuesday. This campaign has been carried on by the employment of political methods, a deviation from the routine of all previous campaigns.

Figure 2.1. *San Francisco Call*, November 2, 1896
Credit: Courtesy of Newspapers.com

It was left to Anthony and Shaw to bring peace to the rival California factions. Anthony's friend, Ellen Sargent, the widow of the late congressional champion of woman's voting rights, became the compromise candidate for the presidency of the state suffrage association. In the florid newspaper coverage of the day, the friendly *San Francisco Call* announced the rapprochement. "When the sun rose yesterday they were gathered in two camps, as hostile to each other as they have been for a year. When the orb of day had made its half round of earth and dropped into the western ocean, the olive branch had been extended and received." The women were united, ready to march onward against "the obnoxious word 'male' in the constitution."[30]

With the divisions healed and Anthony, now in her mid-seventies, managing the effort in the crucial, more populous North, the campaign began the arduous task of raising money, mobilizing supporters, and educating male electors. Previous campaigns had relied on small "parlor meetings" in the fancy homes of elite women. This campaign, however, began with a mass meeting in San Francisco in late March 1896, with Anthony and Shaw the headliners. The women raised several hundred dollars. In the ensuing weeks, they organized auxiliary clubs throughout the state, and many poor laborers, such as seamstresses and washerwomen, fulfilled campaign pledges in 25-cent installments. Canvassers also gathered 40,000 signatures of support during the spring. Ellen Sargent, who led the

---

[30] "Harmony Reigns in the Suffrage Camps: The Hostile Wings No Longer War with Each Other," *San Francisco Call,* July 3, 1895, 14.

collection effort in Northern California, said it "offered an effective answer to the old stock objection that 'women do not want to vote.'"[31]

The campaign set up a network of local organizations—precinct by precinct in the larger cities and campaign committees in rural areas. Their goal was to target every city, town, or hamlet that had at least 200 residents. National suffrage leaders, and particularly Anthony, undertook grueling schedules stumping the state. Anthony gave up to three speeches a day "lecturing in halls, churches, wigwams, parlors, schoolhouses, and the open air." She spoke from the rear platform of trains and once traveled 40 miles by stage coach to give a talk in Santa Barbara. Shaw gave speeches every night for seven months; others gave daily addresses, as well.[32] Anthony's home base for the entire campaign was Sargent's fashionable Folsom Street home in San Francisco, which also served as campaign headquarters for several months. In time, the headquarters moved to a more suitable downtown location, staffed by teachers, bookkeepers, stenographers, and other working women who volunteered their lunch hour to the cause. For the most part, however, native-born, middle-class, educated, white Protestant women made up the core of the movement.

In an article for the California Supreme Court Historical Society, Susan Scheiber Edelman noted that woman suffrage was a radical idea in the nineteenth-century context, "Yet the suffrage workers in California pursued their reform goals through conventional politics—persuasion. . . ."[33] Throughout the campaign, the women used separate—and competing—messages. A liberal democratic argument held that women should be politically equal to men, the "no taxation without representation" line of reasoning. To that end, the suffragists researched government records of women's tax burden on their separate property only. They discovered that women were being taxed $1 million on $3.35 million worth of real property in Butte County. In San Francisco, they were paying more than $2 million in property taxes. In Santa Clara and Marin counties, women owned one-fifth of all real property.[34] The other argument stressed the differences between men and women. Women were mothers and inherently moral, and only by their full participation in the political process could they purify government and rid it of insidious corruption.

Without funds for advertising, the campaign focused on securing as much editorial support as possible. Emissaries visited the managing editors of hundreds of the state's newspapers and had remarkable success. In her history of the campaign, Ida Husted Harper said the women "were received with the greatest cour-

---

[31] Harper, 889; Donald G. Cooper, "The California Suffrage Campaign of 1896: Its Origin, Strategies, Defeat," *Southern California Quarterly*, Vol. 71, No. 4 (Winter 1989): 314.

[32] Stanton, et.al., 490; Harper, 876, 881.

[33] Susan Scheiber Edelman, "'A Red Hot Suffrage Campaign': The Woman Suffrage Cause in California, 1896," *California Supreme Court Historical Society Yearbook, Vol. 2* (Berkeley: Institute of Governmental Studies Press, 1995), 73.

[34] "Suffragists Talk Business," *San Francisco Chronicle*, May 9, 1896, 9.

tesy" and treated with respect. Even many of those newspapers that didn't support the constitutional amendment turned over column space to the suffragists. For seven months, Anthony wrote a Sunday column for William Randolph Hearst's *San Francisco Examiner*, which took no position on the suffrage amendment. The newspaper did, however, print 2,000 leaflets—at its own expense—for suffragists to distribute at their state convention. Harper was even given space in the *San Francisco Chronicle*—which urged a "no" vote two days before the election. In all, more than 250 newspapers endorsed the suffrage effort, while 27 did not.[35] The *Sacramento Record-Union* and the *Los Angeles Times*—owned by the crusty, fiercely anti-union Harrison Gray Otis—were the other major newspapers denouncing the suffrage effort. Otis called suffragists an insignificant band of "ballot-hungry females," motivated by a "craving for notoriety or by mercenary motives. He predicted that if women were allowed to vote, "every woman whose vote could be purchased or influenced would be dragged out to the polls. . . ."[36]

The Campaign Wins Major Endorsements

Overall, however, the women's campaign was pleased with the newspaper coverage it received. The *San Francisco Call*, with Clara Foltz's brother, Charles Shortridge as editor, was the women's most consistent supporter. In a well-timed editorial the day before the state Republican convention met in Sacramento, the *Call* said it "cannot ignore that portion of humanity which seems to have more than half the goodness, wisdom, wit and beauty of the world." It devoted nearly a full page to the suffrage effort. In advance of publication, the newspaper informed key suffrage leaders of its decision. Anthony absorbed the news and seemed stunned. "She remained seated in her chair, the tears rolling over her wrinkled cheeks, for a good three minutes," the *Call* reported. "Then, without a note of warning, she jumped from her seat and seizing her hostess, Mrs. A. A. Sargent, about the waist, executed a triumphal waltz. . . ."[37] In an adjoining article, Anthony wrote that she had been active in a dozen woman suffrage campaigns, but that this was the first time "in which any of the great dailies has exhibited sufficient public spirit to come out boldly in favor of the cause."[38] The endorsement made such a splash that the *Call* ran out of newspapers and said it had to reprint thousands of copies to send abroad.

Hastily, the campaign moved to leverage the newspaper's glowing endorsement by placing copies on the seats of all the Republican convention delegates. Securing the party's formal support was critical, but Anthony had cautioned California suffrage leaders not to get involved in any other political issues for fear of

---

[35] Harper, 868.

[36] *Los Angeles Times*, May 17, 1896, 26.

[37] "The 'Call' Declares for Woman Suffrage," *San Francisco Call*, May 3, 1896, 16.

[38] "Miss Susan B. Anthony on 'The Call's' Attitude on Woman Suffrage," *San Francisco Call*, May 3, 1896.

antagonizing potential supporters. In a letter to Mary McHenry Keith, Berkeley's suffrage leader, Anthony wrote: "We can belong to no party. . . . Now, we are beggars of each and all. . . ."[39] Women flooded the convention with literature, flowers, and suffrage badges for delegates to wear. Anthony made a personal appeal to the platform committee, a majority of whom, it was believed, did not favor a suffrage plank in the party's platform. She reminded the committee members that Republicans had emancipated African Americans more than four decades earlier, and that they needed to do the same with women. "The power of the ballot," she told the committee, "is given to all but criminals, idiots, and women. . . . [Y]ou keep putting us off. You promise, but you do not fulfill." Men, she said, would rise up and "strike down any man who would deny to you your right to vote and remember that women hold that privilege fully as dear." In response to Anthony's plea, the committee voted its approval and the full convention nearly unanimously endorsed the platform plank.[40]

With the Republican endorsement in hand, the women secured favorable treatment from the People's Party (populists), Socialist Labor Party, and the Prohibition Party, but the Democrats couldn't be budged. The national party was against suffrage. As well, many California county conventions had opposed giving women the vote, and they so instructed their state convention delegates. Anthony pleaded with the party's platform committee, but the measure was tabled almost immediately. The women tried to get a minority report read into the record, but that also failed. The women didn't expect an endorsement, but were angered to be treated so cavalierly. "We came up to the convention expecting nothing," Ida Harper wrote to one newspaper, "and we got it."[41] In a comment dripping with disdain, Harper later described a one a.m. incident outside the suffragists' hotel. The women had been awakened by loud laughter and female voices. They looked out the window and saw two carriages with "several gaily dressed women." A number of convention delegates climbed into the carriages, passed around a few bottles of wine and, with their arms around the women's waists, headed up the street. "The ladies returned to their slumbers thoroughly convinced that they had not used the correct methods for capturing the delegates of a Democratic convention."[42]

As it turned out, the Republican convention endorsement was a hollow victory, because support from the party quickly and quietly dissolved. The suffrage platform plank stood, but the November vote coincided with the 1896 presidential election between Republican William McKinley and Democrat William Jennings Bryan—and Republicans were concerned they might risk losing California and its eight electoral votes. The liquor lobby was extremely powerful in San Francisco, the nation's eighth largest city, and it supported the Republican Party with

---

[39] Letter from Anthony to Mary McHenry Keith, dated March 20, 1896, Keith Pond Family Collection, Bancroft Library, University of California, Berkeley.

[40] Cooper, 316.

[41] "Women Are Disgusted," San *Francisco Call*, June 18, 1896, 3.

[42] Harper, 873, n.874.

money and votes. It also feared woman suffrage, assuming that women—given the vote—would use the franchise to enact prohibition and destroy the region's wine-growing and brandy-distilling industries. That perception was fueled by the prominence of the Women's Christian Temperance Union in the suffrage campaign, which provided organization and experienced ground troops. In weighing the support of the suffragists on one side, and the liquor industry on the other, Republicans found it more politically advantageous to unofficially abandon their suffrage plank and heed the interests of the antitemperance movement.

Suffragists were stunned when the state party's chairman notified county leaders not to permit the women to speak at local Republican meetings, and party leaders refused to mention the state constitutional amendment in their speeches. Aside from being abandoned by Republicans, suffrage leaders also believed they were victims of systemic fraud. Ida Husted Harper, in her voluminous biography of Susan B. Anthony, noted, "Some of the women going the rounds with suffrage petitions in San Francisco found a house consisting of one room with three cots, where were registered 27 voters."[43]

The Liquor Industry Strikes a Blow

Aside from being snubbed by the Republican hierarchy, the campaign appeared to be doing well as the election approached. There was little overt opposition, and newspaper support was overwhelming. Supporters heeded advice to keep the campaign positive and not challenge the liquor industry and other interests head-on, "but these watchdogs of privilege had been sleeping with one eye open . . . they were getting ready to bite," Selina Solomons reported.[44]

Ten days before the election, the Liquor Dealers League met in San Francisco and unleashed a devastating broadside against the suffrage campaign. It sent a letter to grocers, saloon keepers, hotel proprietors, and druggists, declaring, "It is in your interest and ours to vote against this amendment. We request and urge you to vote and work against it and do all you can to defeat it."[45] In an interview with the *San Francisco Call*, a league official estimated that 14,000 voters in San Francisco were proprietors or employees in the liquor trade. He said they'd be out in force on Election Day to get like-minded voters to the polls and boasted that similar efforts were organized in more than three dozen other California counties. "Never before in the history of the State have the liquor forces been so well and widely organized as the liquor forces for this campaign. . . ."[46]

Still, the suffragists appeared hopeful on the eve of balloting. They predicted victory "if the men will stand by their promises and pledges."[47] But there were

---

[43] Ibid., 887.
[44] Solomons, 3.
[45] Stanton, et.al., 492.
[46] "Liquor-Men in Battle Array," *San Francisco Call*, October 25, 1896, 25.
[47] "Suffragists Hopeful," *San Francisco Call*, November 2, 1896, 9.

LIQUOR-MEN IN BATTLE ARRAY

Dealers Are Taking an Active Part in the Local Fight.

Are Opposed to the New Charter and to Woman's Suffrage.

Figure Figure 2.2. *San Francisco Call,* October 25, 1896
Credit: Courtesy of Newspapers.com

too many broken promises and forces arrayed against them. Harper wrote that on Election Day agents of the liquor lobby escorted hundreds of men from the San Francisco slums to the polls. Each man had a sample ballot showing him where to place his "X" against the state amendment. "Each had been informed if the referendum carried, there would never be another glass of beer sold in the city."[48] Solomons had walked through two precincts prior to the election—her own upscale neighborhood and a poor, mostly immigrant community. She found that "the masses of the people in the cities were still in a state of deadly apathy."[49] When all the votes were counted, the suffrage amendment lost by 26,000 votes.

In the wake if their disheartening defeat, angry suffragists alleged that the political machines in California had colluded with the liquor industry to deny their dream. Republicans had abandoned their pledge of support out of concern for their own political survival, and the liquor industry had lulled the suffragists into a false sense of security until it struck shortly before Election Day. Many of the campaign leaders had been members of the WCTU, and the optics of that synergy galvanized antitemperance forces. According to Susan B. Anthony and Ida Harper, hundreds of voters in San Francisco ignored the presidential, municipal, and other elections and cast votes only on a single issue—registering their opposition to the suffrage amendment, which was strongly connected to prohibition.

---

[48] Harper, 886.
[49] Solomons, 3.

Self-Inflicted Wounds

Critics considered some of the wounds to be self-inflicted, however—among them, the campaign's racial exclusivity. Anthony had recruited wealthy society women for leadership positions. It was a tactic that worked during Colorado's successful 1893 suffrage campaign, bringing in money and attracting new members. She believed that upper-class white women were best-suited to bring order to a society threatened with disorder, according to historian Gayle Gullett. In Southern California, for example, the campaign reached out to working-class women, but the "contact was almost exclusively with whites, ignoring other racial groups such as Mexicans." In San Francisco, the campaign did appeal to new male immigrants to register to vote, but it didn't send speakers into the large German and Irish communities until a few weeks before the election. Wealthy suffrage leaders perceived the immigrant population would provide insufficient benefits to the overall suffrage effort.[50]

At times during the campaign, the suffragists' nativist rhetoric was laid out for all to see. In California at that time, there were 5,000 American-born Chinese voters and 170,000 naturalized immigrants—Mexicans, Germans, Irish, Eastern Europeans, and Scandinavians.[51] The campaign hired a veteran of Chinese missionary work to reach out to Chinese voters, but public comments by leading suffragists undercut that effort. Woman suffrage was necessary, they said, in order to negate the votes of the foreign, illiterate element, "the ignorant, vicious, besotted of the sloughs, slums, and purlieus."[52] At the annual Women's Congress, suffragist Eliza Keith had argued that the nation was at risk from unrestricted immigration and that the women's vote would be morally uplifting. "The time is coming," she said, "when American men, acting in self-defense, will give women the ballot to rescue the Nation from the ignorant foreign voters and the criminal elements in our National life."[53] Little wonder the immigrant vote went heavily against suffrage. An embittered Anna Howard Shaw complained that "every Chinese vote was against us."[54]

Pioneering Black Suffragist—
Naomi Anderson

The white, middle-class suffragists' relationship with African Americans tended to be a bit more complicated. Many of the older women had been veterans of the abolition movement and believed African-American voters owed them a

---

[50] Gayle Gullett, "Constructing the Woman Citizen and Struggling for the Vote in California, 1896–1911, *Pacific Historical Review*, Vol. 69, No. 4 (2000): 581, 582.

[51] Edelman, 87, 88.

[52] "Susan B. Anthony Talks Suffrage," *San Francisco Chronicle*, April 13, 1896, 11.

[53] "Noble Women Call for Justice," *San Francisco Chronicle*, May 6, 1896, 10, 11.

[54] Quoted in Edelman, 88.

debt of gratitude. The campaign enlisted Naomi Anderson, a 53-year-old African-American writer of poetry and newspaper articles, to work the black churches and other venues in search of male votes. Born in 1843 to free black parents in Indiana, Anderson had established her reputation lecturing on temperance and suffrage throughout the Midwest until moving to California in 1895. The state remained socially segregated, and black women weren't invited to join white woman suffrage groups, so Anderson organized African-American suffrage clubs. A fiery orator, Anderson addressed the state suffrage convention at the capitol, speaking on behalf of those "who have been compelled to kiss the dust and drink the dregs of womanhood."[55]

Described by one newspaper as "an eloquent colored orator and an ardent apostle of the cause,"[56] Anderson traveled the state for several months, speaking to any black audience she could find and earning solid newspaper coverage. In an interview with the *San Francisco Call* promoting her initial speech at a San Francisco church, she outlined her message. "The colored men know what it is to be deprived of the ballot, and I am sure they will do what they can to release white and colored women from the same humiliating state of silent slavery."[57] In the end, however, Anderson's fervent advocacy wasn't enough, and her target audience was too small to tip the election. According to census data, only 11,000 African Americans—voters and nonvoters—lived in California during the 1890s—less than one percent of the state's total population.[58]

Assessing Defeat

Amendment Six, as the state suffrage measure was designated, had its greatest support in small towns, rural areas, and Southern California where its south-state leadership paid greater attention to working-class voters. The measure lost badly in the more populous north, particularly in San Francisco and Alameda counties. Voters in those counties expressed their conservatism by backing the presidential campaign of Republican William McKinley. Post-election analyses indicate the measure lost in both the wealthiest and poorest precincts in the Bay Area, with all but one precinct in San Francisco going against the amendment.

Suffragists also conceded that despite their best intentions, their organization was insufficient to successfully conduct a statewide election. In every county where the campaign organized precinct clubs to canvass and educate voters, the measure carried. But pockets of apathy prevented campaign leaders from recruiting enough women to establish an adequate number of precinct clubs. Part of the

---

[55] "The Suffrage Convention," *Sacramento Record-Union*, May 31, 1896.

[56] "A Colored Lady Orator," July 23, 1986, *San Francisco Call*, 7.

[57] "A New Apostle to the Negroes," *San Francisco Call*, July 26, 1896, 10.

[58] "Historical Statistics of the U.S., Colonial Times to 1970," US Census Bureau, 25, https://www.census.gov/library/publications/1975/compendia/hist_stats_colonial-1970. html.

problem was finances. Campaign leaders had estimated the election effort would cost $10,000, but they ended up spending $19,000 and still lost. Raising money during a depression—even among the wealthy class—proved to be problematic. Harper later complained that "while hundreds of women worked for their political freedom, thousands contributed absolutely nothing in either money or service," and chalked up their lethargy to domestic duties, the demands of society, or apathetic indifference. [T]hey left the whole burden to be carried by the few, and these could not do the work necessary for success, because human nature has its limits."[59] The outspoken *Los Angeles Times*, of course, had a different take: "The defeat of the Sixth Constitutional Amendment in this State was nothing less than a victory for the women, even if there are a few of the sex who won't admit it."[60]

Two days after the election, women from throughout California convened their annual state suffrage convention in San Francisco with Ellen Sargent presiding. News reports characterized the meeting as being far from funereal in the wake of bitter defeat. Reporters said the delegates were upbeat and cheerful as they analyzed what had just transpired and tried to absorb lessons learned for later battles. Apparently, they also broke down a few myths. Their behavior, one account noted, "should quiet forever the calumny that women do not know how to govern themselves—that they become hysterical in the face of defeat."[61]

The women savored small victories, such as the amendment's success in Los Angeles and the apparent impotence of the *Los Angeles Times* editorial page that had so strenuously urged its defeat there. They also noted, however, the measure's big setback in Alameda County, where every newspaper had urged support. "My faith in the power of the press is somewhat shaken," Harper told a newspaper.[62] The nation's most famous suffragist, Susan B. Anthony, put the best face on the setback. She noted how long she and others had worked and agitated in the suffrage movement in the East and praised activists in California for at least getting the measure on the ballot.

Just before the convention adjourned, the women passed the hat to pay off a $900 campaign debt. Ellen Sargent pledged $100, Susan B. Anthony offered $150 from two of her friends, and others gave as little as $5. In short order, the women not only had covered the debt but had a $225 surplus that was pledged to renew the suffrage fight. Before scattering their separate ways, they passed a resolution acknowledging the defeat "but we do not regard it as final."[63] They agreed to start immediately on yet another vigorous campaign to secure the franchise.

From the ashes of the 1896 setback, suffrage pioneers learned valuable lessons in political strategy and tactics that paved the way for success 15 years later. Although more betrayals and disheartening losses lay ahead, they would summon

---

[59] Harper, 865, 866.
[60] *Los Angeles Times*, November 6, 1896, 24.
[61] "Women Workers' Final Rally," *San Francisco Call*, November 7, 1896, 14.
[62] "Those Who Fought for Suffrage," *San Francisco Call*, November 6, 1896, 9.
[63] Ibid.

this collective wisdom to hitch their wagon to a sweeping insurgent reform movement that finally set them up for victory.

Discussion Questions

1. What reason did Governor Markham give for suggesting that enacting a state law to permit women to vote in school elections in California could be unconstitutional?
2. Given references in the Fourteenth Amendment to the voting rights of adult males, as noted in Chapter 1, would a federal law to permit women to vote have been similarly unconstitutional?
3. Why were Laura de Force Gordon and other suffragists downhearted when the legislature put a state constitutional amendment on the ballot to authorize woman suffrage in California?
4. Opponents of suffrage sometimes argued that women didn't want the vote. What evidence seemed to contradict that during the 1896 campaign? (Which gender votes in greater numbers today?)
5. Given the political clout and popularity enjoyed by the liquor industry, did the suffrage movement commit a strategic error in teaming up with the Women's Christian Temperance Union to promote the state amendment?
6. For what reasons has the suffrage movement been accused of catering to middle-class white women to the exclusion of others?

Recommended Reading

Campbell, Karlyn Kohrs. *Man Cannot Speak for Her: A Critical Study of Early Feminist Rhetoric, Vol I*. New York: Praeger, 1989.

Cherny, Robert W., Mary Ann Irwin, and Ann Marie Wilson, eds. *California Women and Politics: From the Gold Rush to the Great Depression*. Lincoln: University of Nebraska Press, 2011.

Mead, Rebecca. *How the Vote Was Won: Woman Suffrage in the Western United States 1868–1914*. New York: New York University, 2004.

Chapter 3

1896–1910
Grassroots Civic Action Sparks Revival of Suffrage Crusade

"The place for you women is home where you belong."
—Governor James Gillett

It was an explosive confrontation—a strange, fiery case of "he said, she said"—that rocked California in 1909, capturing huge headlines and adding more frustration and disappointment for a cadre of women who had worked for decades to secure the vote. It involved an alleged conversation between Lillian Harris Coffin, one of the leaders of the woman suffrage movement, and Republican gubernatorial candidate James Gillett. By the time the dust cleared, either Gillett was a back-stabbing scoundrel, or Coffin had fabricated the whole story.

The exchange in question was kept a well-guarded secret for three years. It had occurred in Santa Cruz, as state Republicans were meeting to select their 1906 nominee for governor. The powerful, king-making Southern Pacific Railroad wanted to deny the party's renomination of incumbent Republican governor George Pardee, a railroad critic. The railroad hand-picked Gillett to be the party's standard-bearer, and it cut backroom deals with delegates to make it happen. Also in Santa Cruz at that time were a number of woman suffragists, who regularly made the rounds of state political conventions seeking endorsements for their cause, as well as "trying to obtain a few pointers in practical politics," according to Coffin's account.

The suffragists failed to secure the party's support in 1906, but Coffin noted an encouraging development on the Santa Cruz beach where a number of women were relaxing. She said a small group of men emerged from the convention tent and approached the women. "I was sitting a little apart from the rest of the ladies," Coffin related a few years later. "One of the gentlemen walked up to me and said: 'I am James N. Gillett. I know who you are. You are woman suffragists. I believe in your cause and I want to say that if I am elected Governor of California, I will do all in my power to help you in your movement.'" According to suffragist and author Selina Solomons, the conversation was witnessed by Mary Simpson Sperry, president of the state suffrage association.[1]

---

[1] Selina Solomons, *How We Won the Vote in California* (San Francisco: The New Woman Publishing Co., 1912), 8.

Gillett went on to win election, and as governor he successfully pushed legislation that created a state version of the federal Pure Food and Drug Act. He also signed a bill allowing the state to sterilize clinically insane mental patients, sexual predators, and persons with more than three criminal convictions.[2] He didn't have the chance to act on suffrage legislation his first year in office, however, because it never reached his desk; it was defeated in the senate by a large margin.

In the meantime, Coffin tried to figure out the best time to take advantage of Gillett's pledge. She decided to keep it under wraps and use it as a trump card down the road when it would have maximum leverage. That time was in early 1909, when the legislature again debated the wisdom of placing a woman suffrage constitutional amendment on the 1910 statewide ballot. Women lobbied in shifts, spending a few days in Sacramento, then returning home to take care of their families. They packed hearing rooms. As the measure was pending, Coffin—then-head of the Woman Suffrage League—decided to play her ace. A signal of support from the governor might nudge fence-sitting lawmakers to the side of suffrage. She called on the governor in his capitol office to confirm his support but was shocked at his reply:

Gillett: "The place for you women is home where you belong. As long as I am in the Governor's chair in California, a woman suffrage bill shall never become a law."

Coffin: "Why, Governor, what do you mean? Don't you remember the time you came to us unsolicited on the beach at Santa Cruz while the convention which gave you your first nomination was in session and you pledged yourself to our cause?"

Gillett: "Oh no; I was only joshing you. I didn't mean what I said."

Coffin: "You may call that joshing, Governor, but some people would designate it by another word."[3]

Stunned, but still hopeful, the women continued to push for passage of the suffrage amendment. On the assembly floor, the suffrage measure immediately followed debate on antirace track legislation, and "the floors and galleries were so packed with disreputable men that there was no room for the women!"[4] During the suffrage debate, San Francisco assemblyman George Perine suggested that "manly men" should protect women from the grime of politics. If they received the vote, he argued, they "would be compelled to rub elbows with dope fiends and persons of low character." Although Alexander Drew of Fresno responded

---

[2] Greg Lucas, "Happy Birthday, Governor Gillett," *California's Capitol*, September 20, 2012, http://www.californiascapitol.com/2012/09/happy-birthday-governor-gillett/.

[3] Various accounts of the Gillett-Coffin conversation can be found in Solomons, 8–9; "Talking through Her Merrywidow Hat," *Sacramento Union*, October 3, 1909, 1; "Replies Tartly to the Charge That He Broke Faith with Suffagists," *Sacramento Union*, 2; and "Conclave Ends in Wordy War," *San Francisco Call*, October 3, 1909, 17.

[4] Solomons, 11.

that women already come in contact with those people on the streets, the measure was defeated.[5]

Nine months later, Coffin decided to go public with her Gillett story at the statewide suffrage association convention in Stockton. It created an immediate feeding frenzy among the press. In responding to reporters, Gillett not only denied that he had pledged his support for the women's efforts, he also suggested the beach conversation never happened that day in Santa Cruz. "I made no pledge to her, as she did not ask for one. . . . Another thing, I don't go around parading political headquarters addressing myself to women who see fit to hang around such places when they ought to be home raising children. . . ." As a senator, Gillett had voted against suffrage legislation. He argued it would have been illogical for him to back suffrage in return for women's political support. "They cannot . . . give me any votes and their influence amounts to nothing."[6]

The Suffrage Movement on the Verge of Collapse

California suffragists had displayed plenty of public bravado immediately following the ballot defeat of suffrage in 1896, but it was all for show. Losing California not only crushed morale within the California movement, it affected other states as well, and the push for political equality stagnated for several years. After Idaho gave women the vote in 1896, it would be another 14 years before another state—Washington—would follow suit. California women were discouraged and impatient with the slow progress. They were weary of fighting the same battle in the legislature every two years without results, and there was an internal debate as to what strategy should be employed—more militancy or more public education and less agitation? Susan B. Anthony urged Berkeley suffrage leader Mary McHenry Keith to keep the fight alive. Shortly after the election, Anthony wrote, "So I do hope you'll leave nothing undone to secure a majority of the coming legislature to vote for the re-submission of the amendment."[7] But the Republican Party withdrew its support of suffrage, and many leaders expressed concern that association with such a radical issue might cost them votes in the next election. With neither GOP nor Democratic backing, there was no chance the legislature would approve a suffrage amendment.

In the years following the 1896 defeat, the organized suffrage movement nearly collapsed. Only about 100 suffragists remained active in nine organizations maintained by skeleton staffs. The California Women's Congress, which had helped build the suffrage movement earlier in the decade, folded in 1898. The following year, temperance women pushed a watered-down suffrage measure that

---

[5] "Suffrage for Women Denied by Lawmakers," *Los Angeles Herald*, January 29, 1909, 1–2.

[6] "Replies Tartly to the Charge That He Broke Faith with Suffragists," 2.

[7] Letter from Susan B. Anthony to Mary Keith, December 20, 1896, Keith-McHenry-Pond Family Papers, Bancroft Library, University of California, Berkeley.

would have allowed women to vote in school elections. That, too, failed when it was vetoed by Governor Henry Gage. However, some suffragists were ambivalent about that defeat, believing the time had long passed for a partial victory; they wanted full suffrage or nothing. Interestingly, although women weren't allowed to vote in school board elections, they could run as candidates, and by 1900 they served on school boards in nearly every California county.[8]

In frustration, one of the leading stars of the suffrage movement tried guerilla tactics. If the male-dominated political leadership was going to stonewall the woman's vote, Ellen Sargent would try to make her point in other ways. In the fall of 1899, she sought to register to vote but was refused. She then went to the polls anyway, and again she was turned away. The next year, she dutifully paid a roughly $500 property tax bill, and then sued the city and county of San Francisco to recover the money. Her son, George Sargent, argued the case. "In taxing women without allowing them a voice," he said, "you take away their property without their consent . . . taxation and representation are morally inseparable." In a decision that made national news headlines, the judge, however, said the remedy was not to recover the taxes but to enforce the right to vote.[9] That task fell to a handful of indefatigable women who slowly started to rebuild the suffrage movement at the turn of the century. Little known today but critical to what was to come, they energized the grassroots women's civic organizations that would carry the fight through the first decade of the twentieth century.

Bringing the Suffrage Movement Back from the Brink— Mary McHenry Keith

Much of the credit for the rebirth goes to Mary McHenry Keith, who came to be known as Berkeley's "mother of suffrage."[10] She was a friend of Susan B. Anthony and the wife of prominent landscape artist William Keith. She was the daughter of a former Louisiana Supreme Court justice and had been one of eight women in the 64-member class of 1879 at the University of California. Her school yearbook listed her as a petite woman—five-feet-two inches tall and weighing 106 pounds. Her occupational goal was to become a lawyer and, indeed, she was the first female to graduate from the Hastings School of Law. But her law career lasted only one year. Instead, she turned her full attention to suffrage and other issues of female political equality.

One of her Berkeley classmates was George Pardee, who became a physician before getting involved in politics. After a stint as mayor of Oakland, Pardee sought the Republican nomination for governor in 1898 and sent a letter to Keith's husband asking for his support. The formal response came not from William but from Mary, who referred to herself as Mr. Keith's confidential legal adviser. There

[8] Gayle Gullett, *Becoming Citizens* (Urbana: University of Illinois Press, 2000), 144.

[9] "Cause of a Woman in Court," *Minneapolis Journal*, June 5, 1901, 13.

[10] Solomons, 27.

were no niceties in her response, and she made no mention of their four years together as classmates. She indicated that her husband might choose to offer his support, but "before permitting him to do so, I should like to ask, 'What are your views upon the question of suffrage for women? . . . If elected Governor would you do all in your power to enfranchise the women of your State?'"[11] Pardee lost the Republican nomination to Henry Gage, Southern Pacific's favorite, but would attain the governor's office four years later and serve a single term. In his lengthy inaugural address, the new governor outlined his many priorities but made no mention of woman suffrage. After the devastating San Francisco earthquake and fire in 1906, Pardee mobilized the National Guard, ordered them to shoot looters on sight, and became the first governor to seek and receive federal disaster aid.[12]

After four years in the wilderness, the state's suffrage movement started to rebound—albeit slowly—late in the year 1900. In Southern California, activists revived the region's suffrage association. In Northern California, Keith was a one-woman dynamo. She lectured frequently, petitioned the legislature, and recruited new members for the moribund state suffrage association. In September, Keith brought back to life Berkeley's lapsed Political Equality League. Only two women attended the first meeting, but 40 came to the league's November session. Two years later, the league boasted 115 members. The state suffrage association also saw gradual growth. Its tiny membership doubled between 1900 and 1901, when 44 delegates attended its state convention; 100 attended in 1902.[13]

Women's Clubs Divided by Race

As the state's suffrage movement was slowly rebuilding, 6,000 women joined 40 women's groups throughout the state under the umbrella of the California Federation of Women's Clubs. These were apolitical social clubs, but gradually they became involved in civic affairs and pushed for reforms in juvenile justice, conservation, food safety, and improved working conditions for women and children.[14] They also became embroiled in what the *Los Angeles Times* called the "all-absorbing question of the color line."[15] The member organizations of the General Federation of Women's Clubs were exclusively white, but there was persistent pressure to scrap the color barrier and open the federation to African Americans.

In the run-up to the federation's 1902 national conference in Los Angeles, intense debates exposed long-held racial prejudices, animosities, and still-raw emotions four decades after the Civil War. At the Friday Morning Club in Los

[11] Letter from Mary McHenry Keith to George Pardee, February 27, 1898, Keith-McHenry-Pond Family Papers, Bancroft Library, University of California, Berkeley.

[12] Lucas, "Happy Birthday, Governor Pardee," *California's Capitol*, July 25, 2012. http://www.californiascapitol.com/2012/07/happy-birthday-governor-pardee/.

[13] Gullett, 145.

[14] Donald Waller Rodes, "The California Woman Suffrage Campaign of 1911," master's thesis, California State University, Hayward, 1974, 27.

[15] "Women's Clubs," *Los Angeles Times*, February 22, 1902, I8.

Angeles, Mrs. W. L. Graves argued that the laws of nature could not be recast. She drew harsh distinctions between white and black:

> . . . the one of that blood which as for centuries ruled the world, the other a slave for over three thousand years; the one vested with every mark of authority, the other with every badge of inferiority; the one which has pushed forward the civilization of the world, the other which has never civilized itself in any country; the one every dominant, the other ever subservient.[16]

When the federation's conference convened in May, proponents of continuing the color line stressed a seemingly less-distasteful, more-pragmatic reason: maintaining unity among women's clubs. One of its vice presidents, Mrs. Dimies T. S. Denison, noted that southern clubs were strongly represented in the federation, "and the effect on those members is obvious if colored women are admitted on a social equality with white members.[17] Members of the federation voted to exclude African Americans.

In response to their systematic exclusion from white-women's organizations, California black women formed their own service clubs, beginning with Oakland's Fanny Jackson Coppin Club in 1899. Originally, the club provided hospitality and housing services to African-American visitors who were not allowed in whites-only hotels and other establishments.[18] In 1906, Eliza Warner melded five black clubs into a cohesive state federation, becoming its first president and—according to one of her successors—"lighting a torch for race regeneration and race betterment."[19]

Wooing Suffrage Supporters—Phoebe Apperson Hearst

Meantime, as Keith slowly started to rebuild Northern California's suffrage movement, she set out to capture the big prize: philanthropist Phoebe Apperson Hearst, widow of wealthy Senator George Hearst, who had made his fortune in mining before turning to politics. Mrs. Hearst was dedicating her life to improving women's access to higher education. She became a generous benefactor of the young University of California, providing funds for scholarships for female students and new campus facilities, including the Hearst Memorial Mining Building—a tribute to her late husband. Her grandson, William Randolph Hearst, Jr., estimated that she donated between $21 million and $25 million during her life-

---

[16] Ibid.

[17] "Auspicious Beginning of the Biennial," *Los Angeles Times*, May 2, 1902, I12.

[18] Gullett, 123.

[19] Delilah L. Beasley, "Federation of Negro Women Convene Here," *Oakland Tribune*, September 14, 1933, 6.

time. "That was when a dollar was real money," Hearst wrote in a family biography, "and there were no tax benefits in giving to charity."[20]

Born on a farm in Missouri and described as "plain, homespun," Phoebe Hearst adhered to three unbendable rules, her grandson wrote: "Be on time, have good manners, and respect older people."[21] In 1888, she became the first president of the elite Century Club, the first women's club on the west coast. In 1897, Governor James Budd appointed her to the University of California Board of Regents, which made her one of the highest-ranking female officials in the country. Likely reflecting her down-to-earth, rural roots, she believed that women didn't belong with boastful and arrogant men in the gritty world of politics. She once said woman suffrage would surely come, "but I have always held myself apart from the organizations that were working for suffrage because the methods did not appeal to me."[22]

By mid-1900, Keith believed her powers of persuasion finally were working, reporting to Susan B. Anthony that she almost had Mrs. Hearst converted to the suffrage cause. Encouraged by Keith's progress, and with a keen eye on Hearst's bank account, Anthony responded that "the wisest appropriation of her millions" would be to educate young women and men to believe that allowing women to vote would bring about the best government the world had ever seen. "How Mrs. Hearst . . . can possibly persuade herself that a government composed wholly of men can legislate better for themselves and for women than a government composed of both sexes is more than I can understand."[23] Although the suffrage movement had seemed tantalizingly close to securing Hearst's coveted endorsement in 1900, it would have to wait another 11 years to get it.[24]

Creating New Suffrage Clubs—Gail Laughlin

The movement received a major boost when the national suffrage association sent a professional organizer to California in early 1904. Gail Laughlin was one of nine children (two did not survive infancy) whose father had died when she was three. A native of Maine, Laughlin had watched the struggles of her mother

---

[20] William Randolph Hearst, Jr., *The Hearsts: Father and Son* (Niwot, CO: Roberts Rinehart Publishers, 1991), 22.

[21] Ibid., 18.

[22] Mildred Nichols Hamilton, *California Women and Politics*, Robert W. Cherny, Mary Ann Irwin, Ann Marie Wilson, eds. (Lincoln: University of Nebraska Press, 2011), 91.

[23] Letter from Susan B. Anthony to Mary McHenry Keith, July 25, 1900, Keith-McHenry-Pond Family Papers, Bancroft Library, University of California, Berkeley.

[24] Less than a week before male voters went to the polls to decide the suffrage issue in a 1911 statewide election, Mrs. Hearst went public with an endorsement. She said she felt that giving women the vote would work for the betterment of women and children. Mary McHenry Keith's hometown newspaper, the *Berkeley Independent*, announced the endorsement October 6 by covering its entire front page with a portrait of Mrs. Hearst. Its simple headline, in large block letters, read: "MRS. HEARST FOR SUFFRAGE."

to support the family and from the age of 12 had vowed to become a lawyer to improve women's opportunities. After working her way through Wellesley College and Cornell Law School, she opened a law practice and then became an agent for the US Industrial Commission. From that position, she investigated the working conditions of rural, immigrant, and nonwhite female domestic servants.[25] She then joined the National American Woman Suffrage Association as an organizer and campaign manager, working out of Denver to help attain the vote for women in western states. The *Los Angeles Times*, a staunch foe of giving women the vote, described Laughlin as someone who "talks like a phonograph, dresses as near like a man as she can without appearing 'mannish,' and she is quick and decisive in action."[26]

The *Times*—reluctantly, no doubt—credited Laughlin with organizing almost every ward in Los Angeles with a thorough and "machined" effort that surpassed the suffragists' statewide campaign strategies eight years earlier. At the state suffrage association's 1904 convention in Los Angeles, Laughlin reported she had helped create 52 new suffrage clubs in California and that membership had more than doubled in one year.[27]

The convention then turned to finances and an urgent plea from the state treasurer for $300 to pay the association's bills. Keith stood up and quietly said, "I'll give $500." After sustained applause, a few other women offered to donate, as well. On the stage sat Amanda Way, "a tall, aged Quakeress from Whittier," who had entertained the women with a comic routine. She rooted through her purse, then rose and said: "I have nobody to depend on and nothing to live on, only what Uncle Sam gives me for helping to take care of the soldiers during the war—$12.50 a month." She stepped forward and laid a $10 gold piece on the table. "I will give this," she said.[28] By the end of the session, the women had collected more than $1,100. They also began the process of rebranding their organization, changing its name from the California Woman Suffrage Association to the California Equal Suffrage Association in an effort to draw attention to the law's inequities and make it more palatable for men to join the campaign.

Throughout the convention, delegates heard a recurring theme that women must be allowed to take their place alongside men in the political arena, because through politics civic good could result. A few months later, after the movement had endured yet another defeat in the legislature, many suffragists decided to flip the equation, concluding that civic betterment would make good politics.

---

[25] National Women's History Museum, https://www.nwhm.org/education-resources/biography/biographies/gail-laughlin/; Her Hat Was in the Ring, http://www.herhatwasinthering.org/biography.php?id=6242#sthash.Nl1ULJvp.dpuf; Gullett, 148.

[26] "'Equal' Now, 'Woman' Gone," *Los Angeles Times*, October 8, 1904, I6.

[27] Ida Husted Harper, *The History of Woman Suffrage*, vol. 6 (New York: J. J. Little & Ives Company), 31; "Surprise for the Men Folk," *Los Angeles Times*, August 7, 1904, II1.

[28] "'Equal' Now, 'Woman' Gone," *Los Angeles Times*.

Laying the Groundwork for Suffrage:
Civic and Social Reform

Women suffragists approached civic activism from different perspectives. Some, like Maud Younger, sought to improve the lot of working women and immigrants, while the elite women's clubs worked to improve their communities at large. Younger was the daughter of a Gold Rush pioneer, born into a prosperous San Francisco family. She attended private schools and traveled frequently to Europe. On a New York stopover on her way to France, Younger was appalled at the poverty she saw among immigrants; she took a temporary job as a waitress and ended up staying for five years, working for social reform and trade unionism.

When Younger returned to San Francisco, the "millionaire waitress," as she was called, created the state's first union for female food servers. In a column written for the *San Francisco Examiner,* she told heartbreaking stories of girls and young women—exhausted and underpaid garment workers, waitresses, and laundry workers—whose deplorable working conditions had improved since women started organizing in 1901. One 12-year-old, "a dark girl with flashing eyes," told her she used to work up to 16 hours a day, and "no one helped us, no one cared." A waitress told of working seven days a week, up to 14 hours a day, for a weekly wage of $5. Younger's union doubled her wage, reduced her work hours and shortened her work week.[29] Younger believed that "high wages do more to keep a girl 'respectable' than all the rescue missions in existence."[30] She also believed that the solution to many women's labor issues would be advanced by giving women the vote.

Meanwhile, elite women's organizations, white and wealthy, undertook ambitious civic affairs and environmental causes, which had as a byproduct the reinvigoration of the suffrage movement after the 1896 setback. One campaign worked to save millions of birds that were being massacred and stuffed by milliners when they made ornate women's hats. The California Club of San Francisco was created amid the ashes of the failed suffrage campaign, and its members were credited with saving the homes of working-class Italians on Telegraph Hill, which were in danger of collapsing. The foundations were being undermined by contractors who were hauling away large rocks to be used as building materials. After a campaign that included the lobbying of supervisors and park commissioners, the women won their victory and earned plaudits from male political leaders by appealing to their civic pride.

The California Club also saved the Calaveras Grove of ancient sequoias from loggers' saws, engaging in a multi-year effort that eventually led to federal protection legislation. In addition, the women engendered significant political support when they pushed to create a system of juvenile courts, establish parks and build

---

[29] Maud Younger, "What Unions Mean for Women," *San Francisco Examiner*, November 25, 1909, 6.
[30] Ibid.

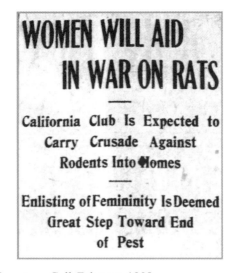

WOMEN WILL AID IN WAR ON RATS

California Club Is Expected to Carry Crusade Against Rodents Into Homes

Enlisting of Femininity Is Deemed Great Step Toward End of Pest

Figure 3.1. *San Francisco Call*, February 1908
Credit: Courtesy of Newspapers.com

public playgrounds—later becoming members of playground commissions—all of which expanded their public personas and allowed them to slowly inch their way into the corridors of municipal leadership.

One of the club's biggest public relations triumphs was its "war on rats" in early 1908 in response to San Francisco's deadly bout with bubonic plague. The city's devastating earthquake and fire two years earlier had sent millions of rats scurrying through drains, sewers, and open streets in search of food from butchers' animal waste, grocers' rotting vegetables, and carelessly discarded garbage by homeowners. The plague was being spread by fleas attached to the rats, and experts said the only way to stanch the spread of the plague was to eradicate the rats. The administration of San Francisco's corrupt mayor, Eugene Schmitz, had been too occupied with the city's rebuilding program and a number of graft trials to devote much time to the rat problem. It was left to citizen volunteers to rid the community of the health scourge. Businessmen, fearful of lost tourism, created the Citizens Health Committee and enlisted the women of the California Club in a high-profile campaign to clean the city—its restaurants, schools, and homes. "Women Will Aid War on Rats," headlined the *San Francisco Call*, suggesting that the citizens committee "has taken its greatest step forward, for the fight will now be carried into the homes of the city where individual effort alone can achieve results."[31] The citizen brigade made sure that grocers and butcher shops carted off their refuse, that bakers kept flour and feed in rat-proof bins, and

---

[31] "Women Will Aid War on Rats: California Club is Expected to Carry Crusade against Rodents in the Homes," *San Francisco Call*, February 7, 1908, 5.

that garbage cans were covered. Devoting a full page to the rat battle, the *Call* said "every kind of club and organization has been called on to assist." Traps baited with cheese, fish heads, fried bacon, fresh liver, and pine nuts nabbed an average 15,000 rats a week.[32]

Building Allies

The California Club's rat campaign, combined with other civic projects, gave the women recognition as local reformers, and the ruling class of white males accepted them as allies. Many club women also had established their credentials as reformers by working actively for the election of Edward Robeson Taylor as San Francisco's mayor. Taylor, a medical doctor and a lawyer, was an unknown dean at the Hastings College of Law when he suddenly was thrust into the political limelight in mid-1907. San Francisco politics was a slimy cesspool of corruption at the time. Former mayor Schmitz was in jail on corruption charges, and the equally sleazy board of supervisors temporarily appointed colleague James Gallagher to the post. A few weeks later, the supervisors decided that yet another board member, Charles Boxton, should be acting mayor. The acerbic *San Francisco Examiner* was not impressed: "Having put our bribe-taking Mayor in jail, and having put in his place a taker of smaller bribes, we have now substituted for Gallagher, Boxton, who differs from Gallagher principally in having sold his vote for still less of the bribing corporations' money."[33]

Boxton lasted eight days. That's when the city's reform element—which included newspaper editor Fremont Older, District Attorney William Langdon and his top assistant, Francis Heney—decided to hand-pick the next mayor and convince the 18-member board of supervisors to accept the selection. Taylor was 68 years old, devoid of charisma, and described as a "shy old man." In Older's autobiography, he described the moment when Taylor was tabbed to become mayor. Older said he and Edward Livernash, a former congressman, were poring over the names of potential candidates who had been untainted by scandal. On a whim, Older asked Livernash if he had a list of those who framed the city's charter a decade earlier. Livernash found a ragged, dusty copy of the charter. "I looked over the names . . . and when I came to E. R. Taylor I said, 'Doctor Taylor is the man.' 'Wonderful,' said Livernash. 'But he's dead.'"

It turned out that Taylor was very much alive. Older found him in a bookstore, convinced him to accept the job, and then helped pressure the supervisors to accept the choice. Taylor then replaced 16 of the 18 supervisors—all of whom had confessed to bribery—as well as the police chief, and set about cleaning city government. Less than four months later, at the next regularly scheduled election,

---

[32] Nathan S. Wood, "Saving a City Is Rather Rough on Rats," *San Francisco Call*, March 1, 1908, 5.

[33] *San Francisco Examiner*, in Walton Bean, *Boss Ruef's San Francisco* (Berkeley: University of California Press, 1967), 228.

Taylor successfully ran to continue as mayor with a cadre of hard-working club women helping him. The women were given much of the credit for his election and continued to amass plaudits with their highly publicized rat extermination efforts. Taylor nominated two California Club members to the city's playground commission, and by the time Taylor's brief 30-month tenure as mayor had expired, the women's club members had established themselves as a major force of civic good.

Despite women's advancements into municipal reform and public affairs, they still couldn't translate it into statewide progress on the suffrage front. Again, there were suggestions of skullduggery. A voting rights bill had been introduced in the 1907 legislative session and was pending in the senate when another set of "peculiar circumstances" led to its defeat. Supporters believed they had enough votes to secure passage, but when the measure was brought to the senate floor and the roll call began, a number of pro-suffrage senators were missing. They were in the cloak room—and the vote was announced before they could be heard on the bill. The explanation afterwards was that the entire mix-up was "unintentional."[34] Absorbing one defeat after another, Mary McHenry Keith lashed out. "Is there not something in the Bible about the kingdom of heaven being taken by violence?"[35]

In the ensuing years, further attempts sought to link suffrage with good government, particularly in the larger cities. Just as San Francisco suffragists had joined reformers to keep E. R Taylor in the mayor's office, women in Los Angeles rallied behind George Alexander—the reformers' 70-year-old, hand-picked successor to that city's corrupt mayor. Alexander repaid the suffragists' electoral assistance by announcing his unambiguous support of the women's quest. "I am unequivocally in favor of political equality, irrespective of the sexes," he told a local suffrage group. He then equated the two crusades, saying that "the agitation for suffrage will in time bring the same results that the agitation for good government has brought."[36] Alexander's comments came on the same day crusading women won another victory—the US Surgeon's declaration that San Francisco was rid of the bubonic plague to become the most "sanitary" city in the United States."[37]

Finding Common Cause with Republican Progressives

Through civic enhancement and political advocacy, suffragists had managed to hitch their wagon to the growing reform movement. In the minds of many, suffrage would rise or fall with the insurgent pursuit of good government, and the women encouraged the optics. When the Los Angeles Political Equality League held a big rally in late 1909, good government and suffrage shared the billing, and

---

[34] "Woman Suffrage Goes by Default: Friends of Measure Not on Hand When the Vote Is Taken," *San Bernardino County Sun*, March 2, 1907, 1.

[35] "Suffrage Plank is Desired," *Berkeley Gazette*, August 20, 1908, 4.

[36] "Mayor Indorses Equal Suffrage," *Los Angeles Herald*, November 13, 1909, 8.

[37] "San Francisco is Sanitary," *Los Angeles Herald*, November 13, 1909, 2.

the newspapers acknowledged the linkage. One speaker "held her audience spellbound" and insisted it was "the duty of women to go into politics and help break the hold of men, machines, and bosses who control public offices for private gain and to the detriment of all the people."[38]

The women's association with political reform wasn't always successful, however. The same year that Los Angeles women actively worked to elect a winning reform ticket, their sisters in San Francisco couldn't duplicate the feat. They had thrown their support behind Francis Heney, a reform candidate for district attorney, announcing in August that they'd "campaign in every residence block in San Francisco."[39] Heney had been selected to lead the prosecution team in the highly publicized graft trial of corrupt political puppeteer "Boss" Ruef. A week into the trial, a former San Quentin inmate who had a beef with Heney walked into the courtroom and shot him point-blank in the face with a hand gun. Heney survived but couldn't continue as Ruef's prosecutor. In a move that ultimately would alter the course of California history, District Attorney William Langdon turned the reins of the trial over to Hiram Johnson, who secured the court victory and quickly became one of the state's leading public figures.

San Francisco suffragists supported Heney and worked hard for his election, but the city had a sizeable antiprosecution element in the business community, and Heney was defeated by Charles Fickert, who was backed by well-funded businessmen who wanted a halt to graft prosecutions. Fickert's claim to fame was that he was a former Stanford football hero who coached his alma mater in the first-ever bowl game in Pasadena on New Year's Day, 1902. (Stanford turned out to be an embarrassment, however, fumbling nine times and trailing Michigan 49–0 before the game was halted with eight minutes left to play.) Once in office, Fickert obliged his benefactors and stopped pursuing graft prosecutions. Despite Heney's defeat, California women continued to make their mark in good-government politics and progressivism, earning praise from reformers and representing virtue in the public arena.

The impact of the suffragists' synergy with reformers cannot be overstated. Reformers believed that direct democracy tools—the initiative, referendum, recall, as well as the direct election of party nominees—would end the Southern Pacific's vise-like grip over the state's politics and economics, leading to "emancipation of the Republican Party from the corrupt domination" of the railroad's political bureau.[40] The suffragists viewed those same tools as vehicles to end the good-old-boys club that employed backroom politics to keep them from enjoying political parity.

---

[38] "Equal Suffrage Cause to Be Formally Launched," *Los Angeles Herald*, December 3, 1909, 3; "Equal Suffrage Given Approval," *Los Angeles Herald*, December 4, 1909, 14.

[39] "Women Organize to Elect Heney," *San Francisco Call*, August 22, 1909, 17.

[40] George A. Van Smith, "Leading Republicans Organized to Fight Boss Rule, *San Francisco Call*, August 2, 1907, 1.

Figure 3.2. *San Francisco Call*, July 4, 1909
Credit: Courtesy of California Digital Newspaper Collection, Center for Bibliographic Studies and Research, University of California, Riverside, http://cdnc. ucr.edu

As early as 1907, the California Equal Suffrage League had formally endorsed political candidates associated with reform Republicans, and the reformers, in turn, endorsed suffrage. The winds of revolt had arisen during informal discussions among reformers and journalists, but the official incorporation of a new reform culture was birthed after a 1907 legislative session that seemed to plumb new depths of corruption. "Scarcely a vote was cast in either house," one senator said, "that did not show some aspect of Southern Pacific ownership, petty vengeance, or legislative blackmail."[41] Journalists covering the session reported often on how the railroad's team of lobbyists strong-armed legislators. On one oc-

---

[41] George E. Mowry, *The California Progressives* (Berkeley: UC Press, 1963), 63.

casion, "the whips of the organization swished before roll call," telling lawmakers how to vote and demonstrating "how nicely [the] little ones could jump backward through the hoops."[42]

When reporters returned to their home bases, they wrote scathing wrap-ups of the just-concluded legislative session and the brazen behavior of the railroad lobbyists. *Los Angeles Times* journalist B. Frank Greaves reported, "It can be said in absolute truth that they directed the majority in both houses as to the course it should take on every bill of any importance."[43] Chester Rowell of the *Fresno Republican* also spared no invective, declaring that in "shameless servility, blatant indecency, and total unfitness, this legislature stands at the very bottom of the long list of boss-ridden legislatures that have disgraced California."[44]

Rowell and his desk-mate in the press gallery, Edward Dickson of the *Los Angeles Express*, were so appalled at what they witnessed in Sacramento that they vowed to start a political movement to run the railroad out of the capitol and retake the Republican Party. On May 21, 1907, meeting in a Los Angeles cafe, they and more than a dozen other reform-minded journalists, lawyers, and businessmen created the Lincoln-Roosevelt Republican League. They produced a 32-page pamphlet stating their principles and offering a tutorial on how to vote in the upcoming 1908 elections. Their platform envisioned a new Republican Party of progressives and sweeping electoral changes that would give voters a direct voice in the selection of party candidates.[45]

The Lincoln-Roosevelt Republican League won its first victory on the local level with the election of Clinton L. White as mayor of Sacramento. According to the *California Weekly*, a contemporary publication with ties to the progressive movement, White didn't like Sacramento's reputation as a wide open gambling town, so he appointed a new police chief "who straightaway drove the gamblers over into Yolo County."[46] The legislative elections of 1908 would be the league's opening offensive on a statewide level, and the results indicated that the progressive movement was gaining a foothold in the Republican Party.

When the new legislature convened in Sacramento in January 1909, the *California Weekly* described it as "apparently 'honest' and reasonably 'capable.'" It noted that the railroad machine continued to control the important senate committees, but when reform-minded Democrats and Republicans were combined, "the

---

[42] "Herrin's Marionettes Reverse Themselves," *San Francisco Call*, March 9, 1907, 2.

[43] B. Frank Greaves, "Looking Backward over the Session," *Los Angeles Times*, March 15, 1907, I4.

[44] Mowry, 65.

[45] "The Lincoln-Roosevelt Republican League," n.d., Los Angeles County Central Committee, Lincoln-Roosevelt Republican League, 20–21. http://digital.library.ucla.edu/campaign/librarian?VIEWPDF=1908_001_001_a.

[46] "Political Table Talk: Interesting Situation at the State Capital," *California Weekly*, July 23, 1909, 553; Spencer C. Olin, "Hiram Johnson, The Lincoln-Roosevelt League, and the Election of 1910," *California Historical Society Quarterly*, Vol. 45, No. 3 (September 1966): 225.

anti-machine element is in definite control of the assembly and nearly in control of the senate. It is organized, militant and victorious."[47] Actually, it was semi-victorious. Although the 1909 legislature was an improvement over its immediate railroad-dominated predecessor in many ways, Southern Pacific continued to exert a significant and powerful presence. Reform lawmakers managed to secure a watered-down railroad regulation bill, and in a move that enabled the progressive takeover of the Republican Party the following year, they passed direct primary legislation—albeit weakened by railroad lobbyists—that gave California voters their first opportunity to nominate candidates for state office. Historian George E. Mowry noted that without that ability to bypass party bosses and take their case directly to the people, the progressives "could not have appealed directly to the people of the state in support of their candidate for governor in 1910."[48]

The legislature may have looked more kindly on a reform agenda, but that didn't include women's voting rights—an indication that the suffragists' bond with reformers required more adhesion. Activists had expected the newly elected progressives to reward their civic engagement and political support by voting for a suffrage bill, but legislation faltered badly. One theory is that reformers had only recently made inroads into the Republican Party and couldn't risk jeopardizing their position by adopting the suffrage agenda. Another theory suggests that some legislators might have been offended by new, more militant tactics that suffragists had recently adopted—marches, protests, confrontations, and a ramped-up publicity campaign. The catalyst had been their patronizing treatment at the 1908 state Republican convention when male delegates refused to endorse suffrage but insulted the women by thanking them for their attendance. After walking out of the Oakland convention hall, an indignant Lillian Coffin recast the battle. "From now on our tactics will change," she announced angrily. "We will make an open war for our rights."[49] Whatever effect the new suffrage strategy might have had on the 1909 legislature, six assemblymen who supported a suffrage bill in 1907 opposed it two years later. [50]

As 1909 drew to a close, women continued to organize themselves like a political party. They received endorsements from the State Federation of Labor, the California State Farmers Institute and other organizations, and they set out to help elect the one constituency that offered them the greatest hope—the men of the fast-growing Lincoln-Roosevelt Republican League. If the reformers could grab hold of the dominant Republican Party and drive the machine out of Sacramento, they hoped they might finally win their prize.

---

[47] *California Weekly*, 145.

[48] Mowry, 82.

[49] Kathleen Thompson, "Women to Wage War on Men Who Opposed Suffrage," *San Francisco Call*, August 29, 1908, 2.

[50] Rodes, 36, 40; *Journal of the Assembly, 37th Session of the California Legislature* (Sacramento: State Printing Office, 1907), 904.

Discussion Questions

1. Which version of the dispute between Lillian Harris Coffin and Governor James Gillett over whether he had pledged to support suffrage are you inclined to believe? How so?

2. Discouraged by the defeat of 1896, suffragists initially debated whether to become more militant or to rely on more public education and less agitation. Their twin arguments of simple fairness—no taxation without representation—or that women's decency would enhance the political system hadn't succeeded. What would you have advised?

3. Mary McHenry Keith became "a one-woman dynamo" in helping to revive California's moribund suffrage movement. Do her persistence and dedication in advancing the cause of women remind you of any prominent women today? If so, how?

4. Millionaire philanthropist Phoebe Apperson Hearst believed women would eventually obtain the vote, yet said she avoided "the organizations that were working for suffrage because the methods did not appeal to me." She may have been referring to Ellen Sargent's tactics—trying to vote at the polls and suing San Francisco to get her taxes back. If so, why might Sargent's aggressive methods have seemed distasteful to Hearst?

5. What were some possible advantages of changing the name "California Woman Suffrage Association" to the "California Equal Suffrage Association" after the defeat of 1896?

6. For what reasons were women's clubs in California divided along a "color line" at the turn of the twentieth century? Is it surprising to you that these social and civic-minded clubs were segregated in California? What kinds of barriers might such segregation have posed for African-American women?

7. In the years after San Francisco's devastating 1906 earthquake, the women of the California Club worked on projects and campaigns to combat the city's political corruption. How did San Francisco's rat infestation help magnify their public image as forces for good?

8. For what reasons did tying the movement to good-government reforms prove a more effective strategy than simply arguing for fairness in obtaining the vote for women?

9. How did the tactics of the suffrage movement become more militant as the new century progressed? Do you agree that such tactics had become necessary?

Recommended Reading

Kraditor, Aileen S. *The Ideas of the Woman Suffrage Movement, 1890–1920.* New York: W. W. Norton, 1981.

Mowry, George E. *The California Progressives*. Berkeley: University of California Press, 1963.

Wheeler, Marjorie Spruill. *One Woman, One Vote: Rediscovering the Woman Suffrage Movement*. Troutdale, OR: NewSage Press, 1995.

Chapter 4

1911
Eureka! California Becomes the Sixth Star

"Give your girl the same chance as your boy."
—College Equal Suffrage League advertisement

California's legions of doggedly determined suffragists—some of whom had been advocating for voting rights for more than four decades—faced a critical dilemma as the state approached its watershed special election on October 10, 1911. Progressives had taken control of the legislature months earlier and placed a series of landmark political reforms on the statewide ballot. Among them was a suffrage constitutional amendment giving women the right to vote. As with the devastating 1896 ballot defeat, it would be the men of California who would decide the issue. Activists believed their message of fair play would resonate with many male voters, but how could they reach them? The suffrage campaign had an active press operation and briefly advertised on street cars. It held rallies, printed posters and circulars, and used billboards and electric signs, but had trouble coaxing persuadable men into meeting halls to hear suffragists' speeches.

Bringing the Message to Male Voters—
Ida Finney Mackrille

The College Equal Suffrage League of Northern California conceived an innovative campaign tactic. If the men were disinclined to come to a suffrage event, why not have the women go to the men? And since men seemed to be fascinated with new, fancy automobiles, why not incorporate the still-novel "horseless carriage" into their campaign by using the cars as props and speech platforms? League member Ida Finney Mackrille recalled the spirited debate when the subject was first broached at a board meeting in San Francisco. Conservatives were adamantly against the stunts, suggesting that "such sensational methods will lose us votes." One member argued, "California men want their women to be dignified and womanly."[1] The more radical element in the league won the day, however,

---

[1] Ida Finney Mackrille, "Winning Equal Suffrage in California, 1913: Reports of Committees of the College Equal Suffrage League of Northern California," National College Equal Suffrage League, 61.

and beginning in mid-August the automobile became a key component of their suffrage campaign.

Automobiles had been introduced in San Francisco after the turn of the century, but the early versions had insufficient power to scale the city's famous steep hills and were considered nuisances, "belching out exhaust, kicking up storms of exhaust, becoming hopelessly mired in the most innocuous-looking puddles, tying up horse traffic, and raising an ear-splitting cacophony that sent buggy horses fleeing."[2] However, days after the 1906 earthquake, one dealer transformed his small fleet of Buicks into rescue vehicles.

The California suffragists used a number of autos during the campaign, but one in particular was a compelling man-magnet. Easily attracting news coverage as well, it was a big, blue, seven-seat, four-cylinder 1910 Packard touring car on loan from a Washington state suffragist and bank president. The vehicle had been employed extensively to ferry speakers and propaganda during that state's successful woman suffrage campaign the previous year. The Blue Liner, as it was called, was an expensive show-piece. It cost more than $4,000, which represented between seven and eight times the average Californian's yearly income.[3] It was bedecked with a suffrage banner and flags. Typically, a young boy with a bugle would accompany the speakers and toot a few bars to attract attention before the suffragists would sing a campaign theme song and deliver short speeches.

Campaign activist Mackrille conceded she was extremely "nervous" the first time the Blue Liner pulled in front of a San Francisco hotel. "[V]oters were in that crowd, and our political freedom depended on the men of the State." After her speech, a man standing in front of the hotel said, "Madam: as soon as you stood up in that automobile I said to my companion, 'Woman Suffrage.'" During another speaking event, a young couple watched for a few minutes before the man scoffed, "Come along, we've had enough of that . . . that woman had better go home to her children, instead of talking on street corners." His companion replied sternly, "She has to do that. She can't make you men listen any other way."[4] During the height of the campaign, one newspaper reported that the car, women, and bugler attracted more than a thousand voters—and many reporters—at three separate downtown San Francisco street corners.[5]

Driven mostly by the suffragists themselves, the Blue Liner was the campaign's workhorse, at times making all-day, all-night treks. It was the centerpiece of the campaign's critical rural outreach, venturing to remote factories, farms,

---

[2] Laura Hillenbrand, *Seabiscuit: An American Legend* (New York: Random House 2001), 4.

[3] Alexander Klein, "Personal Income of U.S. States: Estimates for the Period 1880–1910," Warwick Economic Research Papers, no. 916, Department of Economics, University of Warwick, http://web.stanford.edu/group/spatialhistory/cgi-bin/railroaded/gallery/interactive-visualizations/capita-income-united-states-1880-1910.

[4] Mackrille, 61, 62.

[5] "Women Closing Campaign with Whirl: Auto Canvass Attracting Voters at Many Centers," *San Francisco Call*, October 5, 1911, 4.

Suffrage Auto 'Blue Liner' Will Tour State With Women Making Addresses

Figure 4.1. *San Francisco Call*, August 16, 1911
Credit: Courtesy of Newspapers.com

ranches, and small towns well off the beaten path. For the most part, the roads outside the urban areas were crude and rutty dirt paths. California voters had approved the state's first highway bonds the year before—$18 million for acquisition of land and construction of a state system—but ground wasn't broken for California's first leg, a portion of Highway 1 along the coast, until 1912. The Blue Liner seemed to be the ideal vehicle for the long, difficult trips on uneven roads. In a thoroughly self-serving magazine called "The Packard," the automaker wove customer testimonials in between feature stories on vacation hideaways, sales figures, and maintenance tips. One man from Los Angeles wrote that he had put 5,800 miles on his Packard. "Up to present time I have spent ten cents for repairs," he said. "This was for a broken insulator in the magneto."[6] In the first of several articles on the campaign's new weapon, the *San Francisco Call* noted that

---

[6] "Ask the Man Who Owns One," *The Packard* (Packard Motor Car Company, Detroit), June 16, 1910, https://tinyurl.com/y7plgt72.

"it is planned that no mountain road will be too steep nor any valley too dusty" for the Blue Liner.[7]

Typically, the campaign flooded a community with handbills the day before an appearance, with an advance scout locating an area where men likely would congregate. In one town with 400 voters, more than 200 men showed up. At a Native Sons of the Golden West celebration in Santa Rosa, the Packard parked next to a knife-throwing booth. In Vallejo, the Blue Liner parked amid well-lit cigar stores and nickelodeons on the town's main street and soon was surrounded by curious young men from the Naval Shipyard. In a tiny "burg" in Contra Costa County, the women talked to a couple of men sitting against the walls of two adjacent saloons. "They did not move, they did not resist; possibly none of them understood English," one suffragist recalled. A couple of days later, the women returned to the same town—with the same result. On Election Day, however, the town voted for the suffrage amendment.[8]

The Blue Liner's last day of service was spent transporting hundreds of aging, broken-down men from San Francisco's Relief Home to the polls—men unable to walk, men who couldn't see, men who were close to death. They had listened to speakers sent by the campaign and were determined to perform their civic duty. "We fellows that are on the scrap-heap ain't afraid of the women," one of the men said. As suffragist Louise Herrick Wall later wrote, the Blue Liner "plied back and forth with its crippled loads, until the last old voter had lightened his own cross by stamping one opposite the 'Women's Amendment.'"[9]

Political Synergy—Suffragists and Reformers

California's historic suffrage election could not have occurred in 1911 had the state's young political reform movement not taken hold. After the 1909 legislative session, Los Angeles reformer Meyer Lissner was encouraged enough to suggest "the machine was on the run."[10] The reformers had, indeed, won some victories in the legislature—most notably, stripping party bosses of their right to nominate candidates and enacting an antiracetrack gambling bill—but they couldn't drive a stake through the heart of the all-controlling Southern Pacific Railroad. Wily railroad lawyers had helped block passage of stringent railroad-regulation legislation in favor of a watered-down version. The reformers were forced to turn to women for help.

---

[7] "Workers of Washington and California Map Out Vigorous Campaign for This Fall," *San Francisco Call*, August 15, 1911, 3.

[8] Louise Herrick Wall, "Winning Equal Suffrage in California, 1913: Reports of Committees of the College Equal Suffrage League of Northern California," National College Equal Suffrage League, 68.

[9] Ibid., 72.

[10] Spencer C. Olin, Jr., "Hiram Johnson, the Lincoln-Roosevelt League, and the Election of 1910," *California Historical Society Quarterly* (September 1966): 226.

Suffragist leader Ida Husted Harper wrote that reform-minded males had a "belief that it was only by the help of women's votes they could permanently redeem their State from the evil political influences which had so long controlled it. ... [T]he men were wise enough to realize that, while they might be able to create a spasmodic reform sentiment, it could not be made permanent unless women became a part of the constituency behind it."[11]

When the Lincoln-Roosevelt Republican League met in early 1910, its top agenda item was identifying a man to carry the reform banner in that year's gubernatorial election. Suffragists, who had aligned themselves with the league, expected the chosen candidate to be an ardent supporter of women's voting rights. After all, they had worked hard for upstart league candidates and anticipated the favor to be returned. At first, key league members supported Francis Heney, but he was deemed too radical and antibusiness to be a statewide candidate. In the January 21 issue of the *California Weekly*, an unsigned article extolled the virtues of Hiram Johnson as someone who could "be counted on to head the procession of reform and be no laggard."[12] Less than three weeks later, the league's executive committee decided to draft Johnson as its candidate for the Republican nomination. There was one problem, however. He didn't want the job. According to historian George Mowry, who wrote extensively on California progressives, Johnson was reluctant to give up his lucrative law practice. Further, there was "his wife's opposition to his entrance into politics, [and] her dislike of Sacramento as a place to live. . . . "[13] After dogged lobbying by league leaders, Johnson, the hero of the "Boss" Ruef corruption trial, and his wife acquiesced.

The primary campaign, the first conducted by voters instead of party machinery, would decide once and for all the strength of the reformers' influence with rank and file Republicans. Johnson ran on a singular theme—"kick the Southern Pacific out of politics." The message resonated, both for the victorious Johnson and the slate of league candidates "to give the statewide Republican ticket a distinct reform flavor."[14] The subsequent state Republican convention, now firmly in the hands of insurgent reformers, endorsed a national income tax and woman suffrage, prompting the conservative *San Francisco Chronicle* to editorialize, "For the first time in the history of the conflict between these parties the Republican platform is rather more radical than that of the Democrats."[15]

As a member of the House of Representatives and the California legislature, Grove Johnson, Hiram's father, had been a champion of both the Southern Pacific and woman suffrage. The son, however, was fiercely antirailroad and personally opposed to giving women the right to vote. On the general election campaign trail,

[11] Ida Husted Harper, "Votes for Women," *Harper's Bazaar* (December 1911): 578.

[12] "Political Table Talk: Who is This Man, Hiram W. Johnson?" *California Weekly*, January 21, 1910, 137.

[13] George E. Mowry, *The California Progressives* (Chicago: Quadrangle Books, 1963), 108.

[14] Olin, 234.

[15] "Democrats and Republicans," *San Francisco Chronicle*, September 8, 1910, 14.

he didn't include the women's issue in his speeches and never took a position on suffrage. He also refused to attend the state suffrage association's annual convention, which had adopted Lillian Coffin's militant strategy of "forcing" political parties to endorse their cause. The fall campaign pitted Johnson against three other opponents, most significantly Democrat Theodore Bell, a former district attorney and member of Congress who also campaigned against railroad dominance. In an effort to separate himself from his opponent, Johnson accused Bell of accepting railroad support, and when word leaked that the Southern Pacific backed Bell as the lesser of two evils, Johnson's election was assured in a state weary of the railroad's corrosive influence over more than four decades.

In his inaugural address, Johnson referred to the railroad as "the former political master of this state" and laid out an aggressive reform agenda. He made no mention of woman suffrage. When the new legislature met, it wasted no time in putting progressive campaign promises into practice—placing 23 constitutional amendments on a 1911 special election ballot, including measures dealing with railroad regulation, workers' compensation, working conditions for women and children, nonpartisan local elections, and the direct-democracy tools of the initiative, referendum, and recall. The new-look Republican leadership in Sacramento also moved to include suffrage on the ballot agenda, but holdouts didn't go down without a fight. Some Republicans "tried to wriggle out of supporting the [suffrage] amendment," according to suffragist author Selina Solomons. She insisted that despite Johnson's personal opposition to giving women the vote, and his silence on the campaign trail, the governor "used his influence to prevent them from throwing the suffrage plank overboard."[16]

Opponents first tried a delaying tactic by requiring a women-only advisory vote before the male electorate would get its say. Antisuffrage women had contended the vote was being forced on them, and "antis" saw this as a move to publicly undercut the activists. Suffragists called the move an "insult" and "pure subterfuge," and their supporters in the legislature defeated the provision. Later, when the proposed constitutional amendment was up for a senate floor vote, John Sanford, the legislature's fiercest antisuffrage member and editor of the *Ukiah Dispatch Democrat*, read a letter from "an old mother" in Oakland who said "a suffragette is a woman who wants to raise hell, but no children." That argument didn't work. The measure was approved in the upper house by a seven-to-one margin. Finally, with the amendment needing only assembly approval to go on the ballot, opponents tried appealing to male pride and arrogance as an overflow

---

[16] Selina Solomons, *How We Won the Vote in California* (San Francisco: The New Woman Publishing Co. 1912), 13. Not all suffragists were as charitable to Johnson. When the governor sought female votes during his reelection campaign in 1914, suffrage icon Clara Foltz was indignant, writing in an open letter: "And how, please, can you stand before an audience of women—informed women—and claim any credit for the amendment granting suffrage to women in California? You know that you were opposed to the principle . . . you also know that you tried in every possible way to defeat the amendment." "Not Entitled to Credit," *San Francisco Chronicle*, August 24, 1914, 18.

gallery audience looked on. "I refuse to believe there are 54 men in this assembly who are weak enough to be led around by the nose by women," pleaded San Francisco's Walter McDonald, an old-school, nonprogressive Republican. "You will soon see these women lecturing their husbands instead of cooking their meals." Another San Franciscan argued that putting suffrage on the ballot would promote perjury, because women would balk at revealing their true ages when registering to vote. That plea also failed as lawmakers, by a wide margin, sent the woman suffrage amendment to the voters.[17]

Overcoming Class Divisions

In the 15 years between statewide suffrage votes, California had undergone dramatic changes that altered the state's political contours and affected women's demand for political parity. Thanks in part to economic expansion that helped spur European immigration, California's population grew by 64 percent between the 1900 census and 1910 to more than 2.7 million. Spurred further by rural migration to the cities, much of that growth was in Southern California. San Francisco, long the dominant population center in the state, had lost ground to rapidly growing Los Angeles, and by the 1910 census, Los Angeles County had nearly 90,000 more residents than the city and county of San Francisco.[18] Those trends encouraged activists who were anticipating another tough political battle. During the ill-fated 1896 suffrage vote, Southern California, including agricultural counties east of Los Angeles, had been fertile ground for the suffrage movement. The amendment won majorities in seven counties between Santa Barbara and San Diego, although the well-heeled, antisuffrage liquor industry continued to be politically potent in the Bay Area.

Along with the population shift, California society was changing, as was the role of women. Greater industrialization brought increased job opportunities for women. Many left their traditional roles on the farm or in the home and found work in the textile, canning, and printing industries; there also were new opportunities in teaching, business, and nursing. More women were entering the classrooms of colleges and universities. Political equality, however, was elusive. Several states, particularly in the West, had granted women suffrage in the 1800s, although some of these were only fractional victories—the right to vote in school or municipal elections. "California had granted neither and, as women assumed a more equal role in society, their lack of political equality became more apparently unjust."[19]

---

[17] "Suffragists Are to Have Inning on Wednesday, *San Diego Union*, January 17, 1911, 1; "Suffrage Goes through House with Big Vote," *Sacramento Bee*, February 2, 1911, 5; "Suffrage Bill is Passed by House; Goes to People," Associated Press in the *Los Angeles Herald*, February 3, 1911, 2.

[18] laalmanac.com/population/po02.php; bayareacensus.ca.gov/copop18602000.htm.

[19] Donald Waller Rodes, "The California Woman Suffrage Campaign of 1911," (master's thesis, CSU Hayward, August 1974), 19–21.

In the years since the first statewide suffrage defeat in 1896, suffragists faced their own internal issues concerning equality. Club membership remained racially exclusive and socially stratified, and there was little interaction among the classes. Writing in the *Chapman University Historical Review*, Lauren Abel noted that elite suffragists "did all they could to attract as much support from those in power (men) as possible."[20] They forged alliances with white, male municipal leaders and kept the partnerships intact by shunning American women, as well as Chinese, Japanese, and Mexican immigrants. Further, they didn't want to antagonize working-class male voters who feared immigrants might steal their jobs by working longer hours for less pay. Caroline Severance of Los Angeles, the elder stateswoman of both the abolition and suffrage movements, offered a minority viewpoint. She acknowledged that breaching the color line might jeopardize harmony in the national suffrage federation, but she believed white women should draw "the line of social fellowship at education, character, and good breeding, not race."[21]

If the movement wouldn't unify racially, suffragists understood that it would have to overcome class divides to be successful. The failure to meaningfully include working-class women in the 1896 campaign was seen as a critical flaw, and most clubs remained segregated by class with few clubs combining membership of upper-, middle-, and working-class women. Abel argues that the work of socialist women led to at least partial unification. The Socialist Party had grown significantly in the US after the turn of the century as it allied with many labor organizations in opposition to corporate abuses and income inequality. Socialist suffragists introduced new arguments in an attempt to appeal to and unite all classes. Some traditional messages—that suffrage would be a tool for reform by reducing political corruption, weakening the influence of the liquor industry, and regulating working conditions—proved to be divisive. The Socialist message, however, was broader and more unifying—that all women were entitled to suffrage rights because of their economic contributions. "Women who worked in factories and women who worked from home were considered to be contributors to the social wealth of the state."[22]

Expanding the Suffrage Coalition—Selina Solomons

At the same time, one woman in particular set out to bring self-supporting, working-class women into the movement. Selina Solomons was convinced that a major flaw in the 1896 electoral defeat was the failure of wealthy, white Protes-

---

[20] Lauren Abel, "The California Plan: California's Suffrage Strategy and Its Effects in Other States and the National Suffrage Campaign," *Chapman University Historical Review*, Vol. 5, No. 1 (2013): 10, http://journals.chapman.edu/ojs/index.php/VocesNovae/article/view/636/887.

[21] Ibid.

[22] Ibid., 5.

tant suffragist leaders to broaden their campaign beyond the socially elite. There was "the need of agitation," she said, "among that large class of self-supporting women heretofore hardly approached."[23] Solomons had come from a Sephardic Jewish family that traced its roots to sixteenth-century Spain. Her great-grandfather had participated in George Washington's presidential inaugural in 1789, and her father was a Gold Rush pioneer.[24] In 1910, she founded the Votes-for-Women Club, which operated from a large loft on San Francisco's Sutter Street in the retail shopping district and was designed to attract shop girls, clerks, and other working women into the movement.

The club had a reading room, a kitchenette, and an inexpensive buffet that attracted working women throughout the area drawn by flyers circulated in all nearby stores and offices. All work at the club was donated, except for cooking, dishwashing, and janitor work. Women typically spent 15 cents for lunch. The club's menu included a choice of oxtail soup, tomato bisque, or clam chowder for five cents; salads were a nickel, and five-cent sandwiches included cheese, chicken loaf, smoked tongue, and sardines. Selected meats, including Vienna cutlet, lamb stew, Hamburg steak, and corned beef hash cost a dime.[25] The affordable luncheon buffet was available for three hours each day, and there was an afternoon tea. Further, Solomons brought in entertainment and guest speakers, including British and Australian suffragists and popular writers. According to Solomons, many of the women had not been affiliated with voting-rights groups, but all received suffrage literature and occasionally mixed with the upper crust. One society woman was quoted as saying, "The other day I dropped in for luncheon and a pretty young girl who only an hour before had sold me a pair of gloves sat next to me."[26]

Beyond informational outreach, Solomons and other club leaders weren't above publicity stunts and protests to boost visibility of suffrage issues. Votes-for-Women Club officers initially refused to sign 1910 census documents, telling officials it was the principle—not the questions—they objected to. Solomons also formed the Woman's Committee of Protection to publicly agitate for helping safeguard working women from "the infamous men [who watched] like wolves for the underpaid and underfed working-girls at the noon and dinner hour." She wrote of a young Swedish immigrant who was searching for work as a domestic servant when a strange man offered help. "She was led to a cheap eating-house, drugged, and the next thing she knew, awakened in a low lodging-house in the 'Barbary Coast.'" The woman escaped and wandered the streets, weary and homeless, until

---

[23] Solomons, 16.

[24] "American Jerusalem: Jews and the Making of San Francisco," 2017, http://www.americanjerusalem.com/characters/selina-solomons/28.

[25] "Votes-for-Women Club: Business Women's Lunch," Selina Solomons Papers, Folder 6, Miscellany, Ephemera Re: Woman Suffrage 1908–1912, Bancroft Library, University of California, Berkeley.

[26] Elaine Elinson and Stan Yogi, *Wherever There's a Fight* (Berkeley: Heyday, 2009), 177.

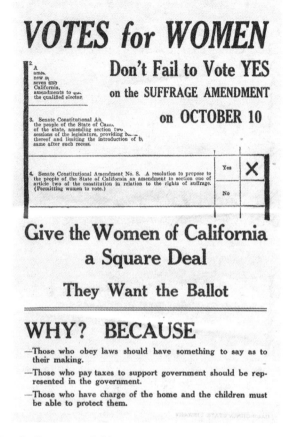

Figure 4.2. Pro-Suffrage Handbill, 1911
Credit: Courtesy of California State Library

she unsuccessfully tried to kill herself by jumping off the top of Telegraph Hill.[27]
The protection campaign continued until the urgency of the suffrage election took
precedence.

The Campaign for Suffrage: Breaking Down Myths

If the suffragists had any hope of winning the election, they would have to
dispel a number of myths that had served their opponents well over the years,
among them: that women were physically and mentally inferior to men, that
women were more emotional than men, that filthy politics would taint and unsex

---

[27] Solomons, 20–21.

women, and that a woman's place was at home caring for children and husbands. In official ballot arguments for the 1911 amendment, H. G. Cattell, speaker pro tem of the state assembly, tackled head-on the male superiority claim. "[I]f we take the number of graduates from our schools and colleges, we must admit that they [women] are farther advanced mentally" than men. He also noted that about 3,000 men were in state prisons but only about 30 women. "Women are better morally," he concluded, "as evidence by the criminals in the penitentiaries." Since it would be men who would decide the suffrage issue, that argument may have been politically risky in those days before messages were forged by focus groups.

In his opposition ballot statement, J. B. Sanford, the long-time senate foe of the suffrage movement, took the mother-in-the-home argument to a new level, suggesting God didn't want women to vote and neglect her children. "The mothers of this country can shape the destinies of the nation by keeping in their places and attending to those duties that God Almighty intended for them." Referring to "mannish female politicians," Sanford concluded, "Let her be content with her lot and perform those high duties intended for by the Great Creator . . . keep woman where she belongs."[28]

It was left to the fanatically antisuffrage *Los Angeles Times* to try to connect suffrage to female physicality in an editorial that employed intriguing logic. "A law that is not backed by physical force is not a law," the *Times* wrote, and since "women are incapable of physically dominating men . . . the enforcement of all law [police forces] must inevitably rest with men." The editorial raised the specter of women getting the vote and passing laws that men didn't want and refused to obey. "[T]he women would pass a law . . . and then ask the men to lock themselves up if they broke it."[29]

The blustery *Times* was relentless throughout the campaign. It accused women in Utah of reneging on a promise to rid the state of polygamy once they received the vote. "On the contrary," it said, "they voted to strengthen it."[30] The newspaper gave ample space to suffrage critics, including one who ridiculed women for wanting to vote so they could pass laws that improved the quality of milk and fresh eggs for their families. "He was mildly curious to know if votes for women will cause every cow to give milk carrying a higher percentage of butter fat, and if the hens . . . will catch the militant suffrage spirit, and lay themselves out for a new record in the egg industry."[31] Perhaps the most hysterical argument on the newspaper's pages was a piece authored by suffrage nemesis Sanford nine days before the election. "Woman suffrage is a disease" that had caused divorces and crime to rise in Colorado, he wrote. "The number of young girls that have gone wrong" also increased, he alleged. In Sanford's mind, who supported suf-

---

[28] Ballot Arguments: Secretary of State Election Papers, 1911 Special Election (Sacramento: Secretary of State).

[29] "Woman-Made Laws," *Los Angeles Times*, January 21, 1911, II4.

[30] "'The Times' and Suffrage," *Los Angeles Times*, September 22, 1911, II4.

[31] "Live Orator on Suffrage," *Los Angeles Times*, September 30, 1911, II3.

frage? Besides the idle rich, "It is the mannish female politician and the little effeminate, sissy man, and the woman who is dissatisfied with her lot and sorry that she was not born a man."[32] Susan B. Anthony once said of Sanford that, "as his species would soon be extinct, she would advise canning him for the benefit of posterity."[33]

The Campaign's Stretch Drive

The *Times* may have had the largest megaphone in Southern California, but the area was a top priority for the suffrage campaign. The liquor industry had less influence in Los Angeles than it did in San Francisco, and the city had delivered a significant majority to the movement in the 1896 election. Campaign leaders expected a similar, perhaps larger victory in 1911. The campaign had split the state in half at the Tehachapis, with the state suffrage association taking responsibility for Northern California, and Southern California groups working the south. Organizers, some from Chicago, Montana, and Colorado, built local and regional clubs in every county. In all, 50 separate suffrage organizations were involved.[34]

The campaign paid special interest to rural voters, farmers, and ranchers who had supported suffrage 15 years earlier. "There was scarcely a corner of the state that went unvisited by good speakers," said Elizabeth Lowe Watson, a preacher and president of the state association.[35] Many of those speakers were transported by the Blue Liner. For her part, suffrage legend Clara Foltz trudged up and down the state, speaking at any place that would have her, including "towns, sheep ranches, cross-roads, and mining camps," according to Solomons' postelection account. Foltz's law office sent out thousands of letters, pamphlets, and leaflets.[36] In mid-August, the *San Francisco Call* ran a story about a society woman in the San Joaquin Valley who gave up her "luxurious home in Madera and is riding horseback through the hills and mountains" giving small, informal talks, "many of them without dismounting." She spread the message to stockmen, forest rangers, and curious wives drawn to the suffrage issue. In the tiny Madera County town of Knowles, Italian quarry workers forbade their wives from attending one talk, but the women rebelled and stood their ground after an interpreter told them they had the right to stay under US laws.[37]

---

[32] Senator J. B. Sanford, "Woman Suffrage Means Disruption of the Home," *Los Angeles Times*, October 1, 1911, V19.

[33] Solomons, 47.

[34] Jane A. Stewart, "Woman's Widening Way," *Journal of Education*, Boston University (August 22, 1912): 175.

[35] Robert P. J. Cooney, "Winning California for Woman Suffrage, 1911," American Graphics Press, http://www.americangraphicpress.com/articlesphotographs.html.

[36] Solomons, 31.

[37] "Society Woman Gives Up Fine Home to Ride for the Cause," *San Francisco Call*, August 16, 1911, 7.

In its outreach to farmers and fruit growers, the campaign appealed to their pride and antagonism to the "evil in the cities," suggesting that women would help make cities cleaner places to live and prevent urban diseases from spreading into the country. Suffragists also stressed that "the cities send delegations to Sacramento that outvote yours" (although the senate was controlled by rural lawmakers at the time), and that women lost their chance to vote in 1896 when urban ballots overwhelmed the prosuffrage support from rural communities. For good measure, the farmers were reminded that their ancestral brethren fired the first shots of the American Revolution on Concord Bridge protesting taxation without representation.[38]

Rural voters, in particular, were targets of the newest innovation in political campaigning, the use of stereopticons—or slide shows—in moving picture theaters. Movie studios had just begun to move west into the new municipality of Hollywood, churning out such silent films as *In Old California* and *Ramona* in 1910 by film pioneer D. W. Griffith. That same year, Tom Mix reached early stardom portraying a bronco buster in *Ranch Life in the Great Southwest*. In many theaters throughout the state, speakers would make a pitch for suffrage by narrating a brief slide-show program that included "actual pictures of many of the lower types of men who are allowed to vote."[39]

The campaign advertised on billboards, in the newspapers, and with pamphlets that flooded the state. In San Francisco, working girls and women gave up their Sundays to hand out leaflets outside every Catholic church during early morning Mass. At one Fourth of July celebration, three suffragist leaders soared 2,200 feet in a hot air balloon and threw literature to thousands of people below. The suffrage messages were everywhere—on blotters distributed in offices, grocery bags, napkins at ice cream parlors, even in the pockets of clothing to be picked up at the tailor.[40] The College Equal Suffrage League spent $237.30 for advertisements on San Francisco street cars, one reading, "Give your girl the same chance as your boy."[41]

---

[38] Millicent Shinn, "To the Farmers and Fruit Growers of California," "Women's Suffrage and Equal Rights" by the College Equal Suffrage League/Ella Strong Denison Library/Claremont Colleges Digital Libraries, http://ccdl.libraries.claremont.edu/cdm/compoundobject/collection/p15831coll5/id/1496.

[39] "Society Woman Gives Up Fine Home to Ride for the Cause, *San Francisco Call*, August 16, 1911, 7.

[40] James A. Stewart, "The Winning of California," *Journal of Education*, Boston University (November 9, 1911): 480; Elinson, "San Francisco Women Helped Forge Suffrage Victory in State," *San Francisco Chronicle*, October 9, 2011, http://www.sfgate.com/opinion/article/S-F-women-helped-forge-suffrage-victory-in-state-2327754.php.

[41] Ernestine Black, "Winning Equal Suffrage in California, 1913: Reports of Committees of the College Equal Suffrage League of Northern California," National College Equal Suffrage League, 88, 89.

Figure 4.3. "Why Shouldn't My Mother Vote?"
Credit: Arthur Buel, Sacramento Bee*, 1911.*

With eight weeks remaining until Election Day, the *Call* reported that the campaign already had broken records for the volume of posters, circulars, and other propaganda in a single state election.[42] Scraping together the funds to pay for those materials, as well as far-flung events, remained a challenge, however. Most of the state's moneyed interests opposed the suffrage amendment, although Solomons reported that a few persons connected with big business, and even the liquor industry, donated anonymously. A fundraising rally at San Francisco's famed Palace Hotel generated $500, and a bazaar netted another $300. A number of suffrage leagues had substantial reserves "well into the thousands," while individual donations—led by Mary Keith's generous $3,000—helped fill the campaign treasury.[43] The national suffrage movement contributed with a "sacrifice week," in which

[42] Ibid.
[43] Solomons, 52–53.

suffragists in New York, Massachusetts, and elsewhere were urged to set aside "a week for self-denial" and send the money saved to the national association so it could be used in California. An August 19, 1911 story in the *Lodi Sentinel* reported that women were avoiding confections, ice cream sodas, "and other delicacies so dear to the feminine heart."[44] Some of that money was used to pay the railroad expenses of speakers who came from the east.

Suffrage campaign leaders considered San Francisco to be a critical challenge. It was hostile territory, yet its population exceeded 400,000 and couldn't be ignored. The city had delivered the movement a strong rebuke in 1896, and the well-heeled liquor interests continued to be powerful and persuasive. Mary McHenry Keith said she was told by a San Francisco senator that "if she could convince all the saloon, hotel, and restaurant keepers, liquor dealers, and other purveyors of alcoholic beverages in his district to support woman suffrage, he would vote in kind."[45] The antisuffragists formed a "Committee of Fifty" to fight the amendment, printing excerpts from J. B. Sanford's senate speech in opposition. They quoted Sanford as saying "he pictures the suffragette seated atop the world she has ruined, crying out, 'Didn't I raise hell?'"[46] While opponents used the term "suffragettes," the women of the suffrage movement called themselves by the weightier-sounding term "suffragists." To counter the "machine politicians, crooks, and the liquor dealers," as the *Journal of Education* put it, the suffragists secured endorsements from labor unions and civic, commercial, and church federations.[47] Prominent men of letters—including Mark Twain, Frank Norris, and Jack London—lent their support, and more than 50 San Francisco stores created window displays supporting the amendment.[48]

In the frenzied campaign finish, and without the benefit of scientific polling, the opposing sides in the suffrage battle each predicted election victory. The secretary of the Men's Political Equality League in Los Angeles took a quick trip to San Francisco and somehow figured "from his observations that San Francisco County will give the women a safe majority." At the same time, an official with the Men's League Opposed to Suffrage who canvassed San Francisco's business district was "confident of a sweeping victory for the antis."[49] Perhaps his confi-

---

[44] Rachel Foster Avery, "Self-Denial Week for the Woman Suffragists of the Nation," McHenry-Keith-Pond Collection, Bancroft Library, University of California, Berkeley; Ralph Lea and Christi Kennedy, "Lodi's Women Were First in State to Vote," October 15, 2011, http://www.lodinews.com/features/vintage_lodi/article_2367c308-35d2-5441-aa82-184ca6f7f011.html.

[45] Susan Englander, *California Women and Politics*, Robert Cherny, Mary Ann Irwin, and Ann Marie Wilson, eds. (Lincoln: University of Nebraska Press, 2011), 213.

[46] Solomons, 46.

[47] James A. Stewart, 481.

[48] Jessica Sewell, *Women and the Everyday City: Public Space in San Francisco 1890–1915* (Minneapolis: University of Minnesota Press, 2011), 143,149.

[49] "Women Claim Big Victory in South," *San Francisco Chronicle*, October 10, 1911, 2.

dence was boosted by an eleventh-hour political trick that rocked the campaign. The day before the election, full-page ads appeared in the *San Francisco Chronicle* and elsewhere attributed to an organization calling itself the Northern California Association Opposed to Woman's Suffrage. It reinforced negative concepts of suffrage and its leading advocates by printing incendiary remarks they purportedly had made. The ad quoted national suffrage leader Anna Howard Shaw as saying: "I would pension all mothers and have them provided for . . . I would place a woman policeman at the door of every saloon and dance hall, every nickel theater and every factory." Carrie Chapman Catt, another national suffrage figure, was accused of saying: "I believe that the time will come . . . when every American woman who does not earn her own living will be considered a prostitute." Catt, the ad continued, had "travestied the Bible, the Declaration of Independence and the American flag." Two angry suffragists, claiming the quotes had been fabricated, stormed the *Chronicle* and confronted a clerk. The women were told the *Chronicle* was paid $500 for the ad and simply could not refuse it.[50]

"You've lost, haven't you, ladies?"

Election Day was balmy in San Francisco. A volunteer force of more than 1,000 women—fearful of tampering at the polls—fanned out throughout the city to keep a day-long watchful eye on the voting and to make a last attempt to persuade men to give voting rights to women. Before sunrise, a woman identified as Mrs. Robert Dean trudged up Telegraph Hill with her husband and stationed herself at a polling place one yard beyond the limit for electioneering. She decorated a barrel with a sign that read, "Votes for Women" and watched vegetable and fish sellers, draymen, and wine merchants file past her to cast ballots. A newspaper account noted that some Italian quarry laborers apparently were unsure of the propriety of the situation, "and a few tried to reach the election booth by crawling on hands and knees behind a miniature sand dune." At Bush and Larkin streets, Marie Parish approached a man and urged him to support the suffrage amendment. He snapped, "You ought to be at home getting breakfast for the family." She responded tartly, "I was up before 6 Mr. Voter, and prepared the family breakfast. Now I am helping them by working here." Outside another voting booth a man elated campaign organizer Gail Laughlin by announcing he would vote for the amendment, "but he said he was doing it on the same theory that he would use in having a bad tooth pulled—it had to be done some time, and he might as well get over it now."[51]

---

[50] "To the Voters of Northern California," *San Francisco Chronicle*, October 9, 1911, 5; Solomons 51.

[51] "Sunrise Sees Women Ready: Mrs. Robert Dean Trudges to Post at Five O'Clock in the Morning," *San Francisco Call*, October 11, 1911, 2; "Suffragist Outposts Watch Voting Booths," *San Francisco Chronicle*, October 11, 1911, 2.

Antisuffragists chose not to engage in last-minute politicking near the polls, convinced that voters already had made up their minds. Instead, they passed out leaflets with the drinks in San Francisco bars. In a statement to the press, the campaign's field manager insisted that more women opposed suffrage than supported it, and said the "anti-women . . . waged the kind of battle that men admire, for, after all, it is the sweet women that we all want—leave the political pool for the men to wade in."[52]

After the polls closed, an overflow throng jammed into the Dreamland Rink to watch the posting of election results. The venue had been donated by the *San Francisco Examiner* whose matriarch, Phoebe Apperson Hearst, had been a late but fervent convert to woman suffrage. A mixture of supporters and opponents filled the skating rink. Selina Solomons, who wrote the only detailed election postmortem, told of groans from her political sisters and despair every time new numbers were posted on bulletin boards. The vote tally was going so poorly, and Solomons and the others were so depressed, they decided to leave early. As they walked out into the night air, a man came up to her and said triumphantly, "You've lost, haven't you, ladies?" The women replied that it looked that way, and as they walked past the man, he said: "You'll never get it in California."[53] All along Market Street, clusters of people watched the results being posted on bulletin boards. Solomons walked into the campaign's headquarters, where "all was gloom," with staffers burying their heads in their hands. As midnight approached, Solomons walked along an unlit street to her car when she overheard one man telling another that suffragists wanted to destroy everyone else's homes. Solomons whirled around and testily confronted the men. "I beg your pardon, gentlemen . . . you are mistaken. We do not desire to destroy homes. But we do desire—*and intend*—*to have a voice in our own government. . . .* If you men continue to withhold it from us, *we'll take it!*"

Undeterred, the head of Sacramento's Equal Suffrage League released a statement declaring that the fight would continue via the newly enacted initiative process, and another campaign spokeswoman said, "We may possibly be defeated, but we are not conquered." The next morning, the *San Francisco Chronicle*, in one of several stories on the election, headlined the suffragists' determination: "Leaders Plan to Renew Battle for the Ballot."[54] Not all the ballots had been tallied, but most newspapers had the suffrage campaign trailing by several thousand votes. Gail McLaughlin, the political organizer from Denver, blamed the apparent defeat on "corruption and 'bought votes.'" She told the *Chronicle* that election officers were drunk and that some poll workers had alleged that prosuffrage ballots had been thrown out. "If there is anything that shows the need of woman

---

[52] "Anti-Suffragists Think They Are Sure Winners," *Los Angeles Times*, October 11, 1911, I 3.

[53] Solomons, 61.

[54] "Leaders Plan to Renew Battle for the Ballot," *San Francisco Chronicle*, October 11, 1911, 2.

suffrage," she said, "it is the way in which the election was conducted in San Francisco."[55] Originally expecting victory, campaign leaders had been scheduled to send a triumphant delegation to be feted at the national suffrage convention in Louisville the following week. Instead, they decided to remain in California and begin plotting strategy for their next suffrage attempt, drafting additional statements for the press that expressed their determination to move forward.

From Despair to Elation

Wasting little time, dejected suffrage leaders held a campaign postmortem. Afterwards, an utterly exhausted Solomons took a ferry to her sister's home in Berkeley in the hopes of getting a solid night's sleep away from the campaign's epicenter. On the passage, she and Mary Keith stood on the deck "and peered through the darkness of doubt, if not despair." Once at her sister's house, she went to bed and slept through the night, unaware that history was being re-written with every late news dispatch. Early Thursday morning, two days after the election, Solomons was awakened by the excited voice of her sister on the telephone, who then made a mad dash up the stairs to tell her the news. Late vote tallies continued to pour into newspaper offices and offered a ray of encouragement to the women. The gap was closing. The amendment had been defeated by a two-to-one margin in San Francisco, but most of those votes had been tallied first. Late returns were coming in from the farmers and miners in the "cow counties," and Los Angeles, Fresno, and Santa Clara showed significant majorities for suffrage. Solomons made a dash for the ferry and a return trip to campaign headquarters, proudly wearing her suffrage badges. When the ferry docked, a newsboy recognized her as a suffragist. He waved his newspaper and excitedly told her, "You'se [sic] are goin' to win out!"[56]

Black Wednesday had morphed into Holy Thursday, Solomons wrote. The voter turnout was heavier in the late-reporting rural counties than in the cities, and by nightfall the suffrage amendment increased its lead from a few hundred votes to nearly 3,000 with ballots in suffrage strongholds—San Diego and mountain areas—still unreported. Where the liquor influence was the weakest, suffrage piled up large majorities; where it was the strongest, San Francisco, it lost, but by a narrower margin than in 1896. Interestingly, the measure carried in the wine-growing regions of Napa, Sonoma, Mendocino, and San Joaquin. Belying the critical importance of the array of ballot measures—including California's support of new direct democracy tools, railroad regulation, and workplace rules—voter turnout was disappointing, although the suffrage issue was more emotional than any other and attracted the most votes. In San Francisco, the suffrage campaign did best in working-class, professional, and middle-class areas and, as expected, worst with the hard-drinking sailors along the Barbary Coast. The final tally showed

---

[55] "Overpowered But Not Conquered," *San Francisco Chronicle*, October 11, 1911, 2.
[56] Solomons, 63.

EQUAL SUFFRAGE WINS BY SAFE MAJORITY

Amendment Is Two Thousand Votes Ahead, With Further Increase Assured.

MISSING PRECINCTS, 244.

The Counties Still to Be Heard From Confidently Claimed by the Women.

Figure 4.4. *San Francisco Chronicle*, October 13, 1911
Credit: Courtesy of Newspapers.com

the amendment winning by a scant 3,587 votes—equal to about one vote per precinct.[57]

California had become the sixth and brightest star in the suffrage banner—after Wyoming, Colorado, Utah, Idaho, and Washington state. Although the election had yet to be certified, the *Los Angeles Times* reported a "rush of newly created voters to register.[58] On the editorial page of his Ukiah newspaper, Senator Sanford took one last swipe at the victorious women, taking aim at his perception of female vanity. When women registered to vote at the county clerk's office, he warned, they would have to "give their visible marks and scars, age and previous condition of servitude, all of which will be a public record open to inspection."[59] A few weeks later, the legislature held a special session in Sacramento to update election laws and required only that all voters state they were over the age of 21. In Santa Rosa, the *Press Democrat* proposed that women be required to attend a

---

[57] "Statement of the Vote of California at the Special Election Held October 10, 1911," California Secretary of State, Sacramento, 1911.

[58] "Votes Piling Up for Suffragism," *Los Angeles Times*, October 14, 1911, I5.

[59] *Ukiah Dispatch Democrat*, October 15, 1911.

"class in politics" to teach them the difference between Democrats and Republicans and help them make the right decisions when they voted. A searing letter to the editor later appeared in the *Santa Rosa Republican*, headlined: "MOST WOMEN ARE NOT IDIOTS."[60]

Six days after the election, California suffrage leaders left on a victory tour. At the national suffrage convention, they were hailed as "victors and conquerors," the architects of the movement's "signal victory." Women wore California poppies and sixth-star badges on their dresses. The convention featured an address by John H. Braly, a businessman who had created the Southern California Political Equality League with about 70 men the year before. He predicted that California's victory would inspire other states to follow.[61] In Boston, Francis J. Garrison, son of the famous nineteenth-century abolitionist William Lloyd Garrison, agreed. "It is impossible," he said, "to exaggerate the importance and far-reaching influence of this conquest."[62]

California's approval of the amendment had enfranchised 600,000 women, overnight doubling the number of American females who could vote.[63] Writing in *Harper's Bazaar*, suffrage historian Ida Husted Harper said the state's experience would strongly influence the movement in other states. "It is not a new State making crude experiments," she wrote, "but has been in the Union over threescore years, and by reason of its great wealth and enterprise holds a position of authority."[64] For campaign strategists in several states, the 71-page election retrospective by Solomons offered helpful hints in tactics and organizing.[65] Months after the California victory, activists in six other states took their case for suffrage to the voters and, once again, there was evidence of the west's progressive streak of independence, as Oregon—on its sixth attempt—Arizona, and Kansas approved ballot amendments. In the Midwest, however, attempts in Ohio, Wisconsin, and Michigan failed. By 1920—42 years after Aaron Sargent's initial effort in Congress—women finally won national suffrage with ratification of the Nineteenth Amendment to the US Constitution.

---

[60] "The Ladies Turn Out to Vote," *Comstock House,* http://comstockhousehistory.blogspot.com/search?q=J.B.Sanford.

[61] Cooney; Ida Husted Harper, ed., *History of Woman Suffrage 1900–1920* (New York: J. J. Little & Ives, Co. 1922), 317–18.

[62] Solomons, 65.

[63] Robert P. J. Cooney, Jr., "Winning California for American Suffrage, 1911," American Graphic Press, http://americangraphicpress.com/articlesphotographs.html.

[64] Harper, "Votes for Women," *Harper's Bazaar*, Vol. 45, No. 12 (December 1911): 578.

[65] Book circular, Solomons Papers, Bancroft Library, University of California, Berkeley.

The First Test for Women Voters

In the weeks after California's suffrage election, voter registration by California women for the most part went smoothly, even though they flooded county clerks' offices. San Francisco added 30 extra clerks to handle the tsunami of new registrations, staying open until midnight. Women waited up to two-and-a-half hours to register. The women weren't asked about scars or their exact ages, but their height had to be reported for identification purposes, which presented a short-lived problem in Sonoma County. Women tended to wear elaborate hats that were difficult to position without a mirror, forcing the county clerk to install one in his office.[66]

Women's interest in voting was staggering. Their first test was in the Los Angeles municipal elections in early December, two months after the statewide franchise vote. Noted feminist author and sociologist Charlotte Perkins Gilman of Pasadena, who gained worldwide fame with her writings on gender inequality, registered women in the city's working-class neighborhoods. Seventy-thousand women hurriedly joined the voter rolls, and an astounding 95 percent of them cast ballots. "Where are the men who used to say, 'The women do not want it?" asked Mabel Craft Deering in an article for *Collier's*. By contrast, the turnout among male voters was 63 percent. In a bit of delicious irony, the fiercely antisuffrage *Los Angeles Times* had begged women to register and vote in order to save the city from Socialist candidates. "The humor of the situation—the '*Times*' on its knees to women whom it had abused for years—was so pungent," Deering wrote, "that many who had worked themselves to the bone for suffrage said it more than repaid them for all their efforts."[67] All Socialist candidates were defeated, and the *Times* gave credit to the women for "the splendid result."[68]

The Los Angeles election also was an initial test of the liquor industry's decades-old fear that women voters, so closely aligned with the temperance movement, would close down all the saloons. Prohibitionists had placed a tough measure on the municipal ballot. In a full-page newspaper ad, the Los Angeles Taxpayers' League argued the proposal was so drastic it would even ban the use of wine in church and the ability of citizens to serve wine in their own homes. "There were fanatics . . . who hoped the women would vote for it," Deering wrote, but the ordinance was handily defeated by a nearly three-to-one margin, and women were given much of the credit for that outcome, as well. Elsewhere, however, women did use their new franchise to go "dry." In an April 1912 special election in a portion of Santa Clara County, voters closed the bars in a number of communities,

---

[66] "M'Lady Your Hat Can Come Off," *Santa Rosa Press Democrat*, January 28, 1912, 6.

[67] Mabel Craft Deering, "The Women's Demonstration: How They Won and Used the Vote in California," *Collier's*, January 5, 1912, 17–18.

[68] "Credit to the Women and Harmony Spirit," *Los Angeles Times*, December 6, 1911, I1.

including Palo Alto, Los Gatos, Sunnyvale, and Mountain View. In this election, turnout was much smaller than anticipated, and "voters were principally women, who exercised their right for the first time."[69] Two years later, California women joined with men to defeat a statewide prohibition initiative. But they also rejected a separate measure that would have forbidden any further prohibition initiatives for eight years. The lesson was that women were discerning voters, committed to their new role in electoral politics. They weren't as frightening as many opponents had feared, and not as helpful as some suffragists had hoped.

Securing the franchise had been an arduous ordeal that spanned 43 years since Laura de Force Gordon had delivered that ground-breaking speech demanding that California women be allowed to vote. In the ensuing decades, suffragists had been ridiculed, ignored, deceived, and out-maneuvered by the male power structure. Most of the suffrage pioneers had passed on before victory finally came. The breakthrough was based partly on a sense of fairness, but also on a realization by many men that the reform movement sweeping through California couldn't be sustained unless women became active participants. From the Blue Liner to town-hall speeches to derringers, the suffragists had set a potent new standard for grassroots political action in California. In the future, women might find it difficult at times to fully assert their power, but they never again would be forced to the fringes.

Discussion Questions

1. In what ways did the Blue Liner seem to make a difference in the final push for achieving suffrage? Do you believe male voters initially attracted to the car stayed to hear the campaign arguments? If you had addressed a crowd of car-struck men from the hood of a Packard, how would you have made your case for suffrage?
2. For what reasons did the quest for woman suffrage in California become intertwined with the drive to loosen the Southern Pacific Railroad's grip over state politics?
3. What arguments against suffrage for women were used in the legislature and during the election campaign? What counterarguments might have refuted them? Do you think some of the longstanding antisuffrage arguments were losing their potency by 1911? If so, for what reasons?
4. Women organized in opposition to the vote for women, known as "antis," lent credence to assertions that women did not want the vote. For what reasons do you suppose some women opposed woman suffrage?
5. How and why did the white-dominated suffragist organizers consciously shun nonwhite immigrants and African-American women?

---

[69] "Prohibition Will Be Enforced in Bulk of Santa Clara County," *San Francisco Call*, April 27, 1912, 12.

6. How did Selina Solomon's Votes-for-Women Club seek to recruit more working-class women to the cause?
7. What persuasive messages did the suffrage campaign use, and how were they transmitted to California voters?
8. What were some impacts of the California suffragists' hard-fought victory? (Did it turn out that women wanted to vote?)
9. The story of winning the right for California women to vote is particularly compelling because suffragists such as Selina Solomons documented their experiences and observations in writing. Newspapers covered the campaign closely. In what ways do the suffragists' own words and personal experiences, as recounted here, enhance the sense of struggle and triumph in the cause of suffrage?

Recommended Reading

Cooney, Robert P. J., Jr. *Winning the Vote: The Triumph of the American Woman Suffrage Movement*. Santa Cruz, CA: American Graphic, 2005.

Silver, Mae, and Sue Cazaly, *The Sixth Star: Images and Memorabilia of California Women's Political History, 1868–1915*. San Francisco: Ord Street Press, 2000.

Solomons, Selina. *How We Won the Vote in California: The True Story of the Campaign of 1911*. San Francisco: The New Woman Publishing Company, 1912 [reprinted 2010].

Chapter 5

1918
Trailblazers Shatter the Capitol's Glass Dome

"State to Have Women Solons"
—*Los Angeles Times* headline

O n January 11, 1911, the tiny *Alturas Plain Dealer* in sparsely populated northeastern California, ran an article containing news items about the town's only high school. Modoc High had five teachers at the time—three women and two men. The article mentioned that a new pupil, Wiley C. Dorris, had just arrived at the school. He wasn't a typical student; he was a bit of an oddity because he was 23 years old. "Mr. Dorris is a young man of somewhat mature years," the article said.[1]

Cyrus Dorris, Wiley's father, was a Midwest pioneer who had homesteaded in Yerba Buena (later renamed San Francisco), two years before gold was discovered in the Sierra foothills. Cyrus, along with much of the Dorris family, eventually settled in far Northern California. The town of Dorris, seven miles from the Oregon state line was named after one of Wiley's uncles.

Born in Alturas in 1887, Wiley had returned to finish high school because he had decided he wanted to become a lawyer. Fatefully, his English teacher at Modoc High was a short, slight woman who also was 23. Grace Storey McMillan had been born in Ventura to a Methodist Episcopal minister and a mother who was a descendent of the Puritans in 1638 New Hampshire. One of her ancestors fought at Bunker Hill and crossed the Delaware River with George Washington during the Revolutionary War.[2] After her mother died when she was one, Grace was adopted and raised by her aunt, Jennie Green, and took the name Grace Storey Green. She attended public schools in Santa Barbara and the University of California in Berkeley, graduating in 1908, before spending a year preparing to be an English, French, and Spanish teacher. After a brief teaching stint in San Rafael, she moved to Alturas and the job at Modoc High.

---

[1] *Alturas Plain Dealer*, January 11, 1911, n.p., in Ethel Bornefeld collection, California State Library.

[2] Kent Miller, "Grace Dorris: Early Political Activist," *Bakersfield Californian,* March 28, 1976, 26.

101

Grace Green, the teacher, and Wiley Dorris, her student, married two years later and settled in Bakersfield, a dusty oil town at the southern end of the Central Valley. Wiley became a successful attorney and Grace gave up teaching to work in his law office, developing a "vision that emphasized 'public progress and civic improvement.'"[3] Propelled by that philosophy and a keen interest in politics, Wiley made it known in Bakersfield Republican circles that he was going to run for the state assembly in 1918. The primary election was in late August, and he had the backing of local progressive Republicans. However, America's brief but intensive leap into World War I in 1918 derailed his promising political career before it had a chance to begin. Dorris enlisted in the Navy, forcing GOP leaders to scramble to find someone else to run.

Shortly before Wiley departed for war, he and Grace were sitting in the office of attorney and civic leader Alfred Siemon discussing Wiley's change of heart and the need to find a replacement candidate for the assembly. "Who will run in your place?" a dejected Siemon asked. Wiley and Grace had thought it out, and they had a plan. Without hesitation, Grace replied, "Why, I will."[4]

Pioneering Political Candidates

Grace Dorris was part of a surge of women in early twentieth-century California who shunned traditional roles as full-time housewives and mothers, instead choosing to carve their own paths and identities. Since statehood, women largely had been denied formal participation in political life, contributing instead on the fringes of the electoral arena. A few brave activists challenged the status quo and risked ridicule by running for office in a man's milieu well before women could vote for them.

In 1881, Marietta Stow, publisher of a woman's newspaper, created the Woman's Independent Political Party and promptly declared herself a candidate for governor the following year. She had been a teacher and lecturer and had run unsuccessfully for San Francisco school director in 1880. Stow fought unfair marital property and estate laws and used her newspaper to crusade on birth control, a shorter work day, crime prevention, and "the mischief resulting from a purely masculine form of government in Church and State." During her campaign for governor, she declared she was "anti-monopoly . . . anti-Chinese" and "unpickled by whiskey and tobacco."[5] Apparently, California's secretary of state recognized neither Stow nor her new political party. She is not listed in official records, and

---

[3] Linda Van Ingen, *Gendered Politics: Campaign Strategies of California Women Candidates, 1912–1970* (Lanham, MD: Lexington Books, 2017), 21.

[4] Bornefeld.

[5] Jill Norgren, *Belva Lockwood: The Woman Who Would Be President* (New York: New York University Press, 2007), 124, 126–27; "Her Hat Was in the Ring, http://www.herhatwasinthering.org/biography.php?id=7740.

her name was not on the ballot, although state documents show a total of 18 write-in votes for unnamed candidates.[6]

Undeterred, Stow created the Equal Rights Party in 1884 and ran for US vice president, collecting a few thousand votes. *The Daily Alta California*, not known for its benevolent treatment of female political activists, covered one of her speeches shortly before the election. "Mrs. Marietta Stow is on the warpath again," the newspaper said, "and has proclaimed herself as the battle-axe of female liberty." It declared that the "ferocity of Woman must be curbed," describing her as wearing a hat that "loomed heavenward like a smoke-stack in an ocean fog." Stow passed the hat for campaign donations among the 30 women and 70 men in attendance. The newspaper said she received less than three dollars.[7]

After the turn of the century, many women began pushing boundaries to build careers in such fields as teaching, law, medicine—even politics. In 1900, for example, women constituted about one-third of all college students, but represented nearly half by 1920. According to historian Barbara Miller Solomon, "the denigration of college as an option for women evaporated, and its desirability became established."[8] In fact, there were complaints that women were "taking over" the universities.[9]

The early years of the twentieth century also saw women allying themselves with America's Socialist Party and its charismatic leader, Eugene V. Debs. Debs was founder of the American Railway Union and champion of the debilitating 1894 Pullman strike. Debs spoke to blue-collar, working-class Americans who demanded better working conditions in "the belief and hope that by proper use of government power, men can be rescued from their helplessness in the wild cycling cruelty of depression and boom."[10] As a candidate for president in 1912, Debs received more than 900,000 votes—six percent of the electorate.

The affinity between the Socialist movement and many mainstream women's groups and activists was the result of shared goals to improve women's standing, prevent exploitation, and promote justice. Since its founding in 1901, the Socialist Party had supported woman suffrage and advocated labor reforms, including unionization and wage-earning equality for women. In Los Angeles, Frances Nacke Noel, a German immigrant and Socialist, achieved success by aligning suffrage with labor reform. "Women, both those who were laborers and sympathetic middle-class clubwomen, supported improving working conditions—in

---

[6] Official Returns of the Vote for State Offices of the State of California, November 7, 1882, California State Printing Office, Sacramento, 1882.

[7] "Troublous Times: Sister Stow Declares Herself the Battle-Axe of Female Liberty," *Daily Alta California*, October 26, 1884, 4.

[8] Barbara Miller Solomon, *In the Company of Educated Women* (New Haven: Yale University Press, 1985), 62.

[9] Linda K. Kerber, *Toward an Intellectual History of Women* (Chapel Hill, University of North Carolina Press, 1997), 231.

[10] Theodore H. White, *Fire in the Ashes: Europe in Mid-Century, 1953* (New York: William Sloan, 1968), 56.

addition to living conditions and protective legislation for women and children," notes Camille Leonhardt, professor of history and women's studies at American River College. "Women who were concerned with those reform activities found the Socialist Party most receptive."[11] Many activist women likely felt they had a more-welcoming home—with a similar vision—with the Socialist Party. Some also may have chosen this electoral route because success for them in the primaries of the major parties was problematic, and at least with minor party nominations they could carry their campaign messages all the way to November.

A majority of the first women candidates for statewide office and the legislature ran under the Socialist banner. Agnes Downing, a Los Angeles attorney who was an active suffragist, ran for state superintendent of public instruction in 1910. The year before, she and three other socialist women had unsuccessfully run for the Los Angeles Board of Education. In a joint newspaper ad in the *Los Angeles Herald* the day before that election, the quartet argued that women knew best the needs of children, were practical and detail-oriented, and had "more time than the business man."[12] In her statewide contest, Downing received nearly 41,000 votes in a losing effort.

California voters had approved woman suffrage as part of sweeping progressive reforms on October 10, 1911. Armed with the newly enacted franchise, 14 women sought elective state and congressional offices in 1912 in the hopes that women would help propel a sister to Sacramento or Washington. Eight of the candidates ran as Socialists and four as members of the Prohibition Party. Mary Ridle, a Democrat from San Luis Obispo, became the first woman to be nominated by a major party. All lost by substantial margins, although Prohibition candidate Gabrella Stickney—president of the state Women's Christian Temperance Union—finished second, ahead of both the Democratic and Socialist Party nominees in a Los Angeles assembly contest.[13] In Sacramento, however, suffragist Luella Johnston tapped 64 women as precinct captains and—aided by a large female turnout at the polls—became the first woman in the state to be elected to a city governing post—the Sacramento city commission. She won by 214 votes but was defeated for reelection the following year.[14]

By 1914, Los Angeles was enjoying unbridled growth and economic success, thanks in large part to water from the Owens Valley, more than 200 miles

[11] Camille Leonhardt interview, Sacramento, February 7, 2017 and May 23, 2017.

[12] "Votes for Women on the Board of Education," *Los Angeles Herald*, December 6, 1909, 12.

[13] Statement of Vote of California at the Direct Primary Election, September 3, 1912, California State Printing Office, Sacramento, 1912; Statement of the Vote of California at the General Election, November 5, 1912, California State Printing Office, Sacramento, 1912.

[14] "Women Organize to Aid Vote for Mrs. Johnston," *Sacramento Union*, May 12, 1912, 17; "Carragher Elected over Mrs. Johnston," *San Francisco Call*, May 4, 1913, 26; Nicolas Heidorn, "Sacramento's First Councilwoman—Part I," Sacramentality, October 13, 2017, https://sacramentality.com/2017/10/13/californias-first-councilwoman-part-i/.

Figure 5.1. California Women Voting in Their First Presidential Election, 1912
Credit: Courtesy of California State Library

away, that surged through the Los Angeles Aqueduct into the San Fernando Valley. Oil exploration helped turn the city into a boomtown, and a new industry—film production—started to take hold and thrive. *Los Angeles Times* publisher Harrison Gray Otis believed that "keeping out the unions remained the key to L.A.'s success,"[15] but many of the newcomers to Southern California were factory workers, carpenters, and longshoremen who had benefited from unionization before resettling in Los Angeles. The *Times* building was bombed early one Saturday morning in 1910, killing 21 nonunion employees who were working late to put the newspaper on the streets. In subsequent news articles and editorials, the blame fell squarely on the heads of "union murderers and anarchists." From the pulpit, a reverend said, "The cause of labor unionism will hereafter be associated in Los Angeles with thugs, bomb-throwers, anarchists and assassins. . . ."[16] Two unionist brothers were convicted of the crime and sent to San Quentin, although Eugene Debs was convinced Otis ordered the bombing himself, as a way to discredit the labor movement. Governor Hiram Johnson was seeking reelection in 1914. Otis saw the year's elections as a crusade to rid the state of Johnson and his progressive cohorts who had taken control of both the Republican Party and

[15] Dennis McDougal, *Privileged Son: Otis Chandler and the Rise and Fall of the* L.A. Times *Dynasty* (Cambridge, MA: Perseus Publishing, 2001), 47–51.

[16] "Ministers Voice Horror at Crime of Assassins: Preachers Denounce Union Murders and Anarchists Who Placed the Bombs," *Los Angeles Times*, October 3, 1910, I1.

state government. California, Otis believed, was being led by a pro-union cabal that favored collective bargaining and other rights for workers, including the right to sue employers. Without the benefit of sophisticated political polling, nonprogressive Republicans theorized that a woman on the statewide ticket would make good politics. They assumed women—particularly suffragists—would vote as a bloc for another woman regardless of political ideology, thus enabling conservatives to recapture both the Republican Party and the state's political machinery. Otis agreed and engineered a remarkable pivot for his newspaper. He had been a vociferous antisuffrage leader three years earlier and had often turned his paper's editorial pages over to the most strident opposition voices. As important as it was to prevent women from voting, however, Otis considered it more critical to prevent unionists from establishing a foothold in Los Angeles.

The *Times*, as expected, cast its lot with conservative gubernatorial candidate John Fredericks, who had served in the infantry during the Spanish-American War and currently was L.A. district attorney. In fact, Fredericks' campaign was being bankrolled by Moses Sherman, the business partner of Otis's son-in-law, Harry Chandler. To round out the top of a ticket dedicated to defeating Johnson and the progressive slate, Otis decided to push the candidacy of a woman for lieutenant governor, seeking to capture the energetic women's vote that he had ridiculed three years earlier. In the process, he turned his newspaper unto an unabashed cheerleader for his chosen candidate, 30-year-old San Francisco newspaper publisher Helen K. Williams.

"I did my small part to help the cause of women"— Helen K. Williams

In the early summer, Williams was one of six women frequently mentioned as possible Republican candidates for the $340-a-month job of lieutenant governor. She had pushed for suffrage in her newspaper, the *Woman Citizen*, and even wrote press releases for Democrat Theodore Bell, Hiram Johnson's unsuccessful 1910 challenger. Shortly before she announced her candidacy, she tested the waters in Southern California, meeting clubwomen at a Van Nuys hotel. The *Times* gushed. In the second paragraph of a lengthy story heralding her appearance, the *Times* printed the following description of Williams: "A smartly-dressed young woman . . . of fine athletic figure with Irish wit brought from her native Wexford, a pair of deep blue eyes that glow and flash and sparkle with her moods, a rich, clear, strong voice, and a personality of strength, and yet winsome—that is Helen K. Williams." The article praised the *Woman Citizen* as a successful, growing publication that dealt with serious matters rather than featuring fashions, crochet patterns, or advice to the lovelorn on its front pages. Assuming the role as the candidate's press agent, the article also reprinted letters sent to Williams from eight of her supporters throughout the state who voiced "unbounded enthusiasm" for her candidacy. One letter, from a part owner of two movie houses in Los Angeles, pledged to "run your picture on the screen with the necessary information that you are to be the next Lieutenant-Governor. Throw your millinery into the ring," he wrote.[17]

Williams did enter the race and faced three Republican men for the party's nomination. Under the state's new system of cross-filing—an innovative reform imposed by the progressives—candidates could run in more than one primary in an effort to land multiple party nominations in a single election. Williams sought nominations in the Democratic and Progressive primaries, as well. But if Williams and her conservative devotees expected blanket support by suffragists, they were mistaken. The influential women's clubs, so critical in the fight for suffrage, turned their backs on Williams and stood by their friends in the Progressive Party, arguing that since progressives had helped them secure the vote, they deserved support.[18] Forming a "Woman's Johnson-Eshleman Nonpartisan League," they threw their support to Progressive John Eshleman, a former legislator and president of the state's railroad commission.

In the days before the August 25 primary elections, the *Times* pushed hard for Williams' nomination, running flattering stories on a near-daily basis. "The charm of her manner and the fascinating simplicity of her demeanor won her a host of friends," the newspaper reported August 20 under the headline, "She Inspires Enthusiasm." Williams insisted her campaign was not a novelty. She outlined proposals to secure pensions for the aged and pay prisoners to work on highway construction, so they could send the money home to their wives and families.[19]

The office of lieutenant governor—then, as now—had few responsibilities beyond casting tie votes in the senate. Williams called it "a political parasite" and promised to make it "something far greater." The office, however, did have one important function, which became a key campaign issue: should the governor die or leave office, the lieutenant governor would become the state's chief executive. Five previous lieutenant governors had assumed the office of governor—three after the governor resigned, one by election, and one after a governor's death; in 1887, Governor Washington Bartlett suffered a severe stroke and died only nine months into his term.[20] On the campaign trail, Williams' male opponents frequently raised the specter of a female governor, which many considered a decisive argument. Williams responded that the candidates for governor "are all lusty, strong men, and they won't die." But if there were an emergency that elevated her to the governorship, she would "call upon the legislators and the people of California to come to my assistance in the emergency." The *Times* took that argument further, reminding readers that Britain's Queen Victoria had relied heavily on the advice of Lord Melbourne after she assumed the throne as an inexperienced 18-year-old

---

[17] "Comes to Meet City's Voters," *Los Angeles Times*, June 9, 1914, II1.

[18] Van Ingen, "The Limits of State Suffrage for California Women Candidates in the Progressive Era," *Pacific Historical Review*, February 2004, 42–43.

[19] "She Inspires Enthusiasm," *Los Angeles Times*, August 20, 1914, II3.

[20] Governors' Gallery, http://governors.library.ca.gov/17-Waterman.html.

in 1837. "Like Queen Victoria, she [Williams] would doubtless accept a little masculine guidance . . . it is to be presumed that our Californian Legislatures [sic] would lose nothing of their prestige by deferring to a woman Governor."[21]

In the end, that question was moot. With editorial support from the *Times*, Williams captured Los Angeles, as well as Ventura, and Alpine counties but was overwhelmed in populous San Francisco and Alameda. She finished second in all three primaries she entered, preventing her from advancing to the general election. Eshleman would go on to win easily in November.[22] After the election, the *Times* characterized Williams as a "thoroughbred" and a trailblazer who would make it easier for the next women seeking elective office. She received press clippings, adoring letters, and telegrams from all over the world, including one from India. Despite significant opposition from California clubwomen, Williams concluded, "I did my small part to help the cause of women."[23]

In all, the number of women running for the legislature, Congress, and state-wide office had nearly doubled since the previous election. All of the women fell short, as did 18 others who sought office in 1916. However, many of them raised money, ran credible campaigns, secured newspaper endorsements, and had solid showings. Nannie Davidson was perhaps the most successful, finishing second among five candidates in the nonpartisan primary for state superintendent of public instruction in 1914 and qualifying for the general election, where she received 290,000 votes as the runner-up. The year before, as the elected superintendent of schools in sparse Kings County, she had become the first female official in the nation to be subjected to a recall. She survived the ouster attempt, but it took its toll on her hometown popularity. In the runoff for state superintendent, Davidson carried six counties but lost in Kings by 34 votes.

Breakthroughs at the Capitol

As the 1918 elections approached, a number of factors offered California women candidates hope for a breakthrough. Most notable among these was a political shift as "the Republican Party healed its rift with progressives and began supporting women in winnable open-seat elections," in the words of Linda Van Ingen, author of *Gendered Politics*.[24] A more supportive Republican Party meant a corresponding drop in Socialist Party activity that previously had attracted many women with little chance of electoral success. The Debs campaign in 1912 had set

[21] Alma Whitaker, "They Believe She'll Win," *Los Angeles Times*, August 21, 1914, II3; "She Inspires Enthusiasm," *Los Angeles Times*.

[22] Statement of Vote at Primary Election held on August 25, 1914, California State Printing Office, Sacramento, 1914; Statement of Vote at General Election held on November 3, 1914, California State Printing Office, Sacramento 1914.

[23] "She's a Good Loser, Helen K. Williams," *Los Angeles Times*, August 30, 1914, I9; Agnes Thurnau, "Women's Work, Women's Clubs," *Los Angeles Times*, October 28, 1914, II6.

[24] Van Ingen, 13.

a high-water mark for the percentage of popular votes for the Socialist Party in a US presidential election. But in the years ahead it would attract waning interest from women candidates trying to break through electoral barriers. Meanwhile, the Prohibition Party was reaching its apex as well, with imminent ratification of the antiliquor Eighteenth Amendment that had been its longtime goal.

The war in Europe cast a large shadow over the late-August primary elections. Any candidate perceived to have divided loyalties could expect vigorous political attacks. In a Sacramento assembly race, as the latest war news dominated the headlines, a last-minute whisper campaign accused two-term Republican incumbent Lee Gebhardt of being a German sympathizer. Gebhardt had to explain that his father's ancestors had come to America in 1650 and fought in every US war since then; his mother's family came to America before the American Revolution. "If ancestry makes an American, then certainly I am 100 percent plus," he told the *Sacramento Union* the evening before the primary.[25] The smear campaign against him didn't work; Gebhardt won.[26]

A critical factor aiding women candidates in 1918 was a reduction of male political aspirants, many of whom—like Wiley Dorris—were fighting in Europe. In 1918, more than 100 fewer men ran for seats in the legislature and Congress than had competed two years earlier, representing a reduction of about 25 percent and creating more open seats where women had better chances. Similarly, from 1914 to 1918 the number of men vying for statewide constitutional offices dropped by one-third. Despite the improved gender balance, only 17 women—a handful as Socialists but most as major-party candidates—competed for Congress and the legislature in 1918,[27] with four of them winning to become the first women state legislators in California history. Grace Dorris, Elizabeth Hughes, and Anna Saylor were married; Esto Broughton was single. All four were well-educated professional women who were active leaders in their communities. They understood their districts, and they mastered the arcane art of politicking to secure victory.

California newspapers disagreed on the election's significance. The *Los Angeles Times* called the women's success an "experiment" under the headline, "No Woman for Next Congress." The *San Bernardino Sun* preferred to stress electoral defeats over victories, concluding, "California is perfectly willing that her daughters should vote, but she is somewhat dubious about the advisability of putting them in office. . . ." The *Oakland Tribune* said it expected the four women to be as competent as other members of the assembly, although it noted, "The record of the legislature of the last several sessions does not impose inordinately severe tests of fitness." The newspaper also said it hoped the women would not "indulge

---

[25] "Gebhardt Resents Loyalty Attack," *Sacramento Union*, August 27, 1918, 7.

[26] Statement of Vote at Primary Election held on August 27, 1918, California State Printing Office, Sacramento, 1916; Statement of Vote at General Election held on November 5, 1918, California State Printing Office, Sacramento 1918.

[27] Statement of Vote at Primary Election held on August 29, 1916, California State Printing Office, Sacramento, 1916; Statement of Vote at Primary Election, August 27, 1918, California State Printing Office, Sacramento, 1918.

Figure 5.2. Grace Dorris, Elizabeth Hughes, Anna Saylor, and Esto Broughton (L-R), 1918
Credit: Courtesy of Sunny Mojonnier, Women in California Politics

their entire time in fads and the special projects of the feminist section of popular thought."[28]

When the *San Francisco Examiner* profiled three of the women a few days after the election, all rejected the notion that they intended to take the assembly by storm or propose radical measures. Broughton said she would not take a gender-specific approach. "I have no definite plans for laws affecting women," she told the newspaper. Hughes reacted similarly: "I have no hobbies to ride, no freak or fad measures to introduce and no pet bills to present."[29]

---

[28] "No Woman for Next Congress," *Los Angeles Times*, November 10, 1918, 5; "Four Women in Next Sessoin [sic]," *San Bernardino Sun*, November 9, 1918, 2; "Women Legislators," *Oakland Tribune*, November 8, 1918, 10.

[29] "4 Women to Go to Assembly," *San Francisco Examiner*, November 10, 1918, 9.

Fighting Kern County's Wealthy Land Barons—
Grace Dorris

In Bakersfield, Grace Dorris had seized upon the war issue to run a populist campaign against the richest and most influential landowners in Kern County. Four companies—Southern Pacific, Tejon Ranch, Kern County Land Company, and Miller & Lux—owned one million acres in her assembly district. Although Dorris was petite, frail looking, and quiet, she excoriated the land barons for refusing to share water rights with neighboring farmers and keeping their land out of production. She proposed a postwar land distribution program in which the large corporations would voluntarily irrigate and sell unused parcels to veterans and farmers at affordable prices with long-term low interest rates. If the landowners didn't cooperate, the property would be condemned. "If it isn't sabotage to hold a million acres out of production, I don't know what is," she said. She told one newspaper, "If we don't offer the thousands of soldiers land or jobs we can hope for no industrial peace."[30]

Dorris believed that, unlike many men, women didn't enter politics as an end to feed their vanity, but as a *means* to an end. She ran as a Republican but called herself a radical. Years later, referring to Paul Scharrenberg, a longtime labor activist, she told an interviewer, "Even Paul used to jokingly call me a Bolshevik."[31] Dorris took advantage of the progressive reform of cross-filing and sought nominations in four different parties. The day after the election, the newspapers proclaimed her the victor in the Republican, Socialist, and Prohibition primaries, but she trailed George E. Wilson (an eventual mayor of Bakersfield) in the Democratic primary by 100 votes. It initially appeared she was headed for a tough November runoff.[32] Not all the ballots had been counted, however, and she ultimately won that primary by a scant 30 votes. She ran unopposed in November. Oklahoma's *Muskogee Times-Democrat* published a story, distributed by the Newspaper Enterprise Association, that played up her David-beats-Goliath victory:

> A quiet, brown-haired school teacher, frail and determined, plunged into a rough-and-tumble fight against four gigantic land corporations. She weighed 103 pounds. They owned 1,000,000 acres. They were fighting for their lives, and knew it. But the little teacher won.[33]

---

[30] Van Ingen, 21; Bornefeld; "Woman Maker of Laws to War against Land Barons," *San Francisco Bulletin*, January 9, 1919, 8.

[31] Bornefeld.

[32] "Newell May Win at Primary," *Bakersfield Californian*, August 29, 1918, 1.

[33] Ernest J. Hopkins, "Schoolmarm Licks Land Kings in Battle Royal: She Weighs Just 103 Pounds, But She Took Capitalists to Trimming," *Muskogee Times-Democrat*, February 4, 1919, 5.

In a letter to the *Bakersfield Morning Echo*, Dorris said she spent part of the legislative session's opening day posing for a newsreel photographer and acknowledged that the four assemblywomen were "curiosities." She said the women were shown "every courtesy and attention" from the men. Dorris and her female colleagues were assigned seats together at desks in the heart of the assembly chamber. She related that she "ordered the cuspidor removed beneath my desk, with a view to providing a safe refuge if the books and ink bottles fly too fast."[34] When the assembly took its recess in late January, Dorris reflected, "They [the men] are not such an awful bunch."[35]

Dorris wasted no time establishing her priorities. She introduced a resolution in support of national woman suffrage, which faced ratification by the states as the Nineteenth Amendment in 1919. (It won approval of the required 36 states by a single vote in the Tennessee legislature to become part of the US Constitution in 1920.) Her first bill sought to make it a misdemeanor to employ a domestic servant for more than 10 hours a day or 60 hours a week. The measure was defeated by one vote when a supporting assemblyman switched his vote. It would be enacted in a later session. She also introduced legislation creating a state-paid public defender. Her land reform battle against the barons of Bakersfield never reached the assembly floor. "Idle land," she argued, "means families kept from happiness, children kept from healthful country homes, food kept from being grown, prices and poverty both kept rising."[36] Eventually, the battle was won. Dorris was 68 years old in 1955 when the Kern County Land Company converted 75,000 acres of grazing land to farms.

Throughout her political career, Dorris had a tenuous hold on Republicans in her heavily Republican agricultural district. Her reelection bid in 1920 brought three challengers, one of whom defeated her by 13 votes out of more than 5,000 cast. Dorris and other staunch prohibitionists in the legislature had been characterized by wine and liquor industries as lawmakers who "have not hesitated to misrepresent their constituents."[37] Dorris ran a write-in campaign in November but was defeated handily. The Bakersfield attorney who trounced her didn't run for reelection in 1922, and Dorris sought a comeback. She narrowly won the Republican primary by 35 votes, as well as the Democratic primary, and won the general election unopposed. Voters returned her two years later to the assembly, where she secured state funding for a sprawling stretch of highway between Bakersfield and Tehachapi. In 1926, Dorris was mentioned as a possible senate candidate, but one of her friends helped dissuade her from running. According to Franklin Hichborn, a prominent political journalist, some of her political enemies were trying to end

---

[34] "Kern Woman is the First Woman to Introduce Bill," *Bakersfield Morning Echo*, January 12, 1919, 1.

[35] Frank Selover, "Capitol Notes," *Sacramento Union*, January 25, 1919, 3.

[36] Hopkins.

[37] H. F. Stoll, ed., "Referending the Wright Act: Dry Leaders Fear Vote of the People," *California Grape Grower*. California Grape Protective Association, June 1, 1921, 3, https://tinyurl.com/yd7h3aqv.

her career by "scheming" to have her run for the upper house in a less-friendly district, knowing that she'd likely lose. In a letter to Dorris, Hichborn wrote, "My own feeling is that the move was intended to eliminate you from the legislature. But I am very glad that you did not fall for it."[38] Dorris took what she thought was the safe way out but lost her campaign for reelection and a second comeback battle two years later.[39]

Bringing Water to the San Joaquin Valley—
Esto Broughton

Reforming the state's community property laws also was a priority of Esto Broughton, a Democrat from the San Joaquin Valley who, at 28, was the youngest of the four victorious women. Her primary focus, however, was bringing water to farms in her district. Esto's father was a bank president who dealt with farmers in the valley, and his daughter, a Modesto native, was excited about the prospects of expanded irrigation systems. Although her given name was Esther, her friends called her Esto from Modesto, and the name stuck. When she was young, she contracted spinal tuberculosis and nearly died. The disease left her with severe curvature of the spine and one leg that was shorter than the other. She limped badly and stopped growing when she reached four-foot, six inches. Biographer Ethel Bornefeld noted that "no word of her crippled condition apparently appeared in any newspapers or other publications . . . no reports mentioned her disability."[40] Broughton did, however, try religious or scientific cures that seemed promising and once visited famed evangelist Aimee Semple McPherson who practiced faith healing in Los Angeles.

Despite her handicap, Broughton learned to ride a motorcycle and was coxswain of the Class of 1915 women's rowing team at the University of California. A photograph in the university's 1914 year book shows her on the Oakland Estuary guiding her boat, which won the lightweight title in the interclass regatta.[41] As an undergraduate, Broughton was a member of the university's honor society and joined a handful of young women studying in the school's jurisprudence program. Its dean, Professor William Carey Jones, made headlines in 1913 when he questioned the ability of women to handle themselves in court. "When male and female minds clash in the courtroom the woman naturally gives in; she becomes confused; she cannot withstand the strain of conflict." Women, he said, "are too emotional to cope with criminal cases." The *San Francisco Call* noted

---

[38] Letter from Franklin Hichborn to Grace Dorris, February 26, 1926, Bornefeld Collection.

[39] Statements of Vote, August 21, 1920; November 2, 1920; August 29, 1922; November 7, 1922;

[40] Bornefeld draft manuscript.

[41] *The 1914 Blue and Gold of the University of California,* published by the junior class in 1913, Sunset Publishing House, San Francisco, 191.

that Broughton and her female classmates "naturally do not believe they will be unequal to men in the arena."[42] After attending law school at Hastings, Broughton practiced law for a while and helped her father in his bank. During the war, she worked for the Red Cross, the Belgian Relief Society, and the Liberty Loan Drive. She also got an early education in politics, working in the office of a Modesto state senator and serving as a clerk for the assembly's irrigation committee.

Broughton had ties to Democratic Party leadership and was "well known throughout Northern California," the *San Francisco Chronicle* noted, "because of her special study of the irrigation laws of this State." [43] She faced two opponents in the August primary and doubled their combined campaign spending. Most of her $354 campaign war chest went to publicity—newspaper ads, advertising cards, circulars, and a screening of her political message at movie theaters.[44] Broughton also had a way of disarming potential adversaries. She told a Sacramento reporter she would not be a "busybody" on the floor of the assembly and was aware that veteran legislators feared that women lawmakers would want them to give up smoking cigars during long sessions. Broughton suggested they needn't worry about her, promising to move that the antismoking rule be suspended "when 'old timers' gave her the high sign."[45] Broughton cross-filed and sought the nominations of five political parties. Like Grace Dorris in Bakersfield, she won them all and had no opposition in November. Her victory made news as far away as Arkansas and Michigan, although the coverage contained some cringe-worthy prose: "The folks at home are going to miss her raisin pies, but she just had to get her fingers into a bigger confection," one reporter wrote."[46]

Broughton put her stamp on the legislature by becoming the assembly's expert on irrigation—not surprising for a representative from farm country in the water-hungry San Joaquin Valley. She co-authored the landmark Broughton-Dennett bill to allow irrigation districts to develop electric power in connection with irrigation projects. As the bill maneuvered through the legislature, the *Pacific Rural Press* helped galvanize votes. "If you want cheaper electricity made by irrigation waters whose mountain power is now wasted it will cost you about three postage stamps and three letters addressed [to legislators] . . . and must be mailed pronto!"[47] The measure became law, and the Modesto and Turlock irrigation districts were the first to profit from it.

Broughton also was the legislature's point person on one of the women's top priorities—a gender-equity measure that would change state law to give either

    [42] "Women Too Emotional for Law," *San Francisco Call*, October 13, 1913, 14.

    [43] "Assembly-Woman Practicing Attorney," *San Francisco Chronicle*, November, 12, 1918, 13.

    [44] Van Ingen, 22.

    [45] Bornefeld draft manuscript.

    [46] "California Legislature Will Sit Up and Notice," *Lansing State Journal*, December 27, 1918, 3.

    [47] "What a Shock! Cheap Electricity," *Pacific Rural Press*, February 22, 1919, 283; "Turlock to Develop Power, *Pacific Rural Press*, December 20, 1919, 856.

spouse right to half of community property, which the *San Francisco Chronicle* conceded is "demanded by 90,000 organized women of California."[48] Over the objections of numerous male lawmakers, Broughton successfully maneuvered the proposal through the legislature and secured the signature of Governor William Stephens, but it was easily defeated in a statewide referendum on the November 1920 ballot. Broughton bided her time. She served four terms, and during the 1923 session she and Senator Herbert Jones moved identical community property bills that one newspaper characterized as "pernicious, unjust in principle and a menace to the business man.[49] The Jones measure eventually became law. This time, however, a referendum fell 844 votes short of qualifying for the ballot.

Defeating a Smear Campaign— Elizabeth Hughes

A third woman to make California political history had a more spirited campaign to deal with. Republican Elizabeth Hughes, of Oroville, faced a determined opponent who tried to use her femininity against her. Born in San Francisco to European immigrants, Elizabeth Lorentzen earned a teacher's certificate from San Jose Normal School and then settled in Butte County with her husband, J. B. Hughes, who took a job as a high school principal. Her campaign against two men focused on issues related to family and education, particularly the need to grant rural schools the same opportunities afforded city schools. A local newspaper described her as an "inspiring" speaker.[50] If elected, she pledged to seek increased funding for Chico State Normal School, which had been created on an eight-acre cherry orchard in 1887 to train and educate rural teachers. Hughes argued that more female legislators would result in better legislation for men, women, and children, and she was helped by the fact that her husband was a prominent educator in Chico and a leading figure in the development of a new junior college. J. B. Hughes received frequent mentions in the local newspaper.

Shortly before the primary election, one of her opponents made a crass appeal to gender stereotypes in a last-ditch effort to derail her campaign. Samuel J. Nunn was a prominent Chico attorney, rice grower, and unsuccessful candidate for district attorney four years earlier. Amid the pages of war news in the *Chico Record*, Nunn placed a newspaper ad questioning the ability of women to do the tough work required of lawmakers. "We are at war with the beast of Berlin," he said, "the perpetuation of democracy is at stake and we want men in the State Legislature that the old timers cannot bluff." He said the business of legislating

---

[48] "Lawmakers Pass Buck on Bill Which Would Give Wife Equal Community Property Rights," *San Francisco Chronicle*, March 23, 1919, 2.

[49] "Community Property Law," *Fresno Bee* quoted *in Modesto Evening News*, August 18, 1923, 5.

[50] "Service is Keynote of Diamond Match Meeting," *Chico Record*, August 15, 1918, 8.

"is no pink tea job. Sledge hammer blows are given and received . . . it takes a virile man who can come back with a punch." Two days later, the Sunday before the election, Hughes ran her own advertisement, angrily repeating Nunn's most inflammatory comments and delivering an impassioned rebuttal. While Nunn had used the war to belittle the candidacies of women, Hughes turned that argument on its head. Service in the assembly, she said, may be strenuous, "but women everywhere, in the hospital, in the office, in the factories, on the farm are today proving the mettle of American womanhood." Arguing that women had bravely answered the country's call during the Great War, she asked, "Are the brace of Red Cross nurses, working night and day at the front, caring for the wounded . . . serving in 'pink tea' jobs?"[51]

Without the benefit of opinion polling, there's no telling how much the last-minute flurry of point-counterpoint affected the contest. But Hughes had the last word, winning the Republican, Democratic, and Socialist party nominations. Nunn captured the inconsequential Prohibition nomination by 13 votes, but the vagaries of election law prevented him from advancing. Hughes won the general election unopposed. Nunn filed for bankruptcy in the middle of Hughes' second term.[52]

True to her district and expertise, Hughes spent much of her political capital on rural and education issues, becoming the assembly's education committee chair and sponsoring legislation to expand the Chico State Normal School. During the 1919 session alone, more than 100 education bills were heard by her committee and several of her measures—including those dealing with compulsory school age, creation of part-time schools, junior colleges, and county school funding—became law. Running for re-election in 1920 against a single opponent, Hughes won the Republican, Democratic, and Socialist party primaries and ran unopposed in November.

After two stints in the assembly, Hughes returned to full-time teaching at Oroville High School. One of her students, 1936 graduate Mamoru Sakuma, recalled that he had difficulties pronouncing words correctly. "She was very persistent . . . I must have made a hundred trips to the large dictionary in her classroom." Sakuma later served with a Japanese-American army combat unit in Europe during World War II (even as his family was relocated to the Tule Lake internment camp), and became the first Asian-American superior court judge in Sacramento County. Another student, future state senator Ray Johnson, said Hughes was unpretentious and never mentioned her political exploits. "[S]he kept her secret well about being a former assemblywoman. Her accomplishments were great and her modesty was even greater."[53]

---

[51] "Mrs. Elizabeth Hughes Answers 'Pink Tea' Accusations," *Chico Record*, August 25, 1918, 3.

[52] "Nunn Creditors File Bankruptcy Papers," *Sacramento Union*, February 7, 1922, 8.

[53] Ray Sehorn, "OUHSD 2013 Hall of Fame: Oroville Native Mamoru Sakuma Blazed Trails for Asian Americans in Sacramento Courts," *Oroville Mercury Register,* September 25, 2013, http://www.orovillemr.com/general-news/20130925/ouhsd-2013-hall-of-fame-

Reforming Criminal Justice and Social Welfare—
Anna Saylor

The fourth woman to win election in 1918 had an incredible backstory of poverty and hardship in Indiana that would frame her political views and lead her to champion disadvantaged children, mental health, and literacy while in the California assembly. In a handwritten autobiography, Republican Anna Saylor said she was born in 1871 during a blinding snow storm in a two-room cottage built by her father near Terre Haute. When she was five, her father had gone into town to buy Christmas gifts during a bitter cold spell, caught pneumonia, and died. "Just before father's fatal illness," Saylor later wrote, "I accidentally hit his nose with my elbow and made it bleed. To tease me, one of my brothers told me that the blow with my elbow caused his final illness." At the funeral, with the ground covered in ice, "I told Father how sorry I was that I made his nose bleed and caused him to go up there alone among the stars and on to heaven."[54] When Anna was 10, her mother fell ill with rheumatism. Anna had to feed their horse and chickens, take care of the garden, chop wood, cook meals, draw water from an 80-foot well, and care for her mother. To make ends meet, she "made men's trousers . . . and for this we received $2.50 per dozen pairs."[55]

Borrowing $200 from the president of the Terre Haute Savings Bank, Anna later enrolled at Indiana State Normal School and within two years was earning $30 a month as a teacher. She worked for her room and board by making beds, washing dishes, and fixing breakfast. "The poverty and ignorance I witnessed during those years fired my soul against child labor of any form."[56] Decades later she would make a plea on the floor of the assembly for ratification of the Child Labor Amendment to the US Constitution. She also was responsible for securing $30,000 to build a library in Elwood, Indiana, after making a personal appeal by letter to steel magnate Andrew Carnegie. Anna and her husband Frank Saylor ended up in California quite by chance. They wanted to find a "better place" to bring up their two children so they toured the west—towns in Washington and Oregon, San Francisco, Oakland, and Berkeley. They chose Berkeley, and within a month

---

oroville-native-mamoru-sakuma-blazed-trails-for-asian-americans-in-sacramento-courts); Letter from Mamoru Sakuma to Ethel Bornefeld, August 17, 1978, Bornefeld collection; Letter from Ray Johnson to Ethel Bornefeld, January 25, 1979, Bornefeld collection.

[54] Mike McCormick, "The impressive triumphs of Anna McBride Saylor," Part I, *Terre Haute Tribune-Star*, October 16, 2016, http://www.tribstar.com/community/the-impressive-triumphs-of-anna-mcbride-saylor/article_eaae4979-275d-5225-99fe-14fc783e-c2a0.html.

[55] Ibid., Part II, October 23, 2016, http://www.tribstar.com/community/historical-perspective-the-triumphs-of-anna-mcbride-saylor-part-ii/article_7e92c3e9-2a48-5350-979a-5afc37714b8d.html.

[56] Ibid.

of their arrival she was invited to join the prestigious Twentieth Century Club for women, later becoming its president.[57]

The Twentieth Century Club played a major role in Saylor's electoral success, engineering "undivided support" among East Bay women for her candidacy. "In union there is strength," the *Oakland Tribune* reported. Club leadership also gave Saylor visibility in the community and enabled her to reach many men in the district who were appreciative of the club's activities on the home front, including leading five war bond drives.[58] Described by the *Sacramento Union* as a "quiet, earnest little woman,"[59] Saylor saw a political opening when Berkeley's popular lower house representative, Assembly Speaker C. C. Young, gave up his seat to run for lieutenant governor. As a former teacher and librarian, Saylor campaigned on a platform to eradicate illiteracy. She wanted to boost state support of elementary schools from $15 per pupil a year to $17.50, and she wanted to raise the annual state support of country schools from $550 to $750. Her Republican opponent, Charles Craig, took to criticizing candidates who made pledges in advance, calling it a "misdemeanor." Like Grace Dorris, Esto Broughton, and Elizabeth Hughes, Saylor successfully cross-filed and wrapped up the election in August. She easily won four different party nominations, faced token opposition from a Socialist in November, and won election by a ten-to-one margin.[60]

Saylor said she was "without any preconceived notions of turning California legislative action upside down," describing her legislative agenda as one that would make California a "better place to live in." She was, however, particularly concerned about the treatment of women in prison. At the time, San Quentin housed 32 women as well as its complement of male convicts. Shortly before being sworn into office, Saylor spent an entire day behind the prison walls investigating conditions for women, as well as the criminally insane. When she emerged, she characterized conditions as "deplorable as far as the women were concerned. Tiny cells, no light, hardly any air." She urged a state farm for women and a separate institute for the criminally insane.[61]

Saylor would serve four terms in the legislature. She amassed a lengthy record of accomplishments, dedicating herself to improving public schools, making significant criminal justice reforms, and aiding vulnerable seniors and children—issues to which women seemed to be more sensitive than men. Befitting her interests, she sat on committees that oversaw education, hospitals and asylums, and prisons and reformatories. As a rookie lawmaker, she also chaired the public morals committee that dealt with such issues as prize fighting, gambling, and liquor. Saylor led a high-profile campaign to abolish the death penalty for minors.

---

[57] Ibid., Part III, October 30, 2016, http://www.tribstar.com/community/historical-perspective-the-triumphs-of-anna-mcbride-saylor-part-iii/article_2325d852-6eec-504e-9253-dd9e8c3993c4.html.

[58] "Woman is Rewarded by Berkeleyans," *Oakland Tribune*, September 1, 1918, 48.

[59] Selover, "Capitol News," *Sacramento Union*, November 10, 1918, 12.

[60] Statements of Vote, August 27, 1918, November 5, 1918.

[61] "Reforms at San Quentin to be Urged," *Oakland Tribune*, December 29, 1918, 19.

"Women, and wealthy young," she said, "never hang. It's always the friendless and poor boy who faces the gallows."[62] One evening, shortly after Governor William Stephens signed the bill into law, Saylor opened her mailbox and found an unsigned letter bearing a postmark from Suisun, a marshland between Berkeley and Sacramento. The letter accused her of "supporting cold-blooded wanton murder." The writer was angry that a young man who had killed a policeman would escape execution. Saylor, the writer insisted, wouldn't be so lucky. "I will be in Berkeley tomorrow or the next day, and I will try to kill you just as I would a dog. You wait and look for me every day from now on."[63] No attempt was made on her life.

Saylor also was dedicated to creating mental health assistance to the elderly and reducing exploitation of children in the workplace. One landmark bill, sponsored by the Berkeley Federation of Mothers, established psychiatric clinics in state prisons, a move hailed as "a big step forward in preventing crime through ascertaining underlying causes. . . ."[64] Saylor credited the enthusiastic support of women in her district for helping to pressure the legislature on behalf of these measures.[65]

After eight years in the assembly, Saylor decided not to run for reelection, instead accepting Governor C. C. Young's offer to become director of social welfare—the first woman to serve in a governor's cabinet. Her agenda expanded with an ambitious plan that included boosting the number of trained social workers, creating a comprehensive state mental hygiene program, reforming the state probation system, and building child detention homes in rural areas so delinquent children wouldn't be sent to county jails with hardened criminals. She told of jails in the basements of courthouses, completely unlit except for an opening in the ceiling not more than an inch square. "This was also the prisoners' air supply. Iron beds, covered with filthy straw tics and two dilapidated dirty blankets, were the only furnishing. Into these foul holes they put child 'criminals' eight and nine years of age."[66] In a speech to clubwomen in Richmond, Saylor said 22,000 babies in California were doomed to become criminals within two decades "unless something is done to prevent problem parents and broken homes."[67] She argued the choice was clear: either build new and larger prisons and spend vast sums on corrections and punishment, or invest in education.

---

[62] "Bill to Save Boys under Eighteen Is Passed by Assembly," *Modesto Evening News*, March 24, 1921, 1.

[63] "'I'll Kill You as a Dog,' Threat Sent Mrs. Saylor," *Oakland Tribune*, August 4, 1921, 1.

[64] "Mrs. Saylor Has Two Measures to Combat Vice," *Oakland Tribune*, Jan. 5, 1921, 2.

[65] Sandra L. Henderson, *California Women and Politics*, Robert W. Cherny, Mary Ann Irwin, Mann Marie Wilson, eds. (Lincoln: University of Nebraska Press, 2011), 179–80,199.

[66] "Program for Social Work Told to Club," *Oakland Tribune*, January 13, 1928, 10.

[67] "Crime Life for 22,000 Babies Here Forecast," *Oakland Tribune*, April 4, 1930, 35.

Saylor's grand plans were short-circuited when Governor Young's bid for reelection was thwarted by James Rolph in the 1930 Republican primary. In the subsequent general election, Rolph failed to receive the endorsement of the San Francisco League of Women Voters, and apparently he held a grudge. According to Helen Velaska Bary, Saylor's deputy director, Rolph "could be a very vindictive person, and he said that he would get even with those women."[68] One of his first moves was to fire Saylor.

Setback in the East Bay

Amid the triumphs in 1918, there was tragedy, as well. While Dorris, Broughton, Hughes, and Saylor were making history in the assembly, Dr. Mabel Anthony, a Republican professor at the College of Professions and Surgeons in San Francisco, sought a seat in the state senate from Oakland. She had come from a family of physicians, and her platform tilted left as she campaigned for public ownership of utility companies and the extension of permanent government control to industries where competition was lacking. She said that "the great wealth-producing organizations should be used primarily for service to mankind and not . . . primarily for profit." She wanted to abolish all child labor and to ensure that women were paid the same as men for equal work.[69] Despite her endorsement from the Alameda County Federation, a nonprofit group of business people that railed against machine politics, Dr. Anthony faltered at the polls, finishing third in both the Republican and Democratic primaries.

In the fall, Dr. Anthony rushed to the copper-mining town of Jerome, Arizona to tend to her sister, who had fallen ill with influenza—the worldwide epidemic that killed tens of millions of people around the globe and more than 500,000 in the US. She also offered her services to local health officials who were dealing with hundreds of cases. Anthony helped save her sister's life and returned to Oakland on Thanksgiving, only to come down with influenza symptoms herself. She battled the illness for 12 days. Her sister, now recovered, rushed west to be at her bedside, but her journey was delayed by a train wreck in Needles. Upon arriving in Oakland, she learned her sister had just passed away from pneumonia.[70] No woman would win election to the state senate until Democrat Rose Ann Vuich, from the farming town of Dinuba, in 1976.

---

[68] Helen Velaska Bary Oral History, "Helen Velaska Bary: Labor Administration and Social Security: A Woman's Life," Conducted by Jaqueline K. Parker, 1974, Regional Oral History Office, Bancroft Library, University of California, Berkeley, 156.

[69] "Political Notes," *Oakland Tribune*, July 21, 1918, 35, https://www.cvbugle.com/news/2009/oct/20/the-killer-flu-of-1918/.

[70] "Funeral Held for Dr. Mabel Anthony," *Oakland Tribune*, Dec. 14, 1918, 2; Helen Peterson, "The Killer Flu of 1918," *Camp Verde Bugle*, October 20, 2009, https://www.cvbugle.com/news/2009/oct/20/the-killer-flu-of-1918/.

California's First African-American Legislator—
Frederick Madison Roberts

The ascension of California's first women legislators had brought headlines and curiosity throughout the state. What wasn't covered to a major extent was another breakthrough that year—the election of the state's first African-American legislator from an assembly district in Los Angeles. Like the new assemblywomen, Frederick Madison Roberts had to overcome ancient prejudices to succeed in politics. His great grandmother was Sally Hemings, one of Thomas Jefferson's slaves who it is widely believed was the mother of six children fathered by Jefferson. Roberts's daughter, Patricia, recalled in an oral history that her parents didn't discuss that very much. But her father did bring up his lineage once when she was young. "I remember him telling me that Thomas Jefferson is my great, great grandfather. I was impressed but at that time it wasn't that meaningful."[71]

In 1900, Roberts had become the first African American to graduate from Los Angeles High School and was a prelaw student for a while at the University of Southern California. Eventually, he took over his father's undertaking business and edited a weekly newspaper. In 1918, he ran for the assembly, defeating four other Republicans in the primary and capturing about half of the November vote. One of his opponents handed out cards reading, "My opponent is a nigger."[72] A lengthy Associated Press election preview that ran in the *Los Angeles Times* noted the significance of electing the first four women legislators but slighted the Roberts candidacy.[73] The *Times* acknowledged the election to the assembly of a hometown African American with a single sentence buried in its story about the legislature's four women. "Also elected," the *Times* said, "Frederick M. Roberts, a negro."[74] Roberts would serve 16 years in the assembly.

Looking Ahead

Despite the historical significance of the 1918 election, the influenza epidemic and World War I had diverted the attention of many Californians. "Never in the memory of the oldest settler has there been an election in this county in which there has been displayed so little interest," wrote the *Red Bluff Daily News* the day after the balloting. There were no squadrons of cars to take voters to the polls, no clusters of interested people gathered around bulletin boards, and no crowds at newspaper offices. Sharing front-page space with election updates in the *Daily*

---

[71] Patricia Roberts oral history, December 5, 1998, Thomas Jefferson Foundation, Inc., https://www.monticello.org/getting-word/people/patricia-roberts.

[72] Robert Fikes, Jr., BlackPast.org, http://blackpast.org/aaw/roberts-frederick-m-1879-1952.

[73] "State to Have Women Solons," Associated Press in the *Los Angeles Times*, November 3, 1918, I5.

[74] "No Woman for Next Congress," *Los Angeles Times*, November 10, 1918, I5.

News were reports of German setbacks along the western front and the death of a local soldier. Prominent coverage also was given to a pair of local deaths from influenza and the county's receipt of a new batch of vaccine. "The war has overshadowed all other events," the newspaper reported, "and the 'flu' restrictions has [sic] taken the pep out of the community."[75] In fact, voter turnout at 59.35 percent was nearly 20 percentage points lower than the previous gubernatorial election and remained the lowest until only 59.26 percent voted during another wartime election in November, 1942.[76]

Grace Dorris, Esto Broughton, Elizabeth Hughes, and Anna Saylor established themselves as serious, earnest lawmakers who had hurdled longstanding political barriers to occupy positions of leadership that women had struggled decades to secure. They learned to organize, build coalitions, raise money, conduct vigorous political campaigns, and legislate—all while earning the admiration of much of the state's male power structure, as well as voters. When veteran assemblywomen Dorris, Saylor, and Broughton were joined by newcomers Eleanor Miller and Cora Woodbridge at the onset of the 1923 legislative session, the *Oakland Tribune* asked, "Do the . . . assemblywomen . . . hold the balance of power? That is the question which is agitating the old-time politicians. . . ."[77] Saylor had surmised that since legislators toiled for so little pay—$1,000 for each legislative session plus 10 cents per mile for transportation—business and professional men would be reluctant to leave their personal interests for lawmaking duties in Sacramento. She expected a quantum leap for women. Instead, female representation atrophied. Incredibly, after those first four women were elected to the legislature in 1918, only 10 others would taste victory in the ensuing 56 years. If women wanted to make a difference in the crafting of California's public policy, they'd have to find other ways to do it.

Discussion Questions

1. Why did many early women activists and candidates believe the Socialist Party was particularly well-aligned with their cause?
2. For what reasons did the editorial pages of the *Los Angeles Times* go from castigating the notion of woman suffrage in 1911 to advocating the election of a woman as lieutenant governor of California in 1914?
3. Why did the women's clubs that had been instrumental in advocating woman suffrage turn their backs on the campaign of the first woman candidate for lieutenant governor?

---

[75] "No Estimate of Final Results Possible from Meager Election," *Red Bluff Daily News*, November 6, 1918, 1.

[76] "Historic Voter Registration and Participation in Statewide Elections 1910–2014, elections.cdn.sos.ca.gov/sov/2014-general/pdf/04-historical-voter-reg-general.pdf.

[77] "Women Active Factor in State Lawmaking," *Oakland Tribune*, January 11, 1923, 13.

4. What key gender issue was raised against Helen K. Williams in her campaign for lieutenant governor? How did she respond to it?
5. How did US entry into World War I in 1917 prove to be a boon to California women running for office in 1918?
6. The first four women elected to the California assembly—Grace Dorris, Esto Broughton, Elizabeth Hughes, and Anna Saylor—arguably were each remarkable individuals. Did they seem to have any qualities in common? How so? Would you describe some of their policy interests as "women's issues"? If so, which ones?
7. What kinds of differences do you believe the presence of these four women legislators might have made?
8. Why do you think so few women followed these first four into the legislature over the ensuing five decades? What may have been some of the consequences?

Recommended Reading

Rice, Richard, and William A. Bullough. *The Elusive Eden: A New History of California*. Long Grove, IL: Waveland, 2017.

Studer, Robert P. "The Pioneer Women in the State Legislature." *California Journal* (February 1979): 65–66, http://www.unz.org/Pub/CalJournal-1979feb-00065.

Van Ingen, Linda. *Gendered Politics: Campaign Strategies of California Women Candidates, 1912–1970*. Lanham, MD: Lexington, 2017.

Chapter 6

1926–1956
Three Blazing Lights Pierce
Dark Times for Women in Politics

"[A man] shouldn't be too interested in who does the job
but whether the job is accomplished."
—Elizabeth Snyder

In 1909 Southern California, babies throughout the region were falling ill from severe digestive disorders that were said to be responsible for a third of all worldwide infant deaths. The women of the exclusive Friday Morning Club in Los Angeles, which was founded by suffragists in 1891, took it upon themselves to find the culprit. They zeroed in on tainted milk. During a nine-month investigation, Katherine Philips Edson, chair of the club's public health committee, made surprise visits to regional dairies and found that at least 10 percent of cows providing milk for Los Angeles "are so tuberculous that it is evident to any veterinarian."[1]

Edson issued a bombshell report that also reported that the city of Los Angeles had neither a staff veterinarian nor sufficient number of inspectors, and that no tuberculin test had been made by the city in the previous two years. Neither did the city have jurisdiction over the quality of milk it imported from dairies as far away as Modesto and San Luis Obispo. Many of the state's best dairy farmers, she said, had abandoned the business because of low milk prices, "leaving many men now supplying milk to this city who are ignorant, careless and utterly unfitted to run a dairy that is not a menace to the health of the babies." Under the headline, "The Milk Peril," a subsequent editorial in the *Los Angeles Herald* praised Edson's work and suggested that "the women might take hold of this question and agitate it until the reforms needed are completely effected." It recommended that Edson head the effort.[2]

Edson's probe landed her a seat on the Los Angeles charter revision commission, and the municipal code was updated to allow for a veterinarian and two additional milk inspectors. She then enlisted California's women's clubs to take the crusade to Sacramento. "If the milk supply is in the hands of politicians," Edson

---

[1] "Mrs. Edison Flays the City Charter," *Los Angeles Herald*, June 18, 1910, 3.
[2] "The Milk Peril," *Los Angeles Herald*, June 19, 1910, 6.

once wrote, "how can a woman who wants to do the right thing by her babies stay at home and keep quiet while they drink impure milk?"[3]

Three years later, despite warnings that a regulatory crackdown would prove too costly to many dairies, Governor Hiram Johnson signed legislation giving the state the authority to oversee the production and sale of milk and milk products. Edison's contribution to public health illustrated that dedicated, reform-minded women didn't have to be members of a formal political structure in order to prove their value as vehicles of social change.

Edson had settled in Southern California quite by happenstance. Born Katherine Philips in 1870 Ohio, she spent a year at a convent, graduated from a seminary, and studied opera at a Chicago conservatory, where she fell in love with music teacher Charles Farwell Edson. After the pair married, Charles borrowed some money from his wealthy parents, and they bought an almond orchard and ranch outside Los Angeles in the high-desert Antelope Valley. Katherine spent many years helping with ranch work while raising two of their three children (one daughter lived with Charles's parents) until a prolonged drought prompted them to give up ranching and move to Los Angeles. There she joined the growing and well-regarded Friday Morning Club.

Edson not only led the battle against impure milk, she played a role in the suffrage movement and had campaigned for Hiram Johnson in 1910. Even before the milk legislation had been finalized, she had been rewarded with an appointment in the Johnson administration as a deputy inspector in the state Bureau of Labor Statistics in 1912.

Creating a Minimum Wage for Women and Children— Katherine Philips Edson

As a state inspector, Edson studied working conditions for women and children in laundries, retail sales, walnut-cracking businesses, and the state's numerous fish, fruit, and vegetable canneries that employed more than 20,000 women. In the canneries, she found women standing "knee deep in waste products and fish residue, breathing poorly ventilated air, and often in pain because of the 10, 12, or more hours per day they had to stand in postures which deformed young and older women alike."[4] Edson documented how many women were living on substandard wages and, at the governor's urging, she drafted legislation to establish a minimum wage for women and children.

During the 1913 legislative session, at the same time that lawmakers were dealing with the impure milk issue, it was Edson's task to help get the minimum wage bill to Johnson's desk. In Sacramento, a controversial minimum-wage bill had stalled in the waning days of the legislative session. Many of the state's

---

[3] Jaqueline R. Braitman, "A California Stateswoman: The Public Career of Katherine Philips Edson," *California History*, June 1986, 86.

[4] Braitman, 87.

Figure 6.1. Katherine Philips Edson
Credit: Courtesy of California State Library

leading merchants supported the measure; a number of unions, however, thought they—not the state—were in the best position to take care of women workers.[5] During its final, frenzied crush of business, the legislature decided to bar lobbyists from floor sessions, but when Edson was told she couldn't enter the chamber, she forced her way through. "Why, of course I can go in," she said. "I am a state officer; I am a deputy of the Labor Commission." According to capitol historian Franklin Hichborn, she had the lobby all to herself.[6] The measure passed, and Hichborn gave credit to the "organizations of women [which] became, on moral issues, the most potent power in the State."[7]

Besides requiring the payment of a living wage to women workers, the new statute established the state Industrial Welfare Commission to enforce wage rates and regulate working conditions. Johnson appointed Edson to the five-member panel and later became its executive director. She surveyed thousands of workers, pored over payroll data, and met with employers to determine a minimum wage to meet an independent woman's cost of living. Her 1914 analysis concluded that, on average, a working woman needed $300 a year for room and board, $10.50

[5] "Union Leaders Oppose Minimum Wage Law," *Oakland Tribune*, January 23, 1913, 2; "Merchants of California for Minimum Wage," *San Francisco Call*, March 14, 1913, 1.

[6] Franklin Hichborn, *Story of the Session of the California Legislature of 1913* (San Francisco: James H. Barry, 1913), 352.

[7] Ibid., 14.

for three pairs of shoes, $4.00 for two corsets, $5 for three petticoats, $18 for two dresses, and additional sums for laundry, amusement, and other expenses. The estimate came to $9.63 a week, and the IWC found that fewer than half of the state's working women received this wage. Subsequently, the commission established a $10 weekly minimum wage in the canning, manufacturing, and laundry industries, as well as in the unskilled and professional occupations.[8]

Edson seemed particularly proud that the state's employers publicly embraced the spirit of the new law. "The employers all seem to agree that the experienced worker should have a good living wage," she wrote in *The California Outlook*.[9] In subsequent years, the commission's jurisdiction was expanded to include workers in restaurants, hotels, motion pictures, and other industries. In 1921, Edson told a disarmament conference, "A life-sustaining wage is more vital to world peace than battleships. Scrapping the avarice in men's souls outranks the junking of navies."[10] Edson retained her high-profile position at the Industrial Welfare Commission through four successive Republican administrations, helping California's working women benefit from improved working conditions and the highest minimum wage in the country. After leaving state service in 1931, many of her efforts were reversed because of new leadership at the Industrial Welfare Commission and Depression-era austerity. She died, at the age of 63, in November 1933, less than three years after her career in government ended. Today, the Industrial Welfare Commission, created by the 1913 legislation that Edson promoted, continues to regulate wages, hours, and working conditions in California.

Rare Women Appointees in State Government

Edson had risen to prominence when a woman's primary avenue for stimulating social change and extending her influence beyond the home was joining a woman's club to work for better conditions. These might include improving public health or dealing with the effects of alcoholism or prostitution—what history and women's studies professor Camille Leonhardt calls "moral housekeeping." Edson argued that if women truly wanted to enact industrial and social reforms affecting working women, they had to participate in politics. Esto Broughton, one of California's pioneering assemblywomen, called Edson "a vivid, energetic iconoclast putting human values above industrial expediency." She noted that Johnson and his lieutenant governor, John Eshleman, may have muscled the women's eight-hour law and minimum wage through the legislature, "but it was Mrs. Edson

---

[8] Susan Diane Casement, "Katherine Philips Edson and California's Industrial Welfare Commission, 1913–1931," master's thesis, Kansas State University, 1987, 142.

[9] Katherine Philips Edson, "Effect of Limited Hours and Minimum Wage on Women in Industry," *The California Outlook*, May 2, 1914, 14.

[10] "Living Wage to End War," *Santa Cruz Evening News*, November 5, 1921, 6.

who put them over with the employer, a far more Herculean task . . . and she made the employer like it, too."[11]

Edson was joined by another prominent woman appointee in government during that era. Promising to make deep cuts in government spending, Governor Friend Richardson in 1923 had put Nellie Brewer Pierce in charge of budgets and accounts for the State Board of Control, which at that time supervised the business and financial affairs of the state. It was her job to trim budget demands made by various state departments and justify those cuts to the legislature. According to a journalist for *Sunset Magazine*, Pierce would closet herself in a room with a large pair of sharp shears and a soft blue pencil, poring over hundreds of volumes of reports and ledgers. "They [the departments] demanded, they requested, they petitioned, they begged, they implored, they threatened, they cajoled, they labored, they all but prayed [and] to every one of them she said firmly, kindly, but irrevocably: 'No!'"[12]

For several decades, Edson and Pierce were among the relatively few women appointees to key administration positions until Jerry Brown succeeded Ronald Reagan as governor in 1975. The year before, Brown as California secretary of state had released a study showing no women in command positions in government in the Reagan administration. Of the top 55 Reagan appointees, all were men.[13] A number of elected and appointed women scattered through government had just formed the California Elected Women's Association for Education and Research (CEWAER) as an answer to the "old boys" club. It presented Brown with a binder of resumes and pressed the new governor to name women to senior positions in the administration, which he did. In his first two terms, Brown appointed more than 1,600 women to boards, commissions, and state agencies and departments, including two to his first cabinet. He named the first woman to the state supreme court, chief justice Rose Bird, a liberal foe of the death penalty who would be defeated by the voters for reconfirmation in 1986. Throughout his record four terms as governor, half of Brown's appointees were women. According to Cassandra Pye, board chair of California Women Lead, CEWAER's successor, "The view was that women leaders were more than role models—they could use their collective influence to help the aspirations of all women."[14]

[11] Esto Broughton, "'In Memoriam,' Katherine Philips Edson," *Political Straws*, November 13, 1933.

[12] Wilbur Hall, "See Mrs. Pierce! The Story of the Woman Who Took the 'Con' Out of Economy and Helped Save Twenty Millions," *Sunset Magazine*, November 23, 1924, 24.

[13] Jennifer Jennings, "Are Qualified Females Available for Executive Posts in Sacramento?" *California Journal*, March 1974, 84–85.

[14] Cassandra Pye, "It's Time for Women to Step Up Their Game," January 27, 2015, http://314comm.net/news/.

A Paucity of Female Political Candidates

After their breakthrough vote for suffrage in 1911, women activists in California had reason to believe that political parity—while still unknowably distant—was at least inching closer. Amid feminist fervor, more women than men cast ballots in the state's 1912 presidential primary, and in 1914 a record 26 women ran for statewide offices, the legislature, or Congress. Four years later, a quartet of women with deep ties in their communities had crushed male adversaries at the ballot box and transitioned from novelties to state legislators, breaking down stereotypes and leaving their imprints on such significant public policy issues as corrections and juvenile justice, education, social welfare, and water and energy. Gender roles appeared to be shifting, albeit slowly, and women were actively embracing political activity as a vehicle to effect social change.

California's pioneering female elected officials had encouraged others to follow in their footsteps. "Women's advice," Anna Saylor said, "is just as important to the state as it is in the home."[15] However, women failed to make significant gains in electoral politics after the mid-1920s. Over several decades, fewer women won elections, in part because fewer even bothered to compete. Their numbers declined considerably as external events and cultural mores in the thirties, forties, and fifties, as well as apathy and arcane election rules, conspired to retard women's electoral advances. Many women concluded that the battle had been waged and won with suffrage and, with their fundamental rights secured, there was no need to continue the fight. The president of the League of Women Voters, the successor of the National American Woman Suffrage Association, declared in 1931 that "nearly all discriminations have been removed."[16]

The Depression threw another roadblock in front of women's electoral progress. With about one-fifth of Californians on public relief in 1934, "society viewed working women as un-American money grubbers, stealing jobs from men who needed them to support their families."[17] Further, if women did seek jobs to fortify the family income, they were expected to stay close to home instead of abandoning the family for months at a time during legislative sessions in Sacramento or Washington, DC. Journalist Norman Cousins once noted that the number of working women in the country equaled the number of unemployed. "Simply fire the women, who shouldn't be working anyway, and hire the men," he said. "Presto! No unemployment. No relief rolls. No Depression."[18]

---

[15] "Women's Place in Politics Urged by Mrs. Saylor," *Oakland Tribune*, September 26, 1922, 7.

[16] Mickey Moran, "1930s America—Feminist Void?" *Loyola University Student Historical Journal, 1988–1989*, http://www.loyno.edu/~history/journal/1988-9/documents/1930sAmericaFeministVoid.pdf.

[17] Ibid.

[18] Marnie M. Sullivan, John Olszowka, Brian R. Sheridan, and Dennis Hickey, *America in the '30s* (Syracuse: Syracuse University Press, 2014), 171; William H. Chafe, *The*

In the post-Depression war years, a different set of forces were at work. Popular opinion suggested women had a patriotic duty to go to work—not in the corridors of government but in the factories, shipyards, and defense plants. At the end of World War II, there were more women in the workforce—nearly 19 million—than at any previous time in the nation's history.[19] In San Francisco, the female labor force doubled between 1940 and 1945.[20] Once the war ended, though, women usually were the first to be fired to make room for returning servicemen, and the popular culture at the time on television and in movies and magazines held that the ideal suburban housewife cared for her children and took advantage of modern conveniences while tending to home duties.

Additionally, purely political influences tended to keep California women out of electoral politics. When Hiram Johnson and the progressives were swept into office in the early 1910s, one of their top priorities was to attempt to rid state politics of partisanship. Political parties and partisanship, they believed, contributed to corruption. To reduce partisanship, they created cross-filing in 1913, which allowed statewide, legislative, and congressional candidates to seek nominations in multiple party primary elections. Candidates were listed on the ballot without their own party identification. The consequence, perhaps unintentional, was that incumbents—at that time, entirely male—had easier paths to reelection; they possessed considerable name identification before the advent of mass-media campaigns, were given favorable ballot positions, and tended to have the support of most newspapers.

With all those advantages, incumbents often ran unopposed in general elections after winning nominations in multiple party primaries. After that 1914 election in which more than two dozen women sought state or congressional elective offices, state records show that the number of women contestants plunged. Only 13 women ran for those offices in 1922, 12 women ran in 1926, 11 in 1930, and 18 in 1932. Not until the legislature ended cross-filing nearly three decades later was there a steady rise in women candidates.[21]

Leone Baxter—A "Talented Huckster"

Despite women's prolonged absence from elective office, several achieved remarkable political influence through other avenues. Six weeks after Katherine Edson's passing—on December 19, 1933—Leone Baxter made the improbable transition from being a small-town business promoter in rural Northern California to becoming one of the most successful political practitioners in history.

Paradox of Change: American Women in the 20th Century (New York: Oxford University Press, 1991), 121.

[19] David M. Kennedy, *Freedom from Fear* (New York: Oxford University Press, 1999), 778.

[20] Chafe, 125.

[21] California Statements of Vote 1914–2018 (Sacramento: State Printing Office).

She was neither elected nor appointed to her position of power, but her future impact on the political process would be unassailable. Along with Clem Whitaker, she invented modern campaign management. "Beyond any doubt," famed California author Carey McWilliams wrote many years later, "these talented hucksters have had more direct influence on California's legislation . . . than any combination of politicians or of special-interest groups. . . ."[22]

McWilliams described Baxter as having a "deceptive mildness of voice and manner." Born in Washington state in 1906, and the daughter of a minister, she spent time as a reporter for the *Portland Oregonian*. In her mid-twenties, elegantly comported and widowed, she moved to Redding, initially to promote a water festival for the chamber of commerce. During the early political maneuvering for the state-federal Central Valley Project to ship abundant northern water to the thirsty Central Valley, the Redding community, eying a financial windfall, needed to convince lawmakers to locate the project's huge centerpiece dam a few miles north of town in Shasta County. Other interests were lobbying that the dam be built in Tehama County. Baxter prepped exhaustively for a series of critical meetings with visiting congress members. Her job, as she explained years later, "was to convince them that Shasta was the perfect locale."[23] In what foreshadowed a lengthy and successful career in political persuasion, Baxter succeeded.

The project was approved by the senate in late July 1933, but even after Governor James Rolph signed the legislation, the battle hadn't been won. The new law required the project to generate power that would be sold publicly. Pacific Gas & Electric, concerned that its private power monopoly was at risk, took advantage of one of Hiram Johnson's direct democracy tools—ironically designed to free the state from special interests—and qualified a late December statewide referendum to invalidate the entire project.

Whitaker, a bright, gangly, and chain-smoking former newspaper reporter, was tapped to manage the campaign against the referendum. On the advice of a prominent CVP supporter, Whitaker brought Baxter into the campaign as a partner. They formed their own consulting business, initially called Campaigns, Inc., and later renamed Whitaker and Baxter. It was an uphill ballot campaign from the start. Powerful Southern California interests rejected the notion that they should pay taxes to help finance a project that benefited only Northern and Central California, and PG&E mustered a seemingly unbeatable war chest. "It was David versus Goliath," noted Greg Mitchell, author of *The Campaign of the Century*. They made a strategic decision to spend their meager dollars only in areas directly benefiting from the project, hoping for anemic voter interest elsewhere in a special election on a single, complex measure a mere six days before Christmas. They placed articles and cartoons in small-town newspapers up and down the

---

[22] Carey McWilliams, "Government by Whitaker and Baxter," *The Nation*, April 14, 1951, 346.

[23] Leone Baxter interview, "The Great Depression," Washington University Film & Media Archive, May 1992, https://www.youtube.com/watch?v=ZKw_OKLkRgg.

valley and "made extensive use of radio, probably the first such use in a statewide campaign, handling everything from scripts to sound effects."[24]

The results were remarkable. As expected, Southern California turned down the project, but in precincts up and down the valley, the CVP won monstrous majorities. The city of Tulare, for example, approved the project by a 2,911-to-14 margin.[25] Despite losing by 102,000 votes in Los Angeles County, the Central Valley Project was approved statewide by 33,000 votes.

Inventors of Political Campaign Management

Whitaker and Baxter were the toast of the Central Valley and Northern California. For a statewide election, they had a tiny campaign account to work with, even by 1933 standards. "Compared to campaigns today," Baxter said many decades later, "it's almost laughable."[26] Their campaign received $40,037.01 and spent all but 53 cents.[27] A few years later, PG&E—obviously impressed—put the pair on an annual retainer.

Few recognized it at the time, but Clem Whitaker and Leone Baxter had created the nation's first professional, full-service political campaign management firm for candidates and public issues. Previously, according to Baxter, "such matters generally were the natural province of broken down politicians and alcoholic camp followers. We were enchanted by the broad horizon—the absolute absence of competition—and frankly by the pride of creating a new profession."[28] California was a natural incubator for this new field. The reform movement of Hiram Johnson and the Progressives had weakened political parties and created a campaign management vacuum. Further, California had fully embraced the relatively new tools of direct democracy—the initiative and referendum—that dramatically expanded the placement of public policy measures on statewide ballots and created a profit incentive for firms like Campaigns, Inc.

The techniques they developed gained national attention in 1934 after muckraking author Upton Sinclair stunned the political establishment by winning the Democratic nomination for governor in California. Sinclair spoke to struggling Californians and offered Depression bromides—the state seizure of unused farmland and idle factories, higher taxes on the wealthy, and government pensions for

---

[24] Greg Mitchell, *The Campaign of the Century* (New York: Random House, 1992), 130.

[25] "Tulare County Votes 19,952 for Plan; 585 Against," *Fresno Bee*, December 20, 1933; Statement of Vote of California at the Special Election held December 19, 1933 on Referendum Measure," California State Printing Office, Sacramento, 1934.

[26] Baxter interview.

[27] Whitaker and Baxter Campaigns, Inc. Collection, California State Archives, Sacramento.

[28] Speech to the 1949 Conference of the Public Relations Society, quoted in Scott M. Cutlip, *The Unseen Power: Public Relations: A History* (Hillsdale, NJ: Lawrence Erlsbaum Associates, 1995), 597.

Figure 6.2. Leone Baxter and Clem Whitaker
Credit: Courtesy of California State Archives

the aged and disabled. California's business community, apoplectic at the thought that Sinclair might defeat Republican Frank Merriam, set up a Northern California front group called the California League Against Sinclairism, and hired Campaigns, Inc.

Working out of a San Francisco office, Baxter and her partner initially locked themselves in a room for three days and read everything the rabble-rousing Sinclair had written. "We read his pamphlets on the meat packing industry, on Wall Street, financiers, on his comments on the church and Christianity, on the institution of marriage," Baxter said. "We wanted to utilize his own words."[29] The couple pulled disparaging quotes out of Sinclair's fictional writings and sent press releases and hard-hitting, mocking cartoons free of charge to every daily and weekly newspaper in the state. The *Los Angeles Times* ran those quotes prominently in front-page boxes. In his bitter election-loss postmortem, Sinclair noted that his opposition "had a staff of political chemists at work, preparing poisons to be let loose in the California atmosphere on any one of a hundred mornings." Having read his own quotes day after day, Sinclair conceded, "It is impossible that the voters will elect a man who has written that!"[30]

The 1934 governor's campaign was a game-changing election remembered for its ground-breaking tactical innovations as well as its viciousness, dirty campaigning, unfair news coverage, and outright lies targeting Sinclair. For her part, Baxter always insisted that she and her partner "had done a fair job" in helping

---

[29] Baxter interview.

[30] Upton Sinclair, *I, Candidate for Governor: And How I Got Licked* (Berkeley: University of California Press, 1994, originally published in 1934), 144.

to defeat Sinclair, "but because he was a good man," she said, "we were sorry we had to do it that way."[31]

Creating "The Faceless Man"

In the aftermath of the 1934 governor's election, Whitaker and Baxter became California's go-to political kingmakers. Whitaker's forte was long-term strategy; Baxter specialized in tactics that supported the strategy. They had replaced the smoke-filled room full of political hacks with sophisticated mass-media politics that entertained and persuaded voters with sharp, stirring appeals and messaging. One little-known campaign in 1946 involved embattled San Francisco mayor Roger Lapham.

Lapham had endured a challenging couple of years in office, and it was promising to get worse. A wealthy shipowner and businessman, Lapham had opted to take a 67 percent pay cut to run for mayor in 1943, defeating the incumbent and capturing 42 percent of the vote in a three-man race.[32] He promised to serve only one term as the city struggled with a surge of wartime growth. A staunch capitalist, Lapham had run-ins with labor, and after World War II ended, he was frustrated that many of the 240,000 wartime workers in the Bay Area's shipyards and other defense plants had settled in the city, straining municipal services.[33] Once, at a news conference, Lapham notoriously asked Thomas Fleming—founder of the *Reporter*, San Francisco's first African-American newspaper—that since the war was over, "How long do you think these colored people are going to be here?" More than 50 years later, Fleming recalled the exchange: "I said, 'Mr. Mayor, you know how permanent the Golden Gate Bridge is out there?' He said, 'yes,' and I said the black population is just as permanent as the Golden Gate. . . . I said you and the city of San Francisco might as well make up your mind right now that you're going to find jobs for these people.'"[34]

In 1945, two months of historic meetings at San Francisco's War Memorial Opera House concluded with the signing of the United Nations Charter by 50 nations, but Lapham's critics said he negligently let the permanent home of the UN slip through his fingers and go, instead, to New York. Lapham raised taxes, but his most controversial decision was to boost fares on city streetcars from seven cents to 10 cents and use the additional revenue to rehabilitate the dilapidated bus system.

---

[31] Irwin Ross, "The Supersalesmen of California Politics," *Harper's*, July 1959, 57.

[32] "Our Campaigns: San Francisco Mayor," http://www.ourcampaigns.com/RaceDetail.html?RaceID=752914.

[33] National Park Service, "World War II in the Bay Area," https://www.nps.gov/nr/travel/WWIIbayarea/text.htm.

[34] "Fillmore Stories, KQED, http://www.pbs.org/kqed/fillmore/learning/people/fleming.html; Thomas Fleming, "Shaping San Francisco," interview by Chris Carlsson, digital editing by Joe Cafentzis, 1999 https://archive.org/details/ssfTomF_1, 1999.

DON'T
SURRENDER
your city to
THE FACELESS MAN
(The Under-cover Candidate
For Mayor)

●

Eleven men—the Board of Supervisors—would pick the man to occupy the Mayor's chair if the recall
succeeds. However strong may be
the confidence of the people in their
Supervisors, the right to name their
own Chief Executive is a privilege
that citizens in a Democracy will
never surrender!

VOTE "NO"
Against the Recall
SPECIAL ELECTION, JULY 16

Figure 6.3. Anti-Recall Ad, 1946
Credit: Courtesy of California Digital Newspaper Collection, Center for Bib-
liographic Studies and Research, University of California, Riverside, http://cdnc.
ucr.edu

Shortly after his election, in a move that seemed inconsequential at the time,
Lapham refused to reappoint Henry Budde, publisher of some weekly throw-
away newspapers and a newsletter for city employees, as park commissioner.
After Lapham raised the transit fares, the 73-year-old Budde found a vehicle for

revenge: he started a recall drive to kick Lapham out of office.[35] That's when Lapham called in the cavalry, the wildly successful husband-and-wife political campaign management firm of Clem Whitaker and Leone Baxter.

Baxter once explained one of the team's inviolate precepts: "You can't wage a defensive campaign and win."[36] To attack, she said, is to define the campaign agenda and wage political war on one's own terms. The Lapham recall inevitably would put the mayor on the defensive, requiring him to justify his record against detractors. Baxter came up with a scheme to go on the attack. Mindful that San Francisco's board of supervisors would appoint a replacement mayor if the recall succeeded, Baxter invented the perfect foil. Drawing on a tablecloth one day, she sketched a picture of a sinister fat man wearing a fancy suit, chomping on a big cigar with a tilted derby hat hiding his face. Baxter gave him a name: the "Faceless Man."

Lapham now had an imaginary campaign opponent. Next, Baxter created an overarching theme. "Who's Behind the Recall? Don't surrender your city to the faceless man" became the campaign's tagline. Baxter's contrivance had turned the recall into a two-man race—Roger Lapham, the sincere and honest mayor, against an unknown, mysterious machine politician who would do the bidding of behind-the-scenes bosses. Voters couldn't escape the relentless barrage of billboards, radio and newspaper ads, speeches, press releases, news interviews, pamphlets, and circulars. In paid radio broadcasts shortly before the election, famed novelist Kathleen Norris wondered who would be mayor if Lapham were recalled: "No one knows . . . he is nameless. He is the faceless man—the faceless candidate of a little coterie of disgruntled politicians." Civic leader Francis Keesling told radio listeners that the recall forces had carefully hidden from view the "puppet boss of the city." [37]

Depictions of the infamous faceless man peered from the pages of San Francisco newspapers.[38] The branding campaign was so successful, even newspaper reporters accepted Baxter's creation as a central issue. Five years later, writing in *The Nation*, Carey McWilliams concluded, "Before the campaign was over, San Franciscans had been pumped so full of sound and fury that they would have lynched this faceless brute if they could have laid hands on him."[39]

Recall advocates hoped a combination of apathy and summer vacations would tilt the mid-July election in their favor. But that was before a hypothetical risk was turned into an imminent threat. In the largest special election turnout in

---

[35] Ibid.

[36] Speech before Los Angeles Area Chapter of the Public Relations Society of America, July 13, 1948, quoted in Stanley Kelley, Jr., *Professional Public Relations and Political Power* (Baltimore: John Hopkins Press, 1954), 48.

[37] A series of radio addresses and newspaper ads can be found in the extensive Whitaker and Baxter Papers at the California State Archives in Sacramento.

[38] *Vestkusten* (Swedish language), July 11, 1946, 4.

[39] Carey McWilliams, "Government by Whitaker and Baxter, III, *The Nation*, May 5, 1951, 419.

city history, Lapham defeated the recall by a four-to-three margin, and the team of Clem Whitaker and Leone Baxter solidified their reputation as the nation's premier political campaign management professionals.

A Permanent Place in US Political History

Until the 1950s, the pair—married in 1938—ran the only full-service professional campaign firm in the country And they were wildly successful—winning 55 out of 60 campaigns during a 15-year period in the thirties and forties. They managed Earl Warren's campaign for governor in 1942, and then defeated his ambitious health care proposal a few years later while working for the state's medical establishment. Their campaigns were expensive, but the return was worth it for those who hired them.

With Whitaker's health failing in the late fifties, the couple sold their firm to Whitaker's son by his first marriage, Clem, Jr., and two partners, who later abandoned campaign management in favor of corporate public relations. Leone and her husband established a smaller, boutique public affairs firm called Whitaker and Baxter International. After the elder Whitaker died in 1961 from emphysema, Baxter remained active into the eighties, having passed on the secrets of campaign management to a flock of younger practitioners.

By adapting public relations to politics, Leone Baxter and Clem Whitaker spawned a behemoth industry that is indispensable to modern-day political hopefuls. To Baxter, voters were consumers to be pitched and persuaded. Writing in the *Public Relations Journal*, Baxter once said that thanks to her profession, never in history had voters been in a better position to understand human affairs. That's because, she said, the public relations and allied professions "know something about presenting abstract ideas, in attractive form, to masses of people who are too occupied with their daily lives to think analytically on their own account. . . ."[40] In 1956, a *San Mateo Times* headline writer put it more succinctly: "Whitaker and Baxter Nearest Thing State Has to Political Boss."[41]

"An Intense Organizing Dynamo"— Elizabeth Snyder

Like Leone Baxter and Katherine Edson, Elizabeth Snyder never ran for political office, but she was responsible for the success of numerous candidates as a dedicated, hard-charging, and pioneering Democratic activist in the 1930s through the '70s. She was the first woman in the nation to be elected to lead a state party and was obsessed with ridding California of the Progressive Era reform of

---

[40] *The Public Relations Journal*, quoted in Stanley Kelley, Jr., *Professional Public Relations and Political Power* (Baltimore: The Johns Hopkins Press, 1956), title page.

[41] Leif Erickson, "Whitaker and Baxter Nearest Thing State Has to Political Boss," Associated Press in the *San Mateo Times*, April 11, 1956, 14.

cross-filing. She instinctively knew that cross-filing, which protected incumbents, kept Democrats and many women out of power. She had overcome childhood poverty, alcoholism, a smear campaign against her, and traditional gender roles to scale the pinnacles of male-dominated party politics.

Elizabeth Carlson was born in 1914 in Minnesota to Swedish immigrants. When she was 13, the family moved to East Los Angeles. Snyder spent two years at Los Angeles Junior College, and then transferred to UCLA where she joined the Young Democrats. After graduation, she became a substitute teacher and met her political hero, Democratic Congressman Jerry Voorhis. Snyder's daughter, Christina, says her mother was drawn to Voorhis's belief that "government's first responsibility is to serve those unable to help themselves." She viewed politics "not as a banal power struggle to be the biggest fundraiser, but rather as an opportunity to mobilize government responsibly to serve the needs of people."[42]

Elizabeth married attorney Nathan Snyder in 1940 and continued digging ever deeper into party politics. It was the Democrats' demoralizing and humiliating defeat in the 1946 gubernatorial election that set the stage for her greatest triumph. Earl Warren, California's popular Republican governor, took advantage of cross-filing provisions in the primary election and won both the Republican and Democratic nominations. He won reelection in November with nearly 92 percent of the vote. Democrats were devastated. [W]e didn't even have a Democratic nominee at the top of the ticket," Snyder reflected years later."[43] Rubbing salt in the wound, Republicans Frank Jordan (secretary of state), Charles Johnson (treasurer), and Thomas Kuchel (controller) successfully cross-filed in the primary and coasted to general election victories. Legislative primary elections were dominated by Republicans, and most of the winners had no Democratic opposition in the general election.

Republicans ruled Sacramento over several decades and drew legislative and congressional districts to their benefit during reapportionment every 10 years. The impact of cross-filing may have been less obvious but was no less important. Since candidates were not identified by party affiliation, their only identification on the ballot was occupation. Republicans—who held most of the offices—used this provision to their advantage by listing their occupations as "incumbent." Since virtually all elected officials were men, women had an even more daunting task in trying to break through the incumbent roadblock. As trailblazing political journalist Mary Ellen Leary noted in 1957, "It got so that death was the only defeat an office holder need worry about."[44]

---

[42] Christina Snyder in Elizabeth Snyder Oral History, "California Women Political Leaders Oral History Project," conducted by Malca Chall, 1977, Regional Oral History Office, Bancroft Library, University of California, Berkeley, vi-vii.

[43] Snyder Oral History, 63.

[44] Mary Ellen Leary, "The Two Party System Comes to California," *The Reporter*, February 7, 1957, 35.

Republican Domination in a Democratic State

What particularly rankled Snyder was the fact that California had become a Democratic state—at least in terms of voter registration—beginning in the mid-1930s during the depths of the Depression. At the time of the 1946 primary election, 2.4 million registered voters were Democrats; 1.5 million were Republicans. Many Democrats, Snyder believed, unknowingly were voting for conservative Republicans who masked themselves as progressives when seeking votes. As Leary put it, "The victory went to the best-camouflaged candidate—and he was usually a Republican."[45]

It took more than 30 years of demoralizing defeats and that embarrassing electoral debacle in 1946 to crystallize the Democrats' opposition to cross-filing. The progressive reform had flown far under the radar when it became law in 1913, buried as the 32nd of 38 amendments in a complex bill on elections. Historians James Rawls and Walton Bean concluded, "The cross-filing system reduced the political party system to a shambles . . . favoring incumbents, encouraging candidates to masquerade as members of parties other than their own, and enabling them to deceive thousands of ill-informed voters."[46] Over a 42-year period, half of all winning legislative candidates successfully cross-filed and avoided November runoff challenges.[47]

Elizabeth Snyder felt that the life of the Democratic Party depended on its ability to field candidates in every contest, and in 1950 she led a campaign that qualified a measure for the 1952 ballot to nullify cross-filing once and for all. With Democratic registration surging, Republicans feared defeat, but they had one more hand to play. As a less onerous "compromise," the legislature placed an alternative measure on the ballot that retained cross-filing but required a candidate's party affiliation to be listed on the primary ballot. In November, Snyder's cross-filing repeal was narrowly defeated, but voters did approve the Republican counter-measure, a Pyrrhic victory for the GOP, as political journalist John Jacobs put it: "the Republicans had outwitted themselves and handed the Democrats an important advantage."[48] By allowing Democrats to be identified on the ballot, the complexion of the state's politics began to change.

The Democrats rewarded Snyder's efforts by electing her to chair the Democrats' Southern California women's division, which was the only vehicle available at the time for women who sought entry into the traditional male work of internal party politics. In 1954, at the age of 40 and still riding high as the champion of cross-filing reform, Snyder shocked the Democratic establishment by seeking the

---

[45] Ibid.

[46] James J. Rawls, Walton Bean, *California: An Interpretive History* (New York: McGraw-Hill, 2003), 269.

[47] Robert Pitchell, "The Electoral System and Voting Behavior: The Case of California's Cross-Filing," *Western Political Quarterly* (June 1959): 463.

[48] John Jacobs, *A Rage for Justice: The Passion and Politics of Phillip Burton* (Berkeley: University of California Press, 1995), 40.

party's statewide chairmanship against two male party stalwarts. In US history, no woman had ever led a state political party.

"She Plays a Pretty Good Game of Poker"

Her opponents made Snyder's past as a rehabilitated alcoholic the center-piece of a smear campaign against her. In 1942, she had given birth to a baby girl who died after one month. She later said that trauma contributed to her alcoholism. "I went in and out of some sanitariums," she said in an oral history for the University of California's Bancroft Library. "I did not try any psychological help because there wasn't anyone to give you that."[49] She said she entered sobriety with the help of Alcoholics Anonymous in June 1945 and never drank again.

As Snyder campaigned for party leadership, one of her supporters, Democratic House member Chet Holifield, made an off-hand remark that generated even more controversy. While trying to promote Snyder among his colleagues in Congress, Holifield suggested she would be a strong leader, "If you knew Liz, she really plays a pretty good game of poker." Her opponents twisted the comment, spreading gossip that Snyder was a professional gambler who owned part of Tony "The Hat" Cornero's gambling ships off the coast of California. They circulated rumors that Holifield was having second thoughts about supporting her. With her candidacy unraveling, Snyder considered withdrawing from the competition. Then, three days before the election, Holifield came to the rescue. He issued an unequivocal statement extolling her qualifications and saying he intended to place her name in nomination at the Sacramento meeting.[50]

The night before the two-day central committee meeting, Snyder checked into Sacramento's Senator Hotel across the street from the capitol. Late in the evening she received a phone call from Earl "Squire" Behrens, the *San Francisco Chronicle* reporter. "Look, Liz, what the hell is all this stuff about you being a professional gambler?" Snyder explained the accusations and promised to resign the chairmanship if any of them proved to be true. Infuriated by lies about her, Snyder then told Behrens, "While we're here in Sacramento this weekend, someone's going to probably locate some red light joint and I expect to be cut in on part of the ownership."[51]

Besides Holifield and her cadre of veteran Democratic women supporters, the besieged Snyder had another weapon—Rosalind Wiener, the toast of Los Angeles, who stunned the political establishment the year before by winning a city council seat as a 22-year-old fresh out of the University of Southern California. Wiener, who would soon marry and change her name to Wyman, had run an all-volunteer, door-to-door campaign so devoid of campaign money that her

---

[49] Ibid., 45.

[50] Ibid., 107, 108; Ursula Vils, "A Pioneer Woman Politician," *Los Angeles Times*, May 18, 1980, VIII, 1.

[51] Snyder oral history, 110.

seven-year-old nephew sold his polliwogs at 10 cents each to help the campaign.[52] Snyder had encouraged Wyman to run for the council as a learning experience, and now Wyman was returning the favor. "I went from caucus to caucus to do whatever I could to help Liz," Wyman said in an interview. "We knew exactly what we were doing. We knew how to count votes."[53]

Despite the whispering campaign and the novelty of a woman running for party chair, Snyder defeated her two opponents handily. After the election, she headed back to the hotel and passed Behrens walking in the opposite direction. "So he sort of nods—a little note of congratulations," Snyder recalled. "Then he came over to me and he says, 'Say, when you open that red light place, give me the address!'"[54]

Two days after her election, Snyder told a television interviewer that men seemed reconciled to a woman assuming an important political position. [T]he more secure and the more mature a man is, the easier it is for him to accept a woman," she said. "He shouldn't be too interested in who does the job but whether the job is accomplished."[55] The next day, the *Los Angeles Daily News* published a lengthy article on her recipe for peppermint stick candy cake.

Throughout her two-year stint as party chair, Snyder told a reporter, she set out to break down prejudices "that virtually barred women from top political jobs."[56] Too often, she said, men in charge would appoint women they could control, "not real feminists and not women who can really stand up and express some strong, individual points of view." She believed that such problems as housing, drugs, delinquency, education, mental illness, and healthcare were not being solved "because there are not enough women in Sacramento and Washington, D.C."[57]

Snyder's tenure as party chair began two months after the 1954 primary election, the first in more than 40 years in which candidates were identified by their party affiliations. The November results were marginally better for Democrats than they had been in 1952, but she remained resolute in her efforts to rid the state of cross-filing once and for all, even as Democrats started winning more elections and began using the system for their own benefit.

Working 60 hours a week, Snyder formed a corps of 30,000 volunteer workers and greatly expanded the number of Democratic clubs throughout the state. The Associated Press called her "an intense organizing dynamo."[58] As Snyder left

---

[52] Mary Ann Callan, "Miss Wiener Had Expected Vote Victory," *Los Angeles Times*, May 28, 1953, 12.

[53] Rosalind Wyman interview, by telephone, Los Angeles, June 13, 2017.

[54] Snyder oral history, 110–11.

[55] KNXT Radio & Television Aircheck, August 10, 1954, in Snyder oral history, 113b.

[56] Art Hewitt, "Mrs. Snyder Retires as Dem. Chairman, *Los Angeles Herald-Express*, August 31, 1956, in Snyder oral history, 177a.

[57] Norma Goodhue, "Need Seen for Women in Politics," *Los Angeles Times*, June 18, 1956, III7; Snyder oral history, 172.

[58] Bill Becker, Associated Press, "The Infighters: Woman, Man Lead Adlai's State Campaign," in *San Bernardino Sun*, April 13, 1956, 6.

her leadership role in August 1956, the Democratic Party—politically impotent for more than a half century—was making public policy gains at the capitol and gradually increasing strength. After the 1956 elections, Democrats almost reached parity with Republicans in the legislature and the state's congressional delegation. Then, in 1958, Pat Brown won a million-vote victory over US Senator William Knowland to become only the second Democratic governor since the turn of the century. Democrats also captured both the assembly and senate—breaking an 80-year string when Republicans controlled at least one legislative house.

The newly empowered Democrats moved quickly to send cross-filing to the scrap heap. Although the Democratic resurgence wasn't permanent—Republican Ronald Reagan defeated Brown for governor in 1966 and the GOP briefly controlled the legislature in 1969–1970—Snyder can be credited with rebuilding her party. She overcame considerable personal, political, and cultural obstacles to improve party organization and boost Democratic registration. "She took the party and opened it up," Rosalind Wyman recalls. "It had been run by a clique in our party—a certain group of men, no women—and when she was elected, it was stunning, because she changed the direction of the party."[59] The two women remained close friends until Snyder's death in 1998 at the age of 84. One of her lasting regrets was the nation's failure to ratify the Equal Rights Amendment by 38 states before its deadline in the early 1980s. California was one of 35 states that did ratify the amendment designed to enshrine women's rights into the US Constitution.

In their own ways and under different circumstances, Katherine Edson, Leone Baxter, and Elizabeth Snyder left remarkable legacies on politics, public policy, and social justice at a time when women were withdrawing from the electoral arena. They challenged historical biases about the role of women in government and politics in an era when men had a virtual monopoly on leadership. They reinforced the perception of women's abilities and demonstrated yet again that women could be tough and effective while taking charge in a man's world.

Discussion Questions

1. Do you think Leone Baxter's "Faceless Man" strategy would work today to oppose ballot measures that are bankrolled by corporate donors who pool their contributions in "independent expenditure committees"? (If so, should the word "man" be used after "faceless" or some other noun?)

2. For what reasons did candidacies among California women taper off significantly after the 1914 elections and into the fifties? Do you find this surprising, or not surprising, given the difficulty of winning suffrage for women in the first place?

---

[59] Wyman interview.

3. For what purpose did Katherine Philips Edson analyze how much money working women spent on petticoats and corsets in her capacity as a member of the Industrial Welfare Commission?

4. Discuss in what ways Edmund G. (Jerry) Brown, Jr.—who served two terms as governor from the mid-seventies to early eighties and, historically, another two terms from 2011 to 2019—smashed all records in becoming a champion of women in government.

5. How did creating and preserving the federal-state Central Valley Project lead to forming the nation's first campaign management firm?

6. In what ways might Leone Baxter have seemed ahead of her time as a strategizing businesswoman in the 1930s? If you were to describe her, what qualities would you attribute to her? Do you think honesty mattered to her? She eventually trained younger generations of consultants. What advice do you think she would give political consultants today?

7. For what reasons did the longstanding practice of cross-filing in California elections harm newcomer women candidates?

8. In what ways was Elizabeth Snyder an ultimate Democratic Party insider? What lasting changes did she help bring to fruition? Do you believe it was more effective for her to work outside rather than inside of elective office? For what reasons?

9. Discuss how Snyder saw herself as a woman who helped pave the way toward greater gender equality in political life. For what reasons did she think this mattered?

Recommended Reading

Chafe, William H. *The Paradox of Change: American Women in the 20th Century.* Oxford University Press, New York, 1991.

Johnson, Dennis J. *Democracy for Hire: A History of American Political Consulting.* New York: Oxford University Press, 2017.

McWilliams, Carey. *The Great Exception.* Santa Barbara: Peregrine Smith, Inc., 1976 [1949].

Chapter 7

1900–1970
Activist Women Kickstart California's Conservation
and Clean Air Movements

"How Los Angeles Women Are Fighting Smog—and Winning"
—*Family Circle*

In early 1886, *Science* magazine devoted an entire edition to birds. Several stories, in particular, shocked the nation. In an article titled, "The Present Wholesale Destruction of Bird-Life in the United States," author J. A. Allen singled out the "slaughter of birds in obedience to the dictates of fashion."[1] Hats adorned with bird parts were status symbols and all the rage in the fashion centers of Paris, London, and New York. Marie Antoinette was said to have started the trend in the late 1700s by adorning her hair with feathers. A century later, the millinery industry was using feathers from herons, egrets, peacocks, birds of paradise, terns, and others to spur hat sales to fashionable ladies. Sometimes, entire small stuffed birds decorated women's hats. A second article in *Science* cited 40,000 terns killed along the shores of Cape Cod during a single season.[2] Over a two-day period in New York's fashion district, an ornithologist counted 700 hats, three quarters of which contained bird parts.[3]

Science, as well as *Forest and Stream* magazine, issued calls to arms. The women who wear birds on their hats and bonnets, *Science* said, "have doubtless done so thoughtlessly . . . without any appreciation of its extent or results. They have therefore sinned, for the most part, unwittingly and thus are not seriously chargeable with blame."[4] But ignorance, the magazine stated, could no longer be used as an excuse. Newspapers piled on. A Chicago reporter, observing the fashion craze, said, "It will be no surprise to me to see life-sized turkeys or even . . . farmyard hens, on fashionable bonnets before I die."[5] The *New York Times* noted

---

[1] J. A. Allen, "The Present Wholesale Destruction of Bird-Life in the United States," *Science*, February 26, 1886, 191.

[2] Ibid., "The Destruction of Birds for Millinery Purposes," 196.

[3] Michelle Kleehammer, "Citizen Bird," in *California Women and Politics*, Robert W. Cherny, Mary Ann Irwin, and Ann Marie Wilson, eds. (Lincoln: University of Nebraska Press, 2011), 125.

[4] "An Appeal to the Women in the Country in Behalf of the Birds," *Science*, 204.

[5] "Notes," *Club Woman* 1, November, 1897, 5, quoted in Jennifer Price, *Flight Maps* (New York: Basic Books, 1999), 59.

that the attack on "feminine vanity" was being met with a favorable response in Europe. It reprinted portions of a French newspaper editorial: "Do you know, oh, lovely woman with heart so tender, how many little birds are killed every year for the plumage that garnishes your hats? Pas moins de trois-cents millions [not less than 300 million]!"[6]

Amid withering criticism and public chiding, putting dead birds on bonnets fell out of favor among the well-to-do. To combat the millinery slaughter, two women in Massachusetts created the Audubon Society in 1896, and in quick order, state chapters were started coast to coast. A California chapter was added two years later.[7] Nature historian Jennifer Price suggests that the bird-hat debate ignited the first wide-scale public conservation protest movement. "The new Audubon arguments reduced the lovely fashions of Marie Antoinette to an antifeminine bone pile."[8] The industry didn't go down without a fight. The *Millinery Trade Review* evoked the image of fanatical rabble-rousers ridding society of decency. "There is very little that woman wears that does not cost life," the magazine noted, "and if these Audubon notions were to be carried to extremes, we blush to think of the possibilities of her future appearance."[9] In an unsigned letter to the *New York Times*, a writer referred to "unthinking reformers" and ventured that an "ugly, large hen suffers the same pang when killed that the heron or the oriole experiences, and yet nobody—except the vegetarians, and they, being obviously mad, do not count"—takes exception to killing animals for their meat. Men, the writer added, "have just as much right to trim a bonnet with egret plumes as to cover a foot with leather or to fill a platter with roast beef."[10]

Women's Clubs Spread Their Influence at the Century's Turn

The conservation movement in the early twentieth century was driven in large part by women club members and was seen as a natural extension of their traditional roles as caretakers of their homes and families. Further, their push to protect bird species and ancient redwoods—as well as reforming milk safety standards, cleaning up municipal government, and beautifying urban environments—came, with few exceptions, well before women could vote and effect change within formal political structures. These women demonstrated that persistent grassroots activism and public education could shift public opinion and leave imprints on their communities' wellbeing for generations. As historian Carolyn Merchant has written, "[W]ithout the input of women in nearly every locale in the country, con-

---

[6] *New York Times*, February 6, 1898, 26.

[7] "A Brief History of Audubon in California," http://ca.audubon.org/about-us/brief-history-audubon-california.

[8] Price, 82.

[9] *Millinery Trade Review*, April 1887, 10, quoted in Price, 86.

[10] "Personal," *New York Times*, November 19, 1897, 6.

servation gains in the early decades of the century would have been fewer and far less spectacular.[11]

Options for women to participate in business and politics were limited, but the popularity of early civic clubs allowed more affluent upper-class women to expand their influence. In some cases, these clubs consciously represented notions of high social standing—or "high society"—for their members, which, in turn, increased the clubs' influence.[12] Black women's clubs also were highly active dating from an era, at the turn of the twentieth century, when the California Federation of Women's Clubs formally excluded African Americans. A motto—"Lifting as We Climb"—adopted by the California Association of Colored Women's Clubs and its national umbrella association helps illustrate how the causes and approaches of black women's clubs differed from those of well-heeled white women's groups. Black clubwomen promoted African-American achievement through community boosterism,[13] community service, and cultural activities, and in fundraising for youth causes and elder care. Socially and civically aware, the clubs were precursors to a cohesive brand of political activism in black communities and supported African Americans in coping with racial and societal barriers.

For instance, although the University of California had no racial bar to admission, its small stream of black students in the early decades of the twentieth century could be shunned on campus and denied off-campus jobs and housing. Black clubwomen in Oakland responded with social support, urged still more black youth to pursue professional careers, and invited black students to display their skills, leadership, and expertise by addressing club meetings and public assemblies.

Winning New Protections for Songbirds— Catherine Hittell

As they built their focus on conservation, California's well-to-do clubwomen challenged what they considered to be "a system of complacency and negligent stewardship of the nation's resources by male policymakers, businessmen, and scientists."[14] In particular, Catherine Hittell, a member of both the California and Century clubs in San Francisco, took a special interest in wildlife preservation. Described by the *Los Angeles Times* as "a gentle sweet-faced little woman, with

---

[11] Carolyn Merchant, "Women of the Progressive Conservation Movement: 1900–1916," *Environmental Review* 8.1 (1985): 57, https://nature.berkeley.edu/departments/espm/env-hist/articles/17.pdf.

[12] Gayle Gullett, *Becoming Citizens: The Emergence and Development of the California Women's Movement, 1880–2011* (Champaign: University of Illinois Press, 2000), 117–26.

[13] Martha Kendall Winnacker, "Oakland, California, Black Women's Clubs," in *Black Women in America*, Vol. II, Darlene Clark Hine, Elsa Barkley Brown, and Rosalyn Terborg-Penn, eds. (Bloomington: Indiana University Press, 1994) 895–97.

[14] Kleehammer, 123.

wide, blue eyes and a fresh color," Hittell was born into a prominent San Francisco family.[15] Her father was a well-known historian. She was among the earliest female graduates at the University of California in 1882, and when the 1886 university yearbook published its alumni directory, she listed her occupation as, "Devoted to the emancipation of women."[16]

Hittell became a statewide celebrity, credited with saving the meadowlark from extinction. In an interview with the *San Francisco Examiner* in the spring of 1895, Hittell argued that saving songbirds—used in meals in that era—was as much a question of mathematics as sentiment. "A meadowlark, cooked, gives one person pleasure for, at most, ten minutes. A living one gives pleasure to a whole community all its life long."[17] Convincing the state's political power structure of the wisdom of bird conservation wasn't easy, however. Reporting on an early failed attempt to protect the meadowlark, the *Examiner* quoted a rural legislator who said, "What's the good of that? The bird only gullups [sic] out a few notes anyway."[18] Writing to naturalist John Muir, Hittell relayed her disappointment and told of a conversation she had with a man who lived in a San Francisco boarding house. The man "told me they had lark pie for breakfast and as there were one hundred boarders in that house, it meant one hundred 'slaughtered innocents.'"[19] In response, Muir encouraged Hittell to remain vigilant. "Better far and more reasonable it would be to burn our pianos and violins for firewood than to cook our divine midgets of songlarks for food," Muir wrote.[20]

Energetic and persistent, Hittell and her California Club colleagues led petition drives and public education campaigns. She lobbied not only at the capitol, but at the Sportsmen's Convention, a gathering of governmental appointees assigned to recommend amendments to the state's game laws. Confronting the convention's chairman, she pressed her argument. "You men are busy making laws to save the game for your hunting. Don't you think you might make just one little law to save the song birds for the women? That is all we want."[21]

---

[15] "To Her Owe Their Voices," *Los Angeles Times*, March 10, 1907, V21.

[16] "Alumni Directory: 1882," *Blue and Gold '86* (Oakland: Pacific Press Publishing House, 1885), 132.

[17] "Protect Our Songbirds: Some Action Should be Taken Soon to Save the Warblers," *San Francisco Examiner*, n.d., reprinted in "Victorians and Meadowlarks: Two Muir Letters Discovered," *John Muir Newsletter*, Vol. 1, No. 4 (Fall 1991), http://vault.sierraclub.org/john_muir_exhibit/john_muir_newsletter/victorians_and_meadowlarks.aspx.

[18] Ibid.

[19] Letter from Catherine Hittell to John Muir, April 3, 1895, Holt-Atherton Special Collections, http://cdm16745.contentdm.oclc.org/cdm/ref/collection/muirletters/id/19270.

[20] Letter from John Muir to Catherine Hittell, April 30, 1895, in "Victorians and Meadowlarks."

[21] "To Her Owe Their Voices."

Figure 7.1. Hat with Bird Parts, Early Twentieth Century
Credit: Courtesy of National Audubon Society

Double-Teaming with the Audubon Society

In 1901, clubwomen Hittell and Alice Park finally found success in the California legislature with their draft of the state's first bird-protection legislation, the Meadowlark Preservation Act, which made it illegal to kill meadowlarks. In the ensuing 18 years, they and other conservation advocates would have to fend off repeated attempts to repeal the law. A particular assemblyman, J. W. Stuckenbruck of San Joaquin County, caused the women angst in several legislative sessions even though he drew scornful opposition in the press. One newspaper ridiculed the legislator as having a "sinister bloodthirsty . . . mad passion to kill. He listens [to the meadowlark] and immediately introduces another bill to have all meadowlarks killed."[22] All of Stuckenbruck's efforts failed.

Clubwomen joined members of the Audubon Society to double-team the lobbying of legislators. Many women, in fact, belonged to both Audubon and their local women's club. Typically, women would establish a state Audubon chapter and invite male scientists and civic leaders—such as Stanford president David Starr Jordan—to sign on as executive committee members who often became

---

[22] "Stuckenbruck and Meadowlarks," *Sacramento Union*, April 27, 1913, 16.

the public faces of the organization. Women comprised 80 percent of the group's membership and provided the everyday organizational work. In 1905, the women won legal protection of mourning doves, as well as legislation prohibiting the trapping or slaughter of wild nongame birds. They continued to win victories during the Progressive Era, including introduction of nature study in schools, but were stunned in 1913 when Hiram Johnson vetoed legislation that would have protected 38 species of shore-birds. *Bird-Lore*, the official publication of the Audubon Society, took the governor to task: "Just why the man posing as a conservationist should have vetoed such . . . a bill is still a mystery."[23]

After a number of successes in the California legislature, the national bird protection campaign culminated in the 1913 Tariff Act that outlawed the import of wild-bird feathers into the country. In California schools, women secured nature study curricula that taught the value and beauty of bird life and created junior Audubon societies to instill in students for years to come a deep love of nature. As Harriet Williams Myers, Audubon's California secretary, put it: [B]ecause of our labors, the people all over the state have a greater appreciation of bird life and, in consequence, the birds are becoming more abundant in many parts of California.[24] Hittell became a talented artist, but she is best remembered as a determined reformer and conservationist. She pushed beautification projects in San Francisco and helped establish forestries on coastal California islands. She also teamed with her sisters in the California Club and other women's organizations in a second conservation cause—a crusade that saved ancient, majestic redwoods west of Yosemite from the logger's axe.

A Fight to Save the Calaveras Big Trees

The headline in the *Santa Rosa Press Democrat* on January 13, 1900 couldn't have been more ominous: "Calaveras 'Big Trees' Doomed." Word had been received in California that a lumber company, headed by Minnesotan Robert P. Whiteside, had bought a popular resort and thousands of acres of forest land that included two groves of giant sequoias in the Sierra foothill counties of Calaveras and Tuolumne. The groves had been major tourist attractions since the early 1850s. The article went on to say that a sawmill was under construction with "the intention to make the trees into lumber."[25]

California was on the front-end of a building boom and would see the state's population rise by a staggering 60 percent between 1900 and 1910. A growing state needed lumber. Destruction of the groves would bring jobs and short-term wealth, but the resort and these *Sequoiadendron giganteum* redwoods were the

---

[23] Harriet Williams Myers, "Reports of State Societies," *Bird-Lore*, Vol. 15, No. 6 (Harrisburg: D. Appleton & Company), 442, https://www.audubon.org/sites/default/files/bird_lore_v15-1913_national_audubon.pdf.

[24] Myers, 441, 442.

[25] "Calaveras 'Big Trees' Doomed," *Santa Rosa Press Democrat*, January 13, 1900, 1.

region's prime tourist attractions. Once the logging operations were completed, residents knew that tourists—attracted by the giant trees—would no longer come.

Four days after publication of the Santa Rosa newspaper article, women representing civic clubs around the state created the California Federation of Women's Clubs at a meeting in Los Angeles, bringing some cohesion to the disparate activities of their groups. Los Angeles club leader Clara Burdette urged members to focus on two issues—children's welfare and protection of the state's giant redwoods. "Word comes to the women of California that men whose souls are gang-saws are meditating the turnout of our world famous Sequoias into planks and fencing worth so many dollars," Burdette said.[26]

The women of the California Club leapt into action, assigning its vice president, Mrs. A. D. Sharon, who was in Washington at the time, to seek introduction of a congressional resolution calling for acquisition of the grove for public benefit. She met with representatives and even secured an audience with President William McKinley. Sharon watched on March 8, 1900, as the president signed legislation authorizing Congress to purchase the resort and groves. After signing, McKinley presented the pen to Sharon so that she could give it to the women of the California Club. The measure appropriated no funds, however, and as the years progressed, Congress repeatedly turned down legislation to come up with the money. After the California Club presented a million and a half signatures to the White House, President Theodore Roosevelt in 1909 agreed to exchange the Calaveras redwoods for federal land of equal value. Over the next 40 years, negotiations with Whiteside and his lumber company foundered, but the massive sequoias were spared. Ultimately, the women's groups turned to the state for assistance, and in 1954, the Calaveras Big Trees were saved for good, becoming part of the state park system. In his book, *The Fight for Conservation*, Gifford Pinchot, former chief of the US Forest Service, said he knew of no case of "persistent agitation under discouragement finer than the fight that the women of California made to save the great grove of Calaveras big trees."[27]

Near the visitor's center in the protected north grove of the 6,500-acre Calaveras Big Trees State Park is a stark reminder of the decades-long struggle to save the giant sequoias in the Sierra foothills. It's the massive "Discovery Stump," what remains of the awe-inspiring 25-foot diameter "Discovery Tree" that August Dowd had stumbled upon while tracking a grizzly bear in 1852. It had taken five men 22 days to cut it down. Sections of the tree's bark and trunk were sent to San Francisco and New York and put on display like a curiosity in a P. T. Barnum freak show. Ring-dating showed the tree first sprouted in the early seventh cen-

---

[26] Mary S. Gibson, "A Record of Twenty-Five Years of the California Federation of Women' Clubs, 1900–1925" (Pasadena: California Federated Women's Clubs, 1927) 10.

[27] Gifford Pinchot, *The Fight for Conservation* (New York: Doubleday, Page & Company, 1910), 106.

tury.[28] The tree's demise became a rallying cry for those seeking to create nearby Yosemite National Park and today occupies a hallowed spot in the north grove.

Found among naturalist John Muir's papers after his death—and published in 1920—was an essay exalting the Calaveras forest. It is believed to have been written about the same time Clara Burdette was urging women to safeguard the redwoods and Mrs. Sharon was pressing for federal protection in Washington. "Through all the eventful centuries since Christ's time, and long before that," Muir wrote, "God has cared for these trees, saved them from drought, disease, avalanches, and a thousand storms; but he cannot save them from sawmills and fools . . . [and] as they are in California we cannot escape responsibility as their guardians."[29]

Creating California's First State Park—
Josephine Clifford McCracken

In 1900, an unsigned letter from "An Old Californian" appeared in the *Santa Cruz Sentinel* urging that a second stand of mammoth coastal redwoods, about 150 miles to the west, be saved. Under the headline, "Save the Trees," the writer told of San Jose photographer Andrew Hill being run off the property 40 miles south of San Francisco as he tried to take photos of the majestic trees for a British publication. The letter-writer protested "against the selfishness that would debar others from looking at and enjoying one of God's greatest works" and urged the legislature to purchase the property on behalf of the people of California. With logging of the coast redwoods rapidly increasing to meet the demand for lumber, the writer judged the owner as being "capable of cutting down those very trees for fire-wood, or to make fence-rails of, if he could get enough money for them."[30] As it turned out, the owner was a willing seller.

The letter's unidentified author was 61-year-old Prussian-born Josephine Clifford McCracken, a well-known writer of news articles and short stories who traveled in the same literary circles as famed writers Samuel Clemens (Mark Twain), Bret Harte, and Ambrose Bierce. McCracken combined the battle to save songbirds and the redwoods into one women's group, the Ladies' Forest and Songbird Protective Association, of Santa Cruz County. McCracken's most prominent legacy would be to bring public attention to the imminent logging threat that endangered the majestic coastal *Sequoia sempervirens* redwoods in what is now the 18,000-acre Big Basin Redwoods State Park, the oldest park in the state system.

---

[28] "California Big Trees State Park," California State Parks, http://www.parks.ca.gov/pages/551/files/CalaverasBigTreesFinalWebLayout101816.pdf.

[29] John Muir, "Save the Redwoods," *Sierra Club Bulletin*, Vol. XI, No. 1 (January 1920), http://vault.sierraclub.org/john_muir_exhibit/writings/save_the_redwoods_1920.aspx.

[30] "Save the Trees," *Santa Cruz Sentinel*, March 7, 1900, 3.

When she was eight, her family relocated from Europe to St. Louis. She later ran away from a paranoid, abusive husband and settled in San Francisco. By 1880, McCracken was an established writer and with $504 in earnings, she bought 26 acres among the redwoods in the Santa Cruz Mountains. She remarried and moved into the mountain ranch. It was destroyed by fire in October 1899.

As the century turned, McCracken and photographer Hill decided that the magnificent trees—already vulnerable to fire—needed to be protected from the saw. The Big Basin/San Lorenzo Valley region had been prime lumber territory for decades. According to a local newspaper, 28 area sawmills were cutting 34 million feet of lumber per year in the mid-1860s.[31] The California Club's success with its Calaveras "Big Trees" campaign hadn't gone unnoticed in Santa Cruz. Hill brought the San Jose Woman's Club into the movement, and it responded with petitions, letters, press outreach, fundraising, and creation of the Sempervirens Club to lobby for legislative protection, and after passing a hat during its first meeting, the club raised 32 dollars. Not long after, newspaper heiress Phoebe Apperson Hearst agreed to underwrite several thousand dollars in campaign expenses.[32] The club also raised money to build roads so that the ancient trees—some of which pre-dated the Roman Empire and were dozens of feet in diameter—would be accessible to visitors.

To avoid direct competition with their Calaveras sisters, who were seeking congressional protection of the Big Trees, the Sempervirens worked on the state legislature, instead. In rather short order, a bill authorizing the state to buy 3,800 acres for $250,000 was signed by Governor Henry Gage. In 1902, the property became the Big Basin Redwoods State Park. Writing in the *Overland Monthly*, Carrie Stephens Walter, a member of the San Jose Woman's Club, credited the women's clubs with saving the ancient trees from the "axe of commerce." Without their effort, "Think of the sacrilege of it!" she wrote. "[T]hink of the antiquity here displayed! Contemporary with Ramses and the builders of Babylon."[33]

Battle to Save Redwoods Opens Third Front to the North

On the heels of their remarkable success in Calaveras and Santa Cruz, clubwomen in far northern coastal California opened up a third front in the battle to save the redwoods. A catalyst in this latest effort was a nine-week transcontinental train excursion through 24 states and territories in 1903 by President Roosevelt. In California, he took a side trip to see the state's giant redwoods for the first time and was in awe to "see a tree which was old when the first Egyptian conqueror

---

[31] "Movement to Purchase Big Basin Was Commenced by the *Sentinel*," *Santa Cruz Sentinel*, September 26, 1902, 1.

[32] Cameron Binkley, "Saving Redwoods," *California Woman and Politics*, 160.

[33] Carrie Stephens Walter, "The Preservation of the Big Basin," *Overland Monthly*, October 1902, 354–55, 358, https://babel.hathitrust.org/cgi/pt?id=iau.31858036877102;view=1up;seq=387.

penetrated to the valley of the Euphrates."[34] Four years later, Roosevelt told a White House visitor from the north coast: "You Humboldters want to be careful of your great forests." "You should not waste that timber, for it will not be many years before it will be more valuable than you ever dream of."[35]

Women and children in the Eureka area took the president's comments to heart. Within two months, the Humboldt County Federation of Women's Clubs sent the president 2,000 signatures urging creation of a national redwood forest. Whereas "the uncouth hand of man scars and gashes the beautiful face of nature in Humboldt," the local newspaper said, "the smooth and gentle hand of woman" can heal the wounds. [36] Notwithstanding numerous roadblocks thrown in their path, the women of Humboldt County over time would make it happen.

The issue presented a particularly delicate problem for members of the region's clubs who were wives, sisters, or daughters of men involved in the lumber industry. Logging had been the backbone of the local economy since the Gold Rush. In late 1909, however, local male business leaders endorsed the idea of creating a national redwood park in the hopes it would attract tourist dollars and boost efforts to build a railroad linking Eureka and San Francisco. The county's women's clubs signed on enthusiastically and sent petitions to Congress, worked the press, and even personally investigated the suitability of potential park sites, sending their research to political officials.

As the years went on without action in Washington, loggers continued systematically felling the irreplaceable trees. Investigating the situation, Madison Grant, an official with the New York Zoological Society, found that the timber along the Eel River was being completely destroyed: "the landscape presents a scene comparable only to the devastated regions of France" during World War I. It will cost money to preserve the redwoods—many millions; but California has no choice."[37] Grant was so shaken, he and others founded the Save the Redwoods League to raise funds to buy—and save—privately held redwoods.

Responding quickly, the women's clubs in Humboldt County resurrected their moribund political and public education campaign, creating a separate women's Save the Redwoods League that promptly attracted hundreds of members. Both independently campaigned for the legislature and governor to create a state redwood park. The women persuaded the post office to stamp "Save the

---

[34] Doris Kearns Goodwin, *The Bully Pulpit: Theodore Roosevelt, William Howard Taft, and the Golden Age of Journalism* (New York: Simon and Shuster, 2013), 353.

[35] George Burchard, "Birds, Beasts and Trees: Saving the Redwoods," *The Outlook*, March 10, 1920, 428, https://tinyurl.com/y9sbk2u7.

[36] "Work for Eureka's Women," *Humboldt Times*, February 24, 1907, 4, quoted in Cameron Binkley, "No Better Heritage than Living Trees: Women's Clubs and Early Conservation in Humboldt County," *Western Historical Quarterly* (Summer 2002): 187, http://doi.org/10.2307/4144802.

[37] Madison Grant, "Saving the Redwoods: An Account of the Movement During 1919 to Preserve the Redwoods of California," *Zoological Society Bulletin*, New York Zoological Society, September 1919, 109, 112, https://tinyurl.com/yb4gsv4d.

Figure 7.2. Saving the Redwoods, 1918
Credit: Courtesy of the Humboldt Historical Society

Redwoods" on outgoing mail.[38] Two popular silent movies—"The Valley of the Giants" and "The Little Boss"—released in 1919 were set in north coast logging country. Sensing an opening for their cause, the women hired a filmmaker and produced a documentary on the destruction of the giant trees to be shown to captive audiences in tandem with the feature films.[39]

The breakthrough for activists came in 1921 when the state created Humboldt Redwoods State Park and started purchasing the first parcels in what decades later would become a 53,000-acre sanctuary of magnificent trees—"priceless for antiquity and still growing, magnificent for beauty, yet staunchly strong, preserved as a park for the people."[40] Governor William Stephens had balked at signing a parks appropriations bill until Flora Stephens, his club-member wife, insisted.[41] In 1923, local club-women coaxed the statewide federation to hold its convention in

[38] Binkley, "No Better Heritage than Living Trees: Women's Clubs and Early Conservation in Humboldt County," *Western Historical Quarterly*, Oxford University Press, Summer 2002, 195, http://doi.org/10.2307/4144802.
[39] Binkley, "No Better Heritage," 195–96.
[40] Myra Nye, "Redwood Fight Success Told," *Los Angeles Times*, February 18, 1925, III1,2.
[41] Binkley, "No Better Heritage, 197.

Eureka despite its remoteness from the rest of the state. Women from throughout California picnicked among the majestic trees. Most had never seen anything so spectacular. When they learned that a 103-acre parcel was for sale, the convention delegates decided that the federation would buy it. Their goal was to raise one dollar from each of the federation's 60,000 members and eventually, when combined with state matching funds, their contributions saved the trees in what is now called the California Federation of Women's Clubs Grove.[42]

Redwood Country's "Joan of Arc"—
Laura Mahan

Securing property wasn't always easy, however, particularly in dealing with Pacific Lumber, which owned most of the park-suitable land. The two Save the Redwoods Leagues worked tirelessly to identify suitable property and raise money for purchases. At one point, however, Pacific Lumber began quietly logging on part of its property—a magnificent grove called Dyerville Flats—that redwood activists considered a key parcel for park purposes. Laura Mahan, president of the women's Save the Redwood League, discovered the surreptitious felling and alerted the press and county officials. Awash in negative publicity, Pacific Lumber halted its logging and tedious sale negotiations proceeded. "Indignation, aroused everywhere . . . coupled with strong and prompt action on the part of the district attorney, saved the magnificent tract," one newspaper said."[43]

Mahan was characterized as "the Joan of Arc" in the North Coast's conservation movement and the state's women's clubs were hailed as heroes.[44] In 1926, the Save the Redwoods League took a gamble on oil magnate John D. Rockefeller, inviting him for a visit to the North Coast and a "lavish lunch" in Dyerville Flats. In less than a year, Rockefeller wrote the first of two million-dollar checks to the league to help purchase the 9,335 acres of Dyerville Flats. Rockefeller Forest is now the heart of Humboldt Redwoods State Park.[45]

Nearly one million annual visitors would be hard-pressed to escape the influence of women in protecting those 53,000 acres of redwoods along the breathtaking North Coast. At the Laura Mahan Trail at Dyerville Flats, a plaque has been placed at the spot where she first noticed Pacific Lumber's secret logging, and the California Federation of Women's Clubs Grove, next to the South Fork of the Eel River, is one the park's most popular attractions. Inside the grove is a four-sided hearthstone created by famed architect Julia Morgan, designer of Hearst Castle.

---

[42] Ibid., 200.

[43] Ibid., 196–97; "Indignations' Roar Alarmed Lumber Baron: Dyerville Flats Will Not Be Cut—Groves Go to the People," *Ukiah Republican Press*, December 10, 1924, 1.

[44] Nye.

[45] "Humboldt Redwoods State Park History," Humboldt Redwoods Interpretative Association, http://humboldtredwoods.org/park-history.

The monument celebrates the club-women who passed the hat to buy the grove and "the federation's scrupulous protection of this heritage."[46]

Women Go to War on a New Front—Smog

Women's interest in wilderness conservation and nature in the early twentieth century was a precursor to their aggressive grassroots activities in what would become California's environmental movement decades later. And it evolved from their natural, Victorian role of being caretakers of the family and protecting children from the new mid-century scourge—smog.

It was mid-summer 1943, and Los Angeles residents were on edge and preoccupied with the two-pronged war against Germany and Japan. Two events 17 months earlier had brought the conflict alarmingly close to home. On February 23, 1942, a Japanese submarine slipped undetected into California waters and attacked an oilfield north of Santa Barbara. The submarine fired 16 shells from about a mile offshore. "One shell hit a well and blew the pumping plant and derrick to bits," said Lawrence Wheeler, the owner of a roadside inn.[47] Two days later, an anti-aircraft barrage lit up the early-morning skies over blacked-out Los Angeles in response to an unconfirmed sighting of enemy aircraft. Three motorists died in traffic accidents during the black-out, two others had fatal heart attacks, and two persons were wounded by falling shell fragments. The secretary of the navy conceded that there were some "jittery nerves" in Southern California.

Those nerves were jolted again the morning of July 26, 1943, when a thick, brown, acrid cloud seemed to appear out of nowhere and hung over the city for several hours. The *Los Angeles Times* called it a "gas attack." It was the fourth and most severe such incident in recent weeks, and there were rumors at first that the Japanese had launched some sort of chemical strike on Los Angeles. The newspaper reported that thousands of people had "irritated eyes, noses and throats." Visibility was cut to three city blocks in the business district, and office workers "found the noxious fumes almost unbearable.[48] Los Angeles's filthy skyline was making national news, as it would for the ensuing 75 years.[49]

Scientists and headline writers started to use the new term "smog"—a contraction of smoke and fog—to characterize the city's awful air quality. It would take several years before scientists determined that auto exhaust was the major culprit—along with the region's unique geography that traps noxious gases in a

---

[46] Sara Holmes Boutelle, *Julia Morgan: Architect* (New York: Abbeville Press, 1988), 126; "Humboldt County: 101 Things to Do," http://101things.com/humboldt/federation-womens-clubs-hearthstone/.

[47] "Submarine Shells Southland Oil Field: Japanese Make Direct Hit North of Santa Barbara," *Los Angeles Times*, February 24, 1942, I1; "Shelling of Oil Field Described by Eyewitness," *Los Angeles Times*, February 24, 1942, I1.

[48] "City Hunting for Source of 'Gas Attack,'" *Los Angeles Time*, July 27, 1943, I1.

[49] Associated Press, "Los Angeles Gas Attacks Not from Enemy Action," in *Alexandria* (Louisiana) *Town Talk*, 6.

basin with mountains to the north and east. And it would take much longer for policymakers to effect meaningful progress in the battle against smog. Along the way, a group of determined women, fed up watching their children cough and wheeze, decided they had to light a fire under the men who were taking too long to solve a debilitating health hazard.

The Dark Side of Paradise

Beginning in the early twentieth century, Los Angeles business leaders had stoked the perception that the city was a bucolic land of fragrant orange groves, fresh air, warm sun, and nearby snow-capped mountains. Los Angeles is a "Paradise for Automobiles," one magazine ad in 1913 promised.[50] But as far back as 1542, Portuguese explorer Juan Rodriguez Cabrillo had named the region "Bahia de los Fumos," or Bay of Smoke, after sailing into San Pedro Bay.[51] It is believed that Cabrillo saw a pall of smoke hanging low over the basin from cooking fires in the Tongva villages that dotted the region. The smoke rose a few hundred feet, then hit the region's infamous inversion layer and flattened out. In 1903, smoky, brown air was mistaken for an eclipse of the sun.[52]

With the coming of World War II, overnight industrialization bore a heavy price tag—smokestacks belching smoke and fumes. Motorists were starting to traverse expansive Los Angeles suburbs on freeways. Hundreds of thousands of residents regularly burned their trash in backyard incinerators. Perhaps worst of all to civic boosters, the tourists that the business community had cultivated and attracted for so long were starting to complain. Still, the Los Angeles Chamber of Commerce, protective of industry, was accused of weakening local smog-control ordinances and defeating corrective legislation at the capitol. Gladwin Hill, stationed in Los Angeles for the *New York Times* beginning in the mid-forties, recalled that "business and industry . . . thought it was some kind of passing fad and wasn't here to stay."[53]

Dorothy Chandler, wife of *Los Angeles Times* publisher Norman Chandler, recalled that the two were driving over the mountains into the city one day, and she was struck by the ugly, brown haze that had settled over the valley. "Some-

---

[50] "Are You Going to Los Angeles?" Advertising Section, *Out West*, Out West Corporation, Los Angeles, September 1913, n.p., https://tinyurl.com/ycr6765c.

[51] J. Adam, "California in the Eighteenth Century," *Historical Society of Southern California*, 1886, 17, https://tinyurl.com/yarjrmx2.

[52] "The Southland's War on Smog: Fifty Years of Progress toward Clean Air," South Coast Air Quality Management District, 1997, http://www.aqmd.gov/home/library/public-information/publications/50-years-of-progress#The%20Arrival%20of%20Air%20Pollution.

[53] Gladwin Hill oral history, State Government Oral History Program, California State Archives, conducted by Carlos Vasquez, 1987, 146.

thing has to be done," she told Norman.[54] The *Times* created a full-time position of smog editor and asked residents to send in the names and addresses of any sources spewing smoke or fumes.[55]

Between 1946 and the late fifties, experts and politicians attacked the overhead plague with little tangible success. State legislation allowed counties to establish air pollution control districts; Los Angeles was the first, while other Southern California counties delayed. LA banned smudge pots—small fires used at night by citrus growers to prevent frost damage—and the use of backyard incinerators that hundreds of thousands of residents used to dispose of solid waste. "People would complain—especially women hanging up their washing outside—that the ashes and soot from the incinerators would soil their freshly laundered clothing before it got dry," said chemist Margaret Brunelle.[56] Officials imposed new regulations governing factory and oil refinery emissions and open burning in garbage dumps.

Cal Tech scientist Dr. Arie Haggen-Smit, considered the "father" of air pollution control, created artificial smog in his laboratory and concluded that emissions from tailpipes and oil refineries mixed with sunlight to produce smog. Fearing onerous regulation, the oil industry fought back, funding a study by the Stanford Research Institute that said Haggen-Smit's research was unproved speculation. Eventually, Haggen-Smit's theory was confirmed, but California wouldn't impose regulations cutting tailpipe emissions until the late sixties. The catalytic converter wasn't required until the mid-seventies.

The Women of Stamp Out Smog Take Charge

Despite the work of an army of scientists and task forces, plus the attention of governments that adopted a slew of new regulations, nothing seemed to work as wheezing, teary-eyed, throat-sore Southern Californians seethed. Schools, offices, and factories shut down, while traffic at times was kept off the freeways. In the midst of a lengthy smog siege in 1954, Governor Goodwin Knight refused to declare a state of extreme emergency, because it would mean "declaring martial law, stopping all cars and trucks, closing all industry which emits smoke or gas. The presence of the National Guard and soldiers patrolling the streets of Los Angeles will not cure smog."[57] As the smog alerts hit with increased frequency, a restless citizenry looked to gimmicks for help—from using cannons to tear a hole

---

[54] Benjamin Ross and Steven Amter, *The Polluters: The Making of Our Chemically Altered Environment* (New York: Oxford University Press, 2010), 79–80.

[55] Ed Ainsworth,"Citizens Invited to Report on Smog," *Los Angeles Times*, Oct 15, 1946, I1.

[56] The Southland's War on Smog: Fifty Years of Progress Toward Clean Air," South Coast Air Quality Management District, 1997, http://www.aqmd.gov/home/research/publications/50-years-of-progress .

[57] "Knight Pledges Aid for War on Smog," *Los Angeles Times*, October 21, 1954, I2; Daniel Nussbaum, "Bad Air Days," *Los Angeles Times Magazine*, July 19, 1998, http://articles.latimes.com/print/1998/jul/19/magazine/tm-5206.

in the inversion layer to building giant fans to blow the smog away. That idea was quashed when Dr. Haggen-Smit determined that the electricity needed to run the fans for just one day would require the output of Hoover Dam for eight years.[58] The issue turned deadly serious in 1956 when a 63-year-old carpenter fatally shot himself in the head. In a suicide note for his wife, Albion Nelson said, "I simply can't stand to be poisoned any longer by this terrible smog and fumes."[59]

With the battle against smog seemingly as stagnant as the air overhead, a nascent women's-only protest movement began in the mid-fifties. Forty-five hundred angry, foot-stomping citizens held a mass meeting in Pasadena and demanded that the county grand jury "conduct an inquiry to determine if officials have been guilty of dereliction of duty in the war against smog." Outside the auditorium, in one of the first all-women antismog protests, a small group of housewives and mothers demanded government action. The women wore gas masks, as did a three-year-old girl, and even her doll.[60] Citizen agitation helped shine the spotlight on public officials, but local antismog protest groups had short shelf-lives. That is, until the "smog ladies" arrived in late 1958. Margaret Levee of Beverly Hills, the wife of a Hollywood producer, was an early enlistee to the cause after she had to rush her two-year-old daughter to the hospital with a severe asthma attack. Doctors told her that the thick brown haze was bad for her daughter and that she should leave the Los Angeles area. "I decided to stay and do something about air pollution," she said.[61] Levee called eight of her friends—affluent housewives and mothers—most of whom had husbands prominent in the entertainment industry. Described as socialites on a mission, they created a tiny but vocal protest group called Stamp Out Smog.

When that handful of well-connected women created Stamp Out Smog, they did so as protectors of their children. "Women weren't seen as prime movers back then, but their powerful husbands were," says Hedy Govenar, who joined the organization in the early 1970s. "These women belonged to powerful families in the community and took advantage of it. When you have 80 women with kids in their arms coming to a board of supervisors meeting, it not only was newsworthy, but it didn't go unnoticed by the men who had the vote."[62]

---

[58] "Can't We Just Blow All This Smog Away?" South Coast Air Quality Management District, http://www.aqmd.gov/home/library/public-information/publications/unusual-smog-busting-ideas.

[59] "Man Writes Note Assailing Smog, Then Ends His Life," *Los Angeles Times*, September 20, 1956, I5.

[60] "4,500 Hear Demand for Smog Probe," *Los Angeles Times*, October 21, 1954, I2; Nancy Unger, *Beyond Nature's Housekeepers: American Women in Environmental History* (New York: Oxford University Press, 2012), 144.

[61] Lucy Kavaler, "How Los Angeles Women Are Fighting Smog—and Winning," *Family Circle*, September 1968, 55.

[62] Hedy Govenar interview, Sacramento, May 16, 2017.

A Leader of Thousands—Margaret Levee

Margaret Levee became Stamp Out Smog's first leader. In announcing formation of the group, SOS said it hoped to be "a rallying point for a vast regiment of housewives dedicated to the ultimate elimination of smog."[63] The women conducted eye-catching publicity stunts to help galvanize public opinion, and they took turns keeping watch and reporting on the output of black smoke from refineries and factories. They quickly realized that to influence state and local officials and effectively rebut oil and gas industry economists and scientists, they'd have to understand the intricacies of smog science and use their technical expertise to back up their arguments with facts. They described themselves as "amateurs in politics but willing to learn." In short order, they consulted scientists, doctors, and key lawmakers, studied complex technical analyses and papers on smog and cancer, were briefed by the county's Air Pollution Control District, and toured a Southern California Edison plant. Stamp Out Smog quickly outgrew Margaret Levee's living room and soon boasted a respected, influential statewide coalition of groups as disparate as the Los Angeles Optometric Association and United Hostesses that combined had individual membership in the tens of thousands.

SOS leaders understood that smog didn't respect political boundaries and demanded an urgent, coordinated state response. They pushed for auto exhaust standards, changes to fuel composition, better coordinated scientific research, and rapid transit in southern California. Members peppered oil companies with letters demanding that they reduce the smog-producing elements in their gasoline. Less than a year after its formation, Stamp Out Smog had welcomed more than 400 separate women's groups under its umbrella and was earning a reputation as a tenacious fighter for families fed up with dirty air. "SOS probably packs the most concentrated and potent feminine determination ever directed towards achievement of a common goal in the long history of our Golden State," one newspaper editorialized. "Woe betide the hapless politician or industrialist who fails to show complete cooperation."[64]

Leaders of Stamp Out Smog believed working through the legislature rather than the ballot box would deliver the best results. The members' political connections, recognition, and affluence undoubtedly helped them get a private audience with the governor to press their agenda. At Governor Edmund G. (Pat) Brown's request, Southern California assemblyman Ronald Cameron carried a bill to require exhaust control devices on all new cars sold in the state. SOS activated phone trees and chain letters to boost turnout at Sacramento committee hearings and paid for newspaper ads urging readers to send letters to Brown and legisla-

[63] "Women's Group Joins Fight on Air Pollution," *Los Angeles Times*, January 8, 1959, B1.
[64] "What Women Want," *Palm Springs Desert Sun*, October 8, 1959, 4.

tors. "Tell them," the ad said, "our health and well-being are more important than special interests."[65]

The pressure worked; the legislature approved the California Motor Vehicle Control Act, the nation's first-ever statewide air pollution control law.[66] The act created a new board to set standards for the devices. Brown hailed the board as representing the "best . . . expert thinking" on air pollution. It included scientists, public health officers, academics, motor vehicle experts, and Margaret Levee.[67] Later, Levee was the only woman to attend when the auto industry invited board members to a meeting with the heads of the biggest car companies in the nation. Someone leaned over and whispered in her ear, "Tell me—how are you going to scare *them*?" Levee casually responded, "Perhaps I'll tell them that SOS will get the public to decide not to buy a new car every year or so."[68]

Public pressure from Stamp Out Smog and its legions of new environmentalists gave political cover to lawmakers who wanted to oppose the powerful oil and auto industries and often made the difference between victory and defeat. The women would bring their children—wearing gas masks—to colorful news conferences, and they regularly testified at packed governmental hearings in their communities and Sacramento. "I know I can count on them when I need them," acknowledged Dr. Haggen-Smit, who became the first chair of California's Air Resources Board.[69] In 1967, Michigan congressman John Dingell introduced an industry-written amendment to the Federal Air Quality Act to strip California of its authority to write smog rules that exceeded federal standards. Word of the amendment came during one of Los Angeles's notorious smog sieges, and the local media and grassroots organizations reacted angrily and moved quickly. A hasty campaign generated hundreds of thousands of letters and postcards to Congress that were dumped on the capitol steps in Washington, and the amendment was defeated.[70]

Savvy in the ways of publicity, the women of Stamp Out Smog grew ever more effective. As the smog plague showed few signs of abating, their numbers grew, bringing garden clubs, health associations, labor unions, churches, and environmental and other groups under their umbrella, demanding action from public

---

[65] "We're Sick of SMOG!" *Los Angeles Times*, March 2, 1960, I12.

[66] Robert Blanchard, "Legislature Passes Smog Control Bill," *Los Angeles Times*, April 6, 1960, I1; "Governor Signs Car Smog Bill," Associated Press in the *Long Beach Independent*, April 14, 1960, 1.

[67] "Smog Devices Board Named," Associated Press in the *San Mateo Times*, May 26, 1960, 10.

[68] Kavaler, 99.

[69] Ibid.

[70] Chip Jacobs and William J. Kelly, *Smogtown: The Lung-Burning History of Pollution in Los Angeles* (Woodstock, N.Y.: The Overlook Press, 2008), 176–77; Roger Karapin, *Political Opportunities for Climate Policy: California, New York and the Federal Government* (New York: Cambridge University Press, 2016), 122; Ray Kovitz, "Laws Won't Get Rid of Smog, But They Help," *Los Angeles Times*, August 18, 1968, Section G, 3.

Figure 7.3. Stamp Out Smog Rally, Los Angeles, 1969
Credit: Courtesy of Los Angeles Public Library

officials. In 1968, 475 organizations belonged to the coalition. "SOS is more potent than any women's organization I've ever heard of—anywhere," said Louis J.
Fuller, Los Angeles County's chief air pollution officer. "These SOS women are
afraid of no one."[71]

Long-time environmental lobbyist V. John White, who wrote and shepherded
many clean-air measures as a capitol staffer, says the SOS women who uprooted
their lives to come to Sacramento had a decisive impact. "The idea that Detroit had
created this noxious phenomenon in Southern California took root in part because
of outside pressure from groups like the smog ladies. Those days, nobody else
in the world had smog like us. The women created a sense that public wellbeing
was at risk."[72] In the late sixties, two Los Angeles television stations recognized
the booming public interest in air pollution and hired full-time environmental
reporters. KNBC's Stan Atkinson reported on smog issues nearly every day in the

---

[71] Kavaler, 96.
[72] V. John White interview, Sacramento, January 23, 2017.

first half of 1969 and found an accepting audience. "Smog was *the* issue, because people were really fed up with it," he says, "and there were steps being taken that were seen as being useful and starting to produce results."[73]

A New Generation Takes Up the SOS Banner— Sabrina Schiller

Sabrina Scharf was in her mid-twenties when she joined Stamp Out Smog in the late sixties. She would spend two decades as an outspoken volunteer activist, heading large coalitions and serving on the board of the South Coast Air Quality Management District. She was a former Playboy Bunny in the midst of a 10-year acting career that included roles in productions such as The Man from U.N.C.L.E, Easy Rider, and Star Trek. But she acknowledged feeling unfulfilled as an actress and wanted to contribute to L.A.'s fight against smog. When she married TV writer Bob Schiller, who was 25 years her senior, she agonized over his daily commute to work, "being stuck in traffic and breathing that junk. I remember worrying that freeway levels of carbon monoxide can cause heart attacks," she says.[74]

Schiller organized well-attended publicity events and hounded newspaper reporters. She was convinced a few lifestyle changes—particularly ending Southern Californians' love affair with their cars—would make a difference. In 1971, she poured everything into "Share a Ride Day," which was hailed as the city's first organized demonstration of the improvement that could be achieved through carpools and increased bus ridership. SOS partnered with another advocacy group, Operation Oxygen. "We've just got to load those cars and pack those buses," Schiller said in the buildup to the event. "We don't dare make promises, but if 'Share a Ride Day' succeeds, we'll see a decrease in traffic congestion and maybe even a difference in the smog."[75]

"Share a Ride Day" received a big publicity push. Using her Hollywood connections, Schiller enlisted Paramount studios to film free public service announcements featuring Lucille Ball, the cast of the Brady Bunch, and other entertainment stars. The Burroughs Corp., a company that manufactured mainframe computers, volunteered to use its hardware to organize carpools. The Southern California Rapid Transit District agreed to run special ecology express buses nonstop from suburbs to downtown Los Angeles, while one of the city's top-rated radio stations placed reporters on the buses to record the event.

---

[73] Stan Atkinson interview, Sacramento, January 12, 2017. Atkinson's smog beat only lasted six months. On August 9, 1968, police discovered the murdered bodies of actress Sharon Tate, her unborn child, and three others in Los Angeles. Atkinson was reassigned to the sensational Charles Manson story for the ensuing 16 months.

[74] Sabrina Schiller interview, Los Angeles, by telephone, June 25, 2017.

[75] Lynn Lilliston, "Smog Foes Take Aim at the Lone Rider," *Los Angeles Times*, September 15, 1971, View1.

Schiller wasn't prepared for what happened next—"Share a Ride Day" was a complete bust. The freeways were just as clogged as ever with little evidence that commuters had doubled up. They didn't turn to transit, either. A total of six people rode on the special buses, and four of them did it by mistake; they were simply waiting for their regular bus. Schiller was stationed at one of the bus locations and had baked a huge six-foot cake to share with riders. "At our bus center, not one person showed up. Not one person. It was completely devastating," she remembers with a chuckle nearly 50 years later.[76] The fiasco, however, did give activists a powerful new talking point in their parallel campaign to establish a strict vehicle inspection mandate: "If people won't carpool, you'll have to clean up the cars,"[77] Hedy Govenar recalls.

The early seventies was a transition period for Stamp Out Smog, as that first generation of women smog fighters handed the reins to a new group of leaders, and then faded into history. "SOS was *the* group," Schiller told an interviewer in 1980. "But it just plain got tired. There's only so much you can do for so long when no one gets paid."[78] Other groups emerged in its place, most notably, the Coalition for Clean Air. Schiller became its unpaid project coordinator, and promoted approaches that included the state smog-check legislation.

Smog Ladies Helped Reshape the American Auto Industry

The modern environmental movement generally is considered to have begun in the early 1960s after Rachel Carson's searing book *Silent Spring* shocked the nation into thinking critically about how technological progress could be ruining the planet. In the two decades before Carson's revelations, Los Angeles residents had been dealing with their own unique consequence of progress, and the women of Stamp Out Smog were the first to give the protest movement its voice and cohesion. They faced resistance from male policymakers who thought they were uninformed, quixotic, and playing in an arena where women didn't belong. But for these women, their crusade was personal. They learned the science behind smog and quickly figured out how to galvanize public opinion by getting the media to tell their stories. "They [policymakers] just avoided us, ignored us, and patronized us," Schiller remembers, "patting us on the head, saying 'nice girls, nice girls.' But when we put feet on the street, that's when it started making a difference."[79]

By channeling public anger into advocacy, the women of Stamp Out Smog and successor organizations have helped to remake the auto industry by pressuring public policymakers to mandate that car makers design cleaner cars for the huge California market. "[W]e were the first place to discover smog and to begin

---

[76] Schiller interview.

[77] Govenar interview.

[78] Joy Horowitz, "Grass Roots Effort Revived, *Los Angeles Times*, October 9, 1980, View1.

[79] Schiller interview.

to take action to deal with the problem of pollution caused by motor vehicles," says Mary Nichols, who for a generation has been one of the nation's most accomplished smog-fighters—at the California Air Resources Board (twice), the US Environmental Protection Agency, and as Secretary for the state Resources Agency. "California buys about 10 percent of all the new cars that are sold every year. But we have even more influence than that over the design of future vehicles because every car manufacturer from the largest to the most innovative start-ups uses us as a design laboratory."[80]

California's requirements for catalytic converters, reformulated fuels and improved engine efficiency have paid dividends that surprised even researchers, thanks in large part to SOS. A 2010 study by Environment California, a citizen-based environmental advocacy group, found vehicle emissions were 99 percent cleaner than they were in 1960.[81] Scientists at the National Oceanic and Atmospheric Administration reported that vehicle-related air pollution in the Los Angeles basin—which, at high levels, harms lungs and damages crops—had decreased by 98 percent since the sixties.[82]

From the wreckage of Sabrina Schiller's failed ride-sharing experiment sprang a growing public recognition that carpooling can reduce pollution as well as ameliorate traffic congestion. In 1993, there were 58 High Occupancy Vehicle lanes in Los Angeles County. By 2010, the number of carpool lanes had increased nine-fold, and today they carry more people than any other HOV system in the US.[83] Schiller feels vindicated: "Before 'Share a Ride Day,' no one had ever considered carpooling as an antismog measure. I'm happy that social attitudes have changed. It was such an uphill battle."[84]

Despite significant improvements over the decades, many California cities remain the smoggiest in the US. In 2016, scientists at New York University and the American Thoracic Society released a study finding that 3,632 Californians— more than half in the Los Angeles-Long Beach-Glendale area—die prematurely

---

[80] Mary Nichols interview, *YaleEnvironment360,* conducted by Paul Rogers, February 8, 2012, http://e360.yale.edu/features/californias_clean_car_rules_help_remake_us_auto_industry.

[81] "California Makes Clean Car History, Again," Environment California, January 27, 2012, www.environmentcalifornia.org/news/cae/california-makes-clean-car-history-again; "California Cars 99% Cleaner Than in 1960s, But Smog Levels Still High, Study Says*, Los Angeles Times*, November 16, 2010, http://latimesblogs.latimes.com/technology/2010/11/california-cars-99-cleaner-than-in-1960s-but-smog-levels-still-high-study-says.html.

[82] "NOAA, Partners Find 50-Year Decline in Some Los Angeles Vehicle-Related Pollutants," *National Oceanic and Atmospheric Administration*, August 9, 2012, http://www.noaanews.noaa.gov/stories2012/20120809_laairqualitystudy.html.

[83] Los Angeles County Metropolitan Transportation Authority: LA County HOV system, https://www.metro.net/projects/hov/hov_system/.

[84] Schiller interview.

from polluted air each year.[85] The grassroots battle that Margaret Levee and eight of her friends birthed in late 1958—and which continues under different banners and with a new cast of characters—couldn't eliminate the smog scourge in Southern California. Neither could an army of some of the nation's best scientific minds. But from its first news conference and initial shaping of the state's landmark Motor Vehicle Pollution Control Board, the women of Stamp Out Smog helped accelerate government's response to this natural and manmade malady. They amassed vocal adherents numbering in the thousands, changed attitudes, and influenced laws that continue to relieve air pollution for families and communities.

Warren Dorn served 16 years as a Los Angeles County supervisor, roughly coinciding with Stamp Out Smog's lifecycle. An asthmatic, Dorn's primary policy focus was on fighting smog. Shortly before he retired from the board, he noted that about 150 rules governing air pollution had been enacted. "And it certainly would have been difficult to get through without the support of SOS, with their testimony and petitions and children with gas masks."[86] Afton Slade, one of the group's presidents, recalled speaking to Los Angeles area parent-teacher associations. "At one meeting a woman got up and said to me, 'Sure—air pollution is bad, but what can a bunch of women do about it?'"[87]

Discussion Questions

1. In what ways did the goals of white clubwomen described in this chapter seem to differ from the orientation of black women's clubs? How might their missions have been considered similar? Could they conceivably have worked together during these years?

2. What factors contributed to the buildup of Los Angeles smog during the 1940s and '50s and the rise of a female-led movement to combat it?

3. How did the founders of Stamp Out Smog turn it into an especially potent women's organization?

4. Describe the links between the fashion industry and the birth of women's activism in the conservation movement.

5. What legislative victories were achieved by Catherine Hittell and other women advocates of protecting birdlife in the early years of the twentieth century?

6. For what reasons did men become the public faces of Audubon chapters that were organized by women? Do you think women believed this masculinity helped their cause?

---

[85] Kevin Cromar, et al., "Health of the Air," Marron Institute of Urban Management, New York University and American Thoracic Society, August 2016, http://thoracic.org/about/newsroom/press-releases/journal/health-of-air-report.pdf.

[86] Kavaler, 99.

[87] Ibid., 100.

7. What successful strategies did the women of the California Club pursue in the decades-long quest to save the giant groves of Sequoias in Calaveras and Tuolumne counties? (Are the groves available for viewing today?)
8. Josephine Clifford McCracken, a writer and leading conservationist who made a difference in saving the coastal redwoods, traveled in the same circles as Mark Twain, Bret Harte, and Ambrose Bierce. Why do you suppose that, unlike her male contemporaries, she and her legacy are largely overlooked today?
9. For what reasons do you think that saving the ancient redwood groves in the Sierra Nevada foothills and along the central and northern coasts proved to be a well-suited cause for women's clubs? How is tribute paid today to the California Federation of Women's Clubs in Humboldt Redwoods State Park?
10. How did Margaret Levee and the other leaders of Stamp Out Smog ready themselves to do battle with the oil and gas industry? What lasting impacts were achieved by these smog fighters and their successors?

Recommended Reading

Binkley, Cameron. "No Better Heritage than Living Trees: Women's Clubs and Early Conservation in Humboldt County." *Western Historical Quarterly* 33 (2002): 179–203, https://www.jstor.org/stable/4144802?seq=1#page_scan_tab_contents.

Grant, Madison. *Saving the Redwoods: An Account of the Movement during 1919 to Preserve the Redwoods of California* (1919). Whitefish, MT: Kessinger Legacy Reprints, 2010. [Originally in *Zoological Society Bulletin*, September 1919.]

Jacobs, Chip, and William J. Kelly. *Smogtown: The Lung-Burning History of Pollution in Los Angeles*. Woodstock, NY: Overlook Press, 2008.

Unger, Nancy. *Beyond Nature's Housekeepers: American Women in Environmental History*. New York: Oxford University Press, 2012.

Chapter 8

1960–1975
Second Feminist Wave Breaks Down Barriers
for Women and Minorities

> "You need to behave like ladies, but demonstrate
> that you can do the job of men."
> —Kimberly Smith, aide to Assemblywoman March Fong

It was supposed to have been a routine political speech three weeks before primary election day in 1950. Helen Gahagan Douglas, a member of the US House of Representatives from Los Angeles, was running for the Democratic nomination for Senate. A victory would set up a showdown against Republican House member Richard Nixon. Douglas had been invited to the University of Southern California by a young alumnus, Jesse Unruh, who was a rising local figure in the party. After Douglas hopped onto a trailer in front of the school library and began her speech, she was blindsided by pranksters. Members of Skull and Dagger, a campus honorary fraternity, were holding an initiation that day, and they pulled up in a horse-drawn hay wagon wearing only underwear, tuxedo jackets and top hats. Their shouting drowned out her speech, and they sprayed her with seltzer water and covered her with hay.

News of the incident found its way into newspapers all over California. United Press quoted USC president Fred. D. Fagg, Jr., as saying the prank was "unpremeditated but went beyond the bounds of gentlemanly conduct."[1] Douglas took the embarrassing incident in stride. "Boys will be boys," she told the campus newspaper. "I don't know what I was squirted with, but I hope it wasn't beer—I hate beer."[2] One witness later told Douglas that the attack in fact was directed from the edge of the crowd by two USC graduates. He identified one of them as Joe Holt, who later became a staffer in Nixon's Senate office. The other was Patrick J. Hillings, the GOP candidate to succeed Nixon in the House.[3] (In later years, Skull and Dagger included several members who would be sent to prison

---

[1] "Hay, Seltzer Water Greet Helen Douglas," United Press, in the *San Mateo Times*, May 17, 1950, 5.

[2] USC *Daily Trojan*, May 17, 1950, in Greg Mitchell, *Tricky Dick and the Pink Lady* (New York: Random House, 1998), 36.

[3] Helen Gahagan Douglas, *A Full Life* (Garden City, NY: Doubleday & Company, Inc., 1982), 313.

for various Watergate crimes while working in the Nixon White House.) Douglas would go on to capture her party's nomination and face a relentless Richard Nixon who accused her of being a Communist sympathizer.

He and his campaign team shredded her reputation and sent a clear signal that the political arena was not a place for the faint of heart. In an autobiography more than three decades after her defeat, Douglas reasoned that men "have been running the country for the past two hundred years and are meant to do so for centuries to come. In short," she continued, "men would never share power with women willingly. If we wanted it, we would have to take it."

A Liberal in a Conservative Time— Helen Gahagan Douglas

Helen Gahagan Douglas was a former actress and opera singer who became involved in politics after a 1937 concert tour that took her to Hitler's Germany. When she returned to the US, she and her actor/husband Mervyn Douglas started speaking out about Nazism. An unabashed liberal, Douglas served as an official in the California Democratic Party and in 1944 became only the third California woman elected to the House and the first to win without succeeding a deceased husband. In one of her early votes, she sabotaged a bill that was quietly maneuvering through Congress to give control of the nation's atomic arsenal to the military. Douglas mailed copies of the legislation to newspapers across the country urging their editorial support for civilian oversight of atomic weapons. She received their support, and the final product—the Atomic Energy Act—placed atomic energy under civilian control.[4]

Since the end of World War II, a frightened nation had become fixated on the burgeoning Soviet threat and the need for displays of American loyalty against communism. In a speech on the House floor in 1946, Douglas said, "Communism has no place in our society. We have something better."[5] But she deplored the anti-Communist zealots who, she believed, were undermining the fabric of democracy. She was one of only 17 representatives to vote against contempt citations for 10 Hollywood producers and writers who had refused to cooperate with the House Un-American Activities Committee. She also voted to withhold funds from the committee, opposed loyalty checks on federal employees, and later cast a vote against a bill that would have outlawed communism, because she thought the legislation was unconstitutional.

After three terms in the House, Douglas set her sights on the US Senate. She burned some bridges in her party when she decided to challenge incumbent Democratic senator Sheridan Downey, who promptly dropped out of the race citing

---

[4] Maria Braden, *Women Politicians and the Media* (Lexington: The University Press of Kentucky, 1996), 46.

[5] Helen Gahagan Douglas, *A Full Life,* (Garden City, NY: Doubleday & Co. 1982), 232.

health reasons. Many leading Democrats believed she should have stayed in the House. India Edwards, the vice chair of the Democratic National Committee in 1950, said Douglas was surrounded by" idolaters" who told her "there never has been anybody in Congress like you, that you are the greatest thing that has come to Washington since Abraham Lincoln, and you begin to think it's true."[6]

The vicious red-baiting campaign against Douglas didn't start with Nixon. Late in the primary campaign, as Douglas recalled in her autobiography, the *Los Angeles Daily News* "called me 'the pink lady,' a tag that stuck."[7] The newspaper was owned by Matthew Boddy, her Democratic opponent, who defined the contest as freedom versus socialism. Shortly thereafter, the *Santa Monica Evening Outlook* called her an "ally of Communist party hard-liners [who] has given aid and comfort to un-American traitors and conspirators,[8] while the *Santa Ana Register* commented, "Mrs. Douglas has travelled the pink fringe."[9]

The "Pink Lady" vs. "Tricky Dick"

Still, Douglas won the primary easily, setting up the fall showdown with Nixon and his cutthroat campaign pro Murray Chotiner. "The purpose of an election," Chotiner said, "is not to defeat your opponent, but to destroy him."[10] The Nixon team would make Douglas's liberal leanings the singular issue, and the timing was perfect. The Soviets had been flexing their muscles in Eastern Europe and tested an atomic bomb in 1949. Communists had taken control of China, and mere days after the general campaign began, American soldiers started dying in Korea fighting Communists. There were concerns that Communist spies were lurking on street corners and had infiltrated the government.

Nixon's strategists had their issue, but they were uncertain how to attack a female political opponent without appearing to be a bully. There wasn't a great deal of history running a rough-and-tumble political campaign against a woman. Douglas was one of only nine women in the House of Representatives, and Margaret Chase Smith of Maine was the only one in the Senate. At a strategy session in Santa Barbara, the Nixon team hashed out an understated gender line of attack. The candidate, himself, "argued for carefully modulating his approach," according to Greg Mitchell, author of an analysis of the Senate race. But that attitude apparently masked his private deep-seated low regard for women. Nixon biographer Fawn Brodie wrote that press secretary James Bassett, "who was witness to

---

[6] India Edwards oral history, "Helen Gahagan Douglas Project, California Democrats: The View from Washington," conducted by Gabrielle Morris, 1981, Regional Oral History Office, Bancroft Library, University of California, Berkeley, 19.

[7] Douglas, 301.

[8] "The Record of Helen Gahagan Douglas," *Santa Monica Evening Outlook*, May 18, 1950, 4.

[9] "Nixon Outstanding US Candidate," *Santa Ana Register*, 22.

[10] Colleen M. O'Connor, "Pink Right Down to Her Underwear," *Los Angeles Times*, April 9, 1990, B9.

some painful scenes of Nixon humiliating his wife, said he had 'a total scorn for female mentality.'"[11] Nixon decided to subtly introduce the gender issue during campaign appearances by commenting how difficult a rugged campaign was on a woman. Frank Jorgensen, a Nixon campaign manager and fundraiser told the Nixon strategists, "I've learned enough in politics to know the average woman reasons with her emotions rather than her head."[12] The hope was that Douglas eventually would snap under the constant onslaught of having to defend her controversial votes in Congress.

Nixon publicly dismissed any suggestion that he might attack Douglas's qualifications based on her sex. He pledged he would "indulge in no name-calling or smearing tactics," but her voting record was fair game. "If she had had her way," Nixon told rallies, "the Communist conspiracy in the United States would never have been exposed."[13] Chotiner printed a half-million leaflets on pink paper listing Douglas's votes that coincided with those made by accused Communist Vito Marcantonio, a New York congressman. When Douglas wanted to talk about civil rights, reclamation, or the oil industry's influence on public policy, hecklers in the audience quizzed her on the bills on the pink sheet. "Every time I heard myself explaining that I really was a good, loyal citizen," Douglas said, "I felt ashamed and debased."[14] In a carefully crafted whispering campaign, voters received phone calls informing them that Douglas was a Communist who was married to a Jew. Privately, Nixon insinuated that Douglas slept with President Harry Truman, and a prominent book editor told her he once heard Nixon say, "Helen Gahagan Douglas is pink right down to her underwear."[15] Some white Republican women received postcards from a nonexistent "Communist League of Negro Women" touting Douglas.[16] She said her worst campaign experience, however, "a sight I couldn't shake, was when children picked up rocks and threw them at my car, at me."[17]

---

[11] Fawn Brodie, *Richard Nixon: The Shaping of His Character* (New York: W. W. Norton and Company, 1981), 235.

[12] Mitchell, 169; Frank E. Jorgensen oral history, "Richard Nixon in the Warren Era: The Organizations of Richard Nixon's Congressional Campaigns 1946–1952," conducted by Amelia Fry, 1980, Regional Oral History Office, Bancroft Library, University of California, Berkeley, 45.

[13] "Opponent Douglas Assailed by Nixon," *Los Angeles Times*, September 19, 1950, I2.

[14] Douglas, 316.

[15] Douglas, 327; Lamar Waldron, *Watergate: The Hidden History: Nixon, the Mafia, and the CIA* (Berkeley: Counterpoint, 2012), 49; David Halberstam, *The Powers That Be* (New York: Alfred A Knopf, 1979), 263.

[16] Mitchell, 230.

[17] Douglas, 334.

A Two-Front War—Douglas against Nixon and the *LA Times*

Douglas later acknowledged that she didn't respond adequately to the barrage of charges, partly because she was busy splitting time between the campaign and her duties in Congress, and partly because she thought the accusations were so "absolutely ridiculous, absolutely absurd" they were unlikely to stick. It was a grave miscalculation.[18] "I was always off balance," she said in her autobiography. "The fabricated stories came at me like a mudslide; I couldn't keep up with it."[19] While Douglas's reputation and electoral hopes were taking a beating, Nixon was earning a new nickname. The Douglas campaign sent out a press release that referred to Nixon as "this tricky young man." The *Independent Review*, a pro-Democratic weekly publication, picked up on it and mistakenly predicted that voters would send "little Tricky Dick Nixon" into "the gutters of political oblivion."[20]

Much of the fusillade against Douglas came from the news and editorial pages of the *Los Angeles Times*, the state's dominant newspaper. Kyle Palmer, the paper's political editor and GOP kingmaker, had convinced Nixon to run for the Senate in the first place. "The *Times* covered Nixon as if he were a favored son," wrote Bill Boyarsky in his history of the newspaper.[21] While Nixon subtly brought gender into the campaign, the *Times* was blunt. In one column, Palmer characterized Douglas as "emotional" four times and "dramatic" twice. He relayed an occasion where she cried "volatile tears," and called her "a veritable political butterfly flitting from flower to flower."[22] The newspaper attacked her mercilessly and treated Nixon with kid gloves. If Democrats defected to Nixon, it made headlines. A week before the election the *Times* ran on its news pages a last-minute appeal for election-day volunteers to keep "leftwing Helen Gahagan Douglas" out of the Senate.[23] In an editorial the following day, The *Times* called her "The Darling of the Parlor Pinks" who voted the Communist party line innumerable times in Congress.[24] Writing about the *Times*, author David Halberstam said, "Mrs. Douglas's voice was never heard. She was never covered; she was only attacked."[25] Her campaign was forced to buy ads in order to publicize upcoming public appearances. Syndicated columnist Drew Pearson was one journalist who did come to

---

[18] Helen Gahagan Douglas oral history, "Helen Gahagan Douglas Project, Vol. IV: Congresswoman, Actress, and Opera Singer," conducted by Amelia Fry, 1982, Regional Oral History Office, Bancroft Library, University of California, Berkeley, 208.

[19] Douglas, 310, 317.

[20] Mitchell, 184.

[21] Bill Boyarsky, *Inventing L.A.: The Chandlers and Their Times* (Santa Monica: Angel City Press, 2009), 123.

[22] Kyle Palmer, "Is the Play the Thing?" *Los Angeles Times*, September 10, 1950, II4.

[23] "Nixon Women's Group Seeks More Workers," *Los Angeles Times*, October 30, 1950, II4.

[24] "The Four Big Senatorial Races: The Darling of the Parlor Pinks," *Los Angeles Times*, October 31, 1950, II4.

[25] Halberstam, 263.

her rescue. Ten days before the election, he called Nixon's election effort full of distortions and "one of the most skilled and cutthroat campaigns . . . I have ever witnessed." He argued "this brand of unfair politics" would not help him with the fair-minded American electorate in the long run.[26]

Nixon won a smashing victory, earning 60 percent of the statewide vote. He had ridden the national wave of anti-Communist hysteria, and Douglas was caught in the undertow. "It is discouraging to women everywhere," commented New Jersey's Mary Norton, who served with Douglas in Congress.[27] The campaign launched Nixon's political ascent—with a few hiccups along the way—until the Watergate scandal brought down his presidency in 1974. A bumper sticker circulating during the Watergate hearings proclaimed: "Don't Blame Me—I voted for Helen Gahagan Douglas."[28] When Douglas died in 1980 at the age of 79, she rated a front-page story and editorial in the *Times*, which had so plagued her during the Senate campaign. The newspaper under publisher Otis Chandler had moderated its editorial views since his father, Norman Chandler, ran the paper in the 1940s and '50s. The editorial didn't comment on the role the *Times* played in the election 30 years earlier, but it noted Nixon's campaign of "innuendo piled on innuendo," and it called Douglas "a gracious person of many talents . . . best remembered for her political courage."[29]

In her autobiography, Douglas said she harbored no burden of resentment after her defeat. "I wasn't a soul in torment who would brood about Richard Nixon for years to come," she said. "He hadn't touched me." But for many others, the bitter scars of 1950 lingered for years and may have been responsible for a dearth of women coming forward to run for political office. In all, 25 women sought statewide, congressional, or legislative office in 1950. But the number of women candidates dropped precipitously in the following seven elections—including to a low of 11 in 1958.[30]

Champion of Rural Northern California— Pauline Davis

One woman who reversed the trend was Pauline Davis, a no-nonsense Democratic assemblywoman from sparsely populated Plumas County who would leave a legacy of accomplishments in state water policy during a political career that spanned a quarter century. A second-generation Czech-American, she grew up in

---

[26] Drew Pearson, "Washington Merry-Go-Round," *Altoona Tribune*, October 28, 1950, 4.

[27] Quoted in Mitchell, 247.

[28] Patt Morrison, "Helen Gahagan Douglas, Ex-Congresswoman, Dies," *Los Angeles Times*, June 29, 1980, I1.

[29] Morrison; "In Memory of Principle and Courage," *Los Angeles Times*, July 1, 1980, II4.

[30] California Statements of Vote, 1950–1964, California Secretary of State.

a Nebraska farming family that lost everything when the banks closed during the Depression. She married after high school, had two daughters, but her alcoholic husband abandoned the family. To make ends meet, she worked as a housekeeper, a telephone operator, and even found a job plucking chickens. Moving to California for a fresh start in the 1940s, she met and married Lester Davis and had a son. Pauline was working in Lester's office in 1952, when he died from a heart attack during his campaign for a fourth term as a rural assemblyman. The state Industrial Accident Commission judged his death was "caused by his employment as a legislator."[31] At an emergency party convention, she was selected to take her husband's place on the November ballot and narrowly won her first of 12 terms.

In 1953, legislators earned $300 a month in salary and $14 a day in living expenses when they were in session or attended interim committee hearings.[32] "When she was first elected, the only money coming in was this part-time job as a legislator," recalls her son Rodney, who was three years old at the time. "She would finagle her way to be appointed to every committee imaginable, and she'd go to these committee hearings throughout the state and secure whatever per diem she could. That's how she made ends meet," her son said.[33] In between interim hearings, Davis would hit the road—with Rodney in the back seat—and make constituent calls in a far-flung, seven-county district of nearly 26,000 square miles. Sometimes, his older sister would make the trip, as well.

During her first term, Davis was joined by Kathryn Niehouse and newcomer Dorothy Donahoe as the only three women in the assembly. Although Niehouse had been in office for 10 years, the male hierarchy at the capitol was slow to accommodate the women. While the men had a restroom and lounge adjacent to the assembly floor, women lawmakers had to exit the chambers and walk down a hall to a public facility. Reporter John Jervis remembers women finally getting their own restroom in the late '50s. "We called it 'Pauline's potty.'"[34] Women also had to fend off gender-specific political attacks. Rodney remembers when he was nine years old, and his mother was seeking her fourth term in office, an opponent's operatives showed up at his school and met with the principal "to see if I was having trouble in school so they could saddle my mom with the charge that she was being an inadequate mother by having a political career while being a widow."[35]

Women in the Legislature Forced to Prove Themselves

From her first days in the legislature, Davis was concerned about her credibility. Women who ventured into the daunting world of politics were curiosities

---

[31] "The Financial Resources of California's Legislators: Pauline L. Davis (D-Portola)," *Los Angeles Times*, September 15, 1965, IV4.

[32] Ed Capps, United Press, in the *Santa Rosa Press Democrat*, August 20, 1953, 3.

[33] Rodney Davis interview, Sacramento, June 26, 2017.

[34] John Jervis interview, Sacramento, August 10, 2017.

[35] Davis interview.

who had to earn the respect of men who controlled the machinery of government. "Any time any legislator tells you that they have no opposition to a woman in a public office," Davis once said, "don't you believe it."[36] Davis said it took 10 years before she was fully accepted by her male counterparts. She advised the next generation of women legislators to train themselves to understand how men think, and then maneuver around it. Calling her male colleagues "front-page publicity seekers" with big egos, Davis said that to get certain bills passed, there were occasions when she would let the men take the credit.[37]

Davis conscientiously cultivated an image as a blunt, plain-speaking advocate for California's far northeastern counties that encompassed her district. To boost her credibility, she became tougher and stronger on various issues than the men, and she didn't back down from a fight. In an oral history for the Bancroft Library, she told of a particularly bitter dispute with an unnamed assembly speaker (she worked with seven speakers during her career), who demanded she support one of his bills. "No, I am a no vote," she told him firmly. He insisted, "You are going to vote for this bill." Davis responded, "Apparently your hearing is not as good as it should be. I am a no vote." After she voted against his bill in committee, Davis said the speaker went on an "abusive" tirade in which he threatened to kill all her bills. Davis ignored the threat, and after the vote he followed her down a corridor to her office. "Now, look," she said, "if you continue using this type of language—you are welcome to come into my office, but I must tell you that I will not guarantee that I will not slap your face."[38] Davis said the speaker gave her a bad time after that. Former Senator Gary K. Hart, whose legislative career briefly overlapped with Davis's, said "she put the fear of God in you. She was not to be tampered with." John Burton, who worked with Davis for 10 years in the assembly, put it simply: "I liked her. She was a tough broad."[39]

With singular purpose, Davis became a fierce protector of her district's interests—rural transportation, local fairs, and small schools—but it was in water policy and fish and wildlife protection where she made her most lasting contributions. Davis recognized the importance of water to the counties in her district, where much of California's fresh runoff fed other parts of the state. In her free time, she studied water policy with two experts in the legislative counsel's office. When Governor Edmund G. Brown proposed development of the California Water Project in 1959 to transfer northern water to the fast-growing south, Davis sounded the alarm. "You're dealing with liquid gold!" she said. "You're not dealing with something that is a commodity that can be replaced, because once that water wagon leaves Northern California . . . it just isn't comin' back."[40]

---

[36] Pauline Davis oral history, "Women in Politics Oral History Project: Pauline L. Davis, California Assemblywoman, 1952–1976," conducted by Malca Chall, 1986, Regional Oral History Office, Bancroft Library, University of California, Berkeley, 49.

[37] Davis oral history, 47.

[38] Ibid., 126.

[39] John Burton interview, San Francisco, February 17, 2017, by telephone.

[40] Davis oral history, 58.

Figure 8.1. Pauline Davis with Governor Earl Warren
Credit: Courtesy of Rod Davis

Brown met stiff resistance from many north-state legislators who had to approve a whopping $1.75 billion bond measure before it could go to the voters. To
get the support he needed, the governor horse traded for votes—one at a time. He
promised a judgeship to a friend of San Francisco Assemblyman Eugene McA-
teer. Davis held out for a series of small lakes in her vast district for recreation.
Brown acquiesced and signed the Davis-Grunsky Act, which authorized $130
million for the water projects—dubbed "Pauline's Puddles." Brown recalled years
later, "Pauline Davis was a pretty hardnosed politician."[41] When it was suggested
that one of the new reservoirs be named after her, she declined. Instead, Lake
Davis was named after her late husband.

Another measure, the Davis-Dolwig Act, required the protection of fish and
wildlife and recreational opportunities when planning State Water Project facilities. Hammering out the details was difficult. Davis had the support of farmers,
sportsmen's associations, and unions, but the Brown administration objected to
the cost and tried to kill the bill. Davis brought the leaders of various statewide

[41] Edmund G. Brown oral history, "Years of Growth, 1939–1966; Law Enforcement,
Politics, and the Governor's Office," conducted by Malca Chall, Amelia R. Fry, Gabrielle
Morris, and James Rowland, 1982, Regional Oral History Office, Bancroft Library, Uni-
versity of California, Berkeley, 352–55; Norris Hundley, Jr., *The Great Thirst* (Berkeley:
University of California Press, 2001), 283 .

associations to a conference in the governor's office, and the talks became heated. At one point, she said, Brown started "screaming at me like a fishwife, and he swore and said, 'You know, if you don't stop this, you're going to find yourself hanging up there on the wall, and you're going to wonder how in the hell you got there.'"[42] It was a rare display of anger from the affable governor, who eventually signed the legislation. And it was an example of her tough negotiating skills. Assembly Speaker Jesse Unruh once described a fair deal with Davis as: "You give her a multi-million dollar dam, and she compliments you on your tie."[43]

A Collision of Two Worlds for Women

Davis's career straddled two eras in California politics. She was elected at a time when Mom was expected to take care of the home while Dad provided for the family. Such 1950s television staples as "The Adventures of Ozzie and Harriet" and "Father Knows Best" had yet to discover female politicians, let alone employable women. Davis never felt she had a mandate to advocate for women at the capitol's boys club, and she insisted on being called "assemblyman." Still, the first bill she ever introduced—back in 1953—would have required women to be paid the same as men for equal work. The bill didn't survive its first committee test. She'd attend political dinners, which could get quite bawdy at times. But if the discussion got too risqué, she'd quietly and unobtrusively leave without complaint. In the mid-1960s, society was changing. The second wave of activist feminism—the first was the fight for suffrage—was underway. Women, including some of her new female colleagues at the capitol, were demanding more rights and access to male dominions. For the most part, Davis wasn't interested. For her the job was pretty simple, because she never forgot where she came from. "I brought the bacon home," Davis once said of her tenure in Sacramento, "and that's what I was sent there for."[44]

The women's movement had become stagnant nationally in the decades after suffrage was won, except for unique work opportunities in defense plants and elsewhere while American men fought in World War I and World War II. In the half-century since California women had secured the vote, only three women had been elected to Congress, 12 to the state assembly, and none statewide or to the state senate.[45] But a number of unconnected events—scientific, societal, and political—combined to fuel a new wave of activism that saw women confront inequalities and win some milestone victories.

[42] Davis oral history, 64.

[43] Leah Cartabruno, "Davis' One-of-a-Kind versus the Leadership's Royal Flush," *California Journal*, September 1976, 303–05.

[44] Davis oral history, 147.

[45] "Women in Congress," Thought.co, https://www.thoughtco.com/women-in-congress-biography-3528696; California Legislative Women's Caucus, http://womenscaucus.legislature.ca.gov/former-members.

In mid-May 1960, the G. D. Searle Co. announced that its birth control pill had been approved by the US Food and Drug Administration. It went on the market a month later, and within six years an estimated five million women were taking oral contraceptives. "No previous medical phenomenon," *Time* magazine said, "has ever quite matched the headlong US rush to use the oral contraceptives now universally known as 'the pills.'"[46] Although it would take several years before this easy-to-use contraceptive would proliferate among large populations of young, unmarried women, researchers noted that after it came into significant use, women started delaying marriage and childbearing and began entering university professional degree programs in substantially larger numbers.[47] California's rock-bottom cost of tuition at public colleges and universities also helped encourage women to seek degrees. Moving into the workplace was an important first step, but securing equal rights proved more difficult. Shirley Biagi Biondi, a former newspaper columnist and journalism professor emeritus at California State University, Sacramento, remembers trying to get a job with the *Sacramento Bee* after earning a four-year degree in English. "There were 'Help Wanted Female' and 'Help Wanted Male' job offers. That was the only way you could look for work. I would have liked to have been an administrative assistant or editor, but those listings were only under 'Help Wanted Male.'"[48] She did, however, have plenty of job opportunities as a secretary.

Historic Anti-Discrimination Ruling Opened Doors for Women

In 1964, a landmark US Supreme Court ruling—*Reynolds v. Sims*—unintentionally offered unprecedented opportunities for women to seek careers in elective politics. In a decision written by Chief Justice Earl Warren, the court required states to craft legislative districts that were roughly equal in population, forcing California to overhaul both its senate and assembly boundaries. Senate districts, in particular, had disproportionally favored rural, conservative interests. In the most egregious example, sparsely populated Alpine, Inyo, and Mono counties—with fewer than 15,000 combined residents—had their own senate representative, while nearly seven million residents were crammed into a single district in Los Angeles County. New boundaries had been drawn for the 1966 state elections, and ambitious politicians in the assembly jumped at the chance to serve in the prestigious, 40-member senate with its four-year terms—much preferred to seeking re-election every two years in the 80-member lower house. Overnight, urban regions dramatically increased their representation in the senate and made the house more

---

[46] "Contraception: The Safe and Effective Pills," *Time*, August 19, 1966, http://content.time.com/time/ magazine/article/0,9171,836258,00.html.

[47] Claudia Goldin and Lawrence F. Katz, "The Power of the Pill: Oral Contraceptives and Women's Career and Marriage Decisions," *Journal of Political Economy*, Vol. 110, No. 4 (2002): 730–70, http://harvard.edu/urn-3:HUL.InstRepos:2624453.

[48] Shirley Biagi Biondi interview, El Dorado Hills, January 17, 2017.

liberal; Los Angeles County suddenly had 14 representatives rather than one, and shared another with parts of Orange County.[49]

Women and minorities found new opportunities in the open assembly districts vacated in 1966 by entrenched white male incumbents running for the newly created senate seats. More women than ever before ran in those open assembly districts. In fact, 1966 was a banner year overall for women political candidates in California. A record 32 women ran for statewide and legislative offices that year. Ivy Baker Priest ran on a slate headed by Ronald Reagan and captured a close contest for state treasurer, becoming the first woman in California to win statewide office. She previously had served as a Republican National Committeewoman from Utah, mobilized the women's vote for Dwight Eisenhower's successful presidential campaign, and served eight years as US Treasurer.

The surge in political activity followed a prolonged dry spell that had begun 16 years earlier, coinciding with the demoralizing US Senate race between Richard Nixon and Helen Gahagan Douglas. The tenor of that highly visible contest may have had a chilling effect on women's desire to seek public office. The low point had come in1958 when only 11 women sought statewide office, seats in the 30-member congressional delegation, or election to the 120-member legislature.

Taking advantage of newly created open seats in Los Angeles and Oakland, two women were elected to join Pauline Davis in the assembly. They became only the thirteenth and fourteenth assemblywomen since statehood, and they shattered ethnic barriers as well. March Fong became the legislature's first Chinese American and Yvonne Brathwaite the first female African American. A month after their elections, the *San Francisco Examiner* ran a profile piece on the pair, referring to Brathwaite as a "brainy Negro beauty . . . slender, exquisitely groomed," while Fong sported "a trademark cluster of dark curls atop her short glossy locks" and had "turned her coiffure into a campaign asset."[50]

Trailblazing Asian American Lawmaker— March Fong Eu

March Fong was born in the back of a Chinese hand laundry in the small San Joaquin County town of Oakdale. Her father, born in the US, had four years of schooling; her illiterate mother was from China. Driven to succeed while growing up in the East Bay, she became a top student who graduated UC Berkeley in dentistry and eventually earned a PhD in education from Stanford. Fong was a teacher and dental hygienist and served on the Alameda Board of Education before running for the assembly when popular incumbent Nicholas Petris of Oakland sought a newly created senate seat in the watershed 1966 election. Fong challenged a

---

[49] Don A. Allen, Sr., *Legislative Sourcebook* (Sacramento: California Assembly, 1965), 119, 125, 159.

[50] Mildred Schroeder, "California" Dynamic New Politicos: Incidentally, They're Beautiful and Brainy, Too," *San Francisco Examiner*, December 6, 1966, Women Today, 3.

woman and six men in the Democratic primary, including a Petris aide who was endorsed by the assemblyman. Lacking funds, a professional campaign manager, and high-profile endorsements, Fong handed out campaign literature on buses and walked nearly every street in the Oakland district with her two young children, who earned 10 cents a week helping out. "We gave out those ugly potholders and bottle caps that never fit on any bottle," son Matt "Kip" Fong recalled.[51] The retail politics worked; Fong won the primary and was a landslide victor in the general election.

March Fong was the antithesis of Pauline Davis, the consummate protector of her rural district's interests with little concern for broad social change. Rather, Fong championed women's issues, landmark health sex education legislation, water fluoridation, consumer laws, and pesticide regulation. She led a multi-year effort to ban pay toilets that detractors viewed as a trivial publicity stunt, but she considered it a small step toward gender equality. Etched into capitol lore was her brash bit of political theater one balmy April day in 1969.

The Saga of the Smashed Toilet Seat

Reporters snickered, but they recorded every word. News photographers and television cameras captured the moment and sent the images around the world. Politicians sneered, but they couldn't help but take notice. As a Dixieland band played "Brother, Can You Spare a Dime," a carnival-like rally of mostly women gathered on the west steps of the state capitol that day, demanding that the male-dominated legislature outlaw pay toilets in public buildings, because they disproportionately inconvenienced women. Then, to drive the point home, the petite 47-year-old assemblywoman, demurely dressed in heels and a stylish suit, hoisted a six-pound golden-headed sledgehammer and smashed a chain-draped toilet bowl to bits. At a venue that has hosted hundreds of publicity stunts over the decades, this was one of the most unusual and enduring.

Pay toilets had become a symbol of gender inequality at a time when women were asserting their rights and challenging long-held societal norms. They believed requiring women to carry dimes (no change was given) to unlock stall doors in public restrooms was sexist and offensive. In the late 1960s, more than 50,000 pay toilets with coin-operated locks were in use in the nation's bus and train stations, airports, and highway rest stops.[52] They were promoted as devices to protect the privacy of patrons and reduce vandalism. They also helped fill gov-

---

[51] Anthony York, "Former California State Treasurer," *Los Angeles Times*, June 2, 2011, AA6; Caren Daniels Lagomarsino interview, Elk Grove, CA, March 13, 2017.

[52] Aaron Gordon, "Why Don't We Have Pay Toilets in America?" *Pacific Standard*, September 17, 2014, https://psmag.com/economics/dont-pay-toilets-america-bathroom-restroom-free-market-90683.

ernment treasuries, generating $50,000 annual revenue at San Francisco International Airport alone.[53]

At the time, Fong was a second-term Democratic assemblywoman and one of only three women in the 120-member legislature. She wasn't the first to seek a prohibition on pay toilets. Charlie Myers, an assemblyman from San Francisco first elected in 1948, tried unsuccessfully several times. "They called him 'Toilet Seat Charlie,'" Fong recalled in an oral history.[54] A Sacramento legislator made another attempt in 1966 but was defeated largely because of opposition from Sacramento airport officials. For years, Fong said she would make her young son Matt crawl under the door and open it from the inside. "When he got tired of crawling under the stall door, I said, 'Something has to be done.'"[55]

Fong was anxious to broaden her reputation beyond her Oakland and Castro Valley district. Her office hired an aide with a media background who suggested she would attract statewide media attention by demolishing the toilet on the capitol steps. Despite some staff misgivings that the stunt might seem trivial, Fong pushed forward. "We must stand up to the pressures of pay toilets or resign ourselves to a life of fumbling for a dime and occasionally losing," she said.[56] Once her bill was introduced, letters started flooding into her office. An official with the state's plumbing industry wrote, "Having to pay a dime to use the facilities that our industry has provided . . . is an odious practice perpetrated on an already beguiled public who in all probability has been dimed to death before." Another letter writer commented, "The freedom to eat and drink without the freedom to expel is as inconsistent as having freedom of the press without the freedom to read." But there was criticism, as well. "Can't you do something more important?" one person wrote.[57]

Strictly as a publicity generator, the ploy worked. The capitol press corps turned out in force, and wire services sent pictures and words all over the world. Newspapers in Rome, London, Tokyo, and dozens of US cities picked up the story. "I was suddenly being mentioned on Johnny Carson's Tonight Show," Fong noted.[58] The rally had been timed perfectly to precede the legislation's first committee hearing, and rally participants anxiously filled the hearing room anticipating victory. Republican chairman Carl Britschgi and his all-male committee colleagues, however, weren't impressed. In his seventh term, Britschgi didn't appreciate an upstart junior assemblywoman trying to pressure the committee through the media. "She's gonna learn the hard way," he told reporters. At one

[53] Peter Weisser, "Mrs. Fong Bowls a Zero," *Fresno Bee*, April 26, 1969, 17.

[54] March Fong oral history, "High Achieving Nonconformist in Local and State Government," conducted by Gabrielle Morris, 1978, Regional Oral History Office, Bancroft Library, University of California, Berkeley, 1978.

[55] Tim Vandehey, March Fong unpublished biography, Fong family collection, 6.

[56] "The War on Pay Toilets," United Press International, in the *Santa Rosa Press Democrat*, April 25, 1969, 10.

[57] Ibid.

[58] Vandehey, 7.

Figure 8.2. Assemblywoman March Fong Attacks Toilet on Capitol Steps, 1969
Credit: AP Photo/Walter Zeboski

point in the hearing, Britschgi asked Fong if she had staged "a live demonstration" outside the capitol. "We staged a live demonstration," Fong replied, "which you probably will see on TV tonight." Fong replied. "That's what I was afraid of," Britschgi shot back. The measure failed by one vote—Britschgi's.[59]

The press couldn't resist having fun with the story. The bill "gurgled down the drain," wrote one reporter, and Fong acknowledged that the gimmickry of the toilet-smashing stunt generated resentment from some of her more hide-bound legislative colleagues.[60] But as it turned out, she was on the cusp of a national movement. The following year, four teenagers from Ohio started the Committee to End Pay Toilets in America (CEPTIA) to educate legislators about what they considered to be an unethical infringement of basic human rights. Lifetime membership cost a quarter. Its logo was a fist grasping chains and rising out of a toilet bowl. CEPTIA printed a quarterly newsletter, called the *Free Toilet Paper*. In early 1973, CEPTIA held a news conference in downtown Chicago that attracted 30 reporters and news stories across the country. A month later, Mayor Richard J. Daley announced that pay toilets would be removed from the city's airports, saying, "I did it for women's lib." Over the next few years, California and 11 other states banned pay toilets.[61] Governor Ronald Reagan signed Fong's legislation in 1974.

---

[59] Weisser.

[60] Ibid.

[61] "Daley Opens Doors for Many," *Chicago Tribune*, February 28, 1973; "Why Don't We Have Pay Toilets in America? *Pacific Standard*, https://psmag.com/economics/dont-

"March Had to Be Tough . . . "

One of Fong's assembly colleagues, San Fernando Valley's Jim Keysor, said she "was the first really aggressive woman to come into the legislature when the legislature was the domain of men." Keysor said men were jealous of her accomplishments. "They saw her as super tough, sometimes vindictive and with a long memory. My contention is March had to be tough because she was a woman operating in a man's world."[62] Fong's secretary, Kimberly Smith, was more blunt. "It was brutal to be a woman in politics," she said. "The sexism during that time was so rampant that nobody even apologized for it. You need to behave like ladies, but demonstrate that you can do the job of men."[63]

In a speech to Foothill College students during her fourth term in the assembly, Fong—at that time, one of only two female legislators—argued it was time for male lawmakers to rethink their prejudices and perspectives:

> Maybe if some men had to bear and rear unwanted babies themselves, they would understand better our resentment of laws relating to our reproductive systems. Maybe if some men let their wives involuntarily control their income, they would understand better our resentment of present discriminatory statutes directed toward women as a class. And maybe if some men were raped, and, in pursuit of justice, they found that they had to reveal humiliating information about their past lives—maybe then they would understand the anger of women who feel they are doubly wronged by rapists and the laws concerning rape.[64]

Fong's eight years in the assembly paralleled Reagan's tenure as governor, and the two went head-to-head on a controversial, high-profile bill in the early 1970s to allow distribution of information about venereal disease to high school students without having to obtain parental consent. VD in California "had reached epidemic proportions," Fong argued, particularly among teenagers, but Reagan vetoed the measure, saying that the responsibility for such education rested with the family and the church. Fong decried the veto as "a mighty blow for a return to the Dark Ages."[65] In the ensuing year, she conducted a broad statewide publicity campaign, enlisting statewide support from doctors, teachers, PTA leaders,

---

pay-toilets-america-bathroom-restroom-free-market-90683.

[62] Susan Sward, "Governor's Mansion May Yet Be March Fong Eu's Goal," Associated Press, in the *Santa Ana Register*, May 12, 1977, D4.

[63] Vandehey, 171.

[64] Excerpts from speech at Foothill College, "The Self-Sufficient Woman," February 22, 1973, in March Fong Eu oral history, "High Achieving Non-conformist in Local and State Government," conducted by Gabrielle Morris, Bancroft Library, University of California, Berkeley, 1978, 206.

[65] Antionette May, "California State Legislator Rattles Staid Lawmaking Sessions," *Portland Oregonian,* November 29, 1973, 2.

journalists, and even members of Reagan's own healthcare task force. She reintroduced the legislation with minor changes, and this time the governor signed it.[66]

Politically ambitious and adept at seizing media opportunities, March Fong Eu (she had divorced Chester Fong in 1970 and married Henry Eu in 1973) won the first of five consecutive elections for secretary of state in 1974, becoming the nation's first Asian American to win a state constitutional office and, at that time, the biggest vote-getter in California history. The *California Journal* said "she rode to victory on a toilet seat."[67] Despite the fact that women candidates continued to struggle for public acceptance, Eu credited her gender and propitious timing as important assets that separated women from the slime in government. It certainly helped that she was a Democrat during the Republicans' post-Watergate free-fall. As the Nixon White House careened out of control amid a flood of corruption indictments and resignations, California voters easily approved a get-tough political reform measure, propelling one of the measure's architects, Democratic secretary of state Jerry Brown, to the governorship. Eu campaigned for election reform—an easy sell in the Watergate atmosphere—and felt that a strong, viable female candidate to succeed Brown would have a particular advantage because voters didn't associate women with corruption in politics. "It was as if people were saying, 'Look at the men running government; they sure are making a mess out of it . . . they're all a bunch of crooks.'"[68]

Once in the secretary of state's office, Eu established a political reform division and adopted programs to boost voter registration, even collaborating with a snack food manufacturer to attach registration applications to bags of potato chips. She also made it easier for Californians to vote by mail. In 1986, less than a week after winning her fourth term as secretary of state with nearly 70 percent of the vote, a burglar on parole broke into her sprawling, two-story Los Angeles home late at night, bludgeoned her with the blunt end of an ax and demanded money. "He didn't know who she was," recalled Eu's long-time communications aide Caren Daniels Lagomarsino. "He dragged her by her hair screaming throughout the house and up the stairs to an office." She gave the intruder about $100 in a blood-soaked envelope marked "secretary of state." After the intruder left the house, he carelessly discarded the envelope with his bloody fingerprints on it and was arrested after being tracked down by a police dog. Eu underwent surgery for serious cuts and was hospitalized for a week.[69]

As a top vote-getter with a lengthening record of service and a media-savvy staff, Eu's name repeatedly surfaced as a potential candidate for governor or US senator, and she did set her sights on higher office. In some cases, the political stars simply didn't align, but she had a more fundamental problem—Democratic

---

[66] Vandehey, 203–07.

[67] Kerry Drager, "A Woman Governor, March Fong Eu, in '82?" *California Journal*, September 1980, 350–52.

[68] March Fong Eu oral history, 194.

[69] Caren Daniels Lagomarsino interview.

Party power brokers never viewed her as a heavyweight who could secure sufficient financing to sustain an expensive campaign. "I always worried about raising enough money," she acknowledged. Further, once the Watergate headlines about wayward men in Washington started to fade, she felt her gender was holding her back; only Helen Gahagan Douglas 30 years earlier had been a serious woman candidate for either governor or the US Senate.[70] After serving as secretary of state for two decades and becoming President Bill Clinton's US Ambassador to Micronesia, Eu tried to revive her political career at the age of 79 with a 2002 run for a sixth term as secretary of state, narrowly losing in the Democratic primary. As Eu faded from the scene, the woman she made political history with in 1966—Yvonne Brathwaite Burke—was continuing to establish her own electoral dynasty.

An African-American Pioneer— Yvonne Brathwaite Burke

Perle Yvonne Watson, 10 years younger than Eu, was born and raised in southwest Los Angeles. Her father was a janitor at the MGM film studios, and her mother was a real estate agent. She graduated from UCLA in 1953 and was the first black woman in 30 years admitted to the USC Law School. "There were law school quotas against both blacks and women," she told the Christian Science Monitor in 1972. "And when you got out, it was difficult to find work. Getting a job with a law firm was almost unheard of."[71] She opened her own small office, focused on civil, probate, and real estate law, and moved into L.A.'s Crenshaw district in the mid-fifties at the beginning of the integration movement. "The year before, some crosses had been burned on lawns," she remembered. "The day I moved in the woman next door peeked around a shrub at me. When I got home from work that night there was a "For Sale" sign on her house."[72]

After marrying, and later divorcing mathematician Louis Brathwaite, Yvonne kept her married name and organized a legal defense team for Watts's rioters in 1965. She was named to the commission that investigated the conditions that led to the riots. When she sought an assembly seat in a newly reapportioned district a year later, her opponent subtly introduced race into the election by distributing a photo of her in his mailers, "and of course he charged that I was a Communist." She also faced accusations that she was a leftwing black militant. Racial as well as gender issues followed her to Sacramento. Once, she had to seek an injunction to force a property owner to rent her an apartment. And several members of a key finance committee, which included Brathwaite, had to halt its practice of holding

---

[70] A. G. Block, "March Fong Eu: A Political Career Stalled Near the Top?" *California Journal*, November 1986, 547–50.

[71] Judy Petsonk, "Just What Democratic Party Wanted," *Christian Science Monitor*, August 1, 1972, 8.

[72] Schroeder.

informal luncheon meetings at the venerable Sutter Club because it was off-limits to women.[73]

Fights over government spending and higher education dominated state politics in the late 1960s during Brathwaite's first term. Ronald Reagan had surged to a million-vote victory over two-term governor Edmund Brown by promising to bring order to turbulent college campuses and to reduce the size and cost of government. "We stand between the taxpayer and the tax spender," he said in his inaugural address.[74] When faced with a gaping budget deficit, Reagan demanded a 10 percent across-the-board cut in the state budget but eventually agreed to a billion-dollar tax increase, the largest in state history. As a freshman lawmaker in a body that rewarded tenure, Brathwaite was a fringe player in those legislative power struggles. With a perspective forged in part by her personal experiences, however, she directed her efforts toward social legislation—women's rights, consumer affairs, housing, and civil rights.

During her third and final term in the legislature, Brathwaite introduced an ambitious package of bills dealing with sex discrimination in securing retail credit, higher education admissions, employment, and housing. Most were defeated by her colleagues or vetoed by the governor for cost reasons. "Equality for men and women has a pretty high price tag," noted Anne Renner, Sacramento's NOW chapter president.[75] Reagan did sign a Brathwaite bill authorizing child care centers on and off university and college campuses.

Fighting the Good Fight in Washington

Impatient with the pace of social legislation in Sacramento—Brathwaite in 1972 sought a seat in Congress from southwest Los Angeles that had a sizeable African-American constituency and was nearly three-fourths Democratic. She defeated popular black city councilman Billy Mills in the primary, married businessman William Burke, and then won an overwhelming victory in November to become the first female African American from California to enter the House (she joined Barbara Jordan that same year as they became only the second and third black women to sit in Congress). Brathwaite had gained national exposure months earlier as vice-chairwoman of the tumultuous Democratic National Convention that exposed to television viewers raucous platform battles that lasted well past midnight. Controlling the gavel, she helped pass rules giving young voters and minorities greater input in shaping party policy.[76] The convention nominated

---

[73] Yvonne Brathwaite Burke oral history, "New Arenas of Black Influence: Yvonne Brathwaite Burke, conducted by Steven Edgington, 1982, Department of Special Collections, University of California, Los Angeles, 10, 11.

[74] Steve Swatt, "Reagan: The Governor," KCRA-TV, January 20, 1981.

[75] Shirley Biondi and Geri Sherwood, "Tight Fiscal Policies Left Little Change in Women's Rights in 1971," *Sacramento Bee*, January 1, 1972, A13.

[76] Yvonne Brathwaite Burke, "History, Art & Archives," US House of Representatives, http://tinyurl.com/yd6c9vnd.

Figure 8.3. Yvonne Brathwaite Burke
Credit: Courtesy of the National Archives and Records Administration

George McGovern for president and advocated the immediate US withdrawal from Vietnam and abolition of the draft. With the war draining the nation's treasury, Yvonne Brathwaite Burke—as she now called herself—urged an adjustment in national priorities. "We're going to have to spend the same kind of money that we spend in Vietnam to produce schools that can deal with the youngsters of the seventies and the problems of the inner cities," she told *Sepia* magazine.[77]

As in the California legislature, Burke concentrated on social issues in Congress, particularly housing, antidiscrimination, and urban development. She supported feminist issues and fought the Nixon administration's attempts to unravel a number of social programs established under Lyndon Johnson. Her amendments to a federal funding bill ensured equal opportunity for women- and minority-owned businesses in the construction of the huge Trans-Alaskan oil pipeline.[78] Described in a House biography as a behind-the-scenes legislator "who avoided confrontation and controversy," Burke nonetheless made national headlines late in her first term when she became the first woman ever to give birth while in Congress. "The most conservative Republican," she told CSPAN in a 2010 interview, "was the one who made the motion to grant me maternity leave." She said she only received a single complaint from a constituent who said, "You shouldn't be back there having babies, you should be working for us."[79] For four years, Burke and daughter Autumn (who was elected to the California assembly in 2014) commuted together between Washington and California. When Autumn reached

---

[77] Biondi, "Two New 'Black' First Ladies in Congress," *Sepia*, October 1972, 46, 52–56.

[78] Burke, "History, Art & Archives."

[79] "American History TV: CSPAN 3," December 29, 2010, https://www.youtube.com/watch?v=xQtY1pKEKRc American History TV: CSPAN 3.

school age, Burke sought another job change, returning to her home state in 1978 to run for attorney general.

The First Serious Black Woman to Seek Statewide Office

The timing and political optics made Burke's attempt to establish a statewide electoral foothold in California a difficult challenge. Voters were in a more conservative antitax, anticrime mood than they had been four years earlier. In June, while Burke was securing her party's nomination, Californians fired the first volley in the nation's nascent tax revolt by approving Proposition 13, which reduced property taxes and made it more difficult to raise others. Running for reelection, Democratic governor Jerry Brown—a Proposition 13 foe—read the tea leaves and quickly embraced the measure as the fall campaign began.

More germane to the attorney general's contest, violent and property crime rates had steadily increased in California since 1960,[80] and the liberal Burke found herself facing conservative law-and-order state senator George Deukmejian in the November general election. Deukmejian had authored the state's death penalty law, which became one of the campaign's leading issues, and was aided by the presence on the same ballot of a popular initiative to dramatically increase the number of crimes that would be subject to capital punishment. Burke promised to enforce the law if elected but said she had "never been able to observe in any place there was a decrease in crime when we instituted the death penalty." When asked about taking a different approach in the attorney general's office, she said she wanted to boost consumer fraud and environmental protection.[81]

Deukmejian's television commercials attacked Burke on three volatile issues—her opposition to capital punishment, a voting record that critics said cared more for criminals than victims, and her perceived support for court-ordered school busing to desegregate public schools. "I wasn't supporting busing so much, but it was an emotional issue," Burke recalled. "It was a statewide television campaign, and this was the first time the people in the state had the opportunity to see a black woman run for state office. It was easy to categorize me as a liberal."[82] A week before the election, a poll of Los Angeles County prosecutors showed they favored Deukmejian 217–32. Burke abruptly canceled several Bay Area campaign appearances to make a new tough-on-crime TV commercial, but it wasn't enough. After holding a lead during most of the campaign, she lost the

---

[80] Magnus Lofstrom and Brandon Martin, "Crime Trends in California," Public Policy Institute of California, August 2016. http://www.ppic.org/publication/crime-trends-in-california/.

[81] Susan Sward, Associated Press, "Attorney General Hopefuls All Vow to Fight Crime," *San Bernardino Sun*, April 19, 1978, 6.

[82] Yussuf Simmonds, "Yvonne Brathwaite Burke—A Lifetime of Service (Part Two)," *Los Angeles Sentinel*, November 6, 2008, https://lasentinel.net/yvonne-brathwaite-burke-a-lifetime-of-service-part-two.htm.

contest by more than 600,000 votes.[83] Afterwards, Burke acknowledged that "everyone knows that mine was a high-risk candidacy," but she was "not prepared to say" that issues of race or sex contributed to her defeat.

A few months after Burke's defeat, Jerry Brown appointed her to a vacant seat on the LA Board of Supervisors. She subsequently lost her bid for a new four-year term and returned to private law practice until she again sought office and won the first of four terms as supervisor. After a ground-breaking political career in which she won 10 different elections—losing two—Burke looked back on that first setback in 1978 when she unsuccessfully ran for attorney general. She still felt the anguish of defeat but characterized the experience as an important milestone for women in politics. "[W]e have established that a woman can raise enough money," she said, "to put on a campaign and dispelled some of the stereotypes that a woman can't stand up to [the rigors of such] a campaign."[84]

Discussion Questions

1. Although some critics had labeled March Fong Eu's campaign against pay toilets a publicity stunt, for what reasons did the cause became a popular feminist issue?

2. What federal post had Ivy Baker Priest held before becoming the first woman ever elected to a statewide office in California? Do you think her experience helped her win with voters? Might some voters during this transitional time in the mid-1960s have opposed voting for a woman? If so, for what reasons?

3. Why was a steep decline in female candidates during the late 1950s quite possibly tied to Helen Gahagan Douglas's campaign against Richard Nixon for the US Senate? What did the color pink have to do with his attacks on her? How did Nixon come to be labeled "Tricky Dick"?

4. Pauline Davis was one of just three women in the assembly at the time of her election in the 1950s. How long, in her opinion, did it take to win acceptance from her male colleagues? If you had been Davis, how would you have sought to achieve their acceptance?

5. Davis wished to be called "assemblyman." Given her record, goals, and accomplishments, would you describe Davis as a feminist? How did her approach to legislating contrast with that of March Fong Eu?

6. In what ways did race as well as gender pose obstacles for Yvonne Brathwaite Burke during her career? Do you believe they were factors in her defeat for state attorney general?

---

[83] Bill Farr, "Younger Backed by Prosecutors," *Los Angeles Times*, October 31, 1978, I3; Kenneth Reich, "New Burke Ad to Stress Law Enforcement," *Los Angeles Times*, October 31, 1978, I3; Statement of Vote, California Secretary of State, Sacramento, November 7, 1978.

[84] Dorothy Townsend, "Rep. Burke Says She Has 'No Regrets' About Race," *Los Angeles Times*, November 8, I,3.

Recommended Reading

Douglas, Helen Gahagan. *A Full Life.* Garden City, NY: Doubleday & Co., 1982.

Mitchell, Greg. *Tricky Dick and the Pink Lady.* New York: Random House, 1998.

Van Ingen, Linda. *Gendered Politics: Campaign Strategies of California Women Candidates, 1912–1970.* Lanham, MD: Lexington, 2017.

Chapter 9

1975–1990
Advocacy, Triumphs, and Backlash

"I was greeted with nothing much less than shock."
—Rose Ann Vuich

S elf-described feminist Leona Egeland started shaking up the state capitol even before she was elected to the assembly. A former science teacher, Egeland was inspired by biologist Paul Ehrlich, who had warned of the global dangers of overpopulation in his 1968 book, The Population Bomb. In the early 1970s, Egeland became a lobbyist for Zero Population Growth and Planned Parenthood and trekked from her home in the Santa Clara Valley to Sacramento to educate male lawmakers about abortion and contraception. "I got paid to talk to men about sex," she says with a chuckle.[1]

In 1974, with strong support from women's groups, Egeland decided to seek a seat in the legislature. Most of her campaign workers were women. An avid hiker, she particularly enjoyed campaigning door-to-door for the 18 months preceding the election in between shifts as a carpool driver for her child's preschool. She recalls stopping at one house and smelling the distinct odor of marijuana. A man opened the door. "He was stark naked," she remembers. "I looked at his eyes and said, 'Here's my literature. And by the way, my husband has a suit just like that at home.'"[2] The man laughed and promised his vote.

Egeland wasn't the candidate favored by the local Democratic establishment, but she credits her gender and a Watergate ripple effect for securing the nomination. The scandal gripped the nation in 1974 and caused many voters to question their trust in government. "I wasn't an incumbent; I wasn't an attorney; I wasn't a male, so I didn't look like anybody who was in office," she says. "I looked the least like Richard Nixon."[3] Egeland captured the nomination against seven opponents and attracted a large number of Republican women's votes to win the general election to become, at the age of 36, only the fifteenth woman in history to win a California assembly seat. When she arrived in Sacramento, she and Pauline

---

[1] Interview by Sunny Mojonnier, "Women in California Politics," July 16, 2017, http://wicp100.org.
[2] Ibid.
[3] Ibid.

Davis were the only females in the 80-member assembly. She used to joke that there were so few women in office they could meet in a phone booth.

Once in office, Egeland says she didn't fit in. Some of her male colleagues were "downright mean" to her, and she wasn't invited to social functions or meetings. "They are only comfortable with women in one role," she says, "as a romantic involvement."[4] Early on, sergeants-at-arms mistook her for a legislative staffer. In one of her first votes, she backed the wrong candidate in an assembly speakership fight and—in retribution—new Speaker Leo McCarthy banished her to a tiny sixth-floor office near the capitol cafeteria. The cagey Egeland subtly fought back. She put together a statewide meeting in Sacramento of high-powered women leaders—the presidents of political, business, and advocacy groups—and invited the news media to hear their remarks on current women's political issues. Then, she asked McCarthy to address the meeting. Sensing a promising media opportunity and a chance to impress many of the state's women leaders, McCarthy agreed and asked her where the meeting would be held. "In my office," Egeland responded. Years later, she recalled, "And do you know that the next day my office was located on the fourth floor; I had a very big office."[5]

Egeland's six-year legislative agenda (she later became chief deputy of the department of health services) focused heavily on social issues, such as family planning, health care, and alcohol and drug addiction. Savvy in using the media, Egeland earned statewide coverage when she boycotted capital-related events at the nearby Sutter Club, where only men could then be members, and she threatened adverse news coverage to coax Bank of America into issuing credit cards in women's names. She had decided to call out the bank at a capitol news conference. In advance, she invited a bank representative to the media event and explained he had a choice: either tell the press why women with the same income and credit as men couldn't get a credit card, "or you can be the first bank in California to announce that you are going to give credit cards to a woman who qualifies. And that's what he did."[6]

The Slow March into History Picks Up Speed

Leona Egeland had come of age in Arizona during the civil rights movement. Her family was described as "politically passive," and her father had voted for conservative home-state Senator Barry Goldwater in the 1964 presidential contest.[7] She began her career outside of politics but gravitated towards the women's movement and associated with several local women's organizations. Just as the abolitionist movement a century earlier had inspired the fight for suffrage, the new

---

[4] Ibid.

[5] Ibid.

[6] Ibid.

[7] Danelle L. Moon, "Community Feminism and Politics; A Case Study of Santa Clara County as the Feminist Capital, 1975–2006," *Scholar Works*, San Jose State University, 11.

wave of women's protests was fueled by white females who had participated in the civil rights movement, rooted in the 1950s, and antiwar movement, grounded in the sixties, where internal divisions of labor were dominated by men. "Indeed, it is the second-class citizenship within the social movements of the 1960s that impelled one strand of activists to take up feminism by the end of the decade," report Kelsy Kretschmer and David S. Meyer.[8]

This second wave of feminists borrowed many of the tactics and strategies employed by civil rights advocates. On August 26, 1970, the fiftieth anniversary of the passage of the Nineteenth Amendment to the US Constitution that granted women suffrage, activists called for a nationwide "Strike for Equality" to bring attention to inequities the *Los Angeles Times* helpfully listed as discrimination in "employment, divorce and alimony, property rights, pensions, inheritance, and even certain criminal statutes."[9] At the time of the protest, women in the work-force earned 59 percent of what men with comparable jobs were earning. Women traditionally were placed in less-skilled, lower-paying jobs, such as clerical, sales, domestic or service work, and were the last to be hired and first to be fired.[10] In advance of the demonstration, however, the *Times* cautioned women that it might be counterproductive to cease housework, discard bras and hair curlers, and picket stores that "exploit women." The president of the League of Women Voters similarly warned, "History has too many examples of over-brash movements who, through their own efforts, have snatched defeat from the jaws of victory."[11]

Tens of thousands of women demonstrated in cities from coast to coast. Up to 20,000 women marched down Fifth Avenue during rush hour in New York. "Today is the beginning of a new movement," feminist author Kate Millett told the New York crowd. "Today is the end of millenniums of oppression."[12] Only a few women actually had asked for and received permission for a day off, but there were teach-ins, sit-ins, and rallies. The *New York Times* gave the march lengthy page-one coverage, but it also ran a smaller story on its inside pages explaining that feminist author Betty Friedan was 20 minutes late for a radio interview "because of a last minute emergency appointment with her hairdresser."[13] In Los Angeles, male counter-protesters yelled, "Go do the dishes!" as 450 marchers

---

[8] Kelsy Kretschmer and David S. Myer, "Chapter 15: Organizing around Gender Identities," in *The Oxford Handbook of Gender and Politics*, eds. Georgina Waylen, Karen Celis, Johanna Kantola, and S. Laurel Weldon (New York: Oxford University Press, 2013), 397.

[9] "Toward Women's Equal Rights," *Los Angeles Times*, August 26, 1970, II10.

[10] National Committee on Pay Equity, https://www.pay-equity.org/info-time.html; *Long Beach Independent*, ". . . the statistics prove the need," August 26, 1970, B10.

[11] "Voters League Leaders Warn about 'Lib-Lash,'" Associated Press in *Fresno Bee*, August 26, 1970, C4.

[12] Linda Charlton, "Women March Down Fifth in Equality Drive," *New York Times*, August 27, 1970, 1.

[13] "Leading Feminist Puts Hairdo before Strike," *New York Times*, August 27, 1970, 30.

made their way through downtown.[14] San Francisco Mayor Joseph Alioto formally proclaimed "Women's Day," although he warned that city employees who took off time to protest would not be paid. He seemed muddled over the cause itself, even though Union Square had attracted a large rally. "What are they after?" he asked."[15] Had Alioto read the morning newspaper, he would have learned what women were demanding. The day before in Sacramento, the senate had approved legislation—eventually signed by Governor Ronald Reagan—to prohibit outright discrimination against women by employers. According to Marian Ash, publisher of a political newsletter that focused on women's issues, "It was supported by women, housewives, mothers, and primarily working women—whose only real influence lies in their vote."[16]

Ronald Reagan Liberalized Choice in California
before *Roe v. Wade*

Although the nationwide "Strike for Equality" is considered the birth of the modern women's liberation movement, California had dealt with one of the movement's most important issues three years earlier. With Reagan's signature, the state had enacted the Therapeutic Abortion Act of 1967. The legislation revised the state's Gold Rush-era law that declared abortion a crime unless a physician deemed it necessary to save a pregnant woman's life. The new law allowed abortions in the case of rape or incest and when doctors found that pregnancy endangered a woman's physical or mental health.

Anthony Beilenson, a liberal senator in his mid-thirties, authored the legislation and acknowledged, "It was an issue that I had never confronted, or thought about, or known a thing about before." But in meetings up and down the state, women would tell him about their experiences. "Their mother had one, they had one, their college roommate had one and lost her life having an illegal abortion. These were all regular upper-middle-class, perfectly responsible people who . . . had done something that was a felony."[17] Beilenson considered the existing law to be "archaic, barbaric, and hypocritical."[18]

With advocacy help from the newly created National Organization for Women, Beilenson overcame strong religious opposition—primarily from the Catholic Church—and won a hard-fought victory in the legislature. Reagan, in office only six months, agonized over his decision. "Those were awful weeks," he told

---

[14] "Crowd of 450 Women Marches for Equality in Los Angeles," Associated Press in *San Bernardino Sun*, August 27, 1970, 1.

[15] "Women Demand Equal Rights," *Los Angeles Times*, August 30, 1970, F5.

[16] Diane Smith, "Women Earn Equal Job Rights," *Long Beach Independent*, August 26, 1970, B10.

[17] Anthony Beilenson oral history, conducted by Susan Douglass Yates, 1998, State Government Oral History Program, State Archives, 267, 273.

[18] Steve Swatt, "Reagan: The Governor," KCRA-TV, January 20, 1981.

biographer Lou Cannon.[19] "With pressure being applied from all sides, Reagan signed the nation's most liberal abortion law after insisting that Beilenson remove a section that would have allowed abortions if there were "substantial risk" that the baby would be born deformed. In defending his signature, Reagan said "a woman has a right to protect herself against physical harm or death or mental illness from this unborn child, just as she would have the same right to protect herself against an assailant in the street—and to take a human life if need be."[20] In 1967, there were 516 legal abortions performed in California; in 1980, the year Reagan was elected president, more than 109,000 were performed.[21] Years later, Reagan would become ardently pro-life and concede that he made a mistake by signing Beilenson's bill.

"We Are Demanding Real Change"

An enduring symbol of the second wave of feminism is *Ms.* magazine, which emerged in late 1971 and was co-founded by Gloria Steinem, the movement's most prominent figure. Steinem had come of age in the 1950s before women were encouraged to participate in public policy. Her magazine covered politics and women's issues—such as abortion, domestic violence, and workplace inequality—from a woman's perspective. Women, it said, "have begun to articulate our common pain, concern, enthusiasm . . . we are demanding real change."[22]

At that time in California, women had a steep hill to climb. There were no women in the top echelons of state government as appointees or jurists, and only a handful had succeeded in becoming elected officials. Although 53 percent of the population, women comprised less than three percent of the legislature. Many women were rallying around the proposed Equal Rights Amendment, sent by Congress to the states for ratification to become part of the US Constitution. Writing in the *Sacramento Bee*, Shirley Biagi Biondi, a member of the local chapter of the National Organization for Women, argued that even with ERA's passage, women would face a political vacuum. "Women have failed miserably so far in building a political power base to guarantee their rights," she wrote.[23] Women's campaigns for office had suffered from poor organization, political naiveté, and inadequate funding. The *California Journal* noted, "The movement has also failed to interest women who are working, low-income, and nonwhite."[24]

Although the ERA would fail to win approval from the required 38 states, California was among the first to ratify it. Various constituencies organized in

---

[19] Lou Cannon, *Governor Reagan* (New York: Public Affairs, 2003), 213.

[20] Swatt.

[21] Cannon, 213.

[22] "Women Candidates," *Ms.*, September 1972, 64.

[23] Shirley Biondi, "Women Clamor for Reforms in Man-Made Political Realm," *Sacramento Bee*, December 5, 1971, P1.

[24] Vonnie J. Madigan, "The Political Greening of the Women's Movement," *California Journal*, May 1976, 170–72.

the state to support it. They later would play critical roles in supporting women who ran for office and promoting issues of particular interest to women, including legislation dealing with child custody and family law, tax status, and fair employment. It was the galvanizing aspect of the ERA movement, and the growth of such groups as the League of Women Voters and the American Association of University Women that would attract Leona Egeland and others to politics and public policy.

Electoral gains in the 1970s were not made exclusively by liberal women who had been swept up by the women's movement and were bent on pursuing social change. Pauline Davis famously insisted on being called an assemblyman, and Rose Ann Vuich—the first woman in California's 126-year history to crash the state's exclusive senate men's club—proudly announced, "I do not intend to be here just as a women's libber representing only the women." [25] Vuich, an accountant and farmer who was raised near Fresno in rural Dinuba, shocked the establishment with a stunning and unexpected state senate victory in 1976. She thought the women's movement was too strident and noted that women didn't elect her, farmers did. She pledged that the farming community was going to be her primary focus.

Breaking a Senate Barrier—Rose Ann Vuich

Nineteen-seventy-six ushered in a gradual changing of the guard at the capitol. Voters two years earlier had approved the Political Reform Act, which restricted lobbyists' spending and influence. It effectively started to break up the capitol's "old boys' network," in which male lobbyists and lawmakers ate, caroused, and made public policy together. Vuich was one of 27 women nominees from the two major parties to run for the legislature that year—the largest female slate to date in California history—and she was considered one of the least likeliest to succeed. A conservative Democrat with a two-year trade school education, and the daughter of Yugoslav immigrants, Vuich's only previous public office was as an elected board member of a local hospital district. Defying the odds, Vuich ran for an open senate seat as a last-minute substitute when another woman candidate dropped out of the contest after her husband suffered a heart attack. Vuich was pitted against Ernest Mobley, a veteran Fresno Republican assemblyman who was well-financed, well-known, and had no skeletons in his closet. He was considered unbeatable in a Republican-leaning district.

Vuich lived with her widowed mother and brother on a 240-acre family farm and had little money or professional campaign help. She tapped a local phone company official to be her campaign manager, recruited family members to work on the campaign, and went farm to farm talking to voters. Veteran lobbyist Terry McHale said Vuich was perceived by Democratic power brokers as "sincere,

---

[25] Jerry Gillam, "A Woman Senator—Profile of Victory," *Los Angeles Times*, November 15, 1976, III16.

but naïve. They thought her indefatigability and grassroots understanding of the district was more old-fashioned than practical."[26] She scraped together enough money to finance a 30-second television spot that proved to be Mobley's undoing. While in the assembly, he had voted for a $50 million freeway link in Long Beach but failed to support appropriating money to complete a project in his own district. The unfinished local project, called the "freeway to nowhere," was an eyesore and embarrassment, and Vuich mocked Mobley for his inaction. She won by fewer than 3,000 votes. At her swearing in, and with the weight of history on her mind, Vuich started quivering. "I stood there, choking back tears, telling myself, 'Don't flub it. This is a men's club and men don't cry.'"[27]

At first, the men of the staid senate were unsure how to handle a woman's presence. Some called her "our farmer," others called her "Rosie." "I was greeted with nothing much less than shock," she told Copley News Service. "All the fellows would look over their glasses and wonder, 'How did she get here?'"[28] Vuich bought a small porcelain bell and kept it at her desk on the senate floor. Whenever her colleagues addressed the collective members of the senate as "gentlemen," she'd gently ring the bell to remind them that a lady was in the house, as well.

Like Pauline Davis before her in the assembly, Vuich also was confronted with the lack of women's facilities. The capitol building had been completed more than a century earlier, and the thought of a woman in the senate never occurred to the architects who designed a plush men's lounge and restroom a few steps off the senate floor. When Vuich arrived in Sacramento, the capitol building was in the early stages of a six-year, 68-million-dollar restoration—at the time, the largest such project in North american history. Both the senate and assembly chambers had to be moved into temporary outdoor locations adjacent to the building. To accommodate the senate's 39 men and Vuich, temporary men's and women's senate restrooms were constructed, but no one thought to label them. "One day, Senator Vuich came to me on the floor and said there was a problem," recalls former chief senate sergeant-at-arms Tony Beard. "She had been in the female restroom and some male senators walked in." From then on, a plaque bearing the image of a rose adorned the restroom door and the facility became known as the "Rose Room." When the legislature moved back to its newly restored chambers in 1982, another oversight was discovered: there was a sparse bathroom with toilets but no lounge or sitting room like the men had. "It was simply explained as, 'Construction forgot to build it,'" Beard says. Vuich, by then joined by Diane Watson in the upper house, designed a new facility that converted a former mail room that was slated to house electrical panels into the new and improved "Rose Room."

Vuich made it her singular goal to educate urban lawmakers—particularly Governor Jerry Brown, then in his first term—about the importance of agricul-

---

[26] Terry McHale, Rose Ann Vuich, *Capitol Morning Report*, February 4, 2002.

[27] "This Senator 'Played It Cool,'" *Bakersfield Californian*, March 11, 1977, 33.

[28] Margery Craig, Copley News Service, in the *Santa Rosa Press Democrat*, February 21, 1979, 11.

ture. She would bring alluring fresh produce into the senate but deny it to hungry colleagues until she explained the importance of the state's agriculture industry. Apparently, the strategy worked. She said senators told her "they voted for more agriculture bills . . . than in the past" because they were more aware of the importance of agriculture.[29] During her 16 years in the senate, she authored considerable legislation boosting her industry, including the creation of the state's Trade and Commerce Agency.

Minorities Ascendant—Diane Watson, Teresa Hughes, Maxine Waters, and Gwen Moore

With the floodgates against female participation now pried open, it took only two years after Vuich's upset victory for the senate to gain its second woman member—Democrat Diane Watson of Los Angeles, who was elected the senate's first female African American in 1978. Three years earlier, she had become the first black woman elected to the Los Angeles school board as it dealt with the thorny issue of desegregation. Watson was a vocal advocate of school busing. One of her campaign advisers, Jerry Zanelli, recalls that unlike Vuich, who had no demonstrable party support, Watson was acceptable to the political power structure and wasn't adverse to playing hard-ball politics. "I think qualified women were starting to step up, and that was the big difference. They believed they could win. A lot of voters were probably thinking, 'The guys have screwed up so bad, let's try a woman.'"

For some old-guard legislators, however, seeing the inexorable gender modernization of the cozy all-male senate was unnerving. During the campaign, Zanelli recalls that some time before Election Day, he was approached on the senate floor by 68-year-old senator Alfred Alquist. Watson had won the Democratic primary and would be a shoo-in in November. Noting her likely election on the heels of Vuich's victory, Alquist crisply remarked, "Watson's okay, but two women are enough!"[30] In an oral history for the California State Archives, Watson said she frequently lectured male colleagues on what it was like to be a woman in the senate. "I'm one-fortieth of you," she would say. "I got here the same way you did, not through affirmative action or discount points. Every vote was a real vote, someone walked in and voted."[31]

As Vuich and Watson paved the way for greater female participation in the venerable senate men's club, women were slowly reshaping the assembly, as well. By the time Watson made it to the senate, where she would serve for two decades, the assembly had already welcomed several minority women—March Fong Eu

---

[29] Jeannie Esajian, Associated Press, in *Pomona Progress Bulletin*, November 29, 1977, 11.

[30] Jerry Zanelli interview, Sacramento, April 7, 2017.

[31] Diane Watson oral history, conducted by Susan Douglass Yates, 1999, State Government Oral History Program, California State Archives, 212.

and Yvonne Brathwaite Burke in the sixties, and Teresa Hughes and Maxine Waters—both African Americans from Los Angeles—in the mid-seventies. The assembly would add Gwen Moore after the 1978 elections. All would enjoy long, successful careers in electoral politics, with Hughes serving in the legislature for 25 years—longer than any woman in history. Moore in particular would feel the particular women's burden of juggling family life and a career in politics. The mother of a young son, who remained at home in Los Angeles while she split time in Sacramento, Moore acknowledged, "I did a lot of parenting by phone."[32]

Waters was a liberal firebrand who helped lead the fight against apartheid by pushing the state pension system to divest investment funds from any business active in South Africa. The forceful Waters made a splash from the beginning. She chafed at what she considered the condescending treatment of women by some of the men. "The average male members tend to be patronizing and chauvinistic in their remarks without even knowing it," she told a reporter.[33] Women in the legislature were still a rarity, and at times sergeants-at-arms mistook them for secretaries. Waters once flashed her anger at a sergeant who tried to remove her from a row of seats in a committee room reserved for lawmakers. "I got mad one day . . . and said, 'If another damn sergeant puts me off the front row, I'm going to raise hell.'"

During her first month in office, Waters had signaled that her tenure would be progressive and controversial. One of five females in the assembly, she carried a resolution to eliminate the titles "assemblyman" and "assemblywoman" from the authorship of legislation. Instead, all authors would be referred to as "assemblymember." Although Waters insisted the proposal didn't represent part of the women's movement agenda, a number of her older male colleagues viewed the proposal with alarm. The new gender-neutral term, one argued, would "take the masculinity out of it" for male bill authors. The measure was approved over the objections of 26 men and one woman—Carol Hallett—a first-term Republican lawmaker from Atascadero along the central coast. She argued the entire exercise was a waste of time. "What we are called is irrelevant," Hallett contended.[34]

In future years, Waters would continue to hone her fiery reputation as a long-time member of California's congressional delegation. She became a leading voice calling for the impeachment of President Donald Trump, leading to a notorious running battle between them. "If you come for me I'm coming for you," the 79-year-old congresswoman proclaimed at the BET cable network's Black Girls Rock event in August 2017. "I'm simply a strong black woman." Trump would not back down either. "'He must be impeached,' that's all she knows how to say," Trump complained at the venerable Gridiron Club dinner in early March 2018.

---

[32] Gwen Moore oral history, conducted by Susan Douglass Yates, 2003–04, State Government Oral History Program, California State Archives, Sacramento, 92.

[33] "Women Legislators Still Find Sacramento a Masculine World," *San Bernardino Sun*, November 3, 1977, A17.

[34] Jerry Gillam, "Assembly Moves to Desex Its Titles," *Los Angeles Times*, January 14, 1977, I3.

"And then I say . . . I get in trouble for this . . . she has to immediately take an IQ test." Many Washington news reporters and their guests, at what is usually a hilarious roast of the high and mighty, gasped. Waters was undaunted: "Even his secretary of state did not deny he called him a moron. So, he has no credibility," she told an MSNBC interviewer a couple of days later.

A Conservative Voice Sets a Leadership Standard— Carol Hallett

Despite the liberal bent of the women's movement, it was Hallett—the conservative antifeminist—who rose to leadership the quickest among women in the legislature. In 1979, after barely two years in office, the quiet and unassuming Hallett became the first woman to lead a political party in either house. Hallett had been immersed in Republican Party politics since her early twenties when she first volunteered in the 1960 presidential campaign of Nelson Rockefeller. She worked for Barry Goldwater's unsuccessful presidential effort four years later, and then served on the staffs of a pair of GOP assemblymen. As the only woman in a four-person Republican primary, Hallett may have benefited from gender vote-splitting, but she never made a secret of the fact that she was offended by the "belligerent attitude" of the women's movement. "I wasn't elected because I was a woman but because I was the most qualified candidate," she said.[35] When Hallett arrived in Sacramento after her general election victory, Leona Egeland suggested the formation of an informal women's caucus. Hallett said she wasn't interested. "I am not a feminist, period," she insisted.[36]

An accomplished pilot who commuted to work from her ranch house in Atascadero in her Beechcraft Debonair, Hallett rarely participated in floor debates during her first term but, like Rose Ann Vuich in the senate, she burnished a reputation as a top advocate for the state's agricultural industry. Republicans sent a cadre of "Proposition 13 babies" to the assembly in 1978—mostly young, first-time lawmakers who had parlayed their unwavering support of that year's property-tax-cutting Proposition 13 into electoral success. In fact, more than half of all the Republicans in the assembly were freshmen. The GOP newcomers believed they were on a holy mission to cut taxes and reduce the size of government, but many of the more seasoned Republicans viewed the new crop as over-the-top superconservatives who first needed to pay their dues in a system that valued seniority. Not Carol Hallett. With one term under her belt, she skillfully cultivated the Proposition 13 disciples. "She didn't view us as apprentices," said 28-year-old freshman assemblyman Pat Nolan. Hallett quietly put together a coalition with mostly newcomers and ousted the party's moderate minority leader, Paul Priolo, who was viewed as being too cozy with Governor Brown and the Democratic

---

[35] Judith Michaelson, "Carol Hallett's Rise: Swift, Unnoticed," *Los Angeles Times*, June 24, 1979, 13.

[36] *San Bernardino Sun.*

Figure 9.1. Assembly Republican Leader Carol Hallett with Sen. H. L. Richardson and Assemblyman Ross Johnson
Credit: Courtesy of Ross Johnson

leadership. One reporter wrote that Hallett's coup "flabbergasted usually blasé Sacramento.[37]

By virtue of her new position, Hallett became one of Jerry Brown's most vocal critics, particularly on agricultural issues. She gave up her assembly seat to run unsuccessfully for lieutenant governor in 1982, but later held key positions in the Reagan and both Bush administrations and served as president and CEO of the Air Transport Association and counselor to the US Chamber of Commerce.

Latinas Begin to Make Their Mark— Gloria Molina

Given that she would become one of the most accomplished politicos in modern Los Angeles history, Gloria Molina's initial insecurities and self-doubt about seeking public office might seem difficult to understand. It was 1982, and Molina—a 33-year-old community activist advocating for the rights of Mexican-American girls and women—decided to seek election in an open assembly seat in southeast Los Angeles. "I didn't have enough confidence in myself," she recalled in an oral history for the California State Archives. She told herself, "I can't do it. I can't win . . . it's something that I find most Chicanas say to themselves."[38]

---

[37] Eric Brazil, Gannett News Service, in the *San Bernardino Sun*, May 11, 1979, 9.

[38] Gloria Molina oral history, conducted by Carlos Vasquez, 1990, State Government Oral History Program, California State Archives, Sacramento, 206, 207.

Figure 9.2. Gloria Molina
Credit: Courtesy of California Assembly

Molina, the oldest of 10 children, had been reared in a section of Montebello in southeast Los Angeles. Spanish was the only language she knew for the first three years of her life. Her father was a laborer born in Los Angeles and raised in Mexico. Her mother was Mexican. The family lived near a brickyard and a pool hall. "My parents wanted me to grow up and be a very traditional Latina, you know, go out and work for a couple of years, marry someone, have tons of children."[39] But Molina was the product of both the feminist and Chicano movements that took hold in the 1970s. The LA Chicano movement had been spurred by a 1968 walkout of thousands of high school students protesting poor classroom education. Molina became immersed in politics, volunteering in several Democratic campaigns, spending four years in the Carter administration, and working for Assemblyman Art Torres and Speaker Willie Brown before seeking public office herself in an assembly district that was heavily Democratic and 80 percent Latino. Molina ruffled feathers by challenging Richard Polanco, who was hand-picked by the community's powerful political machine. She was told "macho" Latino men would never vote for a woman. When she met with one of the power brokers, a personal friend, he responded tersely, "You can't run. You can't win. What are you talking about? You can't raise money. You can't get endorsements."[40]

---

[39] Abby Sewel, "Molina Aims for New Venture," *Los Angeles Times*, December 1, 2014, AA1.
[40] Molina oral history, 210.

Molina remembers that shortly before the election, the *Los Angeles Times* ran a story in which the reporter indicated that "more than likely, she'll lose that race, because she's a woman." Initial despondence and anger turned into a campaign-defining moment. She sent the article to women's groups, which responded with a flood of campaign contributions that financed a last-minute mailer and radio spot. Molina eked out a narrow victory in the primary, which ensured victory in November, as she became the first Latina to win election to the legislature. It earned her the title of "giant slayer." She credits the women's movement for much of her success.

After five years in the assembly—concentrating on issues such as sexual harassment, school dropouts, and insurance consumer protections—Molina returned to her community and spent the next quarter-century as the city's first Latina city councilwoman and first Latina county supervisor. Her initial victories in both the city and county came in newly created districts in response to lawsuits charging that Latino voting strength had been diluted when district boundaries were designed. Jaime Regalado, a former Cal State University Los Angeles political science professor, says Molina's long record of public service earned her a reputation as a "machine buster [and] vibrant force for women," although she could have a "pointed, harsh, frequently unfriendly and sometimes vindictive governing style."[41] Others say that, although her style might be severe, they never questioned her motives or determination.[42] Termed out as a supervisor in late 2014 at the sage of 66, Molina turned down retirement and once again stunned the establishment by challenging an incumbent city councilman. This time—and the only time in her political career—she came up short.

The Rise and Fall of a Liberal Lightning Rod—Rose Bird

There was no more polarizing figure in California during the 1970s and '80s than Rose Bird, the poster child for Governor Brown's campaign to open up the highest echelons of state government to women and minorities. Bird, the daughter of a chicken rancher, graduated with honors from Long Island University and the University of California's Boalt Hall School of Law. She and Brown had become friends while students at Berkeley. Bird had become the first female law clerk in the Nevada Supreme Court and the first female deputy public defender in Santa Clara County before Brown tapped her in 1975 to become the state's agriculture and services secretary. Bird oversaw California's huge agricultural industry, and

---

[41] Jaime Regalado, "Can Gloria Molina Still Slay Giants?" Zocalo Public Square, January 21, 2015, http://www.zocalopublicsquare.org/2015/01/21/can-gloria-molina-still-slay-giants/ideas/nexus/.

[42] Abby Sewell, "Outgoing L.A. County Supervisor Gloria Molina Opts for New Challenge," *Los Angeles Times*, December 1, 2014. Retrieved from http://www.latimes.com/local/california/la-me-gloria-molina-exit-20141201-story.html.

the governor gave her the task of creating a structure to deal with the longstanding rift between the state's growers and organized labor. Cesar Chavez, a close friend of Brown's and leader of the United Farm Workers Union, for years had led lettuce and grape boycotts to protest working conditions and low pay for Mexican-American field workers. Bird was a key author of the landmark Agricultural Labor Relations Act, which was approved by the legislature and guaranteed farmworkers the right to decide by secret ballot if they wanted to be represented by a union.

In 1977, the unpredictable and iconoclastic Brown shook up the legal establishment by appointing Bird as the first woman to sit on the state supreme court—and as its chief justice, no less. He also placed Wiley Manuel on the court as its first African American. Four years later, Brown would appoint the court's first Latino, Cruz Reynoso, and Allen Broussard, another African American. Despite criticism of her lack of judicial experience, Bird was confirmed by the Commission on Judicial Appointments. Evelle Younger, the Republican attorney general, disappointed conservatives when he cast the deciding vote in her favor.

From the beginning of her tenure on the court, Bird faced attacks for her decisions on school busing, taxes, and crime, and stories leaked that her personality and style were affecting court unity. Associate justice Stanley Mosk, who was passed over for chief justice by Jerry Brown, believed Bird was bright and intelligent, but he also characterized her as aloof and ill-equipped to be the administrative and legal head of the state's judiciary. He once told her, "I certainly cannot blame you for being here, but I blame Jerry Brown for putting you here."[43]

Barely a year after Bird's appointment to the court, a vote to deny her retention fell short by 200,000 votes out of six million cast. But even as Bird celebrated a narrow political victory, the *Los Angeles Times*, citing anonymous sources, suggested the court had deliberately held up release of a controversial criminal case to help Bird's chances at the polls. In public hearings by the Commission on Judicial Performance, Bird lashed out at "faceless, nameless accusers who have thrown delicate china into a laundromat."[44] No formal charges of misconduct were brought, but Bird's political problems would get worse.

By the time Brown left office in 1983 after two terms as governor, he had completely reshaped the court into what critics said was a bastion of liberal activism. Although Broussard argued that the court had affirmed 95 percent of criminal convictions that had been appealed, Bird continued to find herself in the middle of a political maelstrom. One of her most vocal critics, conservative state senator H. L. Richardson noted "the blood and carnage that follows after the decisions that she's made."[45] Critics, including incumbent governor George Deukmejian, who was seeking reelection, took aim at the chief justice again during her retention

[43] Stanley Mosk oral history, conducted by Germaine La Berge, 1998, State Oral History Program, California State Archives, 54.

[44] Steve Swatt, "Brown: The Governor," KCRA-TV, January 2, 1983.

[45] Ibid.

election in 1986, and they also targeted two other liberal justices—Reynoso and 1982 appointee Joseph Grodin—in their well-funded campaign. Bird had heard 61 death penalty cases, and she had voted to strike down lower-court death sentences every time. "Bird, a brilliant student of the law," wrote Brown biographer Chuck McFadden, "had somehow found a legal reason to overturn in every one of the 61 cases, despite an earlier promise to uphold the death penalty if she found that the trial was fair and the law constitutional."[46] Mosk noted that he was as antideath penalty as Bird, "but the difference is that I took an oath to support the law as it is and not as I might prefer it to be."[47]

Voters Reject Governor Jerry Brown's Liberal Supreme Court

Between 1977 and 1986, while Bird led the court, California's population had increased by 23 percent, but overall violent crime rose by 38 percent. Many offenses, however—including murder, rape, and property crime—had increased at a significantly slower pace.[48] Still, Californians overwhelmingly favored capital punishment and crime routinely topped the charts as an issue that concerned Californians the most, particularly with the "if it bleeds, it leads" emphasis on news coverage by the state's leading television stations. After a devastatingly effective campaign that employed emotional television ads featuring the families of crime victims, all three targets—Bird, Reynoso, and Grodin—were ousted from the court. The vote against Bird was two-to-one.

On election night, the vanquished chief justice addressed supporters and faced a bank of television cameras. "How am I taking this?" she offered. "My answer is, "Just like a man." There were laughs all around, and then she turned serious. "I don't think anybody in the state will sit easy if in fact this becomes a court that ensures nothing but executions to satisfy the overweening and insatiable appetite of ambitious politicians." She accused powerful groups of bypassing the legislative process and subverting the independent judiciary so they could have pliant judges do their will.[49] After her ouster, Bird eschewed the spotlight. She taught in Australia, did volunteer work at a food bank and lectured. In 1999, at the age of sixty-three, she died of breast cancer.

With three vacancies to fill on the seven-member court, Deukmejian reshaped the panel from one of the most liberal high courts in the country to one of the most reliably conservative. Aside from criminal matters, the Bird court had issued important decisions on issues such as free speech, social justice, workers' rights, and others. Thirteen years after Bird's ouster, *Los Angeles Times* legal affairs re-

---

[46] Chuck McFadden, *Trailblazer* (Berkeley: UC Press, 2013), 75.

[47] Mosk oral history, 57.

[48] "California Crime Rates," http://www.disastercenter.com/crime/cacrime.htm, California Crime Rates 1960–2016.

[49] KPIX, November 4, 1986, Rose Bird Speaks, http://rosebirdspeaks.blogspot.com, February 16, 2012.

porter Maura Dolan noted, "Scholars can no longer even point to a landmark ruling of the Bird court that has survived and continues to affect the law. The post-Bird courts overturned or sidestepped her rulings to move in a dramatically different direction, not just in criminal matters but also in consumer affairs, the environment, and personal injury cases."[50] Even with the lapse of more than four decades, Rose Bird remains a divisive historical figure in California—courageous to some, but to others an embodiment of "soft on crime" liberalism. However, one part of her legacy endures. She had aggressively campaigned for more female and minority judges, and in later years, the supreme court not only become ethnically diverse, but for several years had a female majority.

A Women's Caucus Forms in the Legislature

In the early 1980s, women comprised 10 percent of the legislature but felt unwelcome at the nightly gatherings of male lawmakers at popular downtown Sacramento bars and restaurants. They had begun monthly informal social meetings that gradually morphed into bipartisan discussions on public policy. Despite their political differences, the women figured they could be persuasive and increase their clout if they came together on behalf of certain issues, and in 1985 the nine Democrats and six Republicans were formally recognized as the Women's Caucus. Assembly Republican Marian LaFollette remembered that male lawmakers jeered and hooted when the subject of a women's caucus arose on the assembly floor. The first official act of the caucus was to denounce Bill Lockyer, the Democratic chair of the senate judiciary committee, who days earlier had publicly characterized as "mindless blather" comments made by Diane Watson during a committee discussion on the death penalty.[51] "He said things that he would never say to another man, and with expletives thrown in," Watson said.[52] "We all felt violated, not just me."[53] Lockyer later apologized.

In the ensuing years, the women accepted their differences on taxes, spending, the size of government, and politically divisive social issues and united where they found common ground. They held high-profile hearings on child care licensing and Norplant, a controversial birth control device. They backed and passed measures concerning child support, Pap smears, breast cancer, domestic violence, divorce, and the distribution of free cigarettes to minors. (Years later, after Pete Wilson became governor, caucus members even asked Gayle Wilson to lobby her husband with "pillow talk.") Official caucus positions required a two-thirds vote, and often the women's support decided the fate of legislation. Crusty and

---

[50] Maura Dolan, "Bird's Legacy More Political Than Legal," *Los Angeles Times*, December 6, 1999, I1.

[51] Mark Gladstone, "Women's Caucus Raps Sen. Lockyer's Outburst," *Los Angeles Times*, August 29, 1985, I3.

[52] Watson oral history, 296.

[53] Ibid., 297.

cantankerous Southern California Assemblyman Richard Floyd—who described himself as "an old male chauvinist SOB"—credited the women with giving him the margin of victory on his signature bill to require motorcyclists to wear helmets, contending that helmetless riders cost state taxpayers $65 million a year in medical costs. During a capitol hearing, more than a hundred angry, leather- and chain-clad members of the notorious Hell's Angels motorcycle gang demonstrated their opposition on the capitol steps. "All the men were afraid if they voted for this, there would be a Hell's Angel on the doorstep the next morning," Floyd said. "The women weren't afraid of anything. I'd rather deal with 150 Hell's Angels than the Women's Caucus if they think I'm wrong."[54]

In a study of new laws affecting gender equity in civil rights, education, and the workplace, California senate researchers pointed to "a burst of legislative activity around women's equality" after the mid-1960s, affecting almost every aspect of public life and giving the state "the equivalent of a state equal-rights amendment."[55]

As the decade of the eighties ended, women were participating in the political process as never before. Nowhere was it more evident than in that bastion of testosterone—the staid state senate. In less than 15 years, female representation had jumped from zero to five. There continued to be challenges, however, as women struggled to be taken seriously as political practitioners. At a committee hearing, Rebecca Morgan, a Republican from the Silicon Valley, recoiled when a lobbyist continually referred to members as "gentlemen of the committee." Morgan snapped, "Sir, are you so sure of your votes on this committee that you don't need mine?"[56] For women, the male-dominated news media was part of the problem. The first time Morgan received national press attention was for wearing a pantsuit on the senate floor. Orange County Republican Marian Bergeson bristled at being called "grandmotherly" in frequent media accounts. She never recalled any of her male senate colleagues "who are perhaps comparable in age levels ever being called 'grandfatherly.'"[57] And Lucy Killea, a Democrat-turned-Independent from San Diego and a former CIA analyst, recalled giving a speech early in her political career. After her talk concluded, a member of the audience turned to Killea's husband and said, "That was a nice speech you wrote."[58] Killea also made national news when she was refused communion by the bishop of the San Diego Roman Catholic Diocese because she supported abortion rights.

---

[54] Virginia Ellis, "Women Gain Clout in the Capitol," *Los Angeles Times*, November 6, 1991, 11.

[55] Kate Sproul, Rebecca LaVally, ed., "Women and Equality: A California Review of Women's Equity Issues in Civil Rights, Education and the Workplace, Senate Office of Research, Sacramento, February 1999, http://sor.senate.ca.gov/sites/ sor.senate.ca.gov/files/Women%20and%20Equality.pdf.

[56] Kim Alexander, "Women Senators in the Old Boys' Club: At the Gates of Power," *Sacramento News and Review,* March 28, 1991, 18.

[57] Ibid.

[58] Ibid.

Historic Campaign for Governor—
Dianne Feinstein

Emboldened by recent legislative successes, women stood at the verge of breaking new ground in 1990, with five female candidates receiving major-party nominations for statewide office. The most-watched contest featured former San Francisco Mayor Dianne Feinstein, who sought to become the state's first female governor. In a race with no incumbent, she had what so many women candidates before her lacked—a lengthy list of groundbreaking accomplishments, skyrocketing name identification and star quality, as well as the ability to raise campaign cash.

As a child, Dianne Goldman was a product of a caring father and an abusive mother. Leon Goldman was a staunch Republican and the first Jewish chair of surgery at the University of California's medical school in San Francisco. Dianne's mother, Betty, was a beautiful Russian immigrant and former model who was raised Orthodox Catholic and insisted Dianne attend the Convent of the Sacred Heart in San Francisco. Betty had an explosive temper, "which filled her rose-trellised San Francisco mansion with screaming curses and secret dread," wrote Feinstein biographer Jerry Roberts.[59] According to a *San Francisco Chronicle* profile in 2012, Feinstein once witnessed her mother try to drown a younger sister in the bathtub, "and as the eldest of three girls, she often took the brunt of her mother's wrath."[60]

In Feinstein's senior year of high school, she was accepted to the University of California, Berkeley, and Stanford. Her father pushed hard for Berkeley, which had a number of prominent Nobel laureates on the faculty. Feinstein favored Stanford, because she wanted to attend a smaller school. "Remember, Dianne," she remembers her father saying, "It's better to sit one-thousand feet away from a genius than one-hundred feet from a mediocrity."[61] Flashing a bit of teen-age rebellion, she chose Stanford, gravitated toward history and politics, and helped establish the school's first chapter of Young Democrats. She also was educated about gender issues in the rough and tumble world of politics when she ran for student body vice president, the highest office women could hold. Running against two men, she nonetheless campaigned on fraternity row where men peppered her with food and hauled her into a shower. She won with 63 percent of the vote.[62]

---

[59] Jerry Roberts, *Dianne Feinstein: Never Let Them See You Cry* (San Francisco: HarperCollinsWest, 1994), 9.

[60] Carolyn Lochhead, "Dianne Feinstein: 4 decades of influence," *San Francisco Chronicle*, October 22, 2012, http://www.sfgate.com/politics/article/Dianne-Feinstein-4-decades-of-influence-3968314.php.

[61] Romesh Ratnesar, "The Making of Dianne Feinstein," *Stanford,* December 17, 2017, 51.

[62] Ibid., 51–52.

After a brief, failed marriage and a remarriage to neurosurgeon Bertram Feinstein, Dianne sought a political future, winning election to San Francisco's board of supervisors in 1969 and later becoming its first female president. Her political ambitions appeared to plateau after two unsuccessful runs for San Francisco mayor. On November 27, 1978, Feinstein walked into the city hall pressroom and told a few reporters that she had decided to finish her term and retire from politics.[63]

About two hours later, Dan White, a former police officer and member of the board of supervisors, eased through a basement window at city hall with a loaded .38 caliber revolver, eluding recently installed metal detectors. Days earlier, White had resigned from the board, then changed his mind and asked Mayor George Moscone for his job back. Moscone initially agreed but reconsidered and decided to replace White with a more liberal appointee. White calmly walked into Moscone's office and fired two shots into the mayor's back and two more into his head, killing him instantly. After reloading, he left through a side door and walked the marbled corridors to the supervisors' offices. According to Assemblyman Willie Brown, who moments earlier had been meeting with Moscone, White walked past Feinstein's office and commented to her, "I'll be back in a minute. I have something to do."[64] Seconds later, Feinstein heard gunshots and discovered the body of Harvey Milk, San Francisco's first openly gay supervisor. White had shot him five times. Finding no pulse, she rushed to Moscone's office and was told he was dead. A few minutes later, a shaken but resolute Feinstein stood on the steps of city hall and declared, "Both Mayor Moscone and Supervisor Harvey Milk have been shot and killed." There were audible gasps from the public and the media.[65]

By a majority vote of the supervisors, Feinstein was named interim mayor to serve out Moscone's term. A year later, she won a full term and was reelected in 1983. She governed from the center-left, bringing the city together after the assassinations and focusing on public safety, fiscal responsibility, international trade, and the emerging AIDS epidemic. Veteran San Francisco reporter Hank Plante noted that there was a time when "Feinstein's AIDS budget for the city was bigger than [President] Reagan's AIDS budget for the entire nation."[66] In 1984, she was on Walter Mondale's short list to be his vice presidential running mate before he picked New York representative Geraldine Ferraro.

Feinstein's second full term as San Francisco's chief executive ended in early 1988. With a long list of accomplishments, she had been selected the nation's most effective mayor by *City and State* magazine and readied her campaign to become the state's first female governor. One veteran political observer boldly

---

[63] John Jacobs, *A Rage for Justice* (Berkeley: University of California Press, 1995), 406.

[64] *Willie Brown, Basic Brown* (New York: Simon and Shuster, 2008), 132.

[65] YouTube, https://www.youtube.com/watch?v=jA1Lj04k-so.

[66] Hank Plante, "AIDS: Bay Area Leadership Brings Hope to Epidemic," *San Francisco Chronicle,* May 27, 2011, http://www.sfgate.com/opinion/article/AIDS-Bay-Area-leadership-brings-hope-to-epidemic-2370127.php.

declared, "1990 qualifies as a watershed year for women—reaching new sexual parity in California."[67]

That observer spoke too soon, however. The 1980s also were a time of backlash, when "women's liberation" was subtly—or not so subtly—blamed for throwing girls and women into a troubled sea of angst, confusion, and despair. Susan Faludi in her 1991 book, *Backlash: The Undeclared War against American Women*, argued that mass media from newspapers to films linked the campaign for women's equality to "nearly every woe besetting women, from mental depression to meager savings accounts, from teenage suicides to eating disorders to bad complexions." Although American culture historically has pushed back against women's rights, Faludi asserted, attacks on the movement typically flare or smolder in tandem with the progress of the cause. And the movement was moving faster now. Ostensibly protected by new laws that defined and banned sexual harassment in the workplace, and sometimes boosted by affirmative action policies that sought out females and underrepresented minorities, women were moving into "nontraditional" jobs in record numbers and even supervising men.

Throughout much of the eighties, though, Republican governor George Deukmejian labored to replace Jerry Brown's maverick legacy with one focused on law and order—there would be no more Rose Birds. Across the continent in Washington, the popular Republican president, Ronald Reagan, had opposed the Equal Rights Amendment. Critics complained that Reagan seemed indifferent at best to feminism—although he had bowed to pressures of the times by appointing Sandra Day O'Connor as the first woman justice on the US Supreme Court.[68]

Into this volatile mix, Feinstein tossed a lit match in the spring of 1990. Campaigning for the Democratic nomination for governor against state attorney general John Van de Kamp, Feinstein pledged to the National Council of Negro Women at a luncheon in Los Angeles that she would name women to half of the government jobs and judicial posts that she would be charged with filling as governor. She also vowed to appoint people of color in percentages equal to their representation in California's population.[69] Voters and political critics responded with a hail of derision. Feinstein was accused of wanting to run a government based on quotas rather than qualifications. Although she won the nomination less than two weeks later, male Californians opposed her parity ideas by a margin of four to one. Even women were opposed, according to a *Los Angeles Times* Poll, by a margin of two to one.

---

[67] Ed Salzman, "The Rise of Women in California Politics," *Los Angeles Times*, March 11, 1990, M4.

[68] See Susan Faludi, *Backlash: The Undeclared War against American Women* (New York: Doubleday, 1991), xii; and Lynn Hecht Schafran, "Reagan vs. Women," *The New York Times*, October 13, 1981, http://www.nytimes.com/1981/10/13/ opinion/reagan-vs-women.html.

[69] John Balzar, "Feinstein Vows Hiring Quotas by Race, Sex." *Los Angeles Times*, May 27, 1990, A1.

The poll also found men disagreeing, three to two, that it was "time we had a woman governor," while women disagreed slightly.[70] Feinstein's call for making history clearly held the potential to backfire among men. Yet there was no rule book for how to become a state's first woman governor—whether to emphasize or downplay the change. Only three states—Vermont, Nebraska, and Arizona—had female governors in 1990. (And one of those, Democrat Rose Mofford of Arizona, had succeeded an impeached governor because she was secretary of state.)

By the start of the general election campaign against Republican US Senator Pete Wilson, Feinstein was on the defensive. She released an early ad contending she always opposed quotas for women and minorities in public jobs. Instead, her campaign told reporters, she had been talking about "goals."[71] Feinstein played down the historic nature of her candidacy until the final stretch. "Are you ready to elect the first woman governor in the state?" she exhorted seniors at a Leisure World in Southern California.[72] Women comprised more than half the electorate, but Wilson had overtaken her in the polls after he endorsed a ballot measure to impose term limits on state officeholders. Democratic political consultant David Townsend, however, had a theory that at the last moment, in the privacy of the voting booth, thousands of Republican women would cast votes to make history. "They're going to stand there for a couple of seconds and they're going to say, "You know: imagine what this would mean for a woman to be governor of the biggest state in America. Imagine what message this sends to our daughters."[73]

That year, two of the five California women who ran statewide campaigns won their races. Democrat Kathleen Brown, Jerry Brown's sister, would become state treasurer. March Fong Eu was elected to her fifth and final term as secretary of state. But the big prize narrowly eluded Feinstein, who lost by just 3.5 percentage points. (Perhaps savoring the twist, Wilson as governor would push a successful voter initiative to end public affirmative action in California.) California women who hoped that 1990 would become a dramatic "Year of the Woman" had to wait one more election cycle. Even so, no California woman as of this writing has ever come as close to becoming governor.

Discussion Questions

1. For what reasons did Leona Egeland believe the Watergate scandal helped her as a woman candidate for the assembly in the mid-seventies? How many other women were serving in the legislature in 1975 when she was sworn

---

[70] George Skelton, "Wilson, Feinstein about Even in Race for Governor," *Los Angeles Times*, June 22, 1990, OCA1.

[71] Bill Stall, "Feinstein on Defensive with TV Ad Opposing Quotas," *Los Angeles Times*, August 3, 1990, A3.

[72] Cathleen Decker, "Governor's Race Close at the Wire," *Los Angeles Times*, November 4, 1990, A1.

[73] Steve Swatt, KCRA-TV, November 2, 1990.

in? In what ways did her feminism make a difference in her approach to legislating?

2. In what ways were the civil rights and second-wave women's movements entwined? How was this reminiscent of the abolitionist and suffrage movements?

3. For what reasons might it have been surprising that Republican Governor Ronald Reagan signed the Therapeutic Abortion Act of 1967? What did it seek to do? Why did Senator Anthony Beilenson sponsor it?

4. How did the Equal Rights Amendment fare in California? For what reasons do you supposed it failed to win ratification from sufficient states by the early eighties? What would have been some possible objections to it?

5. Assemblywomen Pauline Davis and Carol Hallett and the first state senator, Rose Ann Vuich, did not see themselves as primarily advocating the cause of feminism, although Egeland saw herself that way. Do you believe that representation by Davis, Hallett, and Vuich made a difference for California women, regardless?

6. Conservative women may become successful trailblazers because they are viewed by voters as less threatening to the status quo. Discuss why, or why not, this may have been the case with Vuich, who broke a 126-year-old glass ceiling in the state senate. Was it the case with Hallett?

7. The concept of "intersectionality" suggests that qualities such as gender, race, ethnicity, class, age, and sexuality combine to create unequal experiences for individuals and unequal impacts on them. Discuss in what ways the experiences and impacts of Diane Watson, Teresa Hughes, Maxine Waters, and/or Gwen Moore as legislators might have been influenced by race as well as gender.

8. What effects might the intersection of ethnicity and gender have had on the ways Gloria Molina approached political office?

9. For what reasons did Governor Jerry Brown's nomination of Rose Bird as chief justice of the state supreme court prove to be highly controversial? Do you believe his choice of Bird was useful or mistaken?

10. Why was Dianne Feinstein's quest for governor hindered by her vows to name women to half of the appointed jobs in the executive and judicial branches, and also to make representative appointments of people of color? Do you agree with these pledges, or were they misguided? Would public reaction to them be similar or different today?

Recommended Reading

Cairns, Kathleen A. *The Case of Rose Bird: Gender, Politics, and the California Courts*. Lincoln: University of Nebraska Press, 2016.

McFadden, Chuck. *Trailblazer: A Biography of Jerry Brown*. Berkeley: University of California Press, 2013.

Morris, Celia. *Storming the Statehouse: Running for Governor with Ann Richards and Dianne Feinstein.* New York: Scribner's Sons, 1992.

Chapter 10

1940s to Present
Women Protesters Agitate for Change

"I have given my life to the struggle. My life belongs to the struggle."
—Angela Davis, 1970

On a cool spring Los Angeles evening in 1976, things got hot. It was only a few weeks after a PTA mom named Bobbi Fiedler decided she had to stand up against a massive plan to desegregate Los Angeles schools with wholesale teacher reassignments and mandatory busing for thousands of schoolchildren. At the third in a series of meetings intended to rally parents against the busing plan, Fiedler stood on the stage of an auditorium in West Los Angeles, looking out at hundreds of agitated moms and dads. Police helicopters circled overhead while armed officers kept watch backstage. Outside, "radical elements . . . of the Communist party came marching down and in fatigues and bullhorns screaming 'burn Miller, burn,'" Fiedler recalled, referring to Los Angeles School Board member Howard Miller, then a busing opponent who was the featured speaker that night. "At that time we were still, you know, fairly innocent, just parents trying to protect the futures of our kids, and we had no idea" that such radical opponents would show up to disrupt things.[1]

Nobody was hurt, but the inflamed tensions that night caused some of the more timid members of the group to argue that the meetings should be stopped. Fiedler, the daughter of an ex-prizefighter, would have none of it. "I wasn't particularly concerned, I was mad! I was really angry that they tried to prevent us from being able to communicate, because we still have the First Amendment in this country."[2]

Fiedler and other affluent parents—most from hillside communities overlooking the San Fernando Valley—early-on formed a grassroots organization they called Bustop, which quickly became "the biggest and most effective opponent of mandatory busing in Los Angeles."[3] The group readily embraced a role spear-

---

[1] Bobbi Fiedler Oral History Interview, conducted by Richard McMillan, November 17, 1988. Urban Archives General Oral Histories Collection, 1967–2004, Delmar T. Oviatt Library, California State University Northridge.

[2] Ibid.

[3] Bill Boyarsky, "How Bustop Became a Force in School Suit," *Los Angeles Times,* May 15, 1977, C1.

heading lawsuits against the court-ordered plan to transport kids out of their local neighborhoods as well as election challenges to incumbent school board members who supported forced integration. Other parents eagerly pushed Fiedler out to the point of the spear.

The *Los Angeles Times* called her "the San Fernando Valley's version of Everywoman—a suburban housewife who built a national political career by challenging the status quo."[4] She was a 38-year-old mother of two, working days in the family pharmacy and meeting an increasing number of evenings with PTA parents at Encino's Lanai Road Elementary School in late 1975. "I'd get up early to make the kids' sandwiches and take them to school," she explained in one interview. "Then I'd go to work and get off in time to pick the kids up and take them to Little League, girls' softball, whatever they had going that day. I had no political aspirations at all," she said.[5] Fiedler insists she was a supporter of *voluntary* integration: "I'm Jewish, so I was strongly opposed to segregation."[6] However, she believed forced busing deprived parents of the right to choose where their children attended school. Then came the school busing order and "I felt I had to stop it."[7] She started attending school board meetings, taking notes and reporting back to her growing group of distressed, mostly white neighbors.

From PTA Mom to Revolt Leader— Bobbi Fiedler

Her rise was meteoric. Within weeks she had become a protest leader, rallying thousands of parents across Los Angeles. Despite telling folks she "couldn't stand politics or politicians,"[8] Fiedler heeded urgings from her supporters at Bustop to campaign for a school board seat, even though "I was scared to death."[9] Little more than a year after forming Bustop, as a savvy Republican political neophyte, she defeated progressive LA School Board President Dr. Robert Doctor in a citywide election. Her appeal as a suburban homemaker taking on the establishment didn't fade, either. *Daily News of Los Angeles* reporter Dennis McCarthy colorfully captured her allure to those suburban parents:

---

[4] Sandy Banks, "Fiedler Remains a Force in Politics," *Los Angeles Times,* August 10, 1997, http://articles.latimes.com/1997/aug/10/local/me-21232.

[5] Dennis McCarthy, "Fiedler Rode the Buses to a New Career," *Daily News of Los Angeles,* January 8, 1986, 3.

[6] Fiedler Oral History.

[7] Susan Khanweiler Pollock, "Bobbi Fiedler," Jewish Women's Archive, Sharing Stories Inspiring Change, https://jwa.org/encyclopedia/article/fiedler-bobbi.

[8] James Sweeney, "Bobbi Fiedler—She's Beaten the Odds Many Times in the Past," *Daily News of Los Angeles,* January 25, 1986, 8.

[9] Kathleen Neumeyer, "The Fiedler Formula: Busing . . . Children . . . Boston," *California Journal,* December 1981, 427.

She was hot. This woman with the bow-tie blouses and wide smile was not some polished, handpicked, machine candidate. She came from the streets—from the carpools, the PTA meetings, and the antibusing picket lines.

Voters liked this image. It was as if one of their own had cracked the starting lineup and damned if they weren't going to go out there and support her.[10]

In 1980, she tapped the vein of rising Reagan Republicanism in the Valley to defeat longtime Democratic Congressman James Corman and move to the US House of Representatives. There she toiled for three terms as a faithful supporter of President Ronald Reagan, delivering a renomination speech for him at the 1984 Republican National Convention.

That a Republican woman could beat venerable and popular liberals in a 60 percent Democratic city demonstrated just how volatile the busing issue had become and how quickly Fiedler had taken to protest leadership. The school district had been waging a simmering court fight against mandatory integration since 1964. The California Supreme Court's eventual order to desegregate in 1975 ignited a culture war across the city. Many white parents feared their children could be bused as much as 35 miles and an hour each way from their homes to east and south LA schools dominated by Latino and black children.

While even many minority families joined in opposition to busing that would take their children so far away, civil rights groups and many neighborhood leaders believed it would improve the quality of education that culturally underrepresented children were receiving, expose white children to greater diversity, and reduce the social challenges presented by disadvantaged schools. Ultimately about one in 10 of the district's more than half-million children were bused out of their neighborhoods.[11] Meantime, the white population of the city fell from nearly 2.2 million in 1970 to 1.84 million in 1980.[12]

Fiedler deftly tapped that white anxiety. With the Watts riots of 1965 still a troubling memory for many Valley parents, "white flight" had become a reality in Los Angeles. Overall, the nation's second-largest school district already had a majority of minority students, although that wasn't true in its schools in the San Fernando Valley north of the city center. Enrollment in the sprawling district dropped by nearly 100,000. The Los Angeles district was forced to close about 20

---

[10] McCarthy.

[11] Robert Lindsey, "Los Angeles Schools End Busing Program," *New York Times,"* March 17, 1981.

[12] Schneider, Jack, "Escape from Los Angeles: White Flight from Los Angeles and Its Schools, 1960–1980," *Journal of Urban History* 34 (2008): 995–1012. 10.1177/0096144208317600.

schools—most of them in the Valley—by the time the courts accepted a voluntary busing plan in 1981.[13]

California Voters Embrace Fiedler

California's experience with court-ordered school busing didn't take the more riotous turns seen in Boston and some southern cities like Louisville. It was fought most intensely in the courts and at the ballot box. Fiedler was staunchly persistent in opposing forced busing after she won that first campaign in 1977 and helped to elect other antibusing activists to the board. On the other side, Superior Court Judge Paul Egly was equally unrelenting in ordering the board to follow through on the 1975 state supreme court ruling to desegregate. He accused Fiedler and her colleagues on the board of "foot-dragging" after they failed repeatedly to comply with his and other court orders. California voters sided overwhelmingly with Fiedler, giving 70 percent support to Proposition 1, a state constitutional amendment she pushed for in 1979 mandating that California courts should be limited in school desegregation cases to standards created by the Fourteenth Amendment's Equal Protection Clause in the US Constitution. Courts could no longer follow more expansive California laws and court rulings. And in 1980, the US Supreme Court upheld Proposition 1.

Feeling that she had accomplished her goals on the school board, Fiedler turned to Congress. She rode President Ronald Reagan's coattails in 1980 to defeat Corman by just 750 votes out of 200,000 cast and became California's only woman in Congress at the time. By then, as a *California Journal* profile asserted, she had built "a political machine in Southern California that has dominated the city school board. . . ."[14]

In Washington, her record tended to support her insistence that she was an independent Republican, fiscally conservative and socially progressive. She largely adhered to Republican fiscal dogma as a member of the House Budget Committee but refused to toe the party line on such charged issues as abortion and the Equal Rights Amendment, which was aimed at specifically securing women's rights in the Constitution. She fought a plan by Reagan to cut federal support for disabled people and sponsored child care tax credit and pension reform legislation. Fiedler earned an A+ rating from the American Israel Public Affairs Committee (AIPAC), the pro-Israel lobby, for her unwavering support of Israel.[15]

She went on to win two more congressional elections by large majorities before deciding to enter the 1986 Republican primary election to select a challenger to Democratic incumbent US Senator Alan Cranston. She faced six men in the primary, including state senator Ed Davis, whose home district overlapped

---

[13] Naush Boghossian, "Kids Volunteer for Long Rides to School," *Los Angeles Daily News,* February 22, 2006.

[14] Neumeyer.

[15] Pollock.

Figure 10.1. Bobbi Fiedler, from PTA Mom to Congress
Credit: Collection of the U.S. House of Representatives

hers. In a bizarre turn, Davis accused Fiedler of trying to bribe him out of the race with an offer of $100,000 to help cover his campaign debt—a charge Fiedler vehemently denied. She and her longtime aide and political advisor, Paul Clarke, were indicted in January, only five months before the election. Thirty-three days later, a judge threw out the indictments as groundless, but the damage had been done. She lost the election, gaining only seven percent of the vote, and moved on to become a lobbyist and political commentator. The following year, she and Clarke were married.

While her elective career ended amid political recrimination and legal brawls, Fiedler never shied away from a fight. She was always convinced, however, that her longstanding image as a homemaker who jumped into politics to protect her children was a "decided asset" that endured in all her election races. Reluctant to call herself a feminist, she still acknowledged while in Congress that she felt a "special obligation" to represent the concerns of women because nobody else was doing it. In a 1988 oral history interview, Fiedler asserted, "I began to realize that most men have very little real knowledge of the problems women face."

The Immigrant Mom Who Launched School Integration— Felicitas Mendez

It's an historic irony that a female leader whose name has been largely lost to history paved the way for the school desegregation upon which Bobbi Fiedler would build her antibusing crusade and political career three decades later. Immigrant Felicitas Mendez, angered at discrimination against her children, waged a legal battle in the Orange County community of Westminster in the mid-1940s that helped topple the school segregation laws that had been part of California's social fabric for nearly a century. Her efforts set the stage for one of the US Supreme Court's most momentous and far-reaching decisions—*Brown v. Board of Education of Topeka, Kansas.*

Much of the drama in the Orange County case would play out in a federal courtroom and the state legislature. But the primary protagonists were Felicitas Mendez and her husband Gonzalo Mendez, Mexican immigrants who had no connections to California's political power structure. Whereas Gonzalo was analytical—fighting school segregation because he believed it was unconstitutional—Felicitas passionately seethed over the hurtful treatment of the couple's daughter and two sons. Sometimes, she said years later, "a person gets tired of being pushed around."[16]

Separating students by their ethnicity and skin color had been a California practice since the early years of statehood, when African-American schoolchildren in San Francisco became the first in the state to be officially segregated. Under the headline, "The Inferior Races in the Public Schools," the *Sacramento Union* quoted that state law as reading: "Negroes, Mongolians and Indians shall not be admitted into the public schools."[17] California's third state superintendent of schools, Andrew Jackson Moulder, was blunt on the issue: "The great mass of our citizens will not associate in terms of equality with these inferior races, nor will they consent that their children do so."[18]

After six years as state superintendent, Moulder became chief of San Francisco's schools. In the mid-1880s, Mamie Tape, a young Chinese girl, was barred from attending schools in the city. Her mother, Mary Tape, sued and won a ruling based on the Fourteenth Amendment to the US Constitution: "Chinese children born in this country are entitled to admission into public schools." The court stated, however, that Chinese children could be educated in separate but equal schools. A newspaper report of the ruling noted, "The decision creates much surprise and excitement."[19] At a time that public sentiment favored Chinese exclusion, much of that excitement was negative. In response, Mary Tape wrote a scathing letter to the *Daily Alta California* in San Francisco. "Is it a disgrace to be born Chinese?" she wrote. "Didn't God make us all? May you, Mr. Moulder, never be persecuted the way you have persecuted little Mamie Tape."[20]

---

[16] Maria Newman, "A Person Gets Tired of Being Pushed Around," *Los Angeles Times*, May 21, 1989, AJ21, 72–75.

[17] "The Inferior Races in the Public Schools," *Sacramento Union*, May 3, 1864, 2.

[18] "*Mendez v. Westminster*: Paving the Way to School Desegregation," Constitutional Rights Foundation, Summer 2007, http://www.crf-usa.org/bill-of-rights-in-action/bria-23-2-c-mendez-v-westminster-paving-the-way-to-school-desegregation.

[19] "Chinese in Public Schools: Decision in Favor of Children Born in the United States," *Los Angeles Times*, January 10, 1885, 1.

[20] "Board of Education: Letter from Mrs. Tape," *Daily Alta California*, April 16, 1885, 1.

Children of Mexican ancestry would become targets of segregation after 1900, when their numbers mushroomed as agribusiness sought cheap labor in the Southern California citrus belt and the fields of the Imperial and San Joaquin valleys. Between 1920 and 1930, the state's Mexican and Mexican-American population tripled. Responding much as earlier generations of Californians had reacted to an influx of Chinese, a number of restaurants, theaters, and other establishments either banned or separated the dark-skinned newcomers. Many Anglo parents also demanded that their schoolchildren be separated from Mexican and Mexican-American children—either in different schools or separate classrooms. In 1931, the parents of 75 Mexican-American students won a court ruling that sent their children to the white school in the San Diego County town of Lemon Grove. The judge's ruling only applied to Lemon Grove, however.

Separate but Not Equal

Twelve years later, on a fall day in 1943, Soledad Vidaurri took her two children, Alice and Virginia, along with the three children of her brother Gonzalo Mendez and his wife Felicitas, to register at the neighborhood elementary school in Westminster, a city in the heart of Orange County's citrus-growing region. Soledad had married Frank Vidaurri, whose name sounded French or perhaps Belgian to school officials. Their children had fair skin. In contrast, the Mendez children—Sylvia, Gonzalo Jr., and Geronimo—had dark hair, dark eyes, and dark skin. Gonzalo Jr. remembered the school administrator sitting behind a table and telling his aunt, "'We'll take those (pointing to Alice and Virginia), but we won't take those three (pointing at the Mendez children).' We were too dark."[21] The Mendez children "belonged in the 'Mexican school' in the barrio," Felicitas recalled.[22]

Hoover School, where the Mendez children were assigned, was in a Garden Grove neighborhood that locals called "Tortilla Flats." The school was separate but not equal. "It was next to a dairy and a cow pasture," said former student Benevieve Barrios Southgate. An electrified fence separated the school from the cows. "It was muddy; it was messy," she said. The school didn't have a cafeteria; the children ate outside and had to shoo flies away during lunch.[23]

Felicitas and Gonzalo refused to accept the district's order without a fight. They persuaded the board to put a bond measure on the ballot to finance a new, integrated school. After voters turned it down, they sued Westminster and four other districts in federal court. Felicitas helped organize other parents of Mexican-American schoolchildren, and the League of United Latin American Citizens provided strategic and tactical support during trial preparations. The league in-

---

[21] Philippa Strum, *Mendez v. Westminster* (Lawrence: University Press of Kansas, 2010), 1.

[22] Newman.

[23] Ibid.

cluded many young veterans who were angry and disillusioned with their treatment at home once World War II was over. Paratrooper A. H. Gallardo was particularly upset that "our children wouldn't be getting as good an education as the white student was going to be getting."[24]

During the two-week trial, Orange County and the various school districts insisted racial bias played no part in segregating the students. Mexican Americans, they said, needed special instruction in separate schools so they could learn to speak English and understand American values and customs. They conceded, however, that they never checked to see if the students could speak English and gave no language test. To drive the point home, Mendez attorney David Marcus put a number of children on the witness stand, who testified in fluent English how they felt when required to attend the Hoover School.

James L. Kent, superintendent of the Garden Grove schools, testified that people of Mexican descent were intellectually, culturally, and morally inferior to white Americans and Europeans. The plaintiffs called anthropologists and social scientists to debunk Kent's ideas. Felicitas and her husband scraped together what money they could to reimburse Mexican-American neighbors who gave up a day's pay to attend the trial. When it was her turn to testify, Felicitas Mendez told the judge that despite the humiliation and indignities, "We always tell our children they are Americans."[25]

California Leads the Way to School Desegregation

On February 18, 1946, US District Judge Paul J. McCormick handed down his decision. It had taken him nearly a year to develop the ruling, reflecting the care he took in drafting his comments and his recognition of the decision's import. He stunned the school districts by ruling that they had violated the US Constitution's Fourteenth Amendment by forcing children with Spanish surnames to attend schools separate from Anglos. "A paramount requisite in the American system of public education is social equality," he wrote. "It must be open to all children by unified school association regardless of lineage."[26]

For the first time, a federal judge had struck down the notion that education could be "separate but equal" for children of differing races and ethnicities. The American Civil Liberties Union filed an amicus (friend of the court) brief on the side of the Mendezes during the trial. When the school districts appealed the decision, the Japanese-American Citizens League, American Jewish Congress,

---

[24] Stan Oftelie, "Murder Trial Obscured 1946 Integration Landmark," *Santa Ana Register*, August 22, 1976, 1.

[25] Francisco Macias, "Before *Brown v. Board of Education* There was *Mendez v. Westminster*," Library of Congress, May 16, 2014, https://blogs.loc.gov/law/2014/05/before-brown-v-board-of-education-there-was-mendez-v-westminster/.

[26] Strum, 125.

and the National Association for the Advancement of Colored People (NAACP) joined the fight by filing briefs in support of McCormick's ruling.

The appellate court in 1947 unanimously upheld the trial court decision, declaring that the Orange County districts had violated the rights of the children. In a separate concurring opinion, Judge William Denman struck a forceful blow against racial and ethnic discrimination. He called school segregation a "vicious principle" akin to "Hitler's anti-Semitism." He even urged a federal grand jury to criminally indict the offending school district trustees.[27] This time, the four Orange County school districts decided that further appeal would be futile—keeping the case from going to the US Supreme Court. The *Mendez* decision reverberated in Sacramento. Barely two months after the appellate ruling, Governor Earl Warren signed legislation that ended all *de jure*—or legally mandated—school segregation in California.[28]

Had those four Orange County districts continued fighting, *Mendez v. Westminster* might have become the national vehicle for the US Supreme Court's groundbreaking antisegregation decision. Instead, it was *Brown v. Board of Education of Topeka, Kansas*, that reached the high court. Representing the plaintiffs in that case was NAACP chief counsel—and future Supreme Court justice—Thurgood Marshall, whose legal strategy a few years later mirrored the approach in *Mendez*. It was more than coincidence; the NAACP had considered *Mendez* a dry run for its own case. The unanimous *Brown v. Board of Education* ruling would be written in 1954 by Earl Warren, newly appointed by President Dwight Eisenhower as chief justice of the United States.

Felicitas Mendez lived to be 82 years old, surviving her husband by 34 years. She liked to call herself a pioneer in the civil rights movement. "She wanted to be remembered as a person who was for education and for equality," daughter Sylvia said. "She wanted to make sure everyone knew how to read and write." After all the legal wrangling, Sylvia attended desegregated schools, went on to college, and became a pediatric nurse. But the *Mendez* case was barely a footnote—if that—in history books. "They had fought and won," Sylvia said of her parents, "and it hurt her that so many young kids didn't know. She wanted people to know that Hispanics were not just passive and laid-back and that they did fight for their rights."[29]

Five months before she died of heart failure, a frail Felicitas dug a shovel into the dirt on an empty lot in Santa Ana, breaking ground on the new Gonzalo and Felicitas Mendez Fundamental Intermediate School. Finally, some recognition. It was the brainstorm of granddaughter Johanna, who had presented more than 1,700 petition signatures supporting the idea to school district officials. "They

---

[27] "Court Denounces Segregation of Mexican Pupils," Associated Press, in the *San Bernardino Sun*, April 15, 1947, 4; Strum, 144–45.

[28] In the 1960s and '70s, large populations of Mexican Americans moved from rural areas to concentrated urban communities, prompting legal de facto segregation in which schools were separated along racial and ethnic lines.

[29] Greg Hernandez, "Daughter: Mendez Died Content That Accomplishments Will Live," *Los Angeles Times*, April 16, 1998, B1, B5.

are so proud of Grandma," Sylvia said. "They all want to go to school and go to college and show that this is what she fought for."[30]

Land of Protest and Revolt

California's heritage as a promised land for dreamers and innovators may have something to do with its longstanding reputation as a vanguard of protests, resistance, and social movements. In the immediate aftermath of becoming a state, settlers' revolts against Mexican land grants, protests against corporate greed and the Southern Pacific Railroad, and the rise of the Grange movement to champion the interests of farmers stamped bold imprints on the state's second constitution in 1879. The Progressive Movement gained its greatest American foothold in California, leading to historic political reforms in 1911 and Upton Sinclair's quixotic campaign for governor in 1934.

The list of California-born social movements and protests is long if not always on the right side of history. A sample:

- Anti-Asian laws that sprang from California to create the federal government's first immigrant restriction policies, including the Chinese Exclusion Act of 1882 and ultimately the Immigration Act of 1924.
- The unionization of mostly Latino agricultural workers, championed by Cesar Chavez.
- Proposition 13, the 1978 property tax limitation initiative that launched an antitax revolt across the country.
- The protest by Julia Butterfly Hill, who gained headlines worldwide for her cause—protecting California's redwood forests—by climbing into the massive tree she named Luna, where she lived for two years from 1997 to 1999.
- The 2005 march down Wilshire Boulevard in Los Angeles of more than half a million Latino immigrants and their supporters as part of a boycott to demonstrate their collective economic impact on a "Day without an Immigrant."
- The Black Power movement that gained its greatest visibility in Northern California, where the Black Panthers and apologists gave philosophical voice to the most radical and violent advocates in the movement.

Less well known is the critical role of women in some of those movements and how their contributions have been eclipsed in history books by the men who gained the headlines. Dolores Huerta spent years as an equal partner (working just as passionately) on behalf of the United Farm Workers alongside Cesar Chavez. Mario Savio's time at the bullhorn in Berkeley during the Free Speech Movement gained headlines, but Jackie Goldberg went to jail with him and has had a more lasting public career making a difference in elective office. In Oakland, Huey Newton, Bobby Seale, and Eldridge Cleaver built the international celebrity—despite their violent activism—of the Black Panther Party for Self Defense, yet Elaine Brown was an overshadowed equal. And Angela Davis, who spent 16

---

[30] Ibid.

months in jail before being acquitted of murder and conspiracy charges, delivered some of the most important orations in support of the party and the Black Liberation Movement. She would become one of the most influential speakers on behalf of the black experience in America in the 1970s—as a California university professor.

A deeper look at California history properly casts the spotlight on women activists who battled injustice and prejudice, heroically spoke truth to power, and built a better world for other women and men who benefited from their sacrifices.

From the Fields to the Picket Line— Dolores Huerta

As she had done hundreds of times over the years, a 58-year-old grandmother, barely five-feet tall, walked among the large crowd of protesters and onlookers, passing out leaflets calling on people to refuse to buy table grapes at the grocery. It was a Wednesday in September 1988, and inside San Francisco's ornate St. Francis Hotel, Vice President George H. W. Bush was giving a speech before donors to his Republican presidential campaign. Outside, some members of the crowd in this most liberal of cities in America were growing more unruly and aggressive. They were starting to bleed across barricades and interfere with traffic around the hotel. Commanders ordered tactical squads to march in ranks through the streets, batons at the ready, to move the throng along. There was some scuffling and suddenly the small woman with the flyers was on the ground, punched in the ribs by a policeman's baton. She was rushed to the hospital where trauma center doctors treated her for two broken ribs and performed emergency surgery to remove her spleen. It turned out the woman was no anonymous protester. She was Dolores Huerta, the much-admired co-founder, with Cesar Chavez, of the United Farm Workers of America.

An angry Mayor Art Agnos called for an investigation of the beating and announced he would not tolerate a misuse of police authority.[31] The *San Francisco Chronicle* editorialized that it was skeptical of Police Chief Frank Jordan's assurance that an initial review showed that "officers followed correct police protocol and used their batons properly when they moved in on the demonstrators." The paper said the police chief and the police commission "have a duty to find out how Huerta was injured and who did it."[32] Her beating led to the rewriting of the San Francisco Police Department's crowd-control policies and an award of $825,000 for her suffering.

Huerta had not always been shown such deference. Over a half century of fighting on behalf of farmworkers, mostly Latinos like her, she was beaten and

---

[31] Dan Morain, "Police Batons Blamed as UFW Official is Badly Hurt during Bush S.F. Protest," *Los Angeles Times,* September 16, 1988, B3.

[32] "Police Probe is Essential," *San Francisco Chronicle* editorial, September 17, 1988, A14.

jailed numerous times. She was spat upon, verbally abused, and thrown out of fields and vineyards. Toiling with other grassroots community organizations through the 1950s, Huerta and Chavez eventually bonded while working with the Community Service Organization (CSO), a post-World War II self-help group that arose in Latino barrios in California and across the Southwest. Chavez started out as a volunteer for the CSO in San Jose, moving from a community organizer to becoming its general director. Working out of Stockton, Huerta did a little of everything—and did it well—from voter registration to fund raising. Leaders noticed and offered her the position of lobbyist.[33]

Individually, Chavez and Huerta enjoyed success within the CSO, winning some wage and benefit improvements, even if modest at times. They found themselves working together more frequently and realized they were philosophical compatriots. They learned, too, how to negotiate competition among labor unions and the sometimes not-so-subtle rivalry between Mexican-American workers and braceros who were allowed to come into California, most from Mexico, during harvest seasons. Those lessons would serve them for the next four decades. When CSO and other union leaders rejected their plan to organize farmworkers in 1962, Chavez called Huerta to his home and told her, "Look, farmworkers are never going to have a union unless you and I do it."[34] That moment gave birth to the farmworkers union.

Dolores Huerta was born in Dawson, a small mining town in New Mexico, in 1930. Her father, Juan Hernandez, was a miner and scrappy union organizer who would eventually be elected to the New Mexico House of Representatives. Lore had it that he once punched a fellow legislator on the house floor. Huerta said he was "charismatic, intelligent, handsome, and a chauvinist."[35] Her parents divorced when Huerta was six, and her mother, Alicia, brought Dolores and her brothers to Stockton, where Alicia bought a restaurant and 70-room hotel. Dolores remembered watching her mother often accommodate those who couldn't afford the full cost of meals or rooms. Business was good enough to allow Dolores to take violin and dance lessons and to join the Girl Scouts. She was a small girl who gave no indication of the toughness that would become her trademark as a union leader. It was in high school that she first demonstrated her organizing abilities, leading an effort to create a teen center where kids could dance to juke-box tunes, play games, and hang out. She was successful in other ways, too, winning contests for selling war bonds and writing an essay. But school officials never let her

---

[33] Margaret Eleanor Rose, "Women in the United Farm Workers: A Study of Chicana and Mexicana Participation in a Labor Union, 1950 to 1980" (PhD diss., University of California, Los Angeles, 1988), 34–39.

[34] Steve Velasquez, Harry Rubenstein, and Peter Liebhold interview of Dolores Huerta, 2005, "Interview No. 1577," Institute of Oral History, University of Texas at El Paso.

[35] Lisa Genasci, "UFW Co-Founder Comes Out of Shadow," Associated Press via the *Los Angeles Times*, May 11, 1995. D8.

Figure 10.2. Dolores Huerta Leading Rally with Howard Wallace, President of the San Francisco Chapter of UFW, and Maria Elena Chavez, 16, Daughter of Cesar Chavez, in San Francisco, 1988
Credit: AP Photo/Court Mast, File

collect the rewards that went with those successes. She said administrators would never accept a Mexican American as a winner.[36]

Huerta took her first job in the fields at age 14, picking cherries and tomatoes. After high school, she attended Stockton Junior College and the University of the Pacific to get her teaching credential. She lasted one year in the classroom. "I realized one day that as a teacher I couldn't do anything for the kids who came to school barefoot and hungry."[37] It was time to look at serving others, reflecting her growing idealism and the example her mother had demonstrated. Over the next two decades, she would bear 11 children by three fathers. The last four were from an unmarried relationship with Cesar's brother, Richard Chavez. She devoted her life, however, to her other child—her union.

---

[36] James Rainey, "The Eternal Soldadera; To Her 11 Children, She Was an Often Absentee Mom. To Those Who Crossed Her, She Was a Harsh Foe. But to the Thousands of Farm Workers She Still Fights for, Dolores Huerta Is the Ultimate Warrior." *Los Angeles Times Magazine*, August 15, 1999. 12.

[37] Jean Murphy, "Unsung Heroine of La Causa," *Los Angeles Times,* December 21, 1970. I1.

Union Success in the Fields

After they formed the UFW, Cesar Chavez went into the fields, coaxing workers to sign union cards, while Huerta concentrated on administrative functions, including negotiations with farmers and state legislators. But she also drove around the state, almost daily at times, to lead marches, strikes, and boycotts. Huerta and Chavez struggled at first to make headway on behalf of workers in the San Joaquin and Coachella valleys and on the central coast around Watsonville and Salinas. Sometimes Huerta would join Chavez in the lettuce and strawberry fields, and the vineyards, seeking to win new supporters. They were arrested and beaten, at times, for entering fields that they viewed as worksites but farmers considered private property. The grape boycotts Huerta organized in 1970 and 1975 ultimately won higher-paying jobs and better benefits for thousands of UFW members. And she succeeded at the state Capitol, too, winning legislative measures removing citizenship requirements for public assistance and making farmworkers eligible for disability and unemployment insurance.

Huerta has been driven by her view that "growers don't understand relationships in terms of management, in terms of people. They kind of have the old Bracero Program mentality that you just drive people as hard as you can, you know, squeeze as much work out of them as you can, and that's why farm working becomes such brutal work. It doesn't have to be like that."[38]

At the beginning of a planned cross-country hitchhiking journey, recent UCLA graduate Jerry Kay stopped in Delano on his way to San Francisco to spend a couple of days as a volunteer, helping with the UFW's table-grape boycott. He stayed six years. Kay recalls that, early on, he was sleeping with other volunteers on the floor of Huerta's Delano house when he heard her mention that she was going to San Francisco. "'Can I get a ride with you?' I asked. I had never spoken to her before." Sure, she replied, "you can drive while I nap."[39] On that trip to San Francisco they formed a bond that has lasted for years. "Dolores has a temper and a voice that can melt steel and shake foundations when she lets loose," Kay wrote in a personal memoir of his time with the UFW. "Her nonviolence never meant taking a kind, gentle path of action. . . ."[40] In fact, Chavez and Huerta often argued vehemently during their years together.

While he embraced adulation as the American Gandhi of the labor movement, Chavez frequently expressed his admiration for Huerta and occasionally even their status as equals. He once described Huerta as "totally fearless, both mentally and physically."[41] Jerry Brown, who as California governor signed UFW-sponsored legislation to create an Agricultural Labor Relations Board in

---

[38] Steve Velasquez, et al.

[39] Jerry Kay, "Dolores Huerta: A Personal Memoir," *Santa Cruz Sentinel,* April 13, 2003. F2.

[40] Ibid.

[41] Lisa Genasci.

1975, praised her for "embodying the spirit of Cesar Chavez." Brown's statement unwittingly underscored the difficulty Huerta had faced in finding recognition for her own tremendous contributions to the cause. "That's the history of the world," she told an interviewer. "I feel that has to change and women are going to have to change it."[42] She met the challenge for 40 years. John Burton, the former state senate leader, called her "a tough broad. . . . She was a very strong woman, she had a lot of guts, because she got beat up. . . ."[43] Nevertheless, says Camille Leonhardt, professor of women's studies and California history at American River College near Sacramento, Huerta has been ridiculed by some and called a "dragon lady" because of her assertiveness. "If she was a man, it would be she's a tough negotiator."[44]

As much as she surely loved her 11 children, her union service often came first. She raised her children "in her spare time," one writer said. Dolores's daughter, Maria Elena Chavez, acknowledges it was "hard having a mom who always worked and wasn't your typical mother. . . ."[45] For her part, Huerta has pleaded guilty to the critique. "I did take the activist path, and I was never able to spend as much time with my children as I would've liked," she told an interviewer. "But I think my kids turned out pretty well. . . . What we have to give to our children are values, not so much material, [but] a social conscience."[46]

Chavez died in 1993. A quarter-century later, immigration crackdowns by the administration of Donald Trump forced many undocumented workers—who make up a majority of California's farmworkers—to keep their heads down or stay away from the fields altogether. Meanwhile, improved state and federal regulations benefiting farmworkers have cooled some of the old outrages that fueled the cause. UFW President Arturo Rodriguez struggles now with the heavy lift of winning new members and contracts—without Huerta (who turned 88 in 2018) at his side.

A Life in the Movement—
Jackie Goldberg

Berkeley has had a storied reputation for more than half a century as a site of resistance—spawning, among other causes, the 1964 Free Speech Movement and the 1969 People's Park protest, both centered on the University of California campus. The latter was especially violent and bloody after then-Governor Ronald Reagan—who made a campaign pledge to suppress campus protesters—sent National Guard troops to reinforce police who were attempting to clear thousands

---

[42] Ibid.

[43] John Burton, interview by authors, June 8, 2017.

[44] Camille Leonhardt, interview by authors, May 23, 2017.

[45] Lisa Genasci.

[46] Julia Bencomo Lobaco, "Dolores Huerta: The Vision and Voice of Her Life's Work," *AARP Segunda Juventud,* Fall 2004.

of demonstrators from a largely vacant lot owned by the university. On May 15, 1969, police fired teargas and double-aught buckshot into the crowds trying to prevent the university from converting the open field—embraced as a park by the protesters—into a parking lot and dormitories. One person was killed and 128 were admitted to local hospitals.[47]

Barely five years earlier, Berkeley had been the scene of another protest that would have even broader implications across the nation. Often cited by its acronym, the FSM—the Free Speech Movement—with Mario Savio as its leading voice helped set a course for campus unrest across America as a rising tide of antiwar and civil-rights anger and revolt were taking root.

Though upstaged by Savio, Jackie Goldberg was a key leader of the FSM and a radical sorority girl who somehow managed to embrace both Greek life and the life of a revolutionary. Goldberg's mother was a teacher, and her father operated an industrial dry-cleaning service in Inglewood. Theirs was a tradition-steeped Jewish family, though "it had very little to do with faith in God and had everything to do with family and culture," she recalled in an oral history. "And identity."[48] After a brief stint at USC, she enrolled at UC Berkeley 1962. She had trouble finding housing, so she decided to join a sorority, even though she was "really unhappy" about it. "See, I had been a part of this group of people who made fun of the sororities and fraternities."

When she "rushed"—hastening from party to party and being put under a microscope by each Greek house—she was assigned a dorm with others making the party circuit. Soon she started betting her incredulous new friends that a sorority wouldn't take her because she was Jewish. "I made a fortune off of all those San Francisco girls." She ended up joining Delta Phi Epsilon, one of three Jewish sororities on campus, finding it to be "a great refuge" amid the campus turmoil. She also took strength from two of her sorority roommates—Dion Aroner and Susan Davis, both of whom later went on, as she did, to become state assemblymembers.[49]

Unlike most of her sorority sisters, however, Goldberg spent much of her time in social action. "I certainly wouldn't call myself a radical when I arrived at Berkeley," she told an interviewer. Like many her age, she had an evolving interest in civil rights and peace protests after seeing '50s news coverage of the violent clashes over integration and civil rights in southern states. Her principal interest was Campus Women for Peace. The FBI labeled it a Communist organization, but Goldberg said she was focused on issues like Strontium 90 in milk. "As a future mother I was worried about poisoning children. I was involved in . . . trying to debunk the notion that in a nuclear war, the little fallout shelters in the basements of

---

[47] "Flashback: Ronald Reagan and the Berkeley People's Park Riots," *Rolling Stone,* May 15, 2017.

[48] Art and Jackie Goldberg, "Free Speech Movement Oral History Project: Art and Jackie Goldberg" conducted by Lisa Rubens, August 8, 1999, Regional Oral History Office, The Bancroft Library, University of California, Berkeley, 2013.

[49] Ibid.

buildings were really going to save our lives and protect our way of life—absurd really, a very absurd notion.[50]

"My first arrest was probably what radicalized me the most," she says. It happened at San Francisco's Sheraton Palace Hotel, where she and others were protesting discrimination against blacks and other minorities among the city's major hotels. She says she had "great faith in the American court system . . . at least for white people." But what she experienced in two trials that ended in hung juries "was enough to curl my straight hair and to make me think that I had a very seriously incorrect notion of what the American judicial system was all about."[51]

When her brother, Arthur Goldberg, arrived on campus the next year, both linked up, through their leftist associations, with Savio, becoming part of the tight-knit group that organized the FSM. Another member was Bettina Aptheker, daughter of Herbert Aptheker, a Marxist historian and Communist, whose writings on slavery significantly corrected the accuracy of African-American history.

Birth of the Free Speech Movement

The movement erupted when university officials issued a directive on September 14, 1964, saying restrictions on political speech, petitioning, fundraising, and recruitment on campus—quietly tolerated in the past—would be strictly enforced in the future. FSM leaders quickly rallied protests and sit-ins almost daily, drawing ever larger crowds of students and faculty. Several students set up political-action tables in front of Sproul Hall, the campus administration building, on September 30 in planned defiance of the university's edict. The next morning, Jack Weinberg, another movement organizer, was arrested for refusing to fold his table on Sproul Plaza. As police placed him in the back of a squad car, growing crowds of students surrounded it, demanding his release. Over the next 32 hours, the police car, with Weinberg inside and hundreds of supporters outside, became a protest-speaker's podium and a national news story.

Two months later, several thousand students went to Sproul Plaza to demand the university agree to a long-delayed compromise relaxing the restrictions. The scene was mostly peaceful, offering "freedom classes," Joan Baez leading folk songs, and even a Chanukah service. The crowd came to life when Savio delivered his famous "put your bodies upon the gears" speech,[52] and eventually more

---

[50] Jackie Goldberg interview, "The Cold War" (Episode 13—Make Love, Not War—The Sixties), CNN 2014 Documentary Series, archived at National Security Archive, The George Washington University.

[51] Ibid.

[52] "There is a time when the operation of the machine becomes so odious, makes you so sick at heart, that you can't take part; you can't even passively take part, and you've got to put your bodies upon the gears and upon the wheels, upon the levers, upon all the apparatus and you've got to make it stop. And you've got to indicate to the people who run it, to the people who own it, that unless you're free, the machine will be prevented from working at all."

than 2,000 students moved in to occupy Sproul Hall. In the middle of the night, on December 4, police rousted the students sprawling in the halls and offices, arresting 800 of them, including Jackie Goldberg. It took 376 officers more than 12 hours to drag occupiers from the building and book them. It was, at the time, the largest mass arrest in California history.[53] Charges were soon dropped against virtually all of the occupiers except Goldberg, Savio, and the other movement organizers. Eventually, even those were dropped.

Over the next few months, tensions grew among FSM leaders over police actions, the university's new guidelines, and rising nationwide anger over civil rights and the Vietnam War. Some in the group were advocating stronger and more aggressive tactics, including violence if necessary. Art and Jackie Goldberg, whose experiences had been more pacifistic, started to balk and left the movement leadership. "I was purged because I won the debate in the negotiations with Clark Kerr," Jackie Goldberg insists. "Mario and a couple of others were really unhappy that I won" the compromise over the final version of campus speech guidelines. She also had become worried about the dangers facing students who might get caught up in the most violent confrontations. "I really felt a responsibility. I said, 'If we have guns and they have guns and people die, I understand this, but we're just going to get slaughtered out in this open pavement by people who have absolutely no concern for our well-being whatsoever.' I think somebody would have been seriously hurt, if not killed. I didn't feel like those folks sitting there had made that kind of commitment."[54]

Goldberg's suggestion that she was ostracized from the FSM because she wasn't radical enough has been challenged by others, including a report prepared by a California state senate committee in 1965. Amid lingering vestiges of the Senator Joseph McCarthy era of purging suspected Communists along with the antipathy of FBI Director J. Edgar Hoover and other powerful figures to growing campus unrest, the committee noted in part:

> Jacqueline Goldberg, the sister of Arthur Goldberg, came from Los An-
> geles to attend the university at Berkeley. She soon became the head of
> UC Women for Peace, a front organization, and was its delegate to a
> Moscow meeting in 1963. She was also active in the American-Russian
> Institute at San Francisco, cited by the Attorney General of the United
> States as a Communist-dominated organization, and is now a member
> of the Policy Committee for the next World Communist Youth Festival
> which is scheduled to be held in Algeria. She was a member of both the

---

[53] Elaine Elinson and Stan Yogi, *Where There's a Fight* (Berkeley: Heyday, 2009), 244.

[54] Art and Jackie Goldberg Oral History.

executive and steering committees of FSM, and was arrested during the invasion of Sproul Hall.[55]

Goldberg saw much of that quite differently, and much less threateningly. While at USC, she had gone to the first one-day Women's Strike for Peace in November 1961, where she "met people who really did influence my life forever . . . . They really were a big part of my political education." They took her with them to the 1963 World Congress of Women in Moscow, but apparently as a youthful observer rather than a delegate. "I was 19 years old. The next person in age to me . . . was about forty-five, and it was up from there."[56]

From Revolutionary to State Legislator

Goldberg moved to Chicago for an advanced teaching degree after graduating from UC, then made her way back to Los Angeles. She never gave up her activist credentials when she got her teaching credential. At the same time Bobbi Fiedler was earning her activist chops rallying parents against busing to desegregate Los Angeles schools, Goldberg, the Berkeley radical, was waging war on the other side of the same issue in the same city, leading the controversial Integration Project to support a moderate system for mandatory busing of white kids into the ghettos and minority students out to the better suburban schools. She never lapsed in her feminist advocacy, either. In 1983 she ran for the Los Angeles School Board, defeating an incumbent 65 to 35 percent and restoring the board to a liberal majority it had lost shortly after Fiedler won her seat. She handily won a second term, serving as board president from 1989 to 1991, then left the board and returned to the classroom.

After getting a taste of activism inside government, she was ready to move up. In 1993, voters elected her to the Los Angeles City Council as its first openly gay or lesbian member. Some tough policy defeats on the school board trained her to be a more effective negotiator. Over the next two years on the city council, Goldberg helped lead adoption of gun controls, health benefits for domestic partners of city workers, and a "living wage" ordinance, among others. She had no opponent when she ran for reelection 1997.

She ran successfully to succeed Assemblyman Antonio Villaraigosa in 2000, serving six years until term limits ended her tenure at the capitol. While there, she outspokenly advocated for California teachers, women, lesbians, and gays. "Her most notable legacy was legislation in 2003 that gave registered same-sex partners almost all the rights, responsibilities, and benefits of married opposite-sex couples in California," according to an admiring profile. With their newlywed adopted son and daughter-in-law standing as witnesses, Goldberg and her long-

---

[55] Jonathan Leaf, *The Politically Incorrect Guide to the Sixties* (Washington, DC: Regnery, 2009), 5.

[56] Art and Jackie Goldberg Oral History.

time partner, Sharon Stricker, were among the first to wed after San Francisco Mayor Gavin Newsom ordered the city clerk to begin issuing marriage licenses to same-sex couples. Recalling her authorship of the same-sex partner law a year earlier, Goldberg joked: "It's now the conservative position. I've never been in the conservative position."[57]

Hero or Antihero?—
Scholar and Street Radical Angela Davis

She struggled to pull the wig over her outsized Afro. The grim realization that she was now a fugitive brought more anger than fear. Hiding behind drawn curtains, she held her breath any time she heard footsteps or a car slowing down outside. It was Sunday August 9, 1970, and Angela Davis was "hiding from the police and grieving over the death of someone I loved."[58] Two days earlier, heavily armed 17-year-old Jonathan Jackson, Davis's sometimes bodyguard, walked into a courtroom in the Marin County Civic Center, intent on helping three San Quentin inmates make an audacious escape. Before others could react, he tossed guns to convict James McClain, on trial for stabbing a prison guard, and to two other convicts waiting to testify. The group taped a shotgun around the neck of Judge Harold J. Haley and took prosecutor Gary Thomas and three women jurors hostage as they headed for a waiting rental van outside the courthouse. Before the four kidnappers could escape, a firefight erupted. Three of the escapees were killed. Judge Haley was killed with the shotgun, and Thomas was permanently paralyzed by a bullet in his spine. One of the three jurors was wounded but survived. Officials quickly determined that three of the four guns were owned by Angela Davis.

The news headlines reverberated around the world. Davis already had become a celebrity revolutionary because of her high-profile role in providing an articulate voice to the rising Black Power movement. She evangelized on behalf of the Black Panther Party, the Soledad Brothers and her belief that "fair trials for black radicals are impossible in today's courts."[59] And there was a confrontation with California Governor Ronald Reagan, who demanded that the university board of regents fire her from her teaching position at UCLA because she was a Communist and radical activist who called police "pigs" and "murderers." The regents fired her twice in 1970, once before and once after a court ruled they could not do so.

---

[57] Karen S. Wilson, editor, *Jews in the Los Angeles Mosaic,* Autry National Center of the American West (Berkeley: University of California Press 2013), 71.

[58] Angela Davis, *Angela Davis, An Autobiography* (New York: International Publishers, Reprint 1988), 3.

[59] J. A. Parker, *Angela Davis, The Making of a Revolutionary* (New Rochelle, NY: Arlington House, 1973), 171.

Her signature look—her afro and the distinctive gap in her teeth—were well-known to anyone who followed the news. She was a popular hero in many black communities. So, when Davis learned the FBI was coming for her, she knew it would be hard to blend in with the crowd. "I knew they would be after me," she wrote in her 1974 autobiography, much of it written in Cuba, where she'd been invited by Fidel Castro to rejuvenate. "Over the last months I had been spending practically all my time helping to build a mass movement to free the Soledad Brothers—Jonathan's brother George, John Clutchette, and Fleeta Drumgo—who were facing a fraudulent murder charge inside Soledad Prison. . . . No one needed to tell me that they would exploit the fact that my guns had been used in Marin (County) in order to strike out at me once more."[60]

Davis, with her friend and Communist comrade David Poindexter, avoided capture for more than two months. By now she was on the FBI's 10 Most-Wanted List and authorities had charged her with conspiracy, aggravated kidnapping, and first-degree murder. Officials said one of the three weapons registered to Davis was a shotgun she bought in San Francisco only two days earlier. It was the one that killed Judge Haley.[61]

Revolutionary Star Power

On October 13, 1970, police and FBI agents, acting on a tip, arrested her at a Howard Johnson's in Manhattan. President Nixon publicly hailed the "capture of the dangerous terrorist, Angela Davis." But after 16 months in jail, an all-white jury found her not guilty of all charges. She "walked out of the court as she had walked into it, with a Black Power salute—as potent a symbol of rebellion as revolutionary Ché Guevara."[62] The verdict reflected the support that had built up for her around the world as her declarations of innocence competed against the circumstantial evidence put together by her prosecutors. Singer Aretha Franklin offered to put up her bail, and John Lennon and Yoko Ono wrote Angela in tribute to her. Even the Rolling Stones recorded a rock anthem, Sweet Black Angel, dedicated to Davis while she awaited trial:

Well de gal in danger, de gal in chains, but she keep on pushin', would you do the same?

She countin' up de minutes, she countin' up de days.

---

[60] Angela Davis.

[61] "Search Broadens for Angela Davis," Associated Press via *Eugene (OR) Register-Guard*, August 17, 1970.

[62] Sharon Knolle, "Nine Great Documentaries about Women Activists," *Independent Lens*/PBS, March 22, 2017.

She's a sweet black angel, not a gun toting teacher, not a Red lovin'
school marm;

Ain't someone gonna free her, free de sweet black slave, free de sweet
black slave?

It was remarkable how threatening this radical black woman had become to
the establishment in so short a time, even before the Marin County mayhem. And
it was equally remarkable how quickly she could rally support across so many
cultures around the world. She founded the Che-Lumumba Chapter of the Communist Party in Los Angeles. She proselytized on behalf of the Black Panthers.
She had organized a boisterous campaign to free the Soledad Brothers, including
George Jackson, her philosophical soul mate who was killed along with five of
his hostages in a shootout as he tried to escape from San Quentin in 1971. Despite
those revolutionary ties, Davis was able to enlist support from people far more
moderate than she was. Her charisma stemmed from her passion for the down-
trodden, particularly blacks and women, and the eloquence of her arguments on
their behalf.

"Many of us during that period were totally convinced that we could change
the world," she recalled. "We were persuaded that revolutionary change was possible."[63]

Whether it was the prison experience or something else, Davis came away
from those early seventies battles a little gentler. "I remember getting out of jail
and people having these ideas about me from the photographs they had seen, that
I was supposed to be this militant revolutionary, ranting and raving and so forth,"
she recalled in her oral history, recorded with Julian Bond in 2009. "So some people were disappointed when they heard me speak and said, 'what did they do to
you?' And I said, 'this is the way I've always been, the way I've always spoken.'
I had to finally recognize that if I was not true to myself, if I did not have the kind
of style that most reflected my upbringing and my character, my training, then I
definitely would not be able to make a difference in the world. No matter how
others wanted me to rant and rave, I opted for my own quiet style."[64]

From Pop Culture Icon to University Scholar

Davis was an academic throughout her adult life. In her hometown of Bir-
mingham, Alabama, her mother was a teacher and activist, involved with the
Southern Negro Youth Congress and the NAACP. Young Davis excelled in segregated local public schools, and in her junior year in high school, she applied for
and was accepted into a Quaker school program aimed at bringing black students

---

[63] Angela Davis interview in "Dolores," *5-Stick Films*/PBS, 2017.
[64] Angela Davis oral history, "Explorations in Black Leadership," conducted by Julian
Bond, University of Virginia Oral Histories, April 15, 2009.

from the South into urban integrated schools in the North. She selected a school in New York City's Greenwich Village, where she first joined a Communist youth group. Leaning toward philosophy, she decided on Brandeis for her undergraduate studies. One of only three black students in her freshman class at the mostly Jewish university, she soon became enthralled by the lectures of prominent Communist philosopher Herbert Marcuse. She graduated *magna cum laude* and earned Phi Beta Kappa honors.

Marcuse, who contributed to the neo-Marxist "Frankfurt School" of philosophy, was one of Davis's greatest influencers, so it came as no surprise when she spent two years postgraduate at the University of Frankfurt. When Marcuse moved to the University of California at San Diego, she followed. He once described Davis as "the best student I ever had in more than 30 years of teaching."[65] In kind, she asserted "Herbert Marcuse taught me that it was possible to be an academic, an activist, a scholar, and a revolutionary."[66] She proved it in San Diego, where she helped form the Black Student Union, earned her master's degree in philosophy, and agitated for creation of the minority-focused Third College (renamed Thurgood Marshall College by the university in 1993). She received her master's degree from UCSD in 1969.

She next returned more than a decade later, on January 18, 1980, at age 36, this time as a vice presidential candidate for the Communist Party of the United States. (She was to run again in 1984.) The violence of her earlier life was behind her, but she retained the radical point of view that had been so strongly influenced by Marcuse. Now a professor of ethnic and women's studies at San Francisco State University, she spoke to 600 cheering students in San Diego about the fights she faced a decade earlier and the future that could be had in a Communist world. "It was clear that the low-voiced, statuesque academician still can draw a crowd," wrote *Los Angeles Times* reporter Paula Parker, who covered the event.[67] Davis went on to teach at Rutgers and finished her tenured career as a Distinguished Professor Emeritus from the History of Consciousness and Feminist Studies departments at the University of California, Santa Cruz.

Considered "a superb historical scholar" by many of her academic peers,[68] Davis continued her Marxist analyses of the fortunes of blacks and women through history after retiring. When she delivered the Birkbeck Annual Law Lecture in London on October 25, 2013, she dolefully lamented the neglect in historical recollection of the women who helped ignite the 1955 Montgomery, Alabama bus boycott:

---

[65] Paula Parker, "Angela Davis at 36: Still a Fighter: Fanfare Has Faded, But Angela Davis Still Takes Activist Role," *Los Angeles Times*, January 19, 1980, SD1.

[66] Barbarella Fokos, "The Bourgeois Marxist," sandiegoreader.com, August 23, 2007.

[67] Paula Parker.

[68] Gloria I. Joseph, book review of "Women, Race, and Power" by Angela Y. Davis, in *Signs,* Fall 1983 (Chicago: University of Chicago Press), 134.

Even though numbers of books, both scholarly and popular, have been written on the role of women in the 1955 Boycott, Dr. King, who was actually invited to be a spokesperson for a movement when was entirely unknown—the movement had already formed—Dr. King remains the dominant figure.[69]

Reflecting on her life, Davis said: "I think I was a creation of the movement in many respects, in terms of who I am, my own passion for justice, but also a creation of the movement that developed around the demand to free me (while she awaited her murder trial)." She quietly embraced the pop-culture aura that embraced her, though she says that it used to embarrass her when she would see people wearing t-shirts emblazoned with her picture. Then one day, she stopped a young woman and asked her why she wore one. "She said 'it makes me feel strong, it makes me feel powerful. It makes me feel like I can do anything I want to.' I said 'right on.'"[70]

Protest from the Grassroots

Today a youthful new generation of protest leaders is rising from California's grassroots, likely to produce the next Bobbi Fiedler, Felicitas Mendez, or Dolores Huerta. Social media has given Everywoman a way to magnify her voice from scattered commentaries on events of the day to the unified cause of a "Me Too" movement against sexual harassment. Originated by Alabama social activist Tarana Burke in 2006, it was reignited on Twitter as #MeToo in 2017 by Hollywood actress Alyssa Milano.

Protest demonstrations and marches in the wake of Donald Trump's upset election over Hillary Clinton created waves of activism at times reminiscent of the mass demonstrations of the sixties. This time, however, newly activated women protesters of all ages could be seen at peaceful women's marches wearing pink knit "pussy hats" in symbolic ownership of a vulgarity uttered by Trump. (He bragged in a 2005 Access Hollywood tape leaked during the 2016 presidential campaign that as a celebrity he could and did get away with kissing and grabbing women, even by their crotches.) In a Facebook post in late 2016, a retired lawyer in Hawaii named Teresa Shook proposed a Women's March on Washington the day after Inauguration Day, January 20, 2017, to protest Trump's election. Her post went viral.[71] And on Saturday, January 21, more than four million people attended women's marches in the District of Columbia and around the country (even the globe), including countless thousands in San Francisco, Oakland, San

---

[69] Angela Davis, "Freedom is a Constant Struggle: Closures and Continuities," Birkbeck Annual Law Lecture, London, October 24, 2013.

[70] Angela Davis oral history.

[71] Perry Stein and Sandhya Somashekhar, "It Started with a Retiree," *Washington Post*, January 3, 2017.

Figure 10.3. Members of Black Women United at "Ain't I a Woman March" in Sacramento, 2017
Credit: Photo courtesy of Angel Rodriguez

Jose, Sacramento, Los Angeles, San Bernardino, San Diego, and elsewhere in sapphire blue California.[72]

Ironically, just as the early suffrage movement often was seen as a white-woman's crusade, many women of color have felt bypassed by the contemporary #MeToo movement. Tarana Burke, the Me Too originator, told *Ebony Magazine* in October 2017 that she didn't intend to build "a viral campaign or a hashtag that is here today and forgotten tomorrow." She created it as a catchphrase "to let folks know that they were not alone and that a movement for radical healing was happening and possible," she said. "The problem is, black women were quickly isolated from the dialogue before we could familiarize ourselves with it," wrote culture writer Zahara Hill, author of the *Ebony* article. "Black women regularly experience sexual assault as well and are often coerced into silence. Rather, the apathy toward the struggles of people of color infiltrated the movement before we could even consider participating."[73]

---

[72] Linda Gonzales, "Women's March: SF, LA, Cities across California Join 'Sister Marches,'" *Sacramento Bee*, January 21, 2017.

[73] Zahara Hill, "A Black Woman Created the 'Me Too' Campaign against Sexual Assault 10 Years Ago," *Ebony Magazine*, October 18, 2017.

In Sacramento, Imani Mitchell enlisted a group of supporters after the Women's March in 2017 "to create an event that would address the lack of intersectionality in the Women's March and find a space to uplift and center black women."[74] She and her colleagues formed Black Women United and organized an alternative gathering at the state capitol in July 2017. They called it the "Ain't I a Woman March," in tribute to Sojourner Truth's famous women's rights speech delivered in 1851. Several hundred women and men participated—a crowd significantly smaller yet more diverse than the anti-Trump throng the previous January. "California is known for being a liberal state," Mitchell told the *Sacramento Bee*, "but there are a lot of microaggressions that can make black women feel like they're not valued or not respected or heard. We wanted to create a space for all black women from all walks of life to feel like they can come together to rejoice, to heal, to cry—and that it will all be OK."[75] While Mitchell lauded the efforts of her white sisters, she added, "We're not asking to have a seat at the table, we're bringing our own table."[76]

Nevertheless, galvanized by the polarizing election of Donald Trump, thousands of women who in the past might have followed the news only on TV now could find themselves behind bullhorns. Among them was Shareen Barrett, a mother of two young boys in Pacifica, a small coastal town south of San Francisco. Her community involvement until the 2016 election had centered on the Pacifica Mothers' Club and its crochet group. That changed with Trump's victory. Barrett said she had been aghast that "someone with such little knowledge of politics or world issues could be a nominee. I started watching the news a lot. When he won, I couldn't believe it."

Disappointed that she wouldn't be able to attend the large San Francisco version of the Women's March, she and a few friends discussed staging a small local one. The others "decided it was too much work and they weren't going to do it," she recalled. "I thought about it and it really didn't seem too hard to gather some friends and create a walk near our beach path."[77] With a week's notice she started posting plans to social media and contacted the city to get her march approved. She and her friends in the crochet group knit dozens of symbolic "pussy hats." She was excited the day of the march but was stunned at the crowd gathering before her. "I couldn't believe how many people I saw," she said. "I was only expecting people I knew." More than 1,000 people showed up. "I felt united and proud. I felt hopeful."

Barrett was activated. She helped promote a new Facebook page called Pacifica Resist. With a growing file of email addresses, she organized a walk on International Women's Day and another for the March for Science, selling pussy

---

[74] Black Women United, https://www.bwusac.com.

[75] Erika D. Smith, "This March—Like Being a Black Woman—Is About More Than Politics," *The Sacramento Bee*, July 14, 2017.

[76] Nashelly Chavez and Tony Bizjak, "#MeToo Fuels Sacramento Women's March, But Some Feel Left Out," *The Sacramento Bee*, January 18, 2018.

[77] Shareen Barrett, interview with the authors via email, February 15, 2018.

hats and bandanas for charity. "I would love to put on some more events, though I recently moved and had a baby, so it probably won't be for a while," she says. But her view of political activism has changed forever. "The most important thing I've learned is that your vote counts."[78]

Discussion Questions

1. School busing for integration polarized parents in Los Angeles in the 1970s. Busing was intended to improve the quality of education, especially for minority children. What are some reasons parents of minority children might oppose busing?
2. Bobbi Fiedler said she opposed segregated schools but objected to forced school busing. Although she was a Republican, she rejected her party's platform at the time and supported abortion rights and the Equal Rights Amendment. How might her family heritage have factored into her opinions on those issues?
3. At the middle of the twentieth century, courts ruled that schools could no longer be "separate but equal" for racial and ethnic minorities and white children. What are some of the reasons the courts may have had for rejecting the separate-but-equal concept?
4. Jackie Goldberg in the early nineties was the first openly gay member of the Los Angeles City Council—something that would have been politically taboo only a few years earlier. What factors do you think might have contributed to the evolution of public acceptance of LGBT officeholders?
5. Angela Davis was an avowed Communist, a radical supporter of convicted murderers and the owner of guns used in a courthouse escape attempt that left four people dead, including a judge. For what reasons do you think people around the world, including entertainment figures such as Aretha Franklin and the Rolling Stones, rallied to her support?
6. Cesar Chavez is widely celebrated as the founder of the United Farm Workers of America, yet Dolores Huerta was his full partner in creation of the union and achieving its goals. For what reasons do you believe she has been slighted in the history books?

Recommended Reading

Asian Women United of California, ed. *Making Waves: An Anthology of Writings By and About Asian American Women.* Boston: Beacon Press, 1989.

Davis, Angela. *Women, Race, and Class.* New York: Random House, 1981.

Elinson, Elaine, and Stan Yogi. *Wherever There's a Fight: How Runaway Slaves, Suffragists, Immigrants, Strikers and Poets Shaped Civil Liberties in California.* Berkeley: Heyday, 2009.

---

[78] Ibid.

Garcia, Mario T., ed. *A Dolores Huerta Reader*. Albuquerque, NM: University of New Mexico Press, 2008.

Chapter 11

1992 and Beyond
The Movement Heads into the Twenty-First Century

"Don't be afraid to step up."
—Barbara Boxer in her 2016 autobiography,
The Art of Tough: Fearlessly Facing Politics and Life

"I'm Dianne Feinstein. I am woman."
—Opening remarks to state Democratic Party convention,
Los Angeles, April 1992

Perhaps the "Year of the Woman" in 1992 ultimately came down to a backlash against a single crude bit of imagery, startling not only for its raw and revolting nature but for the ornate setting in which it was delivered. It was, to put it frankly, a reference to a pubic hair atop an open can of Coca Cola. The setting: Anita Hill's testimony at a confirmation hearing for US Supreme Court nominee Clarence Thomas in the fall of 1991 before the all-male, 14-member US Senate Judiciary Committee. The scene signaled every trapping of American democracy at its most sacred—but for the shocking words that Hill was uttering on live national television.

Hill, a calmly composed law professor, had worked for Thomas at the US Equal Employment Opportunity Commission and US Department of Education. She told the committee that, as her supervisor, Thomas had described to her various acts he had seen in pornographic films, including bestiality and rape scenes, and discussed "his own sexual prowess" in graphic ways. Committee members grilled Hill on her motives and veracity. At home, countless women watching this lone African-American woman facing a panel of white men to relay her embarrassing testimony likely could recall their own experiences with unwanted innuendos or sexual advances from male colleagues in the workplace—and the seeming hopelessness of trying to report or stop them.

The allusion to pubic hair would become shorthand for Hill's uncomfortable comments, morphing into a kind of national catchphrase for the prurient nature of the verbal harassment that Hill was recounting. As she put it: "Thomas was drinking a Coke in his office, got up from the table at which we were working,

Figure 11.1. Barbara Boxer Leads House Women Up Steps on Senate Side of Capitol, 1991
Credit: Paul Hosefros/New York Times/Redux

went over to his desk to get the Coke, looked at the can and asked, "Who has put pubic hair on my Coke?"[1]

As notorious as the hearing quickly became, it almost hadn't happened at all. The Judiciary Committee, chaired by Democratic Senator Joe Biden of Delaware, earlier had wrapped up its confirmation hearings on Thomas with no mention of the charges. But the sensational allegations were leaked to Nina Totenberg of National Public Radio and predictably produced a public uproar when she reported them. Amid the brouhaha, the committee stalled over reopening its hearings. Congresswoman Barbara Boxer, a nine-year House veteran representing Marin County and part of San Francisco, was among seven female House Democrats who, at the urging of Representative Pat Schroeder of Colorado, took collective action. News photographers in tow, the women marched across the Capitol grounds to the Senate side of the building, intent on making a case to their Democratic Senate colleagues for publicly airing Hill's allegations. As the representatives strode up the outdoor marble steps leading to Senate offices, Boxer, fit from her running workouts, took the lead. The moment was captured by a *New York Times* photographer, producing an image that Boxer liked so much she would hang two copies in the office she later occupied in the Senate. Her autobiography best describes what happened next. Members of the group knocked on two massive mahogany doors concealing a luncheon meeting of the Senate Democrats with their majority leader, Senator George Mitchell. In response, one door swung open a crack and the voice of a female staffer drifted out to them. As Boxer tells it:

"We don't allow strangers in the Senate," she [the voice] said.

"Strangers?" we shouted right back. "Are you kidding? We're your Democratic colleagues from the House!"

She explained that any non-senator was technically called "a stranger" and we shouldn't take it personally.

Weird to be called a stranger. It looked hopeless. Then I made one more try.

"Listen, there are about a hundred cameras out there and they all took our picture coming up the steps. They know why we came here and they'll want to know what happened, so if we don't at least meet with the majority leader . . ." My voice trailed off with what I hoped was an ominous tone.

That's when she got it.

---

[1] Barbara Boxer, *The Art of Tough* (New York: Hachette Books, 2016), 76.

"One moment," she said. "Wait here."

We waited. She came back in a moment.

"Okay," she said. "The majority leader will see you in the side room now."

During the meeting we argued that Professor Anita Hill was credible and believable and to ignore her was wrong. New hearings were scheduled.[2]

Biden, responding to the media furor in a statement at the time, said he initially had kept Hill's charges secret to protect her confidentiality at her request. As it turned out, public hearings on her testimony made little difference in the ultimate outcome for Thomas, whose nomination by President George H. W. Bush was confirmed, 52 to 48, by the Senate. (Biden voted no, and in 2017 acknowledged that he regretted the way Hill was treated by his committee.[3]) As the nation would learn, however, Hill's testimony *did* matter to legions of women voters in California and elsewhere. Although it appeared Hill had little to gain, and perhaps much to lose, by making her awkward allegations public, her male inquisitors challenged her veracity, motives, perceptions, and even her understanding of sexual harassment as she sat alone at a witness table before them.

Thomas had received notably tepid reviews from an evaluation committee of the American Bar Association. From the get-go, his nomination to replace retiring Justice Thurgood Marshall had raised fiery criticisms from civil rights and women's groups, who argued the ultra-conservative Thomas was a poor choice to replace Marshall, a civil rights icon. For his part, Thomas, an African American, asserted that he had been victimized by "a high-tech lynching" in the Judiciary Committee.

Women Voters Would Remember the Grilling of Anita Hill

But it was the committee's panel of men grilling the stoic Hill that many women voters would long remember. In perhaps the most pointed way imaginable, the spectacle illustrated that women were all but invisible in the 100-member US Senate, a governing body that was 98 percent male. That would change, and soon. Meanwhile, Hill would become the poster woman for sexually harassed female employees everywhere—underlings who, if they pushed back against their male bosses, would be summarily and humiliatingly batted down.

Federal and state laws would be passed to give victims greater redress against on-the-job sexual harassment in the aftermath of Hill's testimony, and more wom-

---

[2] Ibid., 74–75.

[3] Derek Hawkins, "Joe Biden on Anita Hill's Sexual Harassment Testimony: 'I Owe Her an Apology,'" *Washington Post*, December 14, 2017, https://tinyurl.com/yat42d3a.

en would run for office. Boxer ran the next year for a seat being vacated by long-time California Senator Alan Cranston. She was among a 1992 crop of women candidates who believed the Judiciary Committee's treatment of Hill—or "vilification," as Boxer called it—helped drive their election victories.[4]

At about the same time, Boxer's sister Californian, Dianne Feinstein, almost from the moment of her concession to Pete Wilson in the governor's race of 1990, had shared with reporters her openness to running for the US Senate, where no California woman had ever served. In a twist of serendipity, Feinstein by losing to Wilson was spared the political agony of facing down a huge budget deficit—tied to the deep national recession of the early nineties—that was growing ever more nettlesome as Wilson assumed office. The new governor would make few friends and many enemies by negotiating a Faustian bargain with the legislature's majority Democrats to raise billions of dollars in taxes—including, perhaps most memorably, a snack tax—while slashing spending programs. Had Feinstein inherited the mess, similar criticisms would have befallen her, perhaps with gendered undertones given old stereotypes about women mishandling finances. Instead, Wilson left his unexpired term in the Senate to become governor in January of 1991—closing one door on Feinstein while opening another. The new governor appointed a little-known Orange County GOP state legislator, John Seymour, to replace him in Washington until the seat could be filled by election.

Political Chess: Filling Two Senate Seats

In a move worthy of political chess, state law required Seymour to win approval from California voters in the next statewide election in 1992 for the two years that, by then, would remain of Wilson's old six-year term. Feinstein actually had her choice of running for either of California's two Senate seats, a highly unusual circumstance. Most tempting was the six-year seat that had opened up with Cranston's retirement. That Democratic primary race would attract Boxer, Lieutenant Governor Leo McCarthy, and Representative Mel Levine of Los Angeles. Alternatively, Feinstein could run for the lesser prize, the two years remaining of Wilson's term. A significant downside would be the need to run again in 1994 for a full six-year term if she wished to stay in the Senate. However, Feinstein had built a statewide political base and a reputation as a moderate in what was then a purplish California despite her San Francisco roots. Her loss to Wilson had been respectably narrow, and she was still popular in her party's opinion surveys. If she survived the primary, which seemed likely as the Democrats' previous gubernatorial nominee, then besting the bland, little-known Seymour in a November general election seemed all but certain. There was another factor, as well. Whoever won the contest would be filling an existing term and, thus, could be sworn into office immediately after the election and gain a valuable boost in Senate seniority.

---

[4] Boxer, *The Art of Tough*, 72.

Feinstein chose the two-year seat. She drew a Democratic primary opponent with a name familiar to voters—state controller Gray Davis. Even so, it seemed possible that this time the heady "Year of the Woman" predicted in past election years would finally come to be. Perhaps both Feinstein and Boxer could survive their primary and general election battles. Perhaps Californians could elect not only their *first* woman US senator but their *first two* women US senators in 1992. No state had ever done such a thing.

In his biography of Feinstein, subtitled *Never Let Them See You Cry*, journalist Jerry Roberts writes that there was, indeed, something different about 1992. Seven years after its founding, EMILY's List was raising millions of dollars for Democratic women candidates who supported abortion rights in the face of threatening court decisions. Fifty-five candidates, including Feinstein and Boxer, would benefit from EMILY's List in 1992; it was the single largest donor to House and Senate races that year, reports Roberts. ("EMILY" is an acronym for "early money is like yeast" because it raises dough.) Hill's televised testimony against Thomas the previous fall had marked a turning point, signaling a national phenomenon that would become transforming. Having seen the overwhelming maleness of the Senate, and what it meant for them, women voters were ready for change. As Roberts writes:

> The Thomas-Hill hearings had a profound effect on the politics of 1992, galvanizing the outrage of women throughout the nation. "No matter what is said, there is a humiliation that a woman feels that a man doesn't feel at all about these things," said Feinstein, watching from California as the dramatic hearings unfolded before the Senate Judiciary Committee. "There is no question that if the Judiciary Committee had a woman on it, the whole issue [of Thomas's nomination] would not have moved until it was explored fully."[5]

Feinstein and Boxer: Feminism on the Campaign Trail

Not coincidentally, Feinstein would join the Senate Judiciary Committee as its first woman member once voters sent her to Washington.[6] In campaigning for the Senate, Roberts notes, she began connecting women's issues and public policies in ways she hadn't done while stumping for governor or during her nine years as mayor of San Francisco. In the past, Feinstein had refrained from a firebrand form of feminism, instead modeling strength and problem solving as her contributions to the cause of promoting women as the equals of men. This low-key approach had riled some in the past, including Boxer.

---

[5] Jerry Roberts, *Dianne Feinstein: Never Let Them See You Cry* (New York: HarperCollins West, 1994), 261–62.

[6] "Committee Assignments," website of US Senator Dianne Feinstein, https://feinstein.senate.gov/public/index.cfm/committee-assignments.

However, early in her Senate campaign, Feinstein seemingly became a born-again feminist. She declared to an interviewer: "The women's agenda is becoming the American agenda. Child care and family leave aren't social niceties, they're economic necessities. And there's been an enormous resurgence of women in all kinds of efforts to shatter the glass ceiling."[7] Putting aside past differences, Feinstein and Boxer began campaigning together, the still-popular former gubernatorial candidate lending her credence to underdog Boxer.

Their dual presence on the trail magnified the historic nature of their argument—that two female voices could best represent a single state.[8] Lieutenant Governor Leo McCarthy, who was bested by Boxer in the Democratic primary, later reflected on the seemingly unstoppable power of female candidates in the pivotal year of 1992:

> It was almost like a holy mission. The "Year of the Woman" was the single driving factor in the race. Every two years, we had heard the same kind of build-up but the Clarence Thomas hearing magnified it to five times as important. The women's fundraising groups were a decisive factor.[9]

In the fall, Feinstein defeated Seymour handily, and Boxer won her tougher fight against conservative television commentator Bruce Herschensohn. "The status quo must go," Feinstein declared on election night at her headquarters in San Francisco. "That change begins tonight. They don't get it yet in Washington, but they will once we get there."[10] For her part, at a victory rally in Los Angeles, Boxer declared: "I promised to take this campaign to the people and the people have responded. They want a fighter in the Senate, don't they? They want someone who will shake up the Senate, don't they? I will be a fighter in the Senate."[11]

The returns that night in 1992 gave victories to record numbers of other women candidates as well. More than 25 percent of local elected seats went to women.[12] In the US Senate, female representation tripled to six. Democrats Carol Mosely Braun of Illinois and Patty Murray of Washington also won new seats, and with Feinstein and Boxer joined Barbara Mikulski, a Maryland Democrat first elected in 1987, and Nancy Kassebaum, a Kansas Republican sent to the Senate in 1978. The "Year of the Woman" resulted in record gains in the House, as well, with 24 female newcomers nudging the ratio of women in the 435-member body to just under 11 percent.

---

[7] Roberts, *Dianne Feinstein*, 262.

[8] Robert Reinhold, "The 1992 Campaign: California; 2 Women Win Nomination in California State Races," *New York Times*, June 3, 1992.

[9] Roberts, *Dianne Feinstein*, 274.

[10] Reinhold, "The 1992 Campaign."

[11] Ibid.

[12] Roberts, *Dianne Feinstein*, 280.

"Last week I wanted to be a nurse or a teacher. This week
I decided to be a United States Senator."

Figure 11.2. Impacts of 1992's "Year of the Woman"
Credit: © Dennis Renault. Used with permission.

Mulling over reasons that 1992 was so successful for women, political scientists note that besides the motivation supplied by the Hill-Thomas hearings,
an unusually large number of seats were open that year in the House. Advances
were aided by California's population growth and the addition of seven representatives to the state's delegation through congressional reapportionment, required
after each 10-year census. Women won four of those seven new seats. Even more
importantly, record numbers of women ran. Sufficient cash from PACS, women's
groups, and party leaders made their races competitive. Importantly, too, the election "hinged on issues such as education, health care, and unemployment—issues
on which women have generally been perceived as more competent than men,"
writes Clyde Wilcox in *The Year of the Woman: Myths and Realities*. "The issues

of the campaign, combined with an electorate interested in political change, re-sulted in increased votes for women candidates."[13]

Rising Anticipation: Another "Year of the Woman"?

Comparisons were inevitable between 1992's "Year of the Woman" and the tumultuous aftermath of Donald Trump's assumption of the presidency—with its women's marches, fast-spreading #MeToo crusades against sexual harassment, and unprecedented numbers of women vowing to run for office. During no-holds-barred campaign rallies, Trump's fans had taunted his history-making opponent, Hillary Clinton, with chants of "lock her up," arguably a metaphor for keeping a politically ambitious woman in her place. An Access Hollywood tape leaked during the campaign captured Trump boasting of groping women and getting away with it.

By the fall of 2017, women across the country were stepping forward to publicly accuse male celebrities in entertainment, media, politics, and other high-profile venues of making unwanted sexual advances toward them, often in the workplace. It was as if long-simmering social tensions dating back to Hill's testimony, and perhaps earlier, were boiling over, initially reignited by a spate of sexual-misconduct allegations published in the *New York Times* against media mogul Harvey Weinstein.[14] The ensuing tsunami of accusations against other men quickly coalesced into a full-blown "#MeToo" political movement. One upshot: Minnesota's Al Franken resigned from the US Senate amid claims of his sexually inappropriate behaviors, first evidenced by a photo showing he had pretended to grab the breasts of a sleeping actress on a plane trip a decade earlier.[15] Allegations of sexual harassment swept through the House, too, prompting resignations and retirements among several male members.[16]

Mirroring its counterpart in Washington, DC, the #MeToo campaign explod-ed in Sacramento. First, there was an October 2017 letter to the *Los Angeles Times* signed by more than 140 women who worked in the state capitol and its environs.

---

[13] Clyde Wilcox, "Why Was 1992 the 'Year of the Woman'?" in *The Year of the Woman: Myths and Realities*, edited by Elizabeh Adell Cook, Sue Thomas, and Clyde Wilcox (Boulder, CO: Westview Press, 1994).

[14] Jodi Kantor and Megan Twohey, "Harvey Weinstein Paid Off Sexual Harassment Accusers for Decades," *The New York Times*, October 5, 2017, https://www.nytimes.com/2017/10/05/us/harvey-weinstein-harassment-allegations.html.

[15] Minnesota Governor Mark Dayton named Lieutenant Governor Tina Smith to Fran-ken's seat pending a November 2018 special election to fill the remaining two years of his term. Cindy Hyde-Smith of Mississippi similarly was appointed to replace Thad Cochran, who resigned due to health issues. The two appointees, sworn into office in 2018, brought the number of women senators to a record-setting 23 in the 100-member Senate that year.

[16] Nathaniel Rakich, "We've Never Seen Congressional Resignations Like This Be-fore," FiveThirtyEight, January 29, 2018, https://fivethirtyeight.com/features/more-peo-ple-are-resigning-from-congress-than-at-any-time-in-recent-history/.

While the letter didn't name alleged offenders, it complained of a "pervasive" culture of sexual harassment or worse by men who included lawmakers.[17] The women labeled their campaign #WeSaidEnough. Both legislative houses, led by men at the time, were accused of fostering a climate of secrecy that protected powerful perpetrators rather than their victims.

New procedures were adopted to turn over complaints of sexual misconduct to outside investigators. Commissions were named to review the capitol climate. And then publicly aired complaints began to snowball, as they had in the #MeToo movement generally. By early 2018, three male legislators accused of inappropriate sexual conduct had resigned,[18] and 16 legislators and staffers were under investigation. Meanwhile, Time's Up, a sister movement to #MeToo, was launched by female Hollywood celebrities to push for changing laws, practices, and policies to promote greater workplace equality, safety, and freedom from harassment.

Some female political players suggested that electing and elevating more women might be the best way to bring more gender equality into politics and workplaces—avoiding not only male harassment but male backlash in a climate so superheated that female allegations could carry the power to end men's careers. Vice President Mike Pence already had made it known he did not meet for meals alone with women other than his wife. "So much good is happening to fix workplaces right now," posted Sheryl Sandberg, chief operating officer of Facebook, in worrying over a potential male backlash. "Let's make sure it does not have the unintended consequence of holding women back."[19]

How women react to this new political environment—and how men respond—could define the women's movement for another generation. The off-putting negativity of politics is often cited as one of the reasons many women have been reluctant to run for office, hampering opportunities for female political gains. However, rather than running from the year's sordid developments, there were signals throughout the country that more women were ready for the fray—eager to challenge the maleness and machismo of their political system.

Still a Rough Road to Political Gender Parity

Even so, a quarter-century after 1992's "Year of the Woman," political gender parity remained a distant goal. The ratio of women in the US House of Representatives stood at just 19.3 percent, and women comprised only 21 of the US

---

[17] Jess Bidgood, Miriam Jordan, and Adam Nagourney, "Sexual Misconduct in California's Capitol Is Difficult to Escape," *New York Times*, October 29, 2017, https://www.newyorktimes.com/2017/10/29/us/sacramento-sexual-harassment-california-html.

[18] Assemblyman Matt Dababneh, D-Los Angeles; Assemblyman Raul Bocanegra, D-Los Angeles; and Senator Tony Mendoza, D-Artesia.

[19] Jennifer Peltz, "Will Misconduct Scandals Make Men Wary of Women at Work?" Associated Press, in the *Sacramento Bee*, December 11, 2017, http://www.sacbee.com/latest-news/article189107859.html.

Senate's 100 members in 2017. The elections of 2016 had added one woman to the Senate yet subtracted one from the House.

Kamala Harris, California's first female and first African-American state attorney general, traded Sacramento for Washington in 2017 after voters elected her to replace the retiring Boxer in the Senate. That left state controller Betty T. Yee the lone woman among California's seven elected statewide constitutional officers.[20] (Yee also was the only female Asian-Pacific American in the country to hold an elected state executive post.[21]) Heading into the 2018 contests, only eight women had ever been elected to any of these statewide offices in the history of California. None had ever won the top spots of governor or lieutenant governor.

In the state legislature, after notching steady gains over the years, the ratio of women peaked at 30.8 percent in 2006. Then it began declining. Throughout much of 2017, women numbered 26 (21.7 percent) of the 120-member legislature, the lowest female representation since 1998. California's ratio of female lawmakers trailed percentages in more than 30 other states, according to the Center for American Women and Politics at Rutgers University.[22]

In December of 2017, the number of female lawmakers nudged up to 27 with Wendy Carrillo's win of a special election to fill a vacated assembly seat. The state capitol's women legislators included one Asian-Pacific American, three African Americans, and a plurality of 13 Latinas.[23] (At 39 percent, Latinos represented the largest plurality in California's population, too, according to US Census Bureau estimates. Closely trailing were white Californians at 37.7 percent, followed by Asian-Pacific Americans at 14.8 percent, and African Americans at 6.5 percent.)

---

[20] Governor Jerry Brown nominated and the state senate confirmed Xavier Becerra to fill the remaining two years of Harris's term as attorney general.

[21] "Women of Color . . . ," http://www.cawp.rutgers.edu/women-color-elective-office-2018.

[22] "State Fact Sheet—California," Center for America Women and Politics, Eagleton Institute of Politics, Rutgers University, 2017, http://www.cawp.rutgers.edu/state_fact_sheets/ca.

[23] "Women of Color in Elective Office 2018: Congress, Statewide, State Legislature, Mayors," Center for American Women and Politics, Eagleton Institute of Politics, Rutgers University, http://www.cawp.rutgers.edu/fact-sheets-women-color#LatinasStateLeg. However, Latinas are not as strongly represented among the 19 women in California's congressional delegation. In 2018, the Center for American Women and Politics reported five Latinas (Nanette Barragán, Norma Torres, Linda Sanchez, Grace Napolitano, and Lucille Roybal-Allard), four African Americans (Kamala Harris, Karen Bass, Barbara Lee, and Maxine Waters), and two Asian-Pacific Americans (Judy Chu and Doris Matsui). "Facts: Women of Color in Elective Office 2018," http://www.cawp.rutgers.edu/women-color-elective-office-2018.

Encouraging More California Women to Run

What might account for the robust representation of Latinas among the capitol's elected women? "It's really demographics meeting preparation," explains Helen Torres, executive director of Hispanas Organized for Political Equality (HOPE). Since Latinas as a demographic group are younger than the state's overall population, she says, those interested in political life have more time "in the pipeline" to develop their interest and skills. It likely helps that the nonpartisan HOPE and a host of other nonprofit organizations are bent on promoting greater political success among women in California.[24] Some are divided strictly along Democratic or Republican lines, while others are interested in taking a more intersectional approach to moving women—especially African Americans and Latinas—into the public sphere. As Torres puts it, they're focused on "breaking down the mystique of running for office" to "build confidence in women that they can succeed. It is about keeping that pipeline strong."[25]

The left-leaning Black Women Organized for Political Action, founded in Oakland in 1968, strives to engage more black women in politics with the goal of solving issues affecting the African-American community.[26] IGNITE, with several chapters in California and elsewhere in the country, nurtures aspirations for political leadership among teens and college-aged women.

The Center for Asian Pacific American Women takes a wholistic approach. Hurdles to entering politics for Asian-American and Pacific-Islander women, it reports, include their own self-doubts about the qualities needed for successful leadership, as well as past stereotypes and discrimination.[27] Although fast fading from living memory, Californians of Asian descent were singled out for particular oppression during the first half of the nineteenth century by various laws and decrees. Notably, 90,000 Californians of Japanese ancestry, two-thirds of them American citizens, were removed from their California homes and businesses during World War II and incarcerated in remote compounds.

Given the challenges of encouraging women of all backgrounds to seek office, the nonpartisan California Women Lead has focused on trying to interest women in local rather than state or congressional races that would mean serving in relatively distant Sacramento or Washington, DC. "It's easier on women's lives, and many men are not interested in local jobs because they don't pay enough,"

---

[24] For a list of some 50 California organizations that recruit, train, and/or support women candidates, see "Political Leadership Resource Map," http://cawp.rutgers.edu/education/leadership-resources.

[25] Helen Torres interview, Los Angeles, April 23, 2018, by telephone.

[26] "Our Mission," Black Women Organized for Political Action, http://www.bwopatileleads.org/about.

[27] "About—History," The Center for Asian Pacific American Women, http://apawomen.org/history/.

says board president Cassandra Pye. "It's retail politics at its best, and it's a great way to build up one's confidence."[28]

Even so, a gender gap in local politics stubbornly persists. Among the state's 482 cities, 85 percent were managed by male-majority city councils in 2017, reported California Women Lead. Fifty percent had only one councilwoman or none. Just one of the 10 most populous cities in California was led by a woman—Mayor Libby Schaaf of Oakland.[29]

Similarly, only five of the 58 county boards of supervisors were female-dominated. However, one of these was in mighty Los Angeles County, with a population of 10 million—greater than the populations of all but 10 states. The county's voters added two new women supervisors—Janice Hahn and Kathryn Barger—in 2016 to join Sheila Kuehl and Hilda Solis for a four-woman majority. Female majorities on boards of supervisors in the other four counties—San Francisco, Marin, Contra Costa and Sonoma—set policy for another 2.6 million Californians.[30]

Although overall numbers suggest gender parity remains an elusive target in elective politics, on one front women did achieve political equality. A once hotly controversial goal that Feinstein proposed decades ago as a gubernatorial candidate was quietly achieved in 2015.[31] California Women Lead reported that, aided by Governor Jerry Brown and his administration, half of the appointed offices at the state's executive level were filled by women.[32]

Mixed Results for Term Limits

California voters in 1990 imposed limits on the number of terms that legislators and statewide officeholders could serve—managing to both help and hinder electing more political women and candidates of color. Initially, the limits cast out dozens of mostly male incumbents who, in some cases, had held their seats for decades. The ceilings of three terms (six years) in the 80-member assembly and two terms (eight years) in the 40-member senate generated new opportunities that swelled diversity in the statehouse.[33]

Open seats—those without incumbents and thus most easily won by newcomers—increased nearly five-fold in the legislature by 2008. Female representation rose by almost 40 percent in the assembly and tripled in the senate. In the 13

---

[28] Cassandra Pye interview, January 30, 2017, Sacramento.

[29] "The Status of Women in California Government in 2017," California Women Lead, http://www.cawomenlead.org/?page=StatewideReports.

[30] Ibid.

[31] See Chapter 9 of this book for a discussion of Dianne Feinstein's pledge.

[32] "The Status of Women in California Government. . . ."

[33] Statewide officeholders, such as governor and lieutenant governor, are limited to two terms. Jerry Brown, who served four terms, was "grandfathered in" because his first two terms occurred before the limits were adopted.

elections before term limits, a total of 10 women of color had been elected to the legislature. In the next 13 elections, their numbers nearly quintupled.[34]

Richard Temple, who has managed hundreds of California legislative campaigns, believes term limits aided women by lessening a need to raise hefty sums to challenge sitting officeholders. The average assembly candidate already raises more than a half-million dollars. "It's extremely hard to beat an incumbent. They have a lot more connections to people district-wide, so they typically have more supporters, more money, and more endorsements. No one wants to alienate a sitting member of the legislature or Congress [by donating to an opponent]."[35] Senate Republican leader Patricia Bates notes that she jumped from local government in Orange County to the assembly after an incumbent was forced from office. "Doors opened," Bates says. "Those opportunities never would have been there for us if term limits hadn't kicked in and provided women new avenues to pursue."[36]

In time, however, the limits began terming out women incumbents as well. In 2012, voters revamped the limits to allow legislators to serve up to 12 years, either all in one house or a combination of both houses. This change, which has yet to fully play out, may enable elected women to consolidate their power within the capitol. Yet it has meant the fewest open seats in 28 years—an unintended effect that potentially could last until 2024.

Temple noted that, aside from occasional retirements, resignations, and office-hopping, the change means that "more elections (for legislative seats) will feature incumbents and that means fewer and fewer races will be competitive and open. Ninety-nine percent of the time," he added, "it's easier to win an open seat."[37]

No Term Limits in Congress

In Congress, which has no term limits, California's two senators and 53 House members are free to run as often as they choose, allowing time to build legacies. Not coincidentally, many of the state's most visible, outspoken ,and enduring women leaders—Feinstein and Boxer, and Representatives Nancy Pelosi, Maxine Waters, Barbara Lee, Jackie Speier, and others—have made their marks in Washington across the decades. Still, 11 of California's 17 female House members in 2017 were former state legislators—thanks partly to the revolving door that term limits created in Sacramento. Overall, California's delegation of House

---

[34] California Statements of Vote, 1966–2016.

[35] Richard Temple interview, Sacramento, February 9, 2018, 2018. According to FollowTheMoney.org, the average assembly candidate raised $563,804 in 2014. The average senate candidate raised $899,235 (J. T. Stepleton, "2014 Candidate Elections Overview, October 23, 2015, www.followthemoney.org/research/institute-reports/2014-candidate-elections-overview/.)

[36] Patricia Bates interview, Sacramento, January 23, 2018.

[37] Interview with Richard Temple, Sacramento, February 16, 2018.

and Senate members was 34.5 percent female—taking it substantially further along the path to gender parity than the legislature's membership.

With the exception of Mimi Walters, all of the California women in Congress in 2017 were Democrats. In the legislature, too, Democrats predominated among women, although by smaller margins. Not only was the state deeply blue by then, but the feminist movement itself has been a progressive political cause over time. While feminism requires no partisan allegiance, female politicians who openly challenge the status quo may lean Democratic. At the same time, however, conservative women may find less voter resistance to paving the way because they are perceived as less threatening to established mores.[38]

This phenomenon may explain an unintended consequence for some political women of another voting reform—the unconventional top-two primary system adopted by Californians in 2010. Rather than an automatic runoff between Republican and Democratic nominees in general elections, the two candidates with the most votes in a primary race now advance to the general election, regardless of party affiliation. It applies not only to state races, but to congressional contests in California as well. This creates a possibility of two Democrats or two Republicans facing each other in November run-offs. The upshot? When two Democrats run against each other, for instance, Republican voters have to choose one of them—and presumably will pick the more moderate candidate. The same goes for Democratic voters in Republican-leaning districts: they will be more likely to choose the less partisan of two Republicans in a general election.

Under this system, when a man and woman compete in a general election, some advocates are concerned a female candidate might be perceived as the more progressive or partisan of the two. For example, even if a Democratic female candidate received the most votes in the primary, conservative Republican voters might perceive her Democratic male opponent as more moderate and swing the election toward him in November.

Hurdles to Leadership for Women

Even without voters' tinkering with election procedures, challenging the status quo has never been easy for the feminist cause. Whether implicit or overt, voters of both genders may push back, as they have since the days of the suffrage movement. When women seek elective offices, especially for legislative bodies, the results show they can win. However, mountains of data also show the hurdles are higher for women who seek leadership posts inside and outside of politics. The defeat of Hillary Clinton—politically experienced, even-tempered, policy-oriented—to the highly unconventional, unpredictable, and unsettling Donald Trump arguably illustrates the point. Studies find that men and women alike are

---

[38] See the discussion of Rose Ann Vuich, California's first female state senator, in Chapter 9 and the discussion of Bobbi Fiedler, who at one time was the only woman in California's congressional delegation, in Chapter 10.

offended by ambitious, power-seeking women although they see nothing wrong with these traits in men.[39] Further, because the stereotypical, nurturing qualities of women are at odds with the male-oriented stereotypes of strong, assertive leadership, a body of research shows "women who wish to be leaders are held to a higher standard of competence than men," observes Susan J. Carroll of the Center for American Women and Politics. "They have to do more to demonstrate their qualifications and abilities."[40] Writes Kathleen Hall Jamieson: "Our expectations of women are more difficult to meet. At the core of this bind is the assumption that woman is other and defective."[41]

These kinds of findings help explain what otherwise might seem inexplicable—that too many competent, accomplished women are missing from the top tiers of the political hierarchies in Washington, Sacramento, and other capitols and city halls. (Just six American women—two Democrats and four Republicans—were governors in 2018, the same number as eight years earlier.[42]) Part of the explanation lies within women themselves, who fail to run in the kinds of numbers needed to narrow the gender gap. Women typically require greater encouragement to enter politics than men do, but are less likely to receive it, researchers find.

Jennifer Lawless, director of the Women & Politics Institute at American University, and colleague Richard Fox found "a substantial gender gap in political ambition" in surveys of nearly 4,000 men and women who seemingly would make strong political candidates. They reported that women tended to be more risk-averse than men, more repelled by the negativity of politics, and more likely to question their own qualifications to run. Women also were more prone to feel held back by childcare and household responsibilities.[43] Even so, Lawless argues, "when they do run, female candidates do just as well as men."[44]

Other scholars, such as Jamieson, suggest that a "double bind" requires women to walk a tightrope while balancing the contradictory traits embedded in cultural expectations of gender and leadership: female candidates must be perceived as

---

[39] Tyler G. Okimoto and Victoria L. Brescoll, "The Price of Power: Power Seeking and Backlash against Female Politicians," *Personality and Social Psychology Bulletin* 36, 7 (2010): 923.

[40] Susan J. Carroll, "Reflections on Gender and Hillary Clinton's Presidential Campaign: The Good, the Bad, and the Misogynic," *Politics & Gender* 5, 1 (2009): 5–6.

[41] Kathleen Hall Jamieson, *Beyond the Double Bind: Women and Leadership* (New York: Oxford University Press, 1995), 18 (italics added).

[42] They were serving in Alabama, Iowa, New Mexico, Oklahoma, Oregon, and Rhode Island. See: "Women in Statewide Elected Office in 2017," Center for American Women and Politics, Eagleton Institute of Politics, Rutgers University, http://www.cawp.rutgers.edu/women-statewide-elective-executive-office-2017.

[43] Jennifer L. Lawless and Richard L. Fox, "Men Rule: The Continued Under-Representation of Women in US Politics," Women & Politics Institute, School of Public Affairs, American University, 2012.

[44] Danny Hayes and Jennifer Lawless, *Women on the Run: Gender, Media, and Political Campaigns* (New York: Cambridge University Press, 2016), 6.

appropriately feminine without being submissive; they must be assertive without seeming macho.

At the same time, political women are expected to be likeable. Voters want this quality in female politicians even though likeability is not a trait they consider important in male leaders. Unfortunately, experiments with hundreds of undergraduate students show that men and women alike project a sense of dislike and other negative traits onto ambitious, capable women who succeed in mostly male fields. Interestingly, when the quality of a woman's job performance was kept unclear, harsh feelings did not surface against her. It was only when women were judged competent in male-dominated environments that people of both sexes disliked them and viewed them as hostile, although they didn't react this way toward men.[45] In a cultural Catch 22, then, women who project proficiency in the macho realm of political leadership may be judged, as feminist political scholar Susan Carroll has put it, "not 'nice' enough" to merit the role.[46]

Against this backdrop, perhaps it is unsurprising that women's collective gains in politics have plateaued at times. Senator Bates, in trying to recruit Republican women for office, believes some "distasteful" aspects of social media are a deterrent to running as well, since harshly critical posts may expose women candidates to an "animus that they never expected in their lives."[47] Kimberly Ellis, former executive director of the Democrat-oriented Emerge California, says it takes extra effort to coax women to enter electoral politics. "A big part of that is recruiting," she says. "Women actually don't self-nominate. They have to be asked . . . seven times."[48] Kristin Olsen, a former Modesto city council member and Republican leader in the state assembly, puts a face on the research: "I never thought about running for city council, ever, until somebody called me and asked me if I would consider it."[49] Or, as former Vermont governor Madeleine Kunin has put it, "At some gut level, the art of politics—combative, competitive, self-asserting—is sometimes difficult to integrate with our feminine selves."[50]

Politicians, journalists, and even ordinary citizens believe politics is fraught with gender biases against women.[51] In her autobiography, Boxer writes that she knows "something about discrimination as a woman in politics." She explains:

---

[45] Madeline E. Heilman, Aaron S. Wallen, Daniella Fuchs, Melinda M. Tamkins, "Penalties for Success: Reactions to Women Who Succeed at Male Gender-Typed Tasks," *Journal of Applied Psychology* 89, 3 (2004): 416.

[46] Carroll, "Reflections on . . . ," 6.

[47] Bates interview.

[48] Kimberly Ellis interview, February 2, 2017, Sacramento.

[49] Melanie Mason, "Too Few Women Hold Political Seats, Report Says," *Los Angeles Times,* September 23, 2014, AA3.

[50] Richard Zeiger and Sherry Bebitch Jeffe, "Women in Politics," *California Journal* (January 1988): 7–11.

[51] Hayes and Lawless, *Women on the Run.*

When I started out, people couldn't accept the fact that I was a woman, hinting that there was something wrong with me for wanting to be in office, abandon my children, and anyway, how much could I know about finance? . . . I wish I had a dollar for every time I was called "brash," or "pushy" or "overemotional."[52]

Politics has always pitted the communal ideals of public service against the paradigm of raw power—in the merciless glare of a public spotlight. It thus matters that women tend to be more risk-averse than men. Women may hesitate to run because they feel less competitive or less confident—or because they believe others see them that way. "It's the idea that you're not necessarily taken seriously, not seen as someone sturdy enough to do this work," says Delaine Eastin, a candidate for California governor in 2018 who served four terms in the California assembly and two as the state's superintendent of public instruction.[53]

Why Female Political Leadership Matters

Yet leadership by women matters for other women, as well as for men and children, both for modeling what is possible and for its policy outcomes. As a *New York Times* headline over an exploration of the topic put it: "Women Actually Do Govern Differently." Research shows women lawmakers give more attention to social issues, tend to be more collaborative and bipartisan than men, and bring more federal money to their districts.[54] What's more, a study that tracked nearly 140,000 bills introduced in Congress between 1973 and 2008 found women lawmakers tended to be more effective than their male counterparts in compromising and deal-brokering.[55] Republican leader Bates has noticed a similar trend in Sacramento. "Women like to deal with details and find a consensus," she says. "Women think, 'A committee can solve this,' and men go, 'Oh no, not another committee.'"[56]

Female citizens may be more politically active when their senators are women, and these feelings of engagement apparently work both ways.[57] A study that interviewed female members of Congress found they invariably spoke of their

---

[52] Boxer, *The Art of Tough*, 198.

[53] Delaine Eastin interview, February 2, 2017, Sacramento.

[54] Claire Cain Miller, "Women Actually Do Govern Differently," *New York Times*, November 10, 2016, https//www.nytimes.com/2016/11/10/upshot/women-actually-do-govern-differently.html?_r=0.

[55] Craig Volden, Alan E. Wiseman, and Dana E. Wittmer, "On Average, Women in Congress are More Effective Lawmakers than Men," LSE US Centre, September 20, 2013, http://bit.ly/18dTecx.

[56] Bates interview.

[57] Lori Cox Han and Caroline Heldman, *Women, Power, and Politics: The Fight for Gender Equality in the United States* (New York: Oxford University Press, 2018).

sense of connection and responsibility to women.[58] Perhaps unsurprisingly, electing more women lawmakers produces more legislation that affects the lives of women.[59]

A sampling of female-authored bills signed by Jerry Brown—arguably the state's most feminist-minded governor to date—attests to the kinds of policies associated with female empowerment. Near the end of the Democratic governor's fourth term, some of these new laws expanded protections for rape victims, required public schools in low-income areas to stock bathrooms with free tampons and menstrual pads, sought to narrow the gender pay gap by forbidding employers to ask for a worker's previous salary, and gave California workers at medium-sized businesses a right to take unpaid family leave to care for new babies. Brown also signed a measure, authored by a lesbian legislator, to make it easier for transgender individuals to change their sex on birth certificates, driver's licenses, and other government documents—or to designate a third, nonbinary gender.

Greater diversity among those who legislate and govern, then, can expand the quality of representation their constituents receive. The record-smashing numbers of women candidates in 2018—whether in response to Trump, the #MeToo movement, or something else—seemed destined to change the way many women saw themselves. Even if ballot-box gains toward political equality once again proved only incremental or even halting over time, sea changes were occurring. In January and April of 2018, the US Senate welcomed a record twenty-second and then a record twenty-third woman senator. First, Minnesota Democratic Lieutenant Governor Tina Smith was named by Governor Mark Dayton to replace the disgraced Al Franken pending November election outcomes. Then, with the same caveat, Mississippi Governor Phil Byrant chose Republican Cindy Hyde-Smith to replace Thad Cochran, who left because of health issues. Hyde-Smith became Mississippi's first woman in Congress.[60]

The June primary elections for the US House drew an unprecedented 57 female candidates from the two major parties in California. That was nearly 25 percent more than in 2012, when the previous record was set.[61] However, many ran against each other or challenged well-established female incumbents, diluting the

---

[58] Debra L. Dodson, *The Impact of Women in Congress* (New York: Oxford University Press, 2006), 85.

[59] Han and Heldman, *Women, Power, and Politics*, 148–49.

[60] "Data Point: With New Addition, Record Number of Women in Senate and Mississippi Sends First Woman to Congress," Center for American Women and Politics, Rutgers University, http://www.cawp.rutgers.edu/sites/default/files/resources/data-point-new-senate-record.pdf.

[61] Christine Mai-Duc, "It Could Be Another Year of the Woman in California, But It Probably Won't Be," *Los Angeles Times*, May 28, 2018, http://www.latimes.com/politics/la-pol-ca-year-of-the-woman-california-20180528-htmlstory.html.

impact of their numbers. Further, in California and nationally, about three-quarters of the House candidates from major parties were men.[62]

Blazing a Political Trail for Senior Women

Feinstein, the oldest member of the Senate at a trailblazing 84, sought a fifth six-year term in 2018 that bookended her "Year of the Woman" win in 1992 with another landmark year of female candidacies. Notably, voters in 1992 had sent her to a *legislative body*, a more communal environment than the *chief executive role* she had lost to Wilson in 1990. In the Senate, a continent away from California's day-to-day fray, she remained a popular figure over the decades, at times ranked as the state's favorite politician. Asked during a CNN interview at her home in early 2017 why she had never run for president, Feinstein quietly replied: "I don't know. I felt I'd never be elected." She paused to glance at a room-length case of political career mementos, then added: "See, look how hard it is. Look at Hillary. Look at what she's gone through." Interviewer Dana Bash prompted: "You've done hard before." Replied Feinstein: "Yeah, I've done hard before. But it's not a bad thing being in the Senate."

Feinstein unabashedly advocated stronger gun controls, memorably chastised then-President Bill Clinton for lying about his Monica Lewinsky affair, persistently prodded a reluctant then-President Barack Obama to make public a full report on CIA torture, and angrily challenged what she called "an old boys' club" of federal railroad regulators over a deadly train collision in Los Angeles.[63] Her verbal style pulled few punches, although some of her moderate stands ruffled liberal feathers in her true-blue home state. Notably, she was booed in her hometown of San Francisco seven months after Trump took office for suggesting he could be "a good president" if he could "learn and change."[64] Nor did she win the endorsement of the state Democratic Party in February 2018. (Her primary-election opponent, former senate leader Kevin de León of Los Angeles, also failed to secure the required 60 percent approval from state party delegates. But they favored him, 54 percent to 37 percent, over Feinstein.)

How did Feinstein negotiate the double bind over her long career in the limelight—finding a balance between the assertiveness of political leadership and the cultural expectations made of women? By melding, it would seem, her take-no-prisoners directness with an aura of warmth. Her Senate website, for instance, invited constituents to join her for breakfast when in Washington. Californians of both genders and parties volunteered to an interviewer that they consid-

---

[62] Ibid.

[63] Steve Hymon and Cynthia Dizikes, "Accord Reached on Rail Bill," *Los Angeles Times*, September 24, 2008, B1.

[64] Casey Tolan, "Sen. Dianne Feinstein Booed at San Francisco Event after Saying She Hopes Trump Can Change," *The Mercury News*, August 29, 2017, https://www.mercurynews.com/2017/08/29/feinstein-san-francisco-booed-donald-trump/.

ered her both likeable and principled. "I'd love to sit down and have a conversation with her over dinner, with a glass of sherry," said a 70-year-old Republican man. A 54-year-old Democratic man called her "a wise, respected, grand old dame."[65] In a 2012 profile, *San Francisco Chronicle* reporter Carolyn Lochhead described Feinstein this way: "She is imperious and warm, charming and intimidating, perfectionist and charismatic, earnest and calculating."[66]

One hundred years after the first four women were elected to the California assembly in 1918, Feinstein's 50-year political legacy continued to pave the way for a new century of female groundbreakers, including women facing down their senior years.

The Nation's First Female House Speaker— Nancy Pelosi

Nancy Pelosi, Feinstein's colleague from San Francisco and the first female speaker of the US House of Representatives from 2007 to 2011, was the most powerful political woman in America during those years. In 2010, she presided over the hard-fought passage of the Affordable Health Care Act, also known as Obamacare. Even after Democrats lost control of the House in that year's elections, Pelosi in her demoted post as minority leader arguably remained the nation's top woman officeholder going into the 2018 elections.

For Pelosi, first elected to represent San Franciscans in the House in 1986, politics is a family business. She is the daughter of Thomas D'Alesandro, Jr., first a congressman from hardscrabble Baltimore and then the city's mayor. A tireless and prodigious fundraiser, Pelosi generated tens of millions of dollars for her single-minded goal of winning back the House for Democrats in the midterm races. She was fond of using three-word alliterations on the stump—and three words that might describe her are dogged, disciplined, and determined. "No one doubts that Pelosi can put points on the board," political reporter Michael Scherer wrote in profiling her for the *Washington Post*. He added later in the story: "Underlying her entire approach is a fierceness, born not from the frontier liberalism of San Francisco but from the calculating, ethnic, big city politics of Baltimore."[67]

For all of Pelosi's gravitas in the political arena, gendered nuances could work their way into stories about her. These may note, for instance, her fond-

---

[65] Rebecca LaVally, "Political Contradictions: Discussions of Virtue in American Life" (PhD diss., University of Texas at Austin, 2010).

[66] Carolyn Lochhead, "Dianne Feinstein: 4 Decades of Influence," *San Francisco Chronicle*, October 22, 2012, from http://www.sfgate.com/politics/article/Dianne-Feinstein-4-decades-of-influence-3968314.php#photo-2085178.

[67] Michael Scherer, "Nancy Pelosi Isn't Going Anywhere. Will It Help or Hurt Democrats in 2018?" *Washington Post*, October 29, 2017, https://www.washingtonpost.com/politics/nancy-pelosi-isnt-going-anywhere-will-it-help-or-hurt-democrats-in-2018/2017/10/28/2ea9baa2-bb17-11e7-a908-a3470754bbb9_story.html?utm_term=.18bce7f1b78f.

ness for good manners and conversational pleasantries or her status as a grand-mother—the kinds of qualities that, with the exception of former House Speaker John Boehner's penchant for bursting into tears, might not appear in pieces about male leaders. But qualities such as these may help traverse a double bind. Anticipating Pelosi's ascent as speaker, *New York Times* reporter Jennifer Steinhauer opened a 2006 story on Pelosi with these lines:

> ATLANTA—The young women on the porch were whispering, their tittering just audible over Bill Clinton's remarks to the three hundred or so Democratic donors gathered here for lunch. Representative Nancy Pelosi, mindful that some guests had paid $10,000 for a plate of chicken and bread pudding, shot a frown—the sort a grandmother gives when someone arrives at Christmas dinner in a wrinkled shirt—and in a split second, the whispers ceased. Ms. Pelosi's face resumed its trademark molar-baring smile.[68]

Other Modern-Day Pavers of the Political Road for Women

With credentials that included former district attorney of San Francisco and former state attorney general, Kamala Harris, California's first biracial senator, quickly attracted media attention in Washington and a rising national profile as a fresh, credible, and outspoken voice from her mega state.[69] She soon was grouped with Democratic stars Elizabeth Warren of Massachusetts and Kirsten Gillibrand of New York as one of the Senate women "who speak forcefully in public."[70] A headline on an opinion column by Washington Post writer Jonathan Capehart cemented her emerging image: "'We Need to Get This Done': Kamala Harris Gets Tough on Russia Probe (and Ignores the Mansplainers)."[71]

Other California trailblazers, even if falling short of the top-tier achievements of leaders such as Pelosi, for instance, have responded to the call, sometimes suffering resounding defeats for their labors. Among them, Republican entrepreneur Meg Whitman pumped nearly 150 million dollars of her own fortune into attempting to become California's first woman governor in 2010. She lost by nearly 13 percentage points to Jerry Brown, then attorney general, who was seeking his

---

[68] Jennifer Steinhauer, "With the House in the Balance, Pelosi Serves as a Focal Point for Both Parties," *New York Times*, October 30, 2006, A20.

[69] Her Senate website biography also described her as the Senate's second African-American woman and first South-Asian American senator at https://www.harris.senate.gov/about.

[70] Elaine Showalter, "Author Explains History's Muzzle on Powerful Women," *Washington Post*, December 18, 2017. Retrieved December 31, 2017, from https://tinyurl.com/y7yfafda.

[71] Jonathan Capehart, "'We Need to Get This Done': Kamala Harris Gets Tough on Russia Probe (and Ignores the Mansplainers)," *The Washington Post*, July 25, 2017, https://tinyurl.com/yc8n3yss.

third gubernatorial term after an extended hiatus from the governor's office. Carly Fiorina, former CEO of Hewlett Packard, took on Boxer the same year, marking the first time two California women had competed against each other for the US Senate. Boxer bested Fiorina by 10 percentage points to win her fourth term.

However, a once-thick glass ceiling dating to statehood was broken in Sacramento as the politically stormy year of 2017 played itself out. In the senate, majority Democrats agreed that San Diegan Toni Atkins, a former speaker of the assembly, would become the senate's first female president pro tempore, its top internally chosen leader. She would be the first lawmaker since 1871 to have led both houses of the legislature.[72] Atkins also was destined to become the first openly lesbian or gay legislator to run the senate day-to-day. She remembers watching Anita Hill on television in 1992, "hoping that people would hear her and change things. And it didn't happen. I've been waiting my whole life to be part of something that helps women be treated equally. . . ."[73]

Asked why so few women have held positions of electoral power in Sacramento, Atkins opined: "Much more than men, women tend to hesitate when opportunities arise. . . . We think about all the juggling acts with career and family we'd have to perform in order to make the opportunity work, and too often we wait for a sign, or permission, that it's OK to go for it." Instead, she suggested, women should heed Sheryl Sandberg's advice to "lean in" to embrace the challenges of electoral politics and "let the rest sort itself out." As for being the senate's first openly gay or lesbian leader, she added:

> I am incredibly humbled, but seriously mindful that I'm breaking ground and making history in California—for women and for the LGBTQ community. I get to be the face of that. And while I'm actually much, much more comfortable as a team member and hanging out in the background—directing action and implementing solutions—I'm aware that I need to take my own advice, and Sandberg's, and lean in heavy for all those trailblazers in the women's movement and the LGBTQ community who made this possible.[74]

Propelled partly by leadership turnovers tied to term limits, three women have been chosen by their colleagues to be speakers of the assembly, beginning with Republican Doris Allen in 1995. However, Allen, who won the post in a political sleight-of-hand masterminded by former Democratic Assembly Speaker Willie Brown, held the job only three months. Her tenure summarily ended

---

[72] John Myers, "New Senate President Pro Tem Toni Atkins Pledges Change in the Capitol on Sexual Misconduct," *Los Angeles Times*, March 21, 2018, http://www.latimes.com/politics/essential/la-pol-ca-essential-politics-updates-new-senate-president-pro-tem-toni-atkins-1521669345-htmlstory.html.

[73] Taryn Luna, "State Senate's First Female Leader Says 'Real Work' Is Needed to Fight Harassment," *Sacramento Bee*, February 5, 2018, 3.

[74] Senator Toni Atkins, email interview, March 5, 2018.

when her conservative Orange County constituents recalled Allen from office in retribution for her alliance with Brown. Karen Bass of Los Angeles became the first female African-American speaker in 2008, and served for two years before winning election to the House. Atkins served two years as the first openly lesbian speaker beginning in 2014 (and was acting governor for a few hours that year).

The Next Wave into a New Century

In keeping with the tenor of feminism's third wave, its beginnings grounded in the "Year of the Woman" a quarter of a century earlier, responses to the sea changes of 2017 and 2018 ultimately may be as varied as women themselves. Unlike the second wave, which pushed for collective gains (at least among white women of relative privilege) in male-dominated workplaces and other institutions, the third wave put its emphasis on individual choices. This was a wave that could readily embrace the rights and freedoms of women of color and the LGBTQ movement. It recognized the concept of *intersectionality*—that gender, race, ethnicity, class, sexual orientation, and other factors overlap to influence each individual's experiences differently. Scholars Lori Cox Han and Caroline Heldman observe, however, that some critics have complained this wave too often overlooked the underlying causes of gender inequality and the energy that can arise from united action. In the third wave, past gains could plateau or stagnate.[75]

Yet Han and Heldman also see an emerging fourth wave that relies on new sets of tools—including social media and scholarly research that increasingly has found its way out of academia—to promote interactive responses on multiple fronts. Epitomized by the #MeToo campaign and millions of pussy-hatted protest marchers, this new wave may portend a reawakening that comes full circle, galvanizing women to continue pushing for eradicating misogyny from political life much as Hill's testimony did decades ago. Others label it a "call-out" movement, bent on publicly challenging, even shaming, longstanding gender inequities.[76] HOPE's Helen Torres says its tenets especially appeal to what is becoming known as Generation Z—the postmillennial cohort that includes high-school and younger college students galvanized by school gun violence and other social issues.

Kristin Goss, in a comprehensive study of women's testimony to Congress dating to the nineteenth century, suggests the wave metaphor—with its notions of cresting and receding—may be less apt for describing the women's movement than the imagery of a river. While a river may meander, it continues to flow even during periods of quietude, Goss observes.[77] During the quiet times for women's

---

[75] Lori Cox Han and Caroline Heldman, *Women, Power, and Politics: The Fight for Gender Equality in the United States* (New York: Oxford University Press, 2018).

[76] Ruth Phillips and Viviene Cree, "What Does the 'Fourth Wave' Mean for Feminism in Twenty-First Century Social Work?" *Social Work Education* 33, 7 (2014): 939.

[77] Kristin A. Goss, *The Paradox of Gender Equality: How American Women's Groups Gained and Lost Their Public Voice* (Ann Arbor: University of Michigan Press, 2013), 7.

rights, as these pages have shown, women collectively have taken on other social causes—from regulating milk to saving redwoods to fighting smog to aiding farmworkers.

Whether it crests in waves or flows in rivers, will the movement dating to California's female pioneers finally find itself on a steady keel to close the political gender gap in this nation-state of 40 million? Might the ship of state in the imaginable future be guided by a woman's hand? Or will the quest for political gender equality once again pause at some new plateau?

Throughout its course, feminism inevitably has drawn counterattacks that nipped at the heels of each forward leap. Yet it also has birthed countless trailblazers, the pathfinding women willing to buck convention and risk defeat to secure ever-higher ground in the struggle for political equality. In California, they have included the known, the lesser-known, and the nearly unknown—from Clara Foltz and Ellen Sargent in the late 1800s, to Katherine Philips Edson and Grace Dorris in the 1920s, to Felicitas Mendez and Margaret Levee in mid-century and, more recently, to Bobbi Fiedler, Dolores Huerta, Maxine Waters, and Toni Atkins.

After her fourth term expired, Barbara Boxer visited Sacramento to promote her autobiography, *The Art of Tough: Fearlessly Facing Politics and Life.* Winding up a luncheon appearance in September 2017 before the Sacramento Press Club, a few blocks from the state capitol, Boxer was asked a final, two-part question. In the wake of the Women's March on Washington, amid the apparent rising interest among women in running for office, did she foresee 1992's "Year of the Woman" coming full circle? What advice might she have? Nodding, Boxer repeated her book's assertion that Anita Hill's testimony had been crucial to her own election in 1992. She recounted that a prominent constituent had told her he'd been skeptical of voting for a woman for the Senate, but changed his mind after watching Hill's treatment in the Senate hearings. Closing, Boxer conveyed that, although marching can matter, voting—participating first-hand in the American brand of democracy—matters even more:

> We are guaranteed nothing. We have a framework. I often read the Declaration of Independence: "We are endowed by our Creator with certain unalienable rights, that among these are life, liberty, and the pursuit of happiness." Yes, we are endowed with those, but who is going to protect those? If you've got the wrong people in positions of power, you can kiss it goodbye.

> And then you read the Preamble to the Constitution. "In order to form a more perfect union" we have to "establish justice, ensure domestic tranquility, provide a common defense, promote the general welfare and confer the blessings of liberty on ourselves and our posterity." . . . [T]o me, that's the unification of the American dream—those words.

But we are not guaranteed any of this. . . . I don't care what side of the fence you're on. Everybody has to understand what is at stake and get out and vote. Because, to sum it up in a word, what's at stake? Everything.

Discussion Questions

1. What were the connections between Anita Hill's 1991 testimony against Clarence Thomas, then a nominee to the US Supreme Court, and the electoral groundswell that led to 1992's "Year of the Woman"? For what reasons did the gender and racial composition of the Senate Judiciary Committee become a subtext of this electoral drama?

2. What parallels might be drawn between the treatment of Hill by members of the Judiciary Committee and the #MeToo movement that surfaced in the fall of 2017? How did the emerging movement play out in the capitol environs of Sacramento and Washington?

3. What paradoxes could be associated with Dianne Feinstein's defeat to Pete Wilson for governor and her subsequent election to the Senate? What circumstances helped facilitate sending more women to both houses of Congress and the legislature in 1992? What was the overall increase in the number of women in the US Senate after the election?

4. What are some reasons for declining percentages of women in state elective offices in the years before the 2018 midterm elections? Why do you believe the 2016 presidential election galvanized women marchers, activists, and candidates in its *aftermath*, rather than *at the time* of Hillary Clinton's historic campaign?

5. Why has challenging the status quo in the quest for political equality been such an arduous task for feminists? For what reasons, do you suppose, has California never elected a woman governor or lieutenant governor? (This parallels the record of the nation. Are the reasons the same at the national level?)

6. What are some of the cultural barriers to achieving female leadership? Why might a woman candidate be advised to seem direct and likable, without appearing overly ambitious? Would a male candidate likely get the same advice?

7. Has the #MeToo movement reshaped cultural expectations of what it means to be a feminist? Might a fourth wave movement, relying on social media to spread ideas and activism, bring greater gender equality to public life than the third wave did? Whatever your answer, what are your reasons?

8. Who was the "most powerful political woman in America" for several years beginning in 2007? For what reasons do you believe she was chosen the first woman to lead a legislative body that was 80 percent male? What qualities did she exude to negotiate "the double bind"?

9. Would you consider running for a local, state or federal office? Why or why not? What would it take to persuade you to run?

Recommended Reading

Boxer, Barbara. *The Art of Tough*. New York: Hachette Books, 2016.

Cook, Elizabeth Adell, Sue Thomas, and Clyde Wilcox, eds. *The Year of the Woman: Myths and Realities*. Boulder, CO: Westview Press, 1994.

Han, Lori Cox, and Caroline Heldman. *Women, Power, and Politics: The Fight for Gender Equality in the United States*. New York: Oxford University Press, 2018.

Roberts, Jerry. *Dianne Feinstein: Never Let Them See You Cry*. New York: HarperCollins West, 1994.

Epilogue

2018

Katie Hill smiled broadly and waved to the cheering crowd on election night as she sensed victory for a congressional seat in a sprawling district in northern Los Angeles County. The 31-year-old Democrat, a first-time candidate with a huge volunteer army of millennials, wore a purple outfit and stood behind a podium adorned with a purple campaign sign. The color purple long has been associated with the women's movement, and Hill had declared her candidacy on International Women's Day in 2017. A wire service photographer snapped a photo of Hill as she raised her hand to acknowledge the well-wishers. After her Republican opponent conceded defeat the following day, that photo showed up on newspaper websites from Virginia to Hawaii.

Hill's victory came in a district never before represented by a woman, and it was one of several watershed triumphs for California women that November night. With the high-profile #MeToo movement and rising political engagement as backdrops, women won three statewide constitutional offices for the first time in history. Further, with Dianne Feinstein's re-election, voters had chosen women to hold both of the state's US Senate seats for three consecutive decades.

Eleni Kounalakis became the only woman elected lieutenant governor in California's 168-year history, conceivably moving the state closer to a day when it might elect its first woman governor. The daughter of a successful immigrant Greek developer and the first in her family to attend college, Kounalakis would become acting governor whenever the chief executive was out of the state. She joined Treasurer Fiona Ma and Controller Betty Yee on a deep Democratic bench as political figures who could demonstrably appeal to a statewide electorate.

Also noteworthy was the June election of London Breed as mayor of San Francisco, making it the largest American city headed by a female chief executive. Breed, an African American, was raised by her grandmother in public housing and had upended an incumbent county supervisor before becoming mayor.

California women also made solid showings in district-wide contests – gaining strength in the state's congressional delegation as well as in the assembly and senate. A harbinger of election-day success had come months earlier when the #MeToo movement was gathering steam. Women won five of six special elections for the legislature to replace men who had vacated their offices – three of whom had resigned amid sexual harassment allegations. Labor activist and El Salvador immigrant Wendy Carrillo parlayed an invigorated female electorate and union fundraising support to win a narrow assembly victory in northeast Los Angeles. Sydney Kamlager-Dove, president of the LA Community College District Board of Trustees, won another assembly seat, as did Luz Rivas, who had founded a local nonprofit organization that encourages girls to become interested in science and technology. Also in Los Angeles County, Montebello Mayor Vanessa Delgado captured a temporarily vacant senate seat (but lost a concurrent campaign to serve a full term), while Ling-Ling Chang won a contest to replace a recalled senator.

The spike in electoral success for California women mirrored election results throughout the nation, where a record number of women were sent to the US House. The overwhelming majority were Democrats. "We've seen important breakthroughs," noted Debbie Walsh, director of the Center for American Women in Politics at Rutgers University, "but deepening disparities between the parties in women's representation will continue to hobble us on the path to parity. We need women elected on both sides of the aisle." The election successes corresponded to a boost in political engagement. More than 190 California women ran for statewide, congressional or legislative office during the 2018 election cycle – surpassed only during 1992's "Year of the Woman."

The surge in female Democratic candidacies was rooted in Donald Trump's upset election over Hillary Clinton for the presidency in 2016. Not only had more than a dozen women accused Trump of sexually assaulting them, he infamously had bragged of taking liberties with women – while denying the nation its first woman president. In interviews with CNBC, Democratic women candidates cited "opposition to Trump and GOP policies on health care, reproductive rights, taxes and national security" as their impetus for running. Republican women, on the other hand, expressed support for GOP economic policies they said had helped their districts.

Only weeks before the midterm elections, Brett Kavanaugh's bruising but successful fight for the US Supreme Court had outraged what Trump and GOP leaders pointedly called a "mob" of mostly women protesters at the US Capitol and Supreme Court buildings. Like Clarence Thomas more than a quarter-century earlier, Kavanaugh navigated a contentious confirmation process after accusations of sexual improprieties had been leaked to the public. While a backlash to the Senate Judiciary Committee's cavalier treatment of Thomas's accuser, Anita Hill, spawned 1992's Year of the Woman, Republicans counted on a conservative backlash against the allegations leveled at Kavanaugh to help counter Democrats' obvious enthusiasm over the midterms.

Although both sides seemed energized in the days before the midterms, history-making breakthroughs went to Democrats. The US House would see its first two Native American women (Democrats from New Mexico and Kansas) and its first two Muslim women (Democrats from Michigan and Minnesota) among more than thirty-five female newcomers, including at least thirty Democrats. The record of more than one-hundred women elected or reelected to the 435-member House trounced a previous high-water mark of eighty-five. When joined with their sisters in the US Senate, ballot counting showed an unprecedented number of women headed for seats in the reconstituted Congress. Yet despite all the attention of women running and often winning in 2018, female members made up less than a quarter of the new Congress overall.

Successes nationally and in California demonstrated, at least for the moment, that women could turn a post-2016 swell of political activism into electoral gains. Between 2016 and 2018, the number of female candidates in California for statewide offices, the US House, and the legislature increased by more than twenty-seven percent. Still, the quest for political gender parity remains sufficiently daunting that, post-election, women represented only a little more than one-third of the state's House delegation and roughly thirty percent of the entire legislative membership. In the House – where there are no term limits and congressional incumbents are reelected about ninety percent of the time – entrenched lawmakers (women and men) are allowed to establish dynasties. Only two of fifty-three House races in California had no incumbents seeking reelection in 2018, offering few opportunities for women to pick up many additional seats.

In the legislature, women reversed a six-year slide in electoral success. Yet women candidates likely will face headwinds in the legislature well into the next decade. As noted in Chapter 11, there are inherent risks for outsiders who take on incumbents, because those already in office have distinct advantages in fundraising, visibility, endorsements and campaign organization. A 2012 voter-approved adjustment to the term limits law allows lawmakers to serve up to twelve years in either legislative house. One unintended consequence was that not a single member of the assembly was scheduled to be termed out of office before 2024, suggesting there might be few occasions to alter its gender make-up absent a spate of resignations. "We're not even close to parity," says Elizabeth Fuller, a consultant for the California Legislative Women's Caucus. "A woman's challenge is so much greater going against an incumbent. There's the name recognition that comes with having district and capitol staffs. Plus state senate races cost about a million dollars. Men are more aggressive fundraisers, while women have a tougher time asking for money."

California thinks of itself as a progressive trendsetter and has led the nation in political and policy innovation throughout much of its history. But it also has erected roadblocks – intentional or otherwise -- that impeded the drive toward gender equity. The 2018 election results expanded the potential for a woman governor, but they also were a reminder that California is one of only twenty states that has never elected a woman chief executive.

The Golden State remains a land of pioneers, however, with a legacy of bold, courageous, and determined female trailblazers that dates to the Gold Rush. If this book's stories prove anything, it is that today's women leaders are hardly ready to surrender their predecessors' long struggle for parity in self-governance. On the contrary, they are certain to continue paving the way for tomorrow's groundbreakers.

Please visit our website at
https://www.pavingthewaycalifornia.com
for updated election information

Acknowledgments

The seeds of *Paving the Way* were sown in late 2015 when we were researching our previous book, *Game Changers: Twelve Elections that Transformed California*. We were struck that so few women graced those pages—the result of considerable political, cultural, and social roadblocks that had obstructed their way.

Unearthing the contributions of some of the remarkable women who helped shape California's rich political history took us to research libraries, newspaper archives, century-old government documents, and academic scholarship. The California Digital Newspaper Collection, a project of the Center for Bibliographical Studies and Research at the University of California, Riverside, is a wonderful online collection of more than 18 million California newspaper articles beginning in 1846 (https://cdnc.ucr.edu/cgi-bin/cdnc).

Reference librarians at the California History Room at the California State Library in Sacramento, which houses an extensive collection of archived newspapers, were particularly helpful. We also offer our thanks to state librarian Greg Lucas and the library's communications manager, Alex Vassar, whose institutional memory of California politics helped guide our research.

For their help at the California State Archives, home to a rich abundance of Californiana, we would like to thank Melodi Andersen, Lisa Prince, and other archivists for guiding us through the Archives' special collections and its oral history project. The project's extensive interviews preserve the recollections of government officials and others who have contributed to the state's storied political history.

The Bancroft Library at the University of California, Berkeley, houses a treasure trove of original documents from individual and family collections that have been given to the university over the decades. In addition, Bancroft's Regional Oral History Office was very useful in our research on women who helped shape public policy and politics. At the university's Doe Library, we found turn-of-the-century newspaper articles we couldn't locate elsewhere.

At the state capitol, we would like to thank assembly chief clerk Dotson Wilson and assistant chief clerk/parliamentarian Brian Ebbert for their help with our research on the legislative achievements of the assembly's first four women—elected in 1918.

This book was enriched by the insights of many political insiders and newsmakers who gave interviews to the authors. Among these were senate President pro Tempore Toni Atkins, senate Republican leader Patricia Bates, former senate President pro Tempore John Burton, former state Superintendent of Public Instruction Delaine Eastin, Assemblymember Cristina Garcia, former state Senator Gary K. Hart, and former Los Angeles City Councilmember Rosalind Wyman.

Other players in the public arena who graciously contributed their perceptions and expertise in interviews were Stan Atkinson, Shareen Barrett, Shirley Biagi, Reverend Rod Davis, Kimberly Ellis, Elizabeth Fuller, Hedy Govenar, Caren Lagomarsino, Camille Leonhardt, Cassandra Pye, Sabrina Schiller, Richard Temple, Helen Torres, V. John White, and Jerry Zanelli.

Throughout this endeavor, we received encouragement, assistance, feedback, and valuable insights from numerous individuals, including Emerald Archer, Bill Bailey, Lisa García Bedolla, Steve Boilard, Maryellen Burns, Jack Citrin, Leonor Ehling, Marsha Evans, Sherry Bebitch Jeffe, state Senator Connie Leyva, former Assemblymember Sunny Mojonnier, Natalja Mortensen, Mike Otten, Nick Robinson, Teala Schaff, Holli M. Teltoe, John Underwood, and Gayle Wattawa. State senate photographer Lorie Shelley was instrumental in helping us use visual images to tell the stories of many long-forgotten political women.

Finally, we'd like to acknowledge Ethan Rarick, associate director of the Institute of Governmental Studies at UC Berkeley, and Maria Wolf, senior editor at Berkeley Public Policy Press, for their support, insights, and valuable editing suggestions.

About the Authors

Steve Swatt is a veteran political analyst and public affairs executive. He is a former award-winning political reporter with 25 years of journalism experience with the *San Francisco Examiner*, United Press International in Los Angeles, and KCRA-TV (NBC) in Sacramento. He received a BS in business administration and a master's degree in journalism, both from the University of California, Berkeley.

Susie Swatt is a member of the National Advisory Council of the Institute of Governmental Studies at UC Berkeley. She spent nearly 40 years as a key staff member in the California legislature. As a special assistant for the Fair Political Practices Commission, she researched and authored a study that won a national award for "investigative work in the public interest."

Rebecca LaVally received her Ph.D. from the University of Texas at Austin in 2010. She teaches rhetorical criticism, persuasion, and political communication at California State University, Sacramento. She is a former editor of the California senate's public policy research office and a former Sacramento bureau chief for United Press International and Gannett News Service.

Jeff Raimundo has spent more than 25 years as a political and public-relations consultant based in Sacramento. Previously, he enjoyed a 25-year career as a newspaper reporter and editor with the *Sacramento Bee* and McClatchy Newspapers in Sacramento and Washington, DC.

Index